OFFICIAL PROCEEDINGS

OF THE

Democratic National Convention,

HELD IN 1860,

AT CHARLESTON AND BALTIMORE.

PROCEEDINGS AT CHARLESTON,

APRIL 23—MAY 3.

PREPARED AND PUBLISHED UNDER THE DIRECTION OF

JOHN G. PARKHURST, Recording Secretary.

CLEVELAND:
NEVINS' PRINT, PLAIN DEALER JOB OFFICE.
1860.

PROCEEDINGS

OF THE

Democratic National Convention

AT CHARLESTON, 1860.

FIRST DAY.

MONDAY, APRIL 23, 1860.

IN accordance with the call of the Democratic National Committee, the Delegates to the National Convention assembled at 12 o'clock this morning, in the Hall of the South Carolina Institute, in Charleston, S. C.

Hon. DAVID A. SMALLEY, of Vermont, Chairman of the Democratic National Committee, called the Convention to order, in the following words:

GENTLEMEN OF THE CONVENTION: We are assembled on this occasion as the National Democratic Convention, called by the National Democratic Committee, pursuant to the authority confided in them by the Convention assembled at Cincinnati, to nominate candidates for the Presidency and Vice Presidency of the United States, and to transact such other business as the interests of the Democratic party may dictate. What is the pleasure of the Convention?

Mr. H. R. JACKSON, of Georgia, nominated THOMPSON B. FLOURNOY, of Arkansas, as President of the Convention *pro tem.* Carried unanimously.

Messrs. H. R. JACKSON, of Georgia, and G. W. McCOOK, of Ohio, were appointed a Committee to conduct the temporary Presiding Officer to the Chair.

Col. FLOURNOY, on taking the Chair, said:

GENTLEMEN OF THE CONVENTION: I thank you most sincerely for the honor you have done me, and I shall endeavor so to demean myself as to bring about a speedy organization of this body; and, I hope, in a satisfactory manner.

The Rev. CHARLES HANCKEL, D. D., of the Episcopal Church, then addressed the Throne of Grace in prayer. The Delegates all in a standing position during the prayer.

Mr. FISHER, of Virginia. We are not yet organized, as I understand, nor has a Secretary yet been appointed. I therefore propose the name of WILLIAM F. RITCHIE, of Virginia, as temporary Secretary of the Convention. Carried unanimously.

Mr. FISHER. I now ask the Presiding Officer to read a letter which I will send to the Chair, and in connection with which I have a resolution to offer.

Gov. J. A. WINSTON, of Alabama, objected to the reception of the communication until the Convention was permanently organized.

Mr. FISHER. The letter relates to the organization.

The PRESIDENT. The Chair decides that if it relates to the organization, it is in order.

Mr. FISHER took the Secretary's stand, and was about to read the communication, when

Mr. JOHN COCHRAN, of New York, claimed to be heard one moment before the letter was read.

Mr. FISHER. That is the very issue involved.

Mr. COCHRAN. I claim to have the floor, and shall retain it until I am properly interrupted. I rise to a question of order. The resolution must be offered before the communication is read, otherwise there is no question before the Convention.

Mr. LAWRENCE, of Louisiana, rose to a point of order. The gentleman from New York has no right to address the Convention.

Mr. FISHER. The gentleman is not properly a member of this body.

Mr. COCHRAN. I rise to a point of order, and shall not yield the floor. The gentleman from Virginia claims that he has a resolution to offer. It is out of order to read a communication when no motion is before the House.

The CHAIR. The Chair decided that if the communication refers strictly to the organi zation, it can be read.

Mr. PUGH, of Ohio. The proper way of the gentleman from Virginia will be to communicate to the Chair, or to the Convention, the substance of the letter; then we shall see to what business it relates.

Mr. FISHER. I have been requested to read the communication, and I shall do so. [Mr. F. proceeded to the Clerk's stand and attempted to read the communication.]

The CHAIR. Before the letter is read, the Chair inquires of the gentleman whether it is a communication from a State?

Mr. FISHER. It is from a Delegatton claiming a seat here.

Mr. COCHRAN. I rise to a point of order. I had been awarded the floor, and had not yielded it. I claim, therefore, that the gentleman from Virginia is out of order.

Mr. FISHER. The State of Virginia is not responsible for my conduct. I am responsible alone for my own acts, and I stand here on the right to the floor, awarded me by the Chair.

The CHAIR. The gentleman from Virginia is out of order. The Chair decides that the communication, being only from a contesting Delegation not now recognized by the Convention, is out of order. The gentleman from New York (Mr. Cochran) has been awarded the floor.

Mr. FISHER. The Delegates from whom this communication comes are representatives of the State of New York. They claim it as a right to be heard—

The CHAIR—[rapping to order.] The gentleman from Virginia has been ruled out of order, and I call upon the Convention to support the Chair.

Mr. FISHER. I have the floor, and I do not mean to be unfairly ruled out of order. [Shouts of "Order! order!"]

Mr. JOHN COCHRAN. I move, Mr. President, that the rules of the last National Convention be adopted as the rules to govern this body.

Mr. L. P. WALKER, of Alabama, rose to address the Convention.

The CHAIR. Debate is out of order, unless some question is before the Convention. Does the gentleman from Alabama make any motion?

Mr. WALKER. I desire to speak.

Mr. WALKER. I appeal from the decision of the Chair by which I am ruled out of order, and that I have a right to do.

The CHAIR. The gentleman has a right to appeal. The question will be, shall the decision of the Chair be sustained?

Mr. WALKER. I desire to be heard—[Cries of "Question! question!"]

The CHAIR. Nothing is in order until the question on the appeal is decided.

Mr. CLARK, of Mississippi, in a loud tone of voice, claimed the right of the gentleman from Alabama (Mr. Walker) to be heard on the appeal he had taken from the decision of the Chair.

The CHAIR. If the Convention will come to order, the Chair will state the question before it.

Mr. WALKER. If the Chair will refrain from entering into a conference with me, and will allow me to speak for a few moments, he will then himself understand what is the question to which I desire to speak.

The CHAIR. The Chair has no desire to prevent the gentleman from being heard, unless the Convention itself shall decline to hear him. He is in order if speaking on the appeal from the decision of the Chair.

Mr. WALKER. The question properly before the Convention is, whether the communication presented by the gentleman from Virginia (Mr. Fisher) shall be read. It is simply a parliamentary rule that any gentleman who offers to a body like this a respectful paper, has the right to demand that it be read. The gentleman from Virginia has presented a communication relating directly to the organization of this Convention, from a State Delegation claiming the right of a seat here. It must be entertained at once, if the right of the contesting delegation is to be respected at all. I hold that the question on the reading of the communication is before the House, and as I rose to speak to that question, I hold that the decision of the Chair ruling me out of order is incorrect.

The CHAIR. The question before the Convention is, shall the decision of the Chair be sustained?

The Chair was sustained by a vote almost unanimous.

The CHAIR. The ayes have it, and the decision of the Chair is sustained.

Mr. FISHER. I now offer the resolution which I purported to offer in connection with the communication which I desired to read.

The CHAIR. A question is already pending. It is the motion of the gentleman from New York, that the rules of the last National Convention be adopted as the rules to govern the present Convention.

The motion was unanimously adopted.

Mr. FISHER. I now ask to read the communication and the resolution which I purport to offer in connection therewith.

The CHAIR. It has already been decided that this subject is not in order. The decision of the Chair in that respect, has been sustained by the voice of the Convention. The Chair is therefore compelled to rule the gentleman from Virginia again out of order.

Mr. GEO. W. McCOOK, of Ohio, offered the following:

Resolved, That a Committee of one from each State be selected by the respective delegations, whose duty it shall be to select permanent officers of the Convention.

Mr. FISHER. I move to amend this resolution, and I presume my right to do so will not be disputed.

The CHAIR. An amendment will be in order if it is pertinent to the question before the Convention.

Mr. BARKSDALE, of Mississippi, obtained the floor, and moved the following as a substitute for Mr. McCook's resolution:

Resolved, That a Committee on Credentials be appointed by the several delegations respectively, to be composed of one from each State in which there is no disputed delegation, whose duty it shall be to report to the Convention the Delegates that are entitled to seats on this floor.

Mr. RICHARDSON said: Mr. President—I hope my friend from Ohio will accept the amendment of the gentleman from Mississippi. There is a controversy in the State which I represent upon this floor. Sir, I want the Convention, and I want the country, to see what are its merits. I shrink from no investigation, and when the Convention comes to see the character of the contest, they will be amazed at what small things contests can be raised about.

It is humiliating to me, at this period of my life, to have a contest of this matter of my Democracy with such opponents as those who are contesting my seat here. I am anxious that the Convention shall have this matter before them, without one word or any action from me, and decide it. With that decision I am sure I shall be satisfied.

Mr. JOHN COCHRAN, of New York, rose to speak, but was interrupted by

Mr. LAWRENCE, of Louisiana, who rose to a point of order. No gentlemen from New York had yet been admitted as regular Delegates by the voice of the Convention, and until that question had been decided, no person had a right to be heard from that State.

Mr. COCHRAN. Mr. Chairman, I ask the gentleman from Louisiana by what right he himself holds a seat on this floor?

Mr. LAWRENCE. As a Delegate from the State of Louisiana, whose seat is not contested.

Mr. COCHRAN. And, Sir, by the same right, as Delegates from the State of New York, do we hold our seats here on this floor.

Mr. LAWRENCE. It is well known that there are two sets of Delegates from the State of New York, both claiming a right to seats in this Convention. One of those delegations is headed by Mayor Wood, the representative man of the New York Democracy. The other, by Mr. Dean Richmond, an equally worthy gentleman and reliable Democrat. I hold that—

The CHAIR. The gentleman from Louisiana is not in order. The Chair has already decided that all discussion is out of order upon this question until the Convention shall have been permanently organized.

Mr. W. S. BARRY, of Mississippi, asked that the roll be called. The Convention could not proceed with any regularity until it is ascertained who are and who are not Delegates.

Mr. COCHRAN obtained the floor. He said: Mr. Chairman—I was well pleased to hear the remarks of the gentleman from Illinois, respecting the resolution offered by the gentleman from Mississippi. The sentiments expressed by him are ours, and the amendment offered meets the unqualified approbation of the Delegates from New York. We are the sole representatives of the regular and orthodox Democracy of that State, but while maintaining that position, we are not actuated by such feelings as to pretend that there may be no controversy respecting our claims. Whether the gentlemen who contest our seats come with claims of greater or less magnitude, we have no objection that every man shall be heard in his own behalf. We of New York have not been educated in that school of ethics or politics to claim that we only can be right, or to desire to sit in adjudication on our own case. If the Convention should offer to us to be judges in our own case, we would decline it as men and as gentlemen, but more particularly as men clothed with the robes of regularity, and as representatives of the Democracy of the great State of New York. Wishing to submit ourselves to the decision of the Convention, we are ready to agree in the adoption of the proposed amendment.

Mr. PUGH, of Ohio, desired that the resolution should set forth the States from which there are supposed to be contested seats.

Mr. BARKSDALE then modified his substitute so as to provide for the appointment of a Committee on permanent organization—one from each State (except in New York and Illinois,) to be selected by the Delegates from each State.

Mr. McCOOK. I accept the amendment proposed by the gentleman from Mississippi, with the understanding that it is to be confined to the Delegates whose seats are contested entirely. If it is so modified, I will accept it.

There is then no objection to it, for we come here as Democrats whose Conventions have always excluded from their Committees the States whose seats are contested.

Mr. W. S. BARRY, of Mississippi, suggested that the resolution be so framed as to create a Committee on the contested seats only. If a general Committee on credentials is formed, it may be five days before they report.

The resolution of Mr. McCook, as proposed to be amended by Mr. Barksdale, was then read.

Mr. MATHEWS, of Mississippi, was about to offer a resolution as a substitute for the original resolution and the amendment, when—

Mr. JOHN COCHRAN rose to a point of order. The original resolution related to a permanent organization of this Convention. The proposed amendment had reference to certain seats alleged to be contested, and was not pertinent to the original motion.

Mr. J. B. CLARK, of Missouri, obtained the floor. He held that the amendment was not pertinent to the original resolution. The National Committee admit to the floor of the Convention such Delegates from the several States as are entitled to seats. Every gentleman here is, therefore, to be regarded as a Delegate. He therefore moved the previous question, with a view of bringing the Convention to a vote on the original resolution.

The CHAIR inquired, before putting the motion for the previous question, whether the gentleman from Ohio (Mr. McCook) had accepted the amendment of the gentleman from Mississippi.

Mr. McCOOK. The amendment of the gentleman from Mississippi was not modified in accordance with my suggestion, and, therefore, I did not accept it. While I am in favor, with him, of a Committee on Contested Seats, I am anxious that the question on organization should be disembarrassed of this issue.

Mr. RICHARDSON, of Illinois, argued that the original resolution contemplated a permanent organization. The amendment offered by the gentleman from Mississippi contemplated a Committee on Contested Seats, but if adopted, would really exclude the two great States of New York and Illinois from a representation on the Committee on Organization. To this he objected.

Judge MEEK, of Alabama, raised the point of order, that none of the resolutions are in order until the roll of Delegates has been called, in order that it may be ascertained who are the representatives properly present in the Convention.

Mr. RICHARDSON. The substitute offered by the gentleman from Mississippi varies the proposition from its original form. The original had reference only to the Committee upon Credentials. The gentleman from Ohio proposes to raise a Committee upon Organization. The gentleman from Mississippi moves to amend by excluding the two States in which there is said to be a contest. From that Committee ought to be excluded only the State that is called up. There is no reason why the State of Illinois and the State of New York should be excluded from the Committee on Organization. There may be, and there are reasons which I acknowledge to be satisfactory to me, why I should not sit in the contested case of Illinois. But there is no reason why a member of our Delegation should not sit in the contested case of New York. But when you come to pluralities, you not only take us from the Committees but strike down the power of the two States in this Convention.

Mr. BARKSDALE desired to correct a misapprehension of some Delegates. He did not desire to discuss the merits of any contested seat, but he referred to the Cincinnati Convention, at which no State from which there were contestants was admitted to a representation on the Committee on Permanent Organization.

Mr. CRAIG, of Missouri, desired to correct the gentleman from Mississippi. The contested seat from that State was decided at Cincinnati before the permanent organization, and the Missouri Delegates were fully represented on the Committee.

Mr. CESSNA, of Pennsylvania, moved to amend by striking out all after the enacting clause in the original resolutions, and inserting as follows:

Resolved, That there now shall be appointed two Committees; each to consist of one member from each State, to be selected by the respective delegations thereof; one a Committee on Permanent Organization, and the other on Credentials; and that in determining the controversy in regard to the disputed seats of the Illinois Delegation, the members of the Committee on Credentials of that State shall not be permitted to vote thereon, and in determining the controversy from the State of New York, the members of the Committee on Credentials from that State shall not be permitted to vote.

Mr. CESSNA moved the previous question, which being ordered, the vote was taken upon the above substitute by States, and the same was adopted, as follows:

	Yeas.	Nays.		Yeas.	Nays.		Yeas.	Nays.
Maine	8		North Carolina	10		Tennessee	12	
New Hampshire	5		South Carolina	8		Kentucky	12	
Vermont	5		Georgia	10		Wisconsin	5	
Massachusetts	13		Alabama		9	Michigan	6	
Rhode Island	4		Louisiana		6	Iowa	4	
Connecticut	6		Missouri	9		Arkansas		4
New Jersey	7		Indiana	13		California	2	2
Pennsylvania	27		Illinois	11		Oregon	3	
Delaware	3		Ohio	28		Minnesota	4	
Maryland	7	1	Mississippi		7			
New York	35		Texas		4		257	48
Virginia		15	Florida	8				

Mr. FISHER. We protest against the vote of the State of New York being received and counted here.

The CHAIR. The protest is not now in order.

Mr. FISHER. We desire to enter it on the journal.

The original resolution, as amended, was then adopted.

Mr. CESSNA moved to reconsider the vote, and to lay the motion on the table. Agreed to.

Mr. MATHEWS, of Mississippi, offered the following:

Resolved, That the Delegates from the States of New York and Illinois, whose seats are contested, be requested not to participate in the proceedings of this body, until the Committee on Credentials shall have determined and reported to the Convention, which of said contestants are entitled to seats.

Mr. CLARK, of Missouri, raised the point of order that a similar motion had been offered, and the Convention had virtually rejected it.

The CHAIR. The point of order is not well taken.

Mr. CESSNA moved to lay the resolution on the table.

Mr. CLARK, of Mississippi, objected to the delegations from New York voting on this question, on the ground that they are parties in interest.

The vote to lay the resolution on the table was then demanded by States, and resulted as follows:

	Yeas.	Nays.		Yeas.	Nays.		Yeas.	Nays
Maine	8		North Carolina	10		Tennessee	12	
New Hampshire	5		South Carolina	8		Kentucky	12	
Vermont	5		Georgia		10	Wisconsin	5	
Massachusetts	13		Alabama		9	Iowa	4	
Rhode Island	4		Louisiana		6	Michigan	6	
Connecticut	6		Missouri	9		Arkansas		4
New Jersey	7		Indiana	13		California		4
Pennsylvania	27		Illinois	11		Oregon	3	
Delaware	3		Ohio	23		Minnesota	4	
Maryland	8		Mississippi		7			
New York	35		Texas		4		259	44
Virginia	15		Florida	8				

So the resolution was laid on the table.

The roll of States was then called, and the following Committees were appointed:

On Permanent Organization—Virginia, John Brannon; Indiana, S. K. Wolfe; Connecticut, A. C. Lippit; Minnesota; J. Travis Rosser; Michigan, A. C. Baldwin; South Carolina, B. H. Wilson; Oregon, John R. Limerick; New York, Sidney T. Fairchild; Louisiana, E. LaSere; Rhode Island, John M. Francis; Massachusetts, Chester W. Chapin; Delaware, John B. Pennington; Iowa, E. H. Thayer; New Jersey, Robert Hamilton; Illinois, A. M. Herrington; Texas, F R. Lubbock; Pennsylvania, John Cessna; Ohio, George W. Houk; Florida, Thomas J. Eppes; California, G. W. Patrick; Mississippi, Charles Clark; Arkansas, John J. Sturman; North Carolina, Wm. A. Moore; Maryland, John B. Emory; Missouri, Samuel B. Churchill; Georgia, John H. Lumpkin; Tennessee, Thomas M. Jones; Kentucky, Colbert Cecil; Wisconsin, E. S. Bragg; Alabama, A. B. Meek; Vermont, H. E. Stoughton; New Hampshire, Robert S. Webster; Maine, Wm. H. Burrell.

On Credentials—Virginia, E. W. Hubbard; Indiana, S. A. Hall; Connecticut, James Gallagher; Minnesota, Henry H. Sibley; Michigan, Benjamin Follett; South Carolina, B. F. Perry; Oregon, Lansing Stont; New York D. DeWolf; Louisiana, F. H. Hatch; Rhode Island, George H. Browne; Massachusetts, Oliver Stevens; Delaware, Wm. G. Whitely; Iowa, D. O. Finch; New Jersey, Albert R. Speer; Illinois, Wm J. Allen; Texas Gen. E. Greer; Pennsylvania, A. M North; Ohio, Jas. B. Steedman; Florida, Charles E. Dycke; California, John S. Dudley; Mississippi, Wm S. Barry; Arkansas, Van H. Manning; North Carolina, R. R. Bridges; Maryland, Wm. S Gittings; Missouri, John M. Krum; Georgia, Julian Hartridge; Tennessee, W H. Carroll; Kentucky, G. T. Wood; Wisconsin, P. H. Smith; Alabama, M. W. M. Brooks; Vermont, Stephen Thomas; New Hampshire, Aaron P. Hughes; Maine, Charles D. Jameson.

Mr. S. H. BUSKIRK, of Indiana, moved the following:

Resolved, That the States be called in their order, and that the list of Delegates from each State be furnished to the Secretary, and, whenever there is a contest, the papers relating to such be referred to the Committee on Credentials.

Adopted, and the list of Delegates handed to the Secretary, by the Chairmen of the different Delegations.

Mr. LAWRENCE, of Louisiana, moved as an amendment, to add at the end of the resolution that the communication of the New York contesting Delegation in the hands of the Chairman be read, and then referred to the Committee on Contested Seats.

Mr. COCHRAN moved to amend, by referring the letter without reading, and called the previous question, which was ordered.

Mr. Cochran's amendment was adopted, and the resolution of Mr. Buskirk amended so as to refer the New York letter to the Committee on Contested Seats without reading, was then agreed to.

Mr. O. B. FICKLIN, of Illinois, offered the following resolution:

Resolved, That a Committee of one Delegate from each State, to be selected by the Delegation thereof, be appointed to report resolutions, and that all resolutions, in relation to the platform of the Democratic party, be referred to said Committee, on presentation, without debate.

Pending the question on this resolution, the Convention, on motion of Mr. DAWSON, of Pennsylvania, adjourned until 10 o'clock to-morrow (Tuesday) morning.

SECOND DAY.

TUESDAY, APRIL 24, 1860.

The Convention re-assembled at 10 o'clock, in the Hall of the Institute. The galleries were filled, the North gallery being reserved exclusively for ladies.

Hon. T. B. FLOURNOY called the Convention to order, and announced that the first business in order was the reading of the minutes of yesterday's proceedings, but these not being in readiness, the reading was suspended.

The PRESIDENT *pro tem.* announced that the next business in order was the report of the Committees.

Mr. PAYNE, of Ohio, suggested that the question pending at the adjournment was first in order. The reports of Committees would only be first in order after the permanent organization was completed.

The PRESIDENT. The question pending at the adjournment is not necessarily in order, but the Chair will entertain a motion to take up the business on the table, if no objections are made.

Judge MEEK, of Alabama, moved that the Committee on Permanent Organization be now requested to report.

The PRESIDENT *pro tem.* That is in order. If the Committee on Permanent Organization is ready to report, their report will be received.

Mr. CESSNA, of Pennsylvania, Chairman of the Committee, made the following report of Permanent Officers of the Convention:

For President—Hon. CALEB CUSHING, of Massachusetts.

For Vice Presidents and Secretaries:

MAINE.
Vice President—Th. D. Robinson.
Secretary—C. Record.

NEW HAMPSHIRE.
Vice President—Daniel Marcy.
Secretary—George A. Bingham.

VERMONT.
Vice President—Jasper Rand.
Secretary—P. W. Hyde.

MASSACHUSETTS.
Vice President—Isaac Davis.
Secretary—B. F. Watson.

RHODE ISLAND.
Vice President—Gideon Bradford.
Secretary—Amasa Sprague.

CONNECTICUT.
Vice President—Samuel Arnold.
Secretary—M. R. West.

NEW JERSEY.
Vice President—Wm. Wright.
Secretary—Jon C. Rafferty.

NEW YORK.
Vice President—Erastus Corning.
Secretary—Edward Cooper.

PENNSYLVANIA.
Vice Pres't—Thos. Cunningham.
Secretary—Franklin Vansant.

DELAWARE.
Vice President—W. H. Ross.
Secretary—John H. Buley.

MARYLAND.
Vice President—W. P. Bowie.
Secretary—E. L. F. Hardcastle.

VIRGINIA
Vice President—O. R. Funston.
Secretary—Robert H. Glass.

NORTH CAROLINA.
Vice President—Bedford Brown.
Secretary—L. W. Humphrey.

SOUTH CAROLINA.
Vice President—B. H. Brown.
Secretary—Franklin Gaillard.

GEORGIA.
Vice President—James Thomas.
Secretary—J. J. Dimond.

ALABAMA.
Vice President—R. G. Scott.
Secretary—N. H. R. Dawson.

MISSISSIPPI.
Vice President—James Drane.
Secretary—W. H. H. Tyson.

LOUISIANA.
Vice President—B. Taylor.
Secretary—Charles Jones.

OHIO.
Vice President—David Tod.
Secretary—W. M. Stark.

KENTUCKY.
Vice President—B. Spalding.
Secretary—Robert McKee.

TENNESSEE.
Vice President—J. O. C. Atkins.
Secretary—John R. Howard.

INDIANA.
Vice President—Isaac C. Elston.
Secretary—Lafayette Devlin.

ILLINOIS.
Vice President—Z Casey.
Secretary—R. E. Goodell.

ARKANSAS.
Vice President—Francis A. Terry.
Secretary—F. W Hoadley.

MICHIGAN.
Vice President—H. H Riley.
Secretary—John G. Parkhurst.

FLORIDA.
Vice President—B. F. Wardlaw.
Secretary—C. E. Dyeke.

TEXAS.
Vice President—H. R. Runnels.
Secretary—Thomas P. Ochiltree.

MISSOURI.
Vice Pres't—Abraham Hunter.
Secretary—J. T. Mense.

IOWA.
Vice President—T. W. Claggett.
Secretary—J. W. Bosler.

WISCONSIN.
Vice President—Fred'k W. Horn.
Secretary—A F Pratt.

CALIFORNIA.
Vice President—J. A. Dreibelbis.
Secretary—John S. Dudley.

MINNESOTA.
Vice President—W. W. Phelps.
Secretary—G. T. Rosser.

OREGON
Vice President—S. P. Denison.
Secretary—R. P. Metcalf.

The announcement of the name of the permanent President was received with loud applause.

The Committee further recommended that the rules and regulations adopted by the National Democratic Convention of 1852 and 1856 be adopted by this Convention for its government, with this additional rule:

"That in any State which has not provided or directed by its State Convention how its vote may be given, the Convention will recognize the right of each Delegate to cast his individual vote."

JOHN N. FRANCIS, Secretary. JOHN CESSNA, Chairman.

Mr. McCOOK, of Ohio, moved that the report of the Committee be accepted, and the Committee discharged. Agreed to.

Mr. McCOOK moved that the report of the Committee be adopted.

Mr. CLARK, of Mississippi, stated that the additional rule had been added by the Committee without the knowledge or consent of a majority of the members. The question on its adoption was brought before the Committee, and voted down on a call of the States.

Mr. CASSIDY, of Pennsylvania, rose to a point of order. The report had been adopted, and there was no question before the Convention.

The CHAIR. The point of order is not well taken.

Mr. CLARK. The report has been accepted, not adopted. The Committee at its regular meeting, had refused to alter the rules of the former Conventions, by the addition of the rule now reported. He did not charge any unfairness to the presiding officer of the Committee, who, doubtless, did his best to get all the Committee together again, to re-consider its original action.

But he, and others of the Committee, had not been notified and had no knowledge of the alteration that had been made, until it was announced here. He therefore moved that the proposed additional rule be stricken from the report.

Mr. Richardson, of Illinois. If I propose to go into an inquiry of what was done by the Committee, it might be proper to say that the proposition now submitted was acted upon in a fuller meeting, as I am told, than that of last night, and adopted unanimously. I do not propose to discuss with the gentleman from Mississippi the subject as to the action of the Committee. I propose to place it upon the basis of its own merits. Where a State Convention has met and instructed its Delegation as a unit, and they have accepted the condition, they are bound by it. Wherever they give no such instruction, wherever they have refused in a State Convention to give such instruction, it is proper to place the right of the Delegate upon the broad and distinct ground of right. But where they have entered into an organization, and are pledged, they are not at liberty to over-run the expressed wishes and will of their constituents. But I propose to place the question of individuality upon the broad ground of right, and right alone. [Applause.] I say upon that ground the report of the Committee ought to be adopted.

Mr. Lubbock, of Texas, made an explanation of the action of the Committee. They had spent some three hours in session, at which this subject was fully, fairly and freely discussed. The resolution now proposed to be added had been voted down. The Chairman of the Committee had called a meeting this morning, in order, as it was understood, to receive the names of the Vice Presidents and Secretaries not reported at the regular meeting. At this adjourned meeting, when many members of the Committee were absent, the alteration had been made. He called upon the Convention to sustain the majority of the Committee, and to discountenance any usurpation of power on the part of a portion of a Committee. They had to-day presented to the Convention, as its permanent presiding officer, a man of ability—a man of intellect—a man of power—[cheers]—and the rights of every Delegate were safe in his hands. The merits of the proposed amendment were fully discussed before the Committee, and no reason was seen, upon a full argument, why the rule that had worked well in 1852 and 1856 should not work well now.

Mr. Barry, of Mississippi, suggested that the Committee on Permanent Organization had no power or right to report rules. He should raise the point of order at the proper time.

Mr. Lubbock continued to argue in favor of striking the proposed amendment from the report.

Mr. Salisbury, of Delaware, desired the reading of the proposed rule, as many of the Delegates did not fully understand the question.

Mr. Cessna explained that, as Chairman of the Committee on Organization, he had labored hard to get the whole of the Committee together, again to consider this question of rules. If he had failed, it had only been because of the limited time. As to the merits of the proposed amendment, he held that the old rule of 1852 and 1856 would be construed to deprive those Delegates who happened to be in a minority from freely and fully expressing their views in the Convention and in reality disfranchising them. The rule which it was proposed to add to the rules of the former National Conventions of the party, was to the effect that in any State, which is not directed by its State Convention how to cast its vote, the Convention will recognize the right of each Delegate to cast his individual vote. Although it was not in order to allude to what had taken place in a Committee, yet as other gentlemen had done so, he might be permitted to say that a similar proposition had only been voted down by a small majority. Upon the re-assembling of the Committee, a large majority had agreed to the rule now reported. As he had stated already, he had endeavored to procure the attendance of all the Committee at the adjourned morning session. Only two had been absent, and with these exceptions, he had been unanimously instructed to make the report as it had been made. They had heard that the rule formerly adopted had worked well in former years, and they were therefore urged to adhere to the old rule.

But, as he had said, should the old rule prevail now and the majority of the Pennsylvania Delegation decide among themselves to cast the vote of the State as a unit, he and the constituency represented by him would be virtually disfranchised. In the Pennsylvania State Convention, of which he was a member, no proposition to cast the vote of the State as a unit was entertained. The Committee on Resolutions in that Convention had, on the contrary, rejected such a proposition. The amended rule was designed simply to explain beyond a misconstruction, what was the honest meaning of the rule that heretofore prevailed, but which was now in danger of misinterpretation. In the Conventions at Baltimore and Cincinnati, the right of every Delegate to vote had been recognized, and several of the States, Ohio amongst the number, had divided their votes on almost every ballot. It might as well be claimed that it was wrong to change the platform, as that it was wrong to alter the rules. He as a Northern man, had come here prepared to change the platform of the party, if it was deemed advisable to do so, and he had also come with a candidate from the extreme South as his first choice for the Presidency. He asked the Convention not to strike out this amendment, and so leave him to be disfranchised if a wrong interpretation should be put upon the old rule.

Mr. C. did not profess to be extreme in his views, but he desired to be protected in his rights. He was not of those to threaten non-concurrence in the will of the majority, but was prepared to submit and to stay in the Convention, even if disfranchised. There were some of his colleagues who were prepared to vote for one man, who was not his own choice. They also were in a minority of the whole Delegation, and it would be an act of injustice to disfranchise them. He again appealed to the Convention not to reject the proposed amendment to the rules. To disfranchise a portion of the Democracy of Pennsylvania might be to give that State to the Republicans, but if the rights of all Delegates were respected, the Democracy would again achieve there a glorious triumph. [Applause.]

Mr. BARRY, of Mississippi, raised the point of order that the Committee on Permanent Organization had no right to report rules, and that so much of their report should be rejected.

Mr. JOSIAH RANDALL, of Pennsylvania, said he, too, was in favor of a candidate from the South, and would vote for no man who had not the entire confidence of the South. If the gentleman from his own State, (Mr. Cessna,) said as much, he would act differently from what was supposed to be his views and wishes at home. He desired that the proposed amendment should be stricken out, because with the two-third rule that prevailed in the Convention, such amendment would virtually disfranchise the majority, and enable one-third of a delegation to neutralize the action of the remaining two-thirds. He reviewed the action of the Pennsylvania State Convention, and protested against any action of the Convention that would destroy the efficacy of the vote of that State in the Convention.

Mr. BISHOP, of Connecticut, claimed that the point of order raised by the gentleman from Mississippi (Mr. Barry) ought to be decided at once by the Chair.

The CHAIR. The point of order must be settled at once by the Chair. The Convention yesterday decided to adopt the rules of the last National Convention, and the Chair is of opinion that in reporting rules, the Committee traveled out of its province, and that so much of its report is out of order. [Applause.]

Mr. BISHOP. I now move the previous question.

The CHAIR. The gentleman from Illinois (Mr. Richardson) was recognized by the Chair, and has the floor.

Mr. BISHOP. I raise the point that the gentleman rose to address the Chair, on a question now declared out of order, and is not, therefore, entitled to the floor.

Mr. RICHARDSON, who had remained standing, said that he had heard the remarks of the gentleman from Pennsylvania (Mr. Randall) with surprise. It might be interesting for the Convention to know how long that gentleman had been a member of the Democratic party.

A VOICE. I hope the President will not allow any personal allusions. [Cries of "Order! order!" "Go on! Go on!"]

Several Delegates rose at once to points of order, without being recognized by the Chair, when

Mr. McCOOK, of Ohio, desired to appeal from a decision of the Chair. It had been decided by the Chair that so much of the report as related to the recommendation of rules to govern the Convention, was out of order. The Chair had based his decision upon the statement that the rules of the last Convention had been adopted yesterday by the present Convention to govern its action. This was an error. The resolution adopted yesterday had reference only to the temporary organization, and only adopted the old rules until the permanent organization should be effected. Ohio, on this ground, desired to appeal from the decision of the Chair.

The PRESIDENT *pro tem* The Chair now remembers that the statement of the gentleman from Ohio, Mr. McCook, is correct. The Chair in making his former decision, labored under a misapprehension, and now recalls and reverses that decision. The report of the Committee on Organization is in order.

Mr. LAWRENCE, of Louisiana, read from the report of the previous day's proceedings, and argued that the resolution contemplated that the Committee on Organization should report permanent officers only, and that they had no power to report rules.

Mr. WHITNEY. I call for a division of the question on the report of the Committee.

Mr. BRIERE, of Alabama, again raised the point of order, that the Committee on Organization had, under the resolution, no power to report rules at all.

Mr. CESSNA rose to a point of order. The Convention was now entertaining questions as to the power of the Committee on Organization to report rules. The report made by that Committee had been received and accepted. It was too late now to entertain such questions of order as had been raised. The point should have been taken before the acceptance of the Committee's report.

Mr. WHITNEY. Do I understand the Chair to rule that the question on the adoption of the report of the Committee on Organization is divisible?

The PRESIDENT *pro tem.* The Chair so decides, the question is divisible.

Mr. RICHARDSON. I claim the right to the floor, which I have not yet yielded. After I have said what I desire to say, then the gentleman can press his motion for a division of the question.

The PRESIDENT *pro tem.* The gentleman from Illinois is entitled to the floor.

A DELEGATE. The Chair has decided the question to be divisible. The question, therefore, is on that portion relating to the permanent organization. The gentleman from Illinois must speak to the question of the permanent organization, unless he appeal from the decision of the Chair.

Mr. SAMUELS, of Iowa. Whether the question is divisible or not, is now immaterial. The call for a division cannot affect the right of the gentleman from Illinois to the floor. He was entitled to the floor, and could not be deprived of it by any such point of order.

The PRESIDENT *pro tem.* The question as to whether the report is divisible came up in order. The Chair has decided that it is divisible. Does the gentleman from Illinois appeal from the decision of the Chair?

Mr. SAMUELS. But I again ask the Chair, if the gentleman from Illinois, when he was entitled to the floor and had not yielded it, can be deprived of his right by such a point of order?

The CHAIR. Certainly not. The point of order having been raised, was decided by the Chair, but the division of the question could not be called for, until the gentleman from Illinois had yielded the floor.

A Delegate raised the point of order that the gentleman from Illinois had spoken once on this question before he had taken the floor the second time, and was not, therefore, entitled to speak again until others desiring the floor had been heard.

The PRESIDENT *pro tem.* When the gentleman from Illinois obtained the floor, the Chair did not observe any other gentleman who desired to speak.

Mr. RICHARDSON was proceeding when the points of order had interrupted him, to pay his respects to the gentleman from Pennsylvania, Mr. Randall. He believed it had been asserted, and not denied by him, that he had recently come into the Democratic fold. About the political history of the gentleman he knew but little. The gentleman has taken upon himself to thrust into this debate the complicated question of the Presidency, and to raise the question between Northern and Southern candidates. He was not here for the purpose of disturbing these questions now. From early boyhood to this hour his manhood had been devoted to the cause of the Democratic party, until his life had fallen into "the sere and yellow leaf." He did not desire to be driven by recruits of yesterday from his position. It might be that some of those who had fought and contended with the Democrats throughout many a campaign, were willing to follow the example of the Greeks of old before Troy, and when they could not make an impression upon its walls, to enter within them concealed in a wooden horse, and thus to effect the capture of the city. When gentlemen who have so recently joined the party come here, they are welcome, and they will, no doubt, in time, do good service in the party; but the gentleman from Pennsylvania, in his attempt to thrust this question of the Presidency upon us, was premature, and he protested against his course. The Convention were engaged in deciding a question of right or wrong respecting a report of the Committee on Organization. The Committee had reported rules for the government of the Convention. In all previous Conventions which he had attended, the Committee on Organization had exercised the same power. This Committee had done no more than former Committees had done, and they had in their report followed out the spirit of the resolutions adopted at Cincinnati.

Mr. WRIGHT, of Pennsylvania, took the floor.

Mr. WRIGHT. "Wright of Pennsylvania" You ought to know me, for I have been in every Convention that ever was held. [Loud laughter.] If there ever was a time or occasion when there should be harmony among the members of the Democratic party it was now. He was surprised that after a Committee composed of representatives of every State in the Union had made a report, with only two States dissenting, any opposition should be made to its adoption. He charged upon those who had made this opposition the consequences that might ensue from the rejection of this report. It was well known that unless some harmony shall prevail in the Convention the nominations made here would be worth but the paper upon which the names of the nominees were written. From the year 1836 to 1860 he had been a member of the National Democratic Convention every time it had assembled, and he never yet had seen an attempt to reject a report of this kind forced upon the Convention. The practice of every Democratic Convention had been to allow every Delegate entitled to a vote to cast that vote as he pleased, unless under instructions from his State. The State of Pennsylvania had given this privilege to her representatives here, and it was the people, not the Delegates, who were heard. When it was agreed by a State that her vote should be cast as a unit, he was the last man to object to it; but when the State Convention fails to exercise that power, or is silent upon the subject, then it is the province of the Delegates who are here, to act in their representative capacity, and to cast their votes in conformity with the wishes of their constituency. It was well known in the Convention of 1844 when the Democratic party did him the honor to make him the presiding officer, the State of Pennsylvania exercised the right to cast its divided vote. In the Convention of 1848, the Delegation of Pennsylvania was again divided from the State, and he was himself one of eight Delegates who cast votes in the minority. In 1852 Pennsylvania presented its own candidate, and was therefore united.

A Delegate. Did not the State of Pennsylvania cast a unit vote in 1844?

Mr. Wright. No. Only upon some points upon the question of the adoption of the two-third rule, the vote stood twelve to thirteen. The minority nominated for the Presidency Richard M. Johnson. He thought he could pledge Pennsylvania as a unit this time for a Presidential candidate. Now the Committee had brought this report into the Convention, and he advocated its adoption. But he was not one who would secede, if the Convention should adopt a rule unpalatable to him. He would stay in the Convention so long as a majority of the body remained here. But if the rule was adopted here as adopted at Cincinnati, it would be construed into the right to deny him the privilege of casting a representative vote for his own district. They would be acting in opposition to the Democracy of his own State, who had agreed that he should have the power he claimed. The Convention had no right to ostracise him, and to deprive him of a power conferred upon him by the State he represented. He moved the previous question.

[Cries of "No! no!" and several Delegates attempting to speak amidst calls for "Question!" and cries of "Hear! hear! hear!"]

Mr. Wright insisted upon the call for the previous question.

The President *pro tem.* The Chair desires to explain the state of the question. The Chair decided the report of the Committee, so far as it related to rules, out of order. The only question now before the House is on that portion of the report which names permanent officers. The previous question has been demanded upon this, and until the Convention shall decide whether or not it will order the previous question, debate is out of order.

Mr. McCook rose to a question of privilege. He desired to remind the Chair that the State of Ohio had appealed from its decision, and that the Chair had receded therefrom.

The President *pro tem.* The gentleman from Ohio is correct. The Chair reviewed its decision, but decided that a division of the question on the report was in order. The previous question has been demanded.

[Loud cries of "Question! question!"]

The previous question was then ordered.

The President *pro tem.* The question now is on the adoption of the report of the Committee naming permanent officers of this Convention. [Cries of "Question! question!"]

The report was then adopted with one dissenting voice.

Several Delegates rose to address the Chair.

The President *pro tem.* No business is in order until the permanent officers now chosen have taken their places.

Mr. Samuels, of Pennsylvania, obtained the floor, and moved the appointment of a Committee of two to conduct the permanent presiding officer to the Chair. Agreed to.

Messrs. Clark, of Mississippi, and Richardson, of Illinois, were appointed such Committee.

The President *pro tem.* then addressed the Convention as follows:

Gentlemen of the Convention:—Before introducing to you the permanent officer of this Convention, I wish to return to you my thanks for the compliment you have paid me. To have presided over such a body as this is indeed honor enough for any gentleman. But before retiring, fellow-citizens, let me exhort you in your councils to moderation and harmony. Recollect we are brethren engaged in the same great cause—embarked on the same vessel, and under such circumstances that one plank of the ship cannot sink without the others being submerged. Recollect that we have a common destiny and a common fame. You should regard each other as brothers, and not as hostile forces marching forward to hostile music, under different flags. The Democratic party has but *one* flag—the flag of our common country—and that teaches us fraternal love and unity. Let us then talk no more about sections. We know no North, no South, no East, no West, where Democrats are concerned. No; we go on the Democratic principle, that it matters not where a Democrat resides—whether in the land of perpetual flowers, or in the land of eternal icebergs and everlasting frosts—if he be a Democrat, he may embark on the same deck, and be protected by the same Stars and Stripes. He is a Democrat, and, all other things being equal, he is entitled to the same consideration from wherever he may come. Let us talk no more of sections. It obliterates the kindest feelings from our hearts. To take a sectional view of Democrats, as compared with the broad ground of Democratic brotherly love, regardless of sections, is like a sluggish, winding, obscure stream, as compared with the noble and gigantic Mississippi, which rolls onward in its course to the Gulf of Mexico. Fellow-citizens, our duty here is plain. We come here to consider the good of the great Democratic party. To effect our object, requires a concentration of efforts. It is our duty to meet all our brethren most cordially, and so to combine all interests as to secure the effect and advantages of a concentration of effort. That concentration of effort may well be illustrated by the course of the great Father of Waters, the river which commences at its source in the mountains, in springs and streams so small, that a hunter would scarcely widen his steps to cross them. But, running on, it mingles with other streams; yet so shallow that the mother duck can scarcely swim her callow young in its waters. Then rolling onward, it mingles with yet other streams, until, at last, it forms the great Mississippi River—so deep and so vast that all the navies of the world could ride in safety upon its waters. It is your duty to gather all these streams of Democracy together into one flood, so that the bark freighted with all our hopes and destinies may ride in triumph and in safety. [Loud and continued applause.]

The Committee appeared upon the platform with the Hon. Caleb Cushing, who advanced and shook hands with the temporary President.

Mr. Flournoy. Gentlemen of the Convention:—It is with great pleasure I introduce to you, as your permanent presiding officer, Col. Caleb Cushing, of Massachusetts, and allow me to congratulate you on the wisdom of your selection.

Mr. Cushing was greeted with loud and long-continued applause. When the cheers had subsided, he spoke as follows:

Gentlemen of the Convention:—I respectfully tender to you the most earnest expression of profound gratitude for the honor which you have this day done me in appointing me to preside over your deliberations. It is, however, a responsible duty imposed, much more than a high honor conferred. In the discharge of that duty, in the direction of business and of debate, in the preservation of order, it shall be my constant endeavor faithfully and impartially to officiate there as your minister, and most humbly to reflect your will. In a great deliberative assembly like this, it is not the presiding officer in whom the strength resides. It is not *his* strength, but *yours*—your intelligence; your sense of order; your instinct of self respect. I rely, gentlemen, confidently upon you, not upon myself, for the prompt and parliamentary dispatch of the business of this Convention

Gentlemen, you have come here from the green hills of the Eastern States —from the rich States of the imperial center—from the sun-lighted plains of the South—from the fertile States of the mighty basin of the Mississippi—from the golden shores of the distant Oregon and California—[loud cheers!] —you have come hither in the exercise of the highest functions of a free people, to participate, to aid in the selection of the future rulers of the Republic. You do this as the representatives of the Democratic party—of that great party of the Union, whose proud mission it has been, whose proud mission it is, to maintain the public liberties—to reconcile popular freedom with constituted order—to maintain the sacred, reserved rights of the sovereign States—[loud and long continued applause]—to stand, in a word, the perpetual sentinels on the outpost of the Constitution. [Cries of "that's the talk," and loud cheers.] Ours, gentlemen, is the motto inscribed on that scroll in the hands of the monumental statue of the great statesman of South Carolina "Truth, Justice, and the Constitution." [Loud cheers.] Opposed to us are those who labor to overthrow the Constitution, under the false and insidious pretense of supporting it; those who are aiming to produce in this country a permanent sectional conspiracy—a traitorous sectional conspiracy of one half the States of the Union against the other half; those who, impelled by the stupid and half insane spirit of faction and fanaticism, would hurry our land on to revolution and to civil war; those, the banded enemies of the Constitution, it is the part—the high and noble part of the Democratic party of the Union to withstand; to strike down and to conquer! Aye! that is our part, and we will do it. In the name of our dear country, with the help of God we will do it. [Loud cheers.] Aye, we *will* do it, for, gentlemen, we will not distrust *ourselves*; we will not despair of the genius of our country; we will continue to repose with undoubting faith in the good Providence of Almighty God. [Loud applause.]

Gentlemen, I will not longer detain you from the important business of the Convention. Allow me a few moments for the purpose of completing the arrangements with the elected officers of the Convention, and then the Chair will call upon you for such motions and propositions as may be in order before the Convention. [Applause.]

The Temporary Secretary proceeded to call the roll of the Vice Presidents, who took their places upon the platform.

The names of the Secretaries were then called.

The PRESIDENT stated that it might occupy some minutes for the Secretaries to make arrangements amongst themselves for the business of the Convention. He therefore suggested a brief recess.

The Convention took five minutes recess.

Upon the Convention being again called to order,

Mr. JACKSON, of Georgia, rose to a question of privilege. That question referred to the Delegation from the State of Georgia, on whose behalf he claimed for one moment the attention of the Convention.

The PRESIDENT. The gentleman will state his question of privilege.

Mr. JACKSON. It is as to the right of the State of Georgia to a larger number of representatives on the floor than the regular number allowed her on the floor of the Convention. The question as to the representation of Georgia had been referred back, by the Committee on Credentials, to the Delegates from the State, on the ground that while a greater number of

2

Delegates than were regularly entitled to seats claimed admission to the Convention, there was yet not a contest as to the seats. The State of Georgia had appointed forty Delegates to come to Charleston, at two Conventions which had been held at different times in that State.

Mr. SAYLES, of Rhode Island, rose to a question of order. The Delegates from Georgia had appeared before the Committee on Credentials, and it was out of order to bring this subject before the Convention in advance of the report of the Committee.

Mr. JACKSON said the Committee on Credentials had already acted on the matter, by referring it back to the Delegation from the State.

The PRESIDENT. The gentleman from Georgia will please pause a few minutes. The question of order has been raised that the subject has been referred to the Committee on Credentials, and that the report of that Committee is not yet in possession of the Convention. The point of order is well taken. The subject cannot now be brought up in order; but any motion the gentleman from Georgia has to make will be in order whenever the report of the Committee on Credentials shall be presented to the Convention.

Mr. BARRY, of Mississippi, moved that the rules of the Democratic Convention of 1856 be adopted as the rules of this, and on this he called the previous question.

Mr. MONTGOMERY, of Pennsylvania, raised the point of order that the report of a Committee on Organization, embracing the question of rules, was yet before the Convention. The resolution, therefore, on the same subject, was not in order.

The PRESIDENT. The question pending before the Convention when the permanent officers took their places, was on the remaining portion of the report of the Committee on Organization; that question is the one now in order.

Mr. BARRY. Then I move to strike out from the report the additional rule.

Mr. McCOOK moved that the Convention take a recess till 4 P. M. The Committee on Credentials had not yet reported, and there is great difference of opinion on the report of the Committee on Organization, now before the Convention. For the convenience of the Convention he made this motion for a recess.

The PRESIDENT. The Chair will take the opportunity, before putting the question for recess, as he is not aware how that will be decided, to give two notices:

The first was a notice that the Committee on Credentials desired the attendance of its members.

The second was a letter from the Trustees of the Charleston College, inviting the members of the Convention to visit their Institution, which was read as follows:

To the Honorable, the President of the National Democratic Convention now meeting in Charleston:

SIR:—In obedience to the directions of the Trustees of the College of Charleston, I beg leave to submit to you, sir, and through you, if you please, to the other members of the Convention over which you preside, the subjoined notice—and to invite you and them, at your individual or collective convenience, to visit the Museum of the College. We flatter ourselves that you will find it deserving of your attention; and we shall be much gratified if your examination of it should hereafter be one of many agreeable recollections of your meeting in our city.

I have the honor to be, with the highest respect, sir, your very obedient servant,
M. KING.

CHARLESTON, April 23, 1860.

COLLEGE OF CHARLESTON.

The Museum of the College of Charleston will be open to visitors every week day during the meeting of the Convention. On Saturday from 9 A. M. to 6 P. M., and on every other week day from noon to 6 P. M.

It contains an extensive collection of highly valuable and many rare specimens in Natural History, Mineralogy, Geology, and Paleontology, of great interest to the scientific inquirer, and well worthy the attention of every intelligent observer. By order of the Board of Trustees,

April 23, 1860. M. KING, President.

The invitation was accepted by the Convention unanimously.

The question was then taken on Mr. McCook's motion for a recess, and the same was lost.

Mr. RUSSEL, of Virginia, called for the reading of the latter portion of the report of the Committee on Organization, which was read.

Mr. STUART, of Michigan, rose to a point of order, when the temporary Presiding Officer left the Chair; the report of the Committee on Organization was before the Convention, and the previous question was called and ordered. A division of the qnestion was called for. The question was put on the first portion of the report of the Committee on Organization, and it was adopted. The present Presiding Officer then took the Chair. The question now was upon the adoption of the latter portion of the report. As the previous question had been ordered, the latter portion of the report must be voted upon without debate or amendment.

The PRESIDENT. If the facts are as stated by the gentleman from Michigan, the point of order is well taken, and the position of the gentleman is correct. The present presiding officer will appeal to his predecessor for information as to the correct position of the question.

Mr. FLOURNOY explained the position of the question, showing that the previous question had been ordered; that the question on the first part of the report had been put and carried, and that the Convention was still under the operation of the previous question, thus preventing amendment or debate.

SEVERAL VOICES "What is the question before the Convention?"

The PRESIDENT announced the question to be on a motion made before the previous question was ordered, to strike out from the report of the Committee on Organization the additional rule.

The vote by States was demanded, and the roll was called.

When Virginia was called, Mr. MOFFIT protested against the whole vote of the State being cast in the negative. He denied the justice of the principle that a district had not the right to decide how it would vote. Whilst he denied the propriety of any interference on the part of this Convention, he contended for the principle, and in the name of his constituents protested against the principle contended for. He claimed and reserved to himself and colleague the right, at any time, to decide for his district. He was appointed by the people of his own district, and was responsible to them alone

When Indiana was called, several Delegates from that State rose to make statements, and great confusion ensued, until the Chair compelled the observance of order.

When the State of Tennessee was called, Mr. Ewing stated that the Delegation at its previous meeting had adopted a resolution that on all questions but the nomination of a President, the vote of the State should be cast as a unit. He had taken the sense of the Delegation, and the majority had voted "no." He was, in casting the vote in the negative, not representing his own individual opinion at all. An affirmative vote on this proposition would virtually abolish the rules adopted at former Conventions. He was, therefore, individually opposed to the vote.

Mr. BURROWS, of Arkansas, cast half a vote in the affirmative.

Mr. Hooker, of Mississippi, protested against his State casting a united vote when he was opposed to the vote thus cast. He was called to order, and the vote was then announced, the motion to strike out the additional rule being lost by the following vote:

	Yeas.	Nays.		Yeas.	Nays.		Yeas.	Nays.
Maine		8	North Carolina	7	3	Ohio		23
New Hampshire		5	South Carolina	8		Indiana		13
Vermont		5	Georgia	10		Illinois		11
Massachusetts	6	5½	Florida	3		Michigan		6
Rhode Island		4	Alabama	9		Wisconsin		5
Connecticut		6	Louisiana	6		Iowa		4
New York		35	Mississippi	7		Minnesota		4
New Jersey		7	Texas	4		California	2½	1½
Pennsylvania	14	10½	Arkansas	½	3½	Oregon	3	
Delaware	1½	1½	Missouri	3	7			
Maryland	3½	4½	Tennessee		12		103½	197
Virginia	15		Kentucky		12			

At the request of Mr. Clark, of Mississippi, the report of the Committee on Organization was again read, and adopted by an almost unanimous vote.

Mr. Stuart, of Michigan, moved to re-consider that vote, and to lay that resolution on the table. Adopted.

Mr. Payne, of Ohio, called for the consideration of the resolution for the appointment of a Committee of one from each State to report a Platform, and that all resolutions relating to the Platform shall be referred to that Committee without debate. Upon that resolution he called the previous question.

Mr. Barlow, of New York, desired to offer an amendment, and asked that it be read for information of the Convention.

Mr. Payne. I object to the reading, and demand that the call for the previous question shall be put.

The previous question was ordered and the resolution adopted.

Mr. Payne moved to re-consider that vote, and to lay the resolution on the table. Adopted.

Mr. Burrows, of Arkansas, offered the following:

Resolved, That this Convention will not proceed to ballot for a candidate for the Presidency, until the Platform shall have been adopted.

The President. The first business in order will be the call of the States, that the names of the Committee on Resolutions may be handed in. The question will then be taken on the motion of the gentleman from Arkansas.

The following names were then reported as the Committee on Resolutions:

Committee on Resolutions and Platform—Maine, A. M. Roberts; New Hampshire, Wm. Beven; Vermont, E. M. Brown; Massachusetts, B. F. Butler; Rhode Island C. S. Bradley; Connecticut, A. G. Hazard; New York, Ed. Cogswell; New Jersey, Benj. Williamson; Pennsylvania, A. B. Wright; Delaware, J. A. Bayard; Maryland, B. S. Johnson; Virginia, J. Barbour; North Carolina, W. W. Avery; South Carolina, J. S. Preston; Georgia, J. Wingfield; Florida, J. B. Owens; Alabama, John Erwin; Louisiana, R. A. Hunter; Mississippi, E. Barksdale; Texas, F. S. Stockdale; Arkansas, N. B. Burrows; Missouri, John M. Krum; Tennessee, Samuel Milligan; Kentucky, R. K. Williams, Ohio, H. B. Payne; Indiana, P. C. Dunning; Illinois, O. B. Ficklin; Michigan, G. V. N. Lothrop; Wisconsin, A. S. Palmer; Iowa, B. M. Samuels; Minnesota, J. M. Cavanaugh; California, Austin E. Smith; Oregon, James J. Stevens.

Mr. Richardson, by consent of the Convention, stated that in a few remarks he made this morning, he had been misinterpreted by a certain gentleman on the floor. He had intended no discourtesy to the gentleman from Pennsylvania, Mr. Randall, or to the Whig party, all of whom he desired to see come into the Democratic fold. He could not, he would not offer a discourtesy to a gentleman so much his senior as the gentleman from Pennsylvania. He deemed this explanation to be a duty—nothing more, and nothing less.

The question then recurring on the resolution of Mr. Burrows, of Arkansas, Mr. Bishop called for the previous question.

Mr. Hamilton, of Maryland, moved to lay the resolution on the table.

The vote was called by States, and the motion to lay the resolution on the table was lost by the following vote:

	Yeas.	Nays.		Yeas.	Nays.		Yeas.	Nays.
Maine	8		North Carolina		10	Ohio		23
New Hampshire		5	South Carolina		8	Indiana		13
Vermont		5	Georgia		10	Illinois		11
Massachusetts		11	Florida		3	Michigan		6
Rhode Island		4	Alabama		9	Wisconsin		5
Connecticut	2	4	Louisiana		6	Iowa		4
New York		35	Mississippi		7	Minnesota		4
New Jersey		7	Texas		4	California		4
Pennsylvania	17	10	Arkansas		4	Oregon		3
Delaware		3	Missouri		9			
Maryland	5½	2½	Tennessee		12		32½	270½
Virginia		15	Kentucky		12			

The question recurring on the adoption of the resolution, the call for the previous question was seconded, and the previous question ordered.

The resolution was then adopted by an almost unanimous vote, only two or three voices being heard in the negative.

Mr. BISHOP, of Connecticut, offered the following:

Resolved, That no member of this Convention be allowed to speak more than once on the same question, nor for a longer time than fifteen minutes.

Mr. BISHOP called for the previous question.

Mr. COOPER, of Alabama, moved to lay the resolution on the table. Lost.

Mr. WHITE, of Massachusetts, called for a division of the question.

The previous question was seconded and ordered before the question was put.

Mr. AVERY, of North Carolina, raised the point of order that the Convention was acting under the rules of the House of Representatives, and that the one hour rule was, therefore, the rule of the Convention. This resolution would consequently be an alteration of the rules, and must lie over one day.

The PRESIDENT decided the point of order well taken, and the mover of the resolution gave notice that he should call it up for adoption to-morrow.

Mr. FISHER, of Virginia, moved the following:

Resolved, That the Presiding Officer of this Convention be, and he is hereby requested, to invite the ministers of different denominations in this city to open the daily proceedings with prayer. Adopted.

MR. WHITING, of Delaware, moved to adjourn until 10 o'clock to-morrow morning. He made the motion because the Committee on Contested Seats desired to hold a session in the Hall this afternoon, and they would be prepared to report to-morrow morning.

The motion was temporarily waived.

Mr. EWING, of Tennessee, suggested that the several resolutions to be referred to the Committee on Platform be handed to the Chairman of that Committee. Agreed to.

Judge MEEK, of Alabama, presented to the Convention the Platform of his State, which was referred under the rule.

The CHAIR announced that the Committee on Resolutions would meet at Masonic Hall at 5 this afternoon.

It was announced that the Committee on Contested Seats would meet at Market Hall at 5 P. M., to adjourn to the Hall of the Convention.

The Secretaries of the Convention were requested to meet in their Room after the adjournment.

Mr. PEARCE, of Louisiana, handed in a resolution from his State, which was referred under the rule.

On motion of Mr. Pearce, the Convention then adjourned until 10 A. M., to-morrow.

THIRD DAY.

WEDNESDAY, APRIL 25, 1860.

The Convention met at ten o'clock, A. M., and the proceedings were opened by prayer by the Rev. Dr. Bachman.

In consequence of the necessary absence of Mr. HYDE, Chairman of the Recording Secretaries, the reading of yesterday's Journal was by unanimous consent dispensed with, and the keeping of the records of the Convention were placed in charge of JOHN G. PARKHURST, of Michigan.

The calling of the roll was by unanimous consent dispensed with.

No Committee being ready to report, the PRESIDENT stated the first business in order to be the resolution of Mr. Bishop, of Connecticut.

The Secretary read the resolution as follows:

Resolved, That no member of this Convention be allowed to speak more than once on the same question, nor for a longer time than fifteen minutes.

Mr. BISHOP demanded the previous question on the resolution.

The call for the previous question was seconded, and on the question, "Shall the main question be now put?" a vote by States was called for by several States.

The question being taken by a vote of States resulted, yeas 121, nays 182, as follows:

	Yeas.		Nays.
Maine	8	New Hampshire	5
Connecticut	1	Vermont	5
New Jersey	7	Massachusetts	18
Pennsylvania	27	Rhode Island	4
Delaware	3	Connecticut	5
Missouri	9	New York	35
Tennessee	12	Maryland	8
Kentucky	11	Virginia	15
Indiana	13	North Carolina	10
Illinois	11	South Carolina	8
Michigan	6	Georgia	10
Wisconsin	5	Florida	3
Iowa	4	Alabama	9
California	4	Louisiana	6
		Mississippi	7
		Texas	4
		Arkansas	4
		Kentucky	1
		Ohio	23
		Minnesota	4
		Oregon	3

So the main question was not ordered.

Mr. WALKER, of Alabama, moved to amend the resolution by adding:

Provided, That it shall not be applied to any discussion upon the platform to be reported to this Convention by the Committee on Resolutions.

Mr. BISHOP accepted the amendment of the gentleman from Alabama, and called the previous question on the resolution as modified.

The call for the previous question was sustained, and the main question ordered to be put.

The question was taken on the resolution as modified, and it was adopted.

Mr. SIMMONS, of South Carolina, offered the following resolution:

Resolved, That such part of the South gallery of this hall as may be necessary for the accommodation of the alternates be reserved for their use, and that the remaining part of the galleries be opened for the public accommodation.

Mr. CRAIG, of Missouri, moved to lay the resolution on the table, which motion was agreed to.

The PRESIDENT laid before the Convention the following communication from the Commissioners of the Orphan Asylum of Charleston.

CHARLESTON, April 24, 1860.

To the Honorable, the President and Delegates of the Democratic Convention:

GENTLEMEN:—The Commissioners of the Orphan House of Charleston respectfully invite the Delegates of the Democratic National Convention, now assembled in this city, to visit the Orphan Asylum of Charleston, situated in Calhoun street, to inspect its organization, domestic arrangements, discipline, and economy, and to examine, more especially, the educational departments of their School.

The Institution will be open to the inspection of the Delegates at all times, but more especially on Wednesday afternoon, the 25th of April instant, at 4 o'clock, when the Public Exhibition of the School takes place.

Respectfully, H. A. DESAUSSURE,
Chairman of Commissioners Orphan House.

Mr. STUART, of Michigan, moved that when the Convention adjourn it adjourn to meet at 4 o'clock, P. M.

A Delegate moved to amend the motion so that it would read five o'clock instead of four.

Mr. DENT, of Pennsylvania, moved that when the Convention adjourn, it adjourn to meet at 7 o'clock P. M.

The question being taken on the motion that when the Convention adjourn, it adjourn to meet at 7 o'clock, it was decided in the negative.

The question being taken on the motion that when the Convention adjourn, it be to meet at 5 o'clock, it was also lost.

The question was then taken on the motion that when the Convention adjourn, it be to meet at four o'clock, and it was agreed to.

On motion, the Convention then adjourned.

AFTERNOON SESSION.

The Convention re-assembled at four o'clock, P. M.

Mr. WRIGHT, of Massachusetts, moved the following resolution, viz :

Resolved, That the Committee on Resolutions be instructed to report in print, so that every member may be furnished with a copy—which was unanimously adopted.

Mr. LOWRY, of Indiana, offered the following resolution, viz :

Resolved, That the Officer of the Convention having charge of that matter, be and he is hereby required to have the doors to the Hall of the Convention opened for the admission of those entitled to enter, at least one hour before the time set for each meeting of this body. Which was adopted.

A communication from the officers of the Citadel Academy, inviting the members of the Convention to attend the parade at 5½ o'clock, Thursday P. M., at the Academy grounds, was read and received with cheers.

Mr. LOWRY, of Indiana, moved the following resolution :

Resolved, That a Committee of one from each State be appointed by the Delegates thereof, to report the names of one person from each State, to constitute the Democratic National Committee, to continue in office until their successors are appointed, whose duty it shall be, in addition to other things, to fix the time and place for the holding of the next National Convention, and said first named Committee shall also consider and report.

Mr. LAWRENCE, of Louisiana, moved that the resolution be laid over one day.

Mr. BURNETT, of Alabama, moved to amend by adding, "and said Committee shall not issue tickets of admission to the floor of the Convention to any Delegates whose seats may be contested."

Mr. TERRY, of Arkansas, offered a further amendment as follows :

"And said Committtee shall have power to fill any vacancy in said Committee."

Mr. PUGH, of Ohio, moved that the resolution and amendments be referred to a committee of thirty-three, one from each State, and upon this he called the previous question.

The call for the previous question was seconded and ordered, and the main question was put, and the motion of Mr. Pugh was carried.

The names of the members of this Committee to be handed in to-morrow morning.

Mr. KRUM, of Missouri, Chairman of the Committee on Credentials, then presented the following report and resolutions, upon which the Convention had agreed, and he claimed for it the attention of the Convention:

MAJORITY REPORT.

To the National Democratic Convention:

Mr. PRESIDENT:—Your Committee on Credentials, immediately after their appointment, entered upon the discharge of the duties assigned them, and carefully examined the credentials of the several Delegates to this Convention.

Your Committee find that all the States in the Union, except the States of Massachusetts, Maryland, Illinois and New York, are represented in this Convention by Delegates duly elected in the several States by State or District organizations of the Democratic party, and your Committee append to this report, as a part thereof, full lists of the Delegates so elected.

Your Committee further report that there were contesting claimants to the seats held by the Delegations in the following cases, viz:

In the Fifth Congressional District of Massachusetts.

In the Fourth Congressional District of Maryland.

In the State of Illinois, and

In the State of New York.

The contestants in these several cases had a full and impartial hearing before your Committee, and, after a full consideration of their respective claims, your Committee are of opinion that the sitting Delegates representing these Districts and States are justly entitled to their respective seats.

All of which is respectfully submitted.

JOHN. M. KRUM, Chairman.

Resolved. That the sitting Delegates to this Convention from the State of Illinois, of whom Col. W. A. Richardson is Chairman, are entitled to their respective seats.

Resolved, That Cornelius Doherty and K. S. Chaffee, Delegates representing the Fifth Congressional District of Massachusetts, are entitled to their respective seats.

Resolved, That F. M. Landham and Robert J. Brent, Delegates representing the Fourth Congressional District of Maryland, are entitled to their respective seats

Resolved, That the Delegates to this Convention from the State of New York, of which Dean Richmond is Chairman, are entitled as such to seats therein.

Adopted.

Mr BROOKS, of Alabama, presented the following Minority Report and Resolutions:

MINORITY REPORT.

To the Honorable President of the National Democratic Convention:

The undersigned, members of the Committee on Credential, under an imperious sense of duty, are constrained to dissent from the report of the majority of this Committee, and respectfully recommend that the two Delegations from the State of New York be authorized to select each thirty-five Delegates, and that the seventy Delegates thus selected be admitted to this Convention as the Delegates of the New York Democracy, and that they be allowed two hours to report their selection—the two Delegations to vote separately, each to be entitled to seventeen votes, the remaining vote of said

State to be cast alternately by the two Delegations, the sitting menbers casting it the first time.

(Signed.) WM. M. BROOKS, Delegate from Alabama.
JOHN S. DUDLEY, Delegate from California.
E. GREEN, Delegate from Texas.
VAN H. MANNING, Delegate from Arkansas.
JULIAN HARTRIDGE, Delegate from Georgia.
W. S. BARRY, of Mississippi.

Mr. Brooks, of Alabama, offered the following resolution:

Resolved, That the two Delegations from New York be authorized to select each thirty-five Delegates, and that the seventy Delegates thus selected, be admitted to this Convention as Delegates from the New York Democracy, and that they be allowed two hours to report their selection. The two Delegations to vote separately, each to be entitled to seventeen votes, the remaining vote to be cast alternately by the two Delegations—the sitting members to cast it the first time.

Mr. McCook, of Ohio, moved the adoption of the Majority Report, together with the Resolutions accompanying said report.

Mr. Brooks, of Alabama, moved the adoption of the Minority Report of the Committee on Credentials and Resolutions, as an amendment to the Majority Report.

The previous question being demanded by Mr. McCook, was then seconded and ordered, and a division of the question called for.

The reso utions and reports were read.

The main question was ordered.

The first, second, and third resolutions of the Majority Report were adopted.

The question then being on the amendment of Mr. Brooks, of Alabama, the State of Alabama called for the vote by States, and the State of Mississippi seconded the call.

The amendment was lost by the following vote:

	Yeas.	Nays.		Yeas.	Nays.		Yeas.	Nays.
Maine		8	North Carolina	5	4	Ohio		23
New Hampshire		5	South Carolina		8	Indiana		13
Vermont		5	Georgia	10		Illinois		11
Massachusetts		13	Florida		3	Michigan		6
Rhode Island		4	Alabama	9		Wisconsin		5
Connecticut		6	Louisiana		6	Iowa		4
New York		...	Mississippi	7		Minnesota		4
New Jersey		7	Texas	4		California	3½	½
Ponusylvania		27	Arkansas	3	1	Oregon		3
Delaware		3	Missouri	1	8			
Maryland		8	Tennessee	9	3		55	210½
Virginia	3½	10	Kentucky		12			

The question then recurring on the adoption of the resolution of the majority, the same was adopted by a large majority.

On motion of Mr. Peck, of Michigan, the entire Report of the Committee was then adopted.

Mr. North, of Pennsylvania, moved to re-consider the motion to adopt the report, and to lay that motion on the table. Agreed to.

Mr. North, of Pennsylvania, moved that the rejected claimants for seats in this Convention be allowed honorary seats on the floor of the Convention.

The resolution was laid over under the rules for one day.

Mr. Montgomery, of Pennsylvania, offered the following resolution:

Resolved, That the appointment of a Committee of one from each State to select a National Committee of the Democratic party, for the next four years, be postponed until after the nomination of a candidate for the Presidency. Which was adopted.

The PRESIDENT. I will entreat the Convention to be in order while the painful announcement of the death of a member of this Convention is announced.

Hon. H. E. STOUGHTON, of Vermont.

Mr. PRESIDENT:—I arise by request of the Delegation from Vermont, to announce to this Convention the sad intelligence of the sudden death of Hon. John S. Robinson, one of the Delegates at large from our State, who but yesterday stood in his place upon this floor, in his usual health, officiating as Chairman of this Delegation.

This morning about six o'clock, and while the deceased was apparently in a quiet slumber, he had an attack of apoplexy, and so sudden was his death that he was not able to utter one word or wish to be communicated to those who ere this are stricken down with anguish by the intelligence of the death of their friend in this far distant city.

The deceased was about fifty-five years of age, a lawyer, standing in the front rank of his profession, always a Democrat, and as such a member of our State Senate, and in 1853 he was elected Governor in the Federal State of Vermont—the only Democratic Governor of that State any of the Delegates present have seen since they were voters therein.

We, in common with all who knew him, held him in high estimation for his purity in public and private life.

His remains, on the adjournment of this Convention, will be taken from the Mills House to the New York steamboat, to be conveyed to New York, and thence to his own mountain home, it being all we have left of him to return to the widow and fatherless.

Col. B. F. WARDLAW, of Florida. The sad announcement of death at any time, Mr. President, chills the heart and deadens every sensibility; but, Sir, when that melancholy announcement is made upon an occasion of this sort, it comes with double force, and falls like a leaden pall upon the inmost recesses of our soul. Our deliberations had scarcely begun ere the unrelenting monster, Death, invades our councils—the councils of this mighty Republic.

One of the Delegates to this Convention, from the Old Green Mountain State, has been suddenly struck down in our midst; and whilst we bow in humble reverence to Omnipotent fiat, as he lies near by, still in the chilly arms of death, far away from his home in the icy mountains of the North, the Peninsula State, Florida, desires, as an humble tribute of respect, to mingle her grief in condolence, and with her rich profusion of flowers, to scatter them around the bier of the lamented son of Vermont. Therefore, I tender the following resolution:

Resolved, That with feelings of deep regret, this Convention has just learned that one of her members, Gov. Robinson, a Delegate from Vermont, has suddenly passed from time to eternity, and in respect to his memory, this Convention will now stand adjourned until 10 o'clock to-morrow.

Capt. ISAIAH RYNDERS, of New York, moved that the Convention, on adjourning, proceed in a body to the Mills House.

The resolutions of Mr. Wardlaw and Capt. Rynders were adopted, and the Convention then adjourned until 10 o'clock to-morrow, and proceeded in a body to attend the remains of Governor Robinson to the boat.

APPENDIX TO THE THIRD DAY'S PROCEEDINGS.

List of Delegates appended to the Report of the Committee on Credentials, with their Post Office addresses.

MAINE.

Bion Bradbury, Eastport.
George F Shepley, Portland.
E Wilder Farley, Newcastle.
Amos M Roberts, Bangor.
S R Lyman, Portland.
Thomas K Lane, Saco.
S C Blanchard, Yarmouth.
Calvin Record, Auburn.
Thomas D Robinson, Bath.
Henry W Owen, Bath.
Henry A Wyman, Snowhegan.
Charles D Jameson, Bangor.
J Withrop Jones, Ellsworth.
P S J Talbot, East Machias.
J Y McClintock, Belfast.
W H Burrill, Belfast.

VERMONT.

John S Robinson, Bennington.
Jasper Rand, Berkshire.
Henry Keyes, Newbury.
E M Brown, Woodstock.
Charles G Eastman, Montpelier.
Pitt W Hyde, Hydeville.
H E Stoughton, Bellows Falls.
Stephen Thomas, West Fairlee.
Lucius Robinson, Newport.
H B Smith, Milton.

NEW HAMPSHIRE.

Josiah Minot, Concord.
Daniel Marcy, Portsmouth.
Robert S Webster, North Birnstead.
George W Stevens, Dover.
Aaron P Hughes, Nashua.
Edward W Harrington, Manchester.
Alpheus F Snow, Claremont.
Ansel Glover, Alstead.
William Burns, Lancaster.
George A Bingham, Bath.

MASSACHUSETTS.

Caleb Cushing, Newburyport.
Jas G Whitney, Boston.
Oliver Stevens, Boston.
Isaac Davis, Worcester.
Wm C N Swift, New Bedford.
Edward Merrill, New Bedford.
Phineas W Leland, Fall River.
Alex Lincoln, Hingham.
Orison Underwood, Milford.
Bradford L Wales, Randolph.
James Riley, Boston.
Isaac H Wright, Boston.
Cornelius Doherty, Boston.
K S Chaffee, East Cambridge.
E G Williams, Newburyport.
C G Clark, Lynn.
F O Prince, Winchester.
Geo Johnson, Bradford.
Benj F Butler, Lowell.
Walter Fessenden, Townsend.
Henry H Stevens, Dudley.
Geo W Gill, Worcester.
C W Chapin, Springfield.
Josiah Allis, Whately.
D N Carpenter, Greenfield.
Charles Heebner, Lee.

CONNECTICUT.

James T Pratt, Rock Hill.
Samuel Arnold, Haddam.
Andrew C Lippitt, New London.
W D Bishop, Bridgeport.
A G Hazard, Enfield.
M R West, Stafford.
E Aug Russell, Middletown.
C M Ingersol, New Haven.
William L Converse, Norwich.
Rufus L Baker, Windham.
James Gallagher, New Haven.
P C Calhoun, Bridgeport

RHODE ISLAND.

Welcome B Sayles, Providence.
Charles S Bradley, Providence.
George H Browne Providence.
John N Francis, Providence.
Edward F Newton, Newport.
Amasa Sprague, Providence.
Gideon Bradford, Providence.
Jacob Babbit, Bristol.

NEW YORK.

Dean Richmond, Buffalo, Erie county.
Augustus Schell New York City.
Isaac V Fowler, New York City.
Delos DeWolf, Oswego, Oswego county.
William H Ludlow, Sayville. Suffolk county.
Tennis G Bergen, Bayridge, Kings county.
H McLaughlin, Brooklyn, Kings county.
Francis H Spinola, Brooklyn, Kings county.
John Y Savage, New York City.
Wm Miner, New York City.
Samuel L M Barlow, New York City.
John Clancy, New York City.
Isaiah Rynders, New York City.
Edmund Driggs, Brooklyn, Kings county.
John Cochran, New York City.
Auguste Belmont, New York City.
Nelson J Waterbury, New York City.
Wm N McIntyre, New York City.
Edward Cooper, New York City.
Samuel F Butterworth, New York City.
Gouverneur Kemble, Cold Springs, Putnam co.
Edwin Croswell, New York City.
Benjamin F Edsall, Goshen, Orange county.
John C Holley, Monticello, Sullivan county.
Wm F Russell, Saugerties, Ulster county.
Geo Beach, Cairo, Green county.
Theodore Miller, Hudson Columbia county.
Henry Staats, Red Hook, Dutchess county.
David L Seymour, Troy, Rensselaer county.
Moses Warren, Troy, Rensselaer county.
Erastus Corning, Albany, Albany county.
Peter Cagger, Albany, Albany county.
John Titcomb, Waterford, Saratoga county.
Charles R. Ingalls, Greenwich, Washington co.
Lemuel Stetson, Plattsburgh, Clinton county.
Henry A Tilden, New Lebanon, Columbia county.
James C Spencer, Odgensburgh, St Lawrence co.
Lorenzo Carryl, Salisbury, Herkimer county.
Alonzo C Page, Schenectady, Schenectady county.
David Spraker, Canajoharie, Montgomery county.
Samuel North, Unadilla, Otsego county.
Alexander H Burhans, Roxbury, Delaware co.
John Stryker, Rome, Oneida county.
D P Bissel, Utica, Oneida county.
Henry S Randall, Cortlandville, Cortland county.
John F Hubbard, Jr., Norwich, Chenango co.
Williard Johnson, Fulton, Oswego county.
Sidney T Fairchild, Cazenovia, Madison county.
D C West, Lowville, Lewis county.
Allen C Beach, Watertown, Jefferson county.
James P Haskin, Syracuse, Onondago county.
John J Peck, Syracuse, Onondago county.
Elmore P Ross, Auburn, Cayuga county.

* At the adjourned session of the Convention at Baltimore, no corrected lists of Delegates were furnished the Secretary; and, consequently, the above is the only list published.

John N Knapp, Auburn. Cayuga county.
Wm W Wright, Geneva. Ontario county.
Darius A Ogden, Penn Yan, Yates county.
Henry D Barto, Trumansburgh, Tompkins county.
Charles Hulett, Horseheads, Chemung county.
C C B Walker, Corning, Steuben county.
A J Abbott, Genesee, Livingston county.
S B Jewett, Clarkson, Monroe county.
B F Gilkeson, Rochester Monroe county.
Marshall B Champlain, Cuba. Allegany county.
Henry J Glowacki, Batavia, Genesee county.
Sanford E Church, Albion, Orleans county.
A H Eastman, Lockport, Niagara county.
John T Hudson, Buffalo, Erie county.
Alpheus Prince, Clarence. Erie county.
John C Devereux, Ellicottville, Cattaraugus co.
H J Miner, Dunkirk, Chautauque co.

NEW JERSEY.

William Wright, Newark.
Benjamin Williamson. Elizabeth.
James W Wall, (absent) Burlington.
John O'Rafferty, New Germantown.
Samuel Hanna, Camden.
John L Sharp. Millville.
George F Fort, New Egypt.
David Naar. Trenton.
Albert R Speer, New Brunswick.
Joshua Doughty, Somerville.
Robert Hamilton, Newton.
John Huyler, Hackensack.
Samuel Westcott, Jersey City.
Jacob Van Arsdale, Newark.

PENNSYLVANIA.

Joseph B Baker, Philadelphia.
William Bigler, Clearfield
Kennedy L Blood, Brookville.
Richard Brodhead, Easton.
N B Browne, Philadelphia.
Edward Campbell, Jr., Pittsburgh.
Lewis C Cassidy, Philadelphia.
John Cessna, Bedford.
Hugh Clark, Philadelphia.
A H Coffroth, Somerset.
Heister Clymer, Reading.
Thomas Cunningham, Beaver.
John L Dawson, Uniontown.
Henry H Dent, Condersport.
James Dunlap, Butler.
Peter Ent, Lightstreet.
E C Evans, West Chester.
William A Galbraith. Erie.
James A Gibson, Pittsburgh.
Robert M. Gibson, Washington.
C D Gloninger, Lebanon.
A J Glossbrenner, York.
H A Guernsey, Willsboro'.
R J Haldeman, Harrisburg.
Charles Hotlestein, Milton.
Francis W Hughes, Pottsville.
Owen Jones, Cabinet.
S P Johnson, West Greenville.
F Lauer. Reading.
Samuel Megargee, Philadelphia.
William Montgomery, Washington.
William H McGee, Allegheny City.
George McHenry, Darby.
Chambers McKibbon, Philadelphia.
James Nill, Chambersburg.
H M North, Columbia.
Asa Packer, Mauch Chunk.
Israel Painter, West Newton.
Henry M Phillips, Philadelphia.
A A Plumer, Franklin.
Josiah Randall, Philadelphia.
John Reifsnyder, Liverpool.
W M Reilley, Philadelphia
John Roberts, Philadelphia.
John Ross, McVeytown.
W P Shattuck, Meadville.
D W Gray, Wendridge.
George N Smith, Johnstown.
H B Swarr, Lancaster.
Franklin Vanzant, Oakford.
C L Ward, Towanda.
H W Weir, Indiana.
Thomas B Wilson, Allentown.
Hendrick B Wright. Wilkesbarre.

DELAWARE.

John H Beverley, Smyrna.
William H Ross Seaford.
James A Bayard, Wilmington.
John B Pennington, Dover.
William G. Whiteley, Newcastle.
William Saulsbury, Georgetown.

MARYLAND.

John Contee. Buena Vista.
William T. Hamilton. Hagerstown.
Levin Woolford, Princess Ann.
John R Emory, Centerville.
Wm S Gittings, Baltimore City.
Samuel S Maffit, Elkton, Cecil county.
Carville S Stansbury, Stemmer's Run.
William Byrne Baltimore City.
E L F Hardcastle, Royal Oak.
Daniel Field, Federalsburgh.
Robert J Brent, Baltimore City.
T M Lanahan, Baltimore City.
Bradley J Johnson, Fredrick City.
John J Morrison, Barton, Allegheny county.
Oscar Miles, Milestown, St Mary's county.
D W Bowie, Prince George county.

VIRGINIA.

Arthur R Smith, Portsmouth.
John J Kindred, Jerusalem.
Lewis E Harvie, Chala, Amelia county.
Wm F Thompson, Crimea, Dinwiddie county.
William H Clark, Halifax Court House.
Walter Coles, Pittsylvania Court House.
Edmund W Hubart, Curdsville.
Robert H Glass, Lynchburg.
William L Early, Madison Court House
Robert A Coghill, New Glasgow.
Walter D Leake Goochland Court House.
James Hobbs, Manchester.
George Booker, Hampton.
M W Fisher, Eastville.
Wm A Buckner, Bowling Green.
Henry T Garnett, Oak Grove, Westmoreland co.
James Barbour, Brandy Station.
John Seddon, Fredericksburg.
John Blair Hoge, Martinsburgh.
O. R. Funston, White Post.
S M Yost, Staunton
S H Moffatt, Harrisonburgh.
Daniel H Hoge, Blacksburg.
James W Davis, Greenville Court House.
Robert Crockett, Wytheville.
William T Cecil, Tazewell Court House.
Henry Fitzbugh. Kanawha Court House.
John Brannon, Weston.
William G Brown, Kingwood.
Charles W Russell, Wheeling.

NORTH CAROLINA.

William W Avery, Morgantown.
William S Ashe, Wilmington.
Bedford Brown, Locust Hill.
William W Holden. Raleigh.
William A Moore, Edenton.
Nicholas M Long, Weldon.
Robert R Bridges, Tarboro'.
Lotty W Humphrey Richland.
Walter L Steel, Rockingham.
James Fulton, Wilmington.
Thomas S Green Warrenton.
J W B Watson, Smithfield.
Robert P. Dick, Greensboro'.
Charles S Winstead, Roxboro'.
Samuel Hargrave, Lexington.
Hampton B Hammond, Wadesboro
William Landers, Lincolnton.

Columbus Mills, Columbus.
Henry T. Farmer, Flat Rock.

SOUTH CAROLINA.

James Simmons, Charleston.
Samuel McGowan, Abbeville Court House.
H B Wilson, Georgetown.
R B Boylston, Winnsboro'
J H Witherspoon, Lancaster Court House.
E W Charles, Darlington Court House.
George N Reynolds, Charleston.
Thomas Y. Simons, Charleston.
James Patterson, Barnwell Court House.
B H Brown, Barnwell Court House.
Arthur Simpkins, Edgefield Court House.
Lemuel Boozer, Lexington Court House.
B F Perry, Greenville.
J P Reid, Anderson Court House.
John S Preston, Columbia.
Franklin Gaillard, Columbia.

GEORGIA.

Henry L Benning, Columbus.
John H Lumpkin. Rome.
Isaiah T Irwin, Washington.
Henry R Jackson, Savannah.
Junius Wingfield, Eatonton.
Hiram Warner, Greenville.
Solomon Cohe , Savannah.
James L Seward, Thomasville.
Julian Hartridge, Savannah.
W B Gaulden, Huntsville.
W J Johnson, Fort Gaines.
John A Jones, Columbus.
James M Clark, Lumpkin.
W M Slaughter. Albany.
E L Stroecker. Macon.
P Tracy, Macon.
O C Gibson, Griffin.
E J McGehee, Perry.
James J Dim nd, Stone Mountain.
J A Render, Greenville.
Samuel C Candler, Carrollton.
G J Fain, Calhoun,
E R Hardin, Dalton.
James Hoge, Atalanta.
Mark Johnston, Cartersville.
William H Hull. Athens.
George Hillyer, Monroe.
A A Franklin Hill, Athens.
Henry P Thomas, Lawrenceville.
L H Briscoe, Milledgeville.
Jeff Lamar, Covington.
J W Burney, Monticello.
James Thomas, Sparta.
L A Nelms, ———.
D C Barrow, Lexington.
H Cleveland, Augusta.
H R Casey, Appling.

FLORIDA.

T J Eppes, Apalachicola.
John Milton, Marianna.
B F Wardlaw, Madison Court House.
C E Dycke, Tallahassee
George L Bowne, Key West.
John B Owens, Ocala.

ALABAMA.

F S Lyon, Demopolis.
A B Meek, Mobile.
W L Yancey, Montgomery.
L W Lawler, Talladega.
J A Winston, Mobile.
L P Walker, Huntsville
H D Smith, Graveley Springs.
G G Griffin, Demopolis.
N H R Dawson, Selma.
R G Scott, Claiborne.
J W Portis, Suggsville.
L L Cato, Eufaula.
T J Burnett, Greenville.
J R Breare, Newton, Dale county.
M J Bulger, Dadeville.
P O Harper, West Point.
J C B Mitchell, Mount Meigs.
W C McIver. Tuskeegee.
John Erwin. Greensborough.
W M Brooks, Marion.
J C Guild, Tuscaloosa.
A W Dillard, Livingston.
F G Norman. Tuscumbia.
R M Patton, Florence.
W C Sherrod, Courtland.
R Chapman, Huntsville.
G C Bradley Huntsville.
T B Cooper, Center.
A J Henry, Guntersville.
J T Bradford. Talladega.
W Garrett. Socopetoy.
P G King, Montevallo.

MISSISSIPPI.

W S Berry, Columbus
Charles Clark, Prentiss, Bolivar county.
E Barksdale, Jackson.
W S Wilson, Port Gibson.
James Drane, Bankston.
Beverly Mathews Columbus.
J M Thomson, Houston.
W H H Tyson, Carrollville.
Joseph R Davis, Canton.
C E Hooker. Jackson.
J T Sims, Delta. Coahema county.
D C Glenn, Mississippi City.
George H Gordon, Woodville.

LOUISIANA.

E LaSere, New Orleans.
E Lawrence, New Orleans.
F H Hatch. New Orleans.
A Talbot, Iberville.
R A Hunter. Alexandria.
Richard Taylor, St Charles Parish.
D D Withers, New Orleans.
John Tarlton. Bayou Bueff, St Mary's Parish.
Charles Jones, Trinity.
B W Pearce, Sparta, Bienville Parish.
A Mouton. Vermillionville.
James A McHatton, Baton Rouge.

TEXAS

H R Runnels, Boston. Bowie county.
E Greer, Marshall, Harrison county.
Thomas P Ochiltree, Marshall, Harrison county.
M W Covey, Jefferson, Cass county.
F R Lubbock, Houston, Harris county.
Guy Bryan, Galveston.
Josiah F Crosby, El Paso.
F S Stockdale, Port Lavaca.

ARKANSAS.

J P Johnson, Laconia.
Thompson B Flournoy, Laconia.
N B Burrows, Van Buren.
F A Terry, Waverly Post Office.
John J Sturman, Dardanelle.
John A Jordan, South Bend,
Van H Manning, Hamburg.
P W Hoadley, Little Rock.

KENTUCKY.

G A Caldwell, Louisville.
D P White, Greensburg.
J C Mason, Owingsville.
R K Williams. Mayfield.
William Bradley, Madisonville.
G H Morrow, Paducah.
Lafeyette Green, Falls of Rough.
S B Greenfield, Hopkinsville.
G T Wood, Munfordsville.
J A Finn, Franklin.
S B Field, Columbia.
John S Kindrick, Somerset.
R Spalding, Lebanon.
W B Read, Hodgesville
John Dishman, Barbourville.

Colbert Cecil, Piketon.
William Garvin, Louisville.
S E Dehaven, La Grange.
R M Johnson, White Sulphur.
J B Beck, Lexington.
N Green, New Liberty.
R McKee, Louisville.
H D Helm, Newport
R P Butler, Carrollton

TENNESSEE.

Andrew Ewing, Nashville.
John R Howard, Lebanon.
J D C Atkins, Paris.
Samuel Milligan, Greenville.
William Henry Maxwell, Jonesborough.
John D Riley, Rogersville.
Thomas M Lyon, Knoxville.
W E B Jones, Livingston.
George W Rowles, Cleveland.
William Wallace, Maryville.
David Bunford, Dixon Springs.
James M Shield, Manchester.
John McGavock, Franklin.
James M Avent, Murfreesboro'.
Robert Mathews, Shelbyville.
W L McClelland, Lewisburgh.
Thomas W Jones, Pulaski.
W C Whitthorne, Columbia.
Alfred Robb, Clarksville
Thomas Menees, Springfield.
William H Wall, Paris.
James Connor, Ripley.
William H. Carroll, Memphis.
Samuel McClanahan Jackson.

MISSOURI

J B Henderson, Louisiana.
W T W McIlhany, St. Charles.
R F Lakeman, Hannibal.
G A Shortridge, Bloomington.
John B Clark, Washington City, D C.
Austin A King, Richmond, Ray county.
George P Norris, Platte City.
James Craig, St. Joseph.
Wm Douglas, Boonville, Cooper county.
N C Claiborne, Kansas City.
P S Wilkes, Springfield
J A Scott, Elk Mills.
C G Corwin, Jefferson City.
J F Mense, Washington, Franklin county.
A Hunter, Benton, Scott county.
John O'Fallon, jr., Sulphur Springs, Jefferson co.
John M Krum, St. Louis.
Sam B Churchill, St. Louis.

IOWA.

A C Dodge, Burlington.
B M Samuels, Dubuque.
D O Finch, Des Moines.
Wm H Merritt, Cedar Rapids.
T W Claggett, Keokuk.
J W Bosier, Sioux City.
E H Thayer, Muscatine.
W H M Pusey, Council Bluffs.

WISCONSIN.

John R Sharpstein, Milwaukee.
Alex S Palmer, Geneva.
Alex F Pratt, Waukesha.
Wm A Barstow, Janesville.
James H Earnest, Shullsburgh.
Charles Whipple, Eau Claire.
Perry H Smith, Appleton.
Fred W Horn, Cedarburgh.
Edward S Bragg, Fond du Lac.
John Fitzgerald, Oshkosh

MINNESOTA.

W A Gormans, St. Paul.
Geo L Becker, St Paul.
Henry H Sibley, Mendota.
A J Edgerton, Mantorville.
A M Fridley, St. Anthony.
J Travis Rosser, Mankato.
W W Phelps, Red Wing.

ILLINOIS.

S S Marshall, McLeansboro'.
O B Ficklin, Charleston.
W A Richardson, Quincy.
R T Merrick, Chicago.
Wm M Jackson, Union
John D Platt, Warren.
John B Turner, Chicago.
A M Herrington, Geneva.
Allen Withers, Bloomington.
R E Goodell, Joliet.
B S Prettyman, Pekin.
R Holloway, Monmouth.
W H Rolloson, Dallas City.
James M Campbell, Macomb.
Murray McConnell, Jacksonville.
Wm F Thornton, Shelbyville.
Aaron Shaw, Lawrenceville.
W F Linder, Chicago.
S A Buckmaster, Alton.
Z Casey, Mount Vernon.
W J Allen, Marion.
W H Green, Metropolis.

OHIO.

George W McCook, Steubenville.
George E Pugh, Cincinnati.
D P Rhodes, Cleveland
Washington McLean, Cincinnati.
Henry B Bowman, Cincinnati
Charles Rule, Cincinnati.
Wesley M Cameron, Cincinnati.
Wm T Forrest, Cincinnati.
A P Miller, Hamilton
Geo W Houk, Dayton.
Sabirt Scott, St Mary's.
Joshua Townsend, Greenville, Darke county.
James B Steedman, Toledo.
Wm Mungen, Findley.
J B Cockerill, West Union.
T C Kennedy, Batavia.
Durbin Ward, Lebanon.
W M Stark, Xenia.
Geo Spence, Springfield.
R E Runkle, West Liberty, Logan county.
Edward F Dickinson, Fremont, Sandusky co.
Abner M Jackson, Bucyrus
Thomas McNally, Chillicothe.
Wells A Hutchins, Portsmouth.
Lot L Smith, Athens.
E F Bingham, McArthur, Vinton co.
Wayne Griswold, Circleville.
Geo B Smythe, Newark
Thos W Bartley, Mansfield.
John Tifft, Norwalk.
J A Marchand, Wooster.
J P Jeffreys, "
J G Stewart, Coshocton.
R H Nugen, Newcomerstown, Tuscarawas co.
S R Hosmer, Zanesville.
W W Cones, Cincinnati.
J S Way, Woodsfield, Monroe county.
W Eaton, Morristown, Belmont county.
S Lahm, Canton.
S D Harris, Jr, Ravenna.
H B Payne, Cleveland.
J W Gray, "
David Tod, Brier Hill.
D B Woods, Warren.
Thomas S Woods, New Lisbon.
B F Potts, Carrollton Carroll county.

INDIANA

E M Huntington, Terre Haute.
S H Buskirk, Bloomington.
Robert Lowry, Goshen.
James B Foley, Greensburgh.
John S Gavitt, Evansville.
Smith Miller, Patoka.
J B Norman, New Albany.
S K Wolfe, Corydon.
P C Dunning, Bloomington.
H W Harrington, Madison.

J V Bemusdaffer, Greensburgh.
John Andregg, Lawrenceburgh
Lafayette Devlin, Cambridge City.
Edmund Johnson, Newcastle.
W H Talbott, Indianapolis
J M Gregg, Danville.
F Read, Terre Haute.
H K Wilson, Sullivan.
L B Stockton, Lafayette
Isaac C Elston, Crawfordsville.
G Hathaway, Laporte.
S A Hall, Logansport.
P Hoagland, Fort Wayne.
G W McConnell, Angola
Wm Garver, Noblesville.
John R Coffroth, Huntington.

MICHIGAN.

George V N Lothrop, Detroit.
Charles E Stuart, Kalamazoo.
H H Riley, Constantine.
George W Peck, Lansing.
Benj Follett, Ypsilanti.
Fidus Livermore, Jackson.
John G Parkhurst, Coldwater.
Philo Wilson, Canandaigua.
Franklin Muzzy, Niles.
Alex F Bell, Detroit.
Augustus C Baldwin, Pontiac.
William S Bancroft, Port Huron.

OREGON.

Lansing Stout, Washington, D C.
J K Lamerick, Jacksonville.
Isaac J Stevens, Washington, D C.
Justus Steinberger, Washington, D C.
R B Metcalfe, Independence, Texas.
A P Dennison, The Dalles, Oregon.

CALIFORNIA.

J Bidwell, Chico, Butte county.
G W Patrick, Sonora, Tuolumne county.
Lewis R Bradley, Stockton.
Austin E Smith, San Francisco
John A Dreibelbis, Shasta.
John S Dudley, Yreka, Siskiyou county.
John Rains, Los Angelos.
D S Gregory, Monterey.

FOURTH DAY.

THURSDAY, APRIL 26, 1860.

The Convention was called to order at 10 o'clock.

The proceedings were opened by prayer, by the Rev. Mr. Forrest.

On motion of Mr. Miller, of Indiana, the reading of the Journal of yesterday was dispensed with.

The unfinished business of yesterday was called up.

The consideration of Mr. North's resolution not being called for by the mover, was passed over.

Mr. FITZHUGH, of Virginia, presented a series of resolutions, which were read and referred to the Committee on Resolutions. The resolutions are as follows:

Resolved, That the rendition of fugitive slaves and other property by one State to another is a right secured by the laws of nations, recognized by the Colonies and the mother country previous to the Declaration of Independence by the Courts of Great Britain and by the Supreme Court of the United States, and by the law and courts of all civilized nations, and *a fortiori* is the duty of the States of this Confederacy under the Constitution and laws.

Resolved, That the refusal of the Governors of the several States to deliver up fugitives from justice and fugitive slaves, is an open and palpable violation of the above natural and international law and the Constitution and laws of the United States, constituting official perjury by such Governors as have evaded or refused to perform this duty, and if persevered in, must lead to the severance of the Union.

Mr. HUGHES, of Pennsylvania, presented a resolution, which was read and referred to the Committee on Platform. The resolution was as follows:

Resolved, That while recognizing the doctrine that the General Government has no power to create in, or exclude from, by legislation, any species of property in any State or Territory, yet we maintain that it is the duty of that Government to provide the Courts with ample process and ministerial officers for the protection and enforcement of any existing right, or the correction of any wrong, over which said Government, under the Constitution, has jurisdiction.

Mr. WATERBURY, of New York, moved to accept the invitations received from the several Institutions of the city of Charleston, to visit the same, and that the President of the Convention return the thanks of the Convention for such invitations—which motion was carried.

Mr. BROWNE, of Pennsylvania, moved the following:

Resolved, That the citizens of the several States, when emigrating into a Federal Territory, retain the right to slave and other property which they take with them, until there is some prohibition by lawful authority; and that, as declared by the Supreme Court, Congress cannot interfere with such right in a Territory, nor can a Territorial Legislature do so, until authorized by the adoption of a State Constitution; and that the attempted exercise of such a function by a Territorial Legislature is unconstitutional, and dangerous to the peace of the Union.

The resolution, after having been read, was referred to the Committee on Platform.

Mr. WALKER, of Alabama. As a pendent to the resolution of the gentleman from Pennsylvania, I offer the following:

Resolved, That it is the duty of the Federal Government, in all its departments within their constitutional sphere, to afford adequate protection and equal advantage to all descriptions of property recognized as such by the laws of any of the States, as well within the Territories as upon the high seas, and every place subject to its exclusive power of legislation.

Mr. BROWNE. I desire to say I accept that very cheerfully as an amendment, if it is intended as such.

Mr. WALL, of Tennessee, offered the following resolutions, being the Platform advocated by that State:

Be it Resolved, That we hereby re-affirm the principles announced in the Platform of the Democratic party adopted in Convention at Cincinnati, in June, 1856, and that we hold them to be a true exposition of our doctrines on the subjects embraced.

Resolved, That the views expressed by the Supreme Court of the United States in the decision of the case of "Dred Scott," are, in our opinion, a true and clear exposition of the powers reposed in Congress upon the subject of the Territories of the United States, and the rights guaranteed to the residents in the Territories.

Resolved, That the States of the Confederacy are equals in political rights; each State has the right to settle for itself all questions of internal policy; the right to have or not to have slavery is one of the prerogatives of self-government—the States did not surrender this right in the Federal Constitution, and Tennessee will not now do so.

Resolved, That the Federal Government has no power to interfere with slavery in the States, nor to introduce or exclude it from the Territories, and no duty to perform in relation thereto, but to protect the rights of the owner from wrong, and to restore fugitives from labor; these duties it cannot withhold without a violation of the Constitution.

Resolved, That the organization of the Republican party upon strictly *sectional* principles, and its hostility to the institution of slavery, which is recognized by the Constitution, and which is inseparably connected with the social and industrial pursuits of the Southern States of the Confederacy, is war upon the principles of the Constitution and upon the rights of the States.

Resolved, That the late treasonable invasion of Virginia by an organized band of Republicans, was the necessary result of the doctrines teachings, and principles of that party; was the beginning of the "*irrepressible conflict*" of Mr. Seward; was a blow aimed at the institution of slavery by an effort to excite servile insurrection; was war upon the South, and as such, it is the duty of the South to prepare to maintain its rights under the Constitution.

Resolved, That if this war upon the Constitutional rights of the South is persisted in, it must soon cease to be a war of words. If the Republican party would prevent a *conflict of arms*, let them stand by the Constitution and fulfill its obligations—we ask nothing more, we will submit to nothing less.

The resolutions were referred.

Mr. WOLFE, of Indiana, moved the following:

Resolved, That the Federal Government has no power to interfere with slavery in the States, nor to introdue or exclude it from the Territories, and no duty to perform in relation thereto, but to faithfully enforce the Fugitive Slave Law, and all the decisions of the Supreme Court of the United States in regard to all the rights of the people of every State and Territory under the Constitution of the United States.

The resolution was referred.

Mr. GLENN, of Mississippi, presented the following:

1. A citizen of any State in the Union may immigrate to the Territories with his property, whether it consists of slaves or any other subject of personal ownership.

2. So long as the Territorial condition exists, the relation of master and slave is not to be disturbed by Federal or Territorial legislation; and if so disturbed, the Federal Government must furnish ample protection therefor.

3. Whenever a Territory shall be entitled to admission into the Union as a State the inhabitants may, in forming their Constitution, decide for themselves, whether it shall authorize or exclude slavery.

The resolution was referred.

Mr. HORN, of Wisconsin, offered the following:

Resolved, That the letter of President Buchanan, accepting the nomination at Cincinnati, where he explains the Cincinnati Platform in relation to the power of a Territorial Legislature on the subject of slavery is eminently sound, and is hereby referred to the Committee on resolutions for their consideration.

The resolution was referred.

Mr. MOUTON, of Louisiana, offered the following:

Resolved, That the Territories of the United States belong to the several States as their common property, and not to the individual citizens thereof, that the Federal Constitution recognizes property in slaves, and as such the owner thereof is entitled to carry his slaves into any Territory of the United States and hold them as property. And in case the people of the Territories, by inaction, unfriendly legislation or otherwise, should endanger the tenure of such property or discriminate against it by withholding that protection given to this species of property in the Territories, it is the duty of the General Government to interpose, by an active exertion of its Constitutional powers to secure the rights of slaveholders.

The resolution was referred.

Mr. GREENFIELD, of Kentucky, offered the following:

Resolved, That it is the duty of the National Government to provide by law, for paying for such fugitives from labor as, by the illegal interposition of State authorities, the owners thereof may be prevented from receiving under the Fugitive Slave Law.

Referred to the Committee on Platform.

Capt. RYNDERS, of New York. If the gentleman from Kentucky will induce the Government to give the United States Marshals sufficient power, he may rest assured the South shall have all her fugitive slaves returned. He was somewhat interested in that matter himself. [Applause.]

Mr. BIDWELL, of California, moved the following:

Resolved, That our States and Territories on the Pacific, and the Territories of the Great Basin, and of both slopes of the Rocky Mountains, demand the early construction of a railroad to connect them with the internal navigation and railway system of the Atlantic States; and that on the ground of postal communication, protection of Territories and States, and of military defense, the General Government has accepted authority under the Constitution.

Mr. CRAIG, of Missouri, offered the following:

Resolved, That the Democratic party are in favor of granting such constitutional aid as will insure the speedy construction of a railroad connecting the Atlantic and Pacific States.

Referred under the rule.

Mr. STOUT, of Oregon, offered the following:

Resolved, That to preserve the Union, the equality of States must be maintained, and every branch of the Federal Government should exercise all their Constitutional powers for the protection of persons and property.

Referred.

Mr. McCONNELL, of Illinois, offered the following:

Resolved, That the Federal Government has no power to interfere with slavery in the States, or to introduce it or exclude it from the Territories, and has no duty to perform in relation thereto, except to secure the rights of the owner by a return of the fugitive slave, as provided by the Constitution.

Referred.

Mr. SEWARD, of Georgia, presented the following:

Resolved, That the Constitution of the United States extends to the several States, and to every citizen, the full protection of persons and property in all the States and Territories; and that those rights, as declared and determined by the Courts, under the Constitution, are to be respected and maintained by the Government of the United States; and that James Guthrie, of Kentucky, be the nominee of the Democratic party for President of the United States, on this platform.

The motion was referred.

Mr. CESSNA, of Pennsylvania, offered the following:

Resolved, That the convictions of the Democratic party of the country remain unshaken in the wisdom and justice and adequate protection of iron, coal, wool, and the other great staples of our country, based upon the necessities of a reasonable revenue system of the General Government; and approving of the views of President Buchanan upon the subject of specific duties, we earnestly desire our Representatives in Congress to produce such modifications of the existing laws as the unwise legislation of the Republican party in 1857 renders absolutely necessary to the prosperity of the great interests of the country.

Mr. PUGH moved that after disposing of such resolutions as are now before the Convention, all further resolutions offered be referred to the Committee on Platform without being read before the Convention.

This resolution was carried.

Resolutions were then presented by Messrs. Brooks, of Alabama, West, of Connecticut, Dudley, of California, Green, of North Carolina, Rosser, of Minnesota, O'Fallon, of Missouri, Tarlton, of Louisiana, and Read, of Indiana; all of which were referred to the Committee on Platform.

Mr. STUART, of Michigan, moved that the Convention adjourn until 4 o'clock P M.

Mr. MONTGOMERY, of Pennsylvania, stated that the Convention had before it a resolution undetermined, and asked to have a vote taken upon it, and desired Mr. Stuart to withdraw his motion for that purpose.

Mr. STUART withdrew his motion.

Mr. INGERSOLL, of Connecticut, renewed the motion to adjourn, upon which a vote was taken, and the motion to adjourn was lost.

Mr. MONTGOMERY, of Pennsylvania, called up the resolution heretofore offered by him, and modified it so as to read as follows:

Resolved, That the Committee appointed to frame rules and regulations for the future action of our Executive National Committee, shall not report until after the nomination of candidates for President and Vice President.

Mr. BIGLER offered as an amendment, the following:

"And they shall report as members of the National Committee, such persons as shall have been selected for that purpose by the respective State delegations for their respective States."

Mr. SEWARD, of Georgia, moved to refer the resolutions to the Committee ordered yesterday, and called for the previous question.

The call for the previous question was seconded, and the main question ordered.

The two propositions were committed to the Committee heretofore ordered.

The Convention then, on motion of Mr. WRIGHT, of Mass., took a recess till 4 o'clcok P. M.

AFTERNOON SESSION.

Mr. SAYLES, of Rhode Island, offered the following resolution :

Resolved, That the Committee on Resolutions be instructed to report forthwith to this Convention, the platform adopted by the Cincinnati Convention, with the following additional resolution :

Resolved, That we recognize to the fullest extent, the principle that to preserve the Union the equality of the States must be maintained, the decisions of the Courts enforced; and that every branch of the Federal Government shall exercise all its Constitutional powers in the protection of persons and property both in the States and Territories ; and upon that moved the previous question.

Mr. BOCOCK, of Virginia, raised a point of order, and insisted upon the resolutions going to the Committee on Platform without debate.

The PRESIDENT sustained the point of order.

Mr. MITCHELL, of Alabama, offered a resolution of inquiry, as to whether the Committee had agreed upon a platform.

Mr. BOWIE, of Maryland, offered as an amendment, the following :

Ordered, that the Committee on Resolutions be requested to report to this Convention the result of its deliberations, to-morrow at 10 o'clock.

Mr. STUART, of Michigan, moved that the Convention adjourn ; which motion was carried, and the Convention adjourned till to-morrow at 10 A. M.

The following is the Committee elected by the States to report rules and regulations for the guidance of the next National Executive Committee :

Committee on Rules and Regulations—Maine. Henry A. Wyman ; New Hampshire, Ansel Glover ; Vermont, Lucius Robinson ; Massachusetts, W. C. N. Swift; Rhode Isiand, Edward F. Newton ; Connecticut, James T. Pratt : New York, Marshall B. Champlin ; New Jersey, Geo. F. Fort ; Pennsylvania, Josiah Randall ; Delaware, John B. Pennington ; Maryland C. S Stansbury ; Virginia, W. F. Thompson ; North Carolina, Samuel Hargrave ; South Carolina, Franklin Gaillarfi ; Georgia John A. Jones ; Florida, Thomas J. Eppes ; Alabama, Thomas J. Burnett ; Louisiana, E. Lawrence Mississippi, J. M Thompson ; Texas, W. H Parsons ; Arkansas, John J. Sturman ; Missouri, J. M. Krum ; Tennessee, W. E. B. Jones ; Kentucky, D. P. White ; Ohio, Wells A. Hutchins; Indiana, John B. Norman ; Illinois, Samuei S. Marshall ; Michigan, Fidus Livermore ; Wisconsin, J. H. Earnest ; Iowa, Wm. H. Merritt ; Minnesota, A. M. Fridley ; California, G. W. Patrick ; Oregon, Justus Steinberger.

FIFTH DAY.

FRIDAY, APRIL 27, 1860.

The Convention was called to order at 10 o'clock A. M., by Gen. CALEB CUSHING, President of the Convention, and he introduced to the Convention the Rev. Mr. SMYTHE, of Charleston, who offered up prayer.

Mr. BUTTERWORTH, of New York, moved to suspend the reading of the Journal. Agreed to.

Mr. COCHRAN presented the following communication from the working men of New York, Brooklyn, and Greenport, which was referred to the Committee on Resolutions :

NEW YORK, April 20, 1860.

To the National Democratic Convention :

At a meeting of the representatives of the working men of the different Wards of this City, Brooklyn, and Green Point, held on the evening of the 16th instant, at Union Hall, 195 Bowery, it was

Resolved, That the officers of the meeting be instructed to address the National Democratic Convention, to assemble at Charleston, and respectfully request the Convention to declare itself opposed to all further traffic in the public lands of the United States, and in favor of laying them out in farms and lots for the *free* and *exclusive* use of *actual settlers.*

We see this singular condition of affairs—that while the wealth of our country is rapidly accumulating—while internal improvements of every description are fast increasing—and while machinery has multiplied the powers of production to an immense extent; yet, with all these material advantages, the compensation for useful labor is getting less and less.

We seek the cause of this anomaly, and we trace it to the monopoly of the land, with labor at the mercy of capital. We, therefore, desire to abolish the monopoly, not by interfering with the conventional rights of persons now in possession, but by averting the further sale of all land not yet appropriated as private property, and by allowing these lands, hereafter, to be freely occupied by those who may choose to settle on them.

We propose that the public lands hereafter shall *not be owned*, but *occupied* only—the occupant having the right to sell or otherwise dispose of his or her improvements to any one not in possession of other lands; so that, by preventing any individual from becoming possessed of more than a limited quantity, every one may enjoy the right. Respectfully,

BENJAMIN HAGUE, Secretary. HENRY BEENY, Chairman.

The unfinished business of yesterday being called up, the resolution of Mr. MITCHELL, of Alabama, was considered in order; but it being understood that the Committee on Platform and Resolutions were ready to report the Platform, Mr. Mitchell withdrew his resolution.

The PRESIDENT here requested the Select Committee heretofore appointed under Mr. Pugh's resolution, to assemble in front of the stand for the purpose of consultation.

Gov. KING, of Missouri, offered a resolution, which was received and read by the Clerk, and which was on motion of Mr. SPINOLA, of New York, referred to the Select Committee. The resolution is as follows:

Whereas, the Democracy of the Territory of Kansas have sent to this Convention Delegates to cast herein the votes of Kansas in the event of her admission into the Union; and whereas, the times indicate that before the meeting of the next National Convention, Kansas will be a sovereign State, and with the view of enabling the proposed State to have upon the next Executive Committee of the party a representative, be it, therefore, by this Convention,

Resolved, That the Delegation here representing the Democracy of Kansas, be, and they are hereby, empowered to select one member for the National Committee, which person thus selected shall be placed upon the National Democratic Committee as a member thereof, upon the admission of Kansas into the Union as a sovereign State.

Mr. OCHILTREE, of Texas, offered a series of resolutions, which were referred to the Committee on Platform and Resolutions without reading.

Mr. STUART, of Michigan, moved that the Convention take a recess of one hour.

Mr. WARDLAW, of Florida, moved to amend by substituting the following, viz: "That the Convention suspend proceedings for one hour;" which amendment was accepted by Mr. Stuart, and the question on suspending business was put and carried.

The hour for a recess having expired, the PRESIDENT called the Convention to order at twenty minntes past eleven o'clock.

Mr. W. W. AVERY, of North Carolina, Chairman of the Committee on the Platform and Resolutions, made a report, and asked leave to make an explanation, which was granted.

The following is the Report on Platform and Resolutions offered by Mr. Avery.

I am instructed, as Chairman of the Committee on Resolutions, to report to the Convention the Platform of Resolutions which they have adopted. I am further instructed by the Committee to state that entire unanimity did not prevail as to several of the resolutions.

The first and third resolutions in reference to slavery in the Territories, and the duty of the General Government to protect the rights of persons and property, were adopted by a majority of the Committee.

The second resolution, in relation to the fugitive slave law, and the fourth resolution, in regard to our foreign born citizens, were unanimously adopted; and the fifth resolution, in reference to the acquisition of Cuba, was adopted without division.

The last resolution of the series, in regard to the Pacific Railroad, was adopted by a majority.

The Committee on Resolutions, by their Chairman, Mr. Avery, submits the following report. W. W. AVERY, Chairman.

PLATFORM.—MAJORITY REPORT.

Resolved, That the Platform adopted at Cincinnati be affirmed, with the following resolutions:

1. *Resolved*, That the National Democracy of the United States hold these cardinal principles on the subject of Slavery in the Territories: First, That Congress has no power to abolish slavery in the Territories. Second, That the Territorial Legislature has no power to abolish slavery in any Territory, nor to prohibit the introduction of slaves therein, nor any power to exclude slavery therefrom, nor any power to destroy or impair the right of property in slaves by any legislation whatever.

2. *Resolved*, That the enactments of State Legislatures to defeat the faithful execution of the Fugitive Slave Law are hostile in character, subversive of the Constitution, and revolutionary in their effect.

3. *Resolved*, That it is the duty of the Federal Government to protect, when necessary, the rights of persons and property on the high seas, in the Territories, or wherever else its Constitutional authority extends.

4. *Resolved*, That the Democracy of the Nation recognize it as the imperative duty of this Government to protect the naturalized citizen in all his rights, whether at home or in foreign lands, to the same extent as its native-born citizens.

5. *Resolved*, That the National Democracy earnestly recommend the acquisition of the Island of Cuba at the earliest practicable period.

Whereas, That one of the greatest necessities of the age, in a political, commercial, postal and military point of view, is a speedy communication between the Pacific and Atlantic coasts. Therefore, be it

Resolved, That the National Democratic party do hereby pledge themselves to use every means in their power to secure the passage of some bill for the construction of a Pacific Railroad from the Mississippi River to the Pacific Ocean, at the earliest practicable moment.

Mr. AVERY, after making his report, proceeded to address the Convention, but on request, yielded the floor for the purpose of receiving the Minority Report of the Committee on Resolutions and Platform.

Mr. PAYNE, of Ohio, a member of the Committee on Platform and Resolutions, offered a Report and Resolutions from a minority of said Committee, which he moved as a substitute for the Majority Report made by Mr. AVERY, which Report and Resolutions offered by Mr. PAYNE are as follows, viz:

MINORITY REPORT OF THE COMMITTEE ON RESOLUTIONS.

The undersigned, a minority of the Committee on Resolutions, regretting their inability to concur with the report of the majority of your Committee, feel constrained to submit the following as their Report, and recommend its adoption as a substitute for the report of the majority.

Respectfully submitted.

AMOS ROBERTS, Delegate from Maine.
W. BURNS, Delegate from New Hampshire.
E. M. BROWN, Delegate from Vermont.
C. S. BRADLEY, Delegate from Rhode Island.
A. G. HAZZARD, Delegate from Connecticut.
BENJ. WILLIAMSON, Delegate from New Jersey.
H. B. PAYNE, Delegate from Ohio.
P. C. DUNNING, Delegate from Indiana.
O. B. FICKLIN, Delegate from Illinois.
G. V. N. LOTHROP, Delegate from Michigan.
A. S. PALMER, Delegate from Wisconsin.
BEN. M. SAMUELS, Delegate from Iowa.
JAS. M. CAVANAUGH, Delegate from Minnesota.
HENDRICK B. WRIGHT, Delegate from Pennsylvania.

In compliance with the wish of the New York Delegation, I concur with this Report as far as it goes.

EDWIN CROSWELL, Delegate from New York.

1. *Resolved*, That we, the Democracy of the Union, in Convention assembled, hereby declare our affirmance of the Resolutions unanimously adopted and declared as a Platform of Principles by the Democratic Convention at Cincinnati, in the year 1856, believing that Democratic principles are unchangeable in their nature, when applied to the same subject matters ; and we recommend as the only further resolutions the following :

2. *Resolved*, That all questions in regard to the rights of property in States or Territories, arising under the Constitution of the United States, are judicial in their character ; and the Democratic party is pledged to abide by and faithfully carry out such determination of these questions as has been or may be made by the Supreme Court of the United States.

3. *Resolved*, That it is the duty of the United States to afford ample and complete protection to all its citizens, whether at home or abroad, and whether native or foreign born.

4. *Resolved*, That one of the necessities of the age, in a military, commercial, and postal point of view, is speedy communication between the Atlantic and Pacific States ; and the Democratic party pledge such Constitutional Government aid as will insure the construction of a Railroad to the Pacific coast, at the earliest practicable period.

5. *Resolved*, That the Democratic party are in favor of the acquisition of the Island of Cuba, on such terms as shall be honorable to ourselves and just to Spain.

6. *Resolved*, That the enactments of State Legislatures to defeat the faithful execution of the Fugitive Slave Law, are hostile in character, subversive of the Constitution, and revolutionary in their effect.

Mr. BUTLER, of Massachusetts, a member of the Committee on Platform and Resolutions, offered another Report as a Minority Report, which he moved be received as a substitute for the resolutions reported by Mr. Avery and Mr. Payne. The following are the resolutions reported by Mr. Butler :

Resolved, That we, the Democracy of the Union, in Convention assembled, hereby declare our affirmance of the Democratic Resolutions unanimously adopted and declared as a Platform of Principles at Cincinnati, in the year 1856, without addition or alteration, believing that Democratic principles are unchangeable in their nature, when applied to the same snbject matter, and we recommend as the only farther resolution the following :

Resolved, That it is the duty of the United States to extend its protection alike over all its citizens, whether native or naturalized.

A minority of your Committee have agreed to report the above as the sole resolutions upon the subject of the principles of the party.

In behalf of a minority of the Committee. B. F. BUTLER.

Mr. COCHRAN, of New York, offered an amendment to the amendment offered by Mr. Butler, of Massachufetts, by substituting therefor the following :

Resolved, That the several States of this Union are, under the Constitution, equal, and that the people thereof are entitled to the free and undisturbed possession and enjoyment of their rights of person and property in the common Territories; and that any attempt by Congress or a Territorial Legislature to annul, abridge or discriminate against any such equality or rights, would be unwise in policy and repugnant to the Constitution; and that it is the duty of the Federal Government, whenever such rights are violated, to afford the necessary, proper, and constitutional remedies for such violations.

Resolved, That the Platform of Principles adopted by the Convention held in Cincinnati, in 1856, and the foregoing resolutions, are hereby declared to be the Platform of the Democratic party.

The PRESIDENT. The Chair will state the condition of the question for the purpose of determining the question of order. The report of the Committee presented by Mr. Avery, of North Carolina, is the first question before the Convention. To the resolutions presented by the gentleman from North Carolina, Mr. Payne, of Ohio, offers a series of resolutions as a substitute or as an amendment in gross. The gentleman from Massachusetts (Mr. Butler) moves an amendment to the amendment. In the opinion of the Chair, amendments can go no further, the proposition of the gentleman from New York being an amendment in the third degree.

Mr. COCHRAN. I give notice, then, that I will offer the amendment I have indicated, as soon as the amendment last offered is disposed of.

Mr. WHITNEY, of Massachusetts. I wish to state that I shall call for a division of the report of the majority, so that the sense of the Convention may be taken separately upon each resolution. I also desire to move an amendment, which, with the permission of the gentleman from North Carolina, I will have read.

Objection was made to the reading of the amendment.

Mr. AVERY. On behalf of the majority of the Committee on Resolutions, I am instructed to say that it is with profound regret we have appeared before this Convention to present a report that has not met the sanction of the entire Committee whom I have the honor to represent upon this occasion; and I desire, before proceeding, to inquire of the gentleman from Ohio, who represents a branch of the minority, whether he represents a greater number of States than are affixed to the report which he has made upon this occasion.

Mr. PAYNE. I read the names of the delegates.

Mr. AVERY. I understood the gentleman from Ohio to say that he represented only thirteen States of this Federal Union, in the report which he has made.

Mr. PAYNE. Fifteen States are represented. I explained that upon the printed copy of the report the names of two States, New York and Pennsylvania, were omitted, which have been supplied.

Mr. AVERY. I did not understand the explanation of the gentleman from Ohio, or I should not have made the inquiry.

Mr. AVERY then proceeded to address the Convention, and occupied his full hour.

Mr. PAYNE, of Ohio, followed Mr. Avery in an address to the Convention.

Mr. B. F. BUTLER, of Massachusetts, obtained the floor, and addressed the Convention for the time allotted him under the rule.

On motion of Mr. BARKSDALE, of Mississippi, the Convention then adjourned until four o'clock P. M.

AFTERNOON SESSION.

The Convention was called to order by the President, at 4 o'clock P. M., when Mr. SAYLES, of Rhode Island, offered the following resolution:

Resolved, That the Committee to whom has been referred the subject of the time and place of holding the next Convention, appointment of National Committee, &c., be requested to consider the propriety of fixing the number of Delegates for whom seats shall be provided in the next National Convention, to be limited to the number of Senators and Representatives to which such State is entitled in the Congress of the United States. The resolution was read and adopted, and referred to the Committee.

The PRESIDENT then proceeded to remark as follows:

The PRESIDENT gave notice that for the convenience of members of the Convention, assuming that most of them were by this time known to the officers at the door, he had given orders to the officers to admit them henceforth with or without tickets. He also desired to say to the Convention that it had thus far proceeded in its deliberations with much decorum and with proper attention to parliamentary rules. The Chair confidently believed that the Convention would so continue to act to the last; and now having arrived at that stage of the proceedings which is of the highest importance, and when much interest and excitement prevailed, he called upon them to preserve their own dignity and self-respect, here, in the metropolis of the State of South Carolina.

Mr. BARKSDALE, of Mississippi, then addressed the Convention.

Mr. KING, of Missouri, then obtained the floor, and addressed the Convention for an hour.

Mr. YANCY, of Alabama, then proceeded to the stand; and, on motion of Mr. SAMUELS, of Iowa, the time for Mr. Yancy's remarks was extended to one hour and a half.

Mr. PUGH, of Ohio, next obtained the floor, and the same courtesy which had been extended to Mr. Yancy was extended to him, and he proceeded to address the Convention. Before Mr. Pugh concluded his remarks, it was suggested that the Convention adjourn for one hour; but before any motion was made,

Mr. WHITNEY, of Massachusetts, gave notice that he would to-morrow call up his motion which he had to-day asked to have read.

A motion was then made that the Convention adjourn for one hour.

Mr. HATCH, of Louisiana, moved that the Convention do now adjourn.

The question being taken first on Mr. Hatch's motion to adjourn, was lost.

A vote was then taken on the motion to adjourn for one hour, which motion was carried.

The hour having expired, the Convention was called to order by the President.

Mr. SPINOLA, of New York, offered a resolution that a final vote be taken on the resolutions and amendments thereto, which are now before the Convention, at 12 o'clock to-morrow.

Mr. CLARK, of Mississippi, objected, and

Mr. PUGH, of Ohio, resumed and concluded his address.

Mr. COCHRAN, of New York, again offered his amendment, and claimed that the friends of a measure had a right to perfect it before any amendments were made.

Mr. CLARK, of Missouri, asked if the gentleman was a friend of the Majority Report.

Mr. COCHRAN. If the amendment I proposed to make is adopted, I shall be.

Mr. STUART, of Michigan, raised the point of order that while the right claimed by the gentleman from New York existed to a certain extent, his alteration was, in fact, to entirely change the whole proposition.

Mr. CLARK raised a point of order, and stated that the proposition of Mr. Cochran took the shape of an amendment, and was not in order.

The PRESIDENT decided the motion of Mr. Cochran to be out of order.

Mr. BISHOP, of Connecticut, demanded the previous question on the resolutions.

Before the demand for the previous question was seconded,

Mr. CLARK, of Mississippi, moved that the Convention adjourn, and upon this motion,

Mr. SAMUELS, in behalf of the State of Iowa, called for a vote by States.

The vote was taken, and the motion to adjonrn was decided in the affirmative. The vote was as foilows:

	Yeas.	Nays		Yeas.	Nays.		Yeas.	Nays.
Maine	8		North Carolina	10		Onio		23
New Hampshire		5	South Carolina,	8		Indiana		13
Vermont,		5	Georgia	10		Illinois	5	6
Massachusetts	7	5½	Florida	3		Michigan		6
Rhode Island		4	Alabama	9		Wisconsin		5
Connecticut	1	5	Louisiana	6		Iowa		4
New York		35	Mississippi	7		Minnesota	1½	2½
New Jersey	7		Texas	4		California	4	
Pennsylvania	8	19	Arkansas	4		Oregon	3	
Delaware	3		Missouri	3	6			
Maryland	8		Tennessee	12			158½	144
Virginia	15		Kentucky	12				

So the motion was carried and the Convention adjourned.

SIXTH DAY.

SATURDAY, APRIL 28, 1860.

The Convention met and was called to order by the President, and no clergyman being present, the Convention proceeded to business without prayer.

The PRESIDENT made some remarks, and admonished the members of the Convention of the necessity of preserving order in their deliberations.

Mr. BIGLER, of Pennsylvania, was proceeding to make some remarks, when

Mr. BISHOP, of Connecticut, arose to a point of order and claimed the floor.

JOHN COCHRAN, of New York, spoke upon the question of order.

Mr. RANDALL, of Pennsylvania, claimed that when the Convention adjourned last night he had the floor, and was now entitled to it.

The PRESIDENT decided that as the previous question had not been seconded when the Convention adjourned, the motion for the previous question fell with the adjournment.

Senator BIGLER, of Pennsylvania, then moved that the majority and minority reports be recommitted to the Committee, with instructions to report in an hour the following resolutions:

Resolved, That the Platform adopted by the Democratic party at Cincinnati be affirmed, with the following explanatory resolutions:

Resolved, That the Government of a Territory, organized by an act of Congress, is provisional and temporary, and, during its existence, all citizens of the United States have an equal right to settle in the Territory, without their rights, either of person or property, being destroyed or impaired by Congressional or Territorial legislation.

Resolved, That the Democratic party stands pledged to the doctrine that it is the duty of Government to maintain all the constitutional rights of property of whatever kind, in the Territories, and to enforce all the decisions of the Supreme Court in reference thereto.

Resolved, That it is the duty of the United States to afford ample and complete protection to all its citizens, whether at home or abroad, and whether native or foreign.

Resolved, That one of the necessities of the age, in a military, commercial, and postal point of view, is speedy communication between the Atlantic and Pacific States; and the Democratic party pledge such Constitutional Government aid as will insure the construction of a railroad to the Pacific coast at the earliest practicable period.

Resolved, That the Democratic party are in favor of the acquisition of the Island of Cuba, on such terms as shall be honorable to ourselves and just to Spain.

Resolved, That the enactments of State Legislatures to defeat the faithful execution of the Fugitive Slave Law, are hostile in character, subversive of the Constitution, and revolutionary in their effect.

He moved the previous question.

Mr. COCHRAN, of New York, submitted, as a question of order, that the previous question, if sustained, would operate on the resolutions reported by the Committee, as well as on the motion to recommit. He hoped, therefore, the gentleman from Pennsylvania would withdraw the motion for the previous question, and in this connection he (Mr. C.) would move to amend the proposed instructions by adding to the series the resolutions which he had offered to the Convention yesterday.

Mr. RICHARDSON, of Illinois, raised a question upon a point of order and stated it.

Mr. STUART, of Michigan, made some suggestions to the Chair.

Mr. COCHRAN made further remarks upon his point of order.

Mr. STUART now made a point of order.

The PRESIDENT decided that Mr. Cochran's question was not properly one of order; that it was an inquiry for information, and could not be entertained by the Chair while the gentleman from Pennsylvania was upon the floor.

Senator BIGLER believed that his motion was understood, and, therefore, insisted on the demand for the previous question.

Mr. PHILLIPS, of Pennsylvania, addressed the Chair, and Mr. STUART called him to order.

Mr. RANDALL spoke upon a privileged question.

Mr. MARSHALL, of Illinois, rose to a point of order.

Mr. MONTGOMERY, of Pennsylvania, moved to lay Mr. Bigier's motion on the table. He did not regard as a compromise, a proposition for a Congressional slave code and the re-opening of the African slave trade.

Mr. PHILLIPS, of Pennsylvania, and several other delegates, inquired if the effect of the adoption of Mr. Montgomery's motion would not be to lay the whole subject on the table.

The PRESIDENT decided that that would be the effect of the motion.

Mr. MONTGOMERY withdrew his motion.

Senator BIGLER again insisted on his demand for the previous question.

Mr. MONTGOMERY inquired whether the previous question, if sustained, would not apply to the whole platform?

The PRESIDENT said that he could answer the question if it was the wish of the Convention. [Cries of "Yes, yes."]

Mr. MILES, of Maryland, desired to know distinctly, from the Chair, whether the previous question would cut off all debate upon the platform? If so, as a representative of the slave district of Maryland, he should claim the privilege of being heard by the Convention, to show that the gentleman who had represented the State of Maryland on the Committee on Resolutions had, by his course, denied his own record at home, and misrepresented the State of Maryland. [Loud cheers.]

The PRESIDENT decided that debate was out of order.

Mr. PRATT, of Connecticut, raised the question of order, that the motion of Mr. Bigler was only a particular form of offering an amendment in the third degree, and was therefore not in order.

The PRESIDENT decided that although such might be the effect of the motion, the practice was perfectly well settled in the House of Representatives that such a motion could be entertained. In reply to the interrogatories as to the effect of the previous question, he stated that by an express rule of the House of Representatives when the previous question was moved on a series of propositions, if seconded, it applied to the whole series. If now seconded, therefore, and the main question ordered, the question would be first on the motion to commit; if that failed, then upon the amendment in third order, and finally upon the majority report of the Committee.

Mr. PUGH, of Ohio, inquired whether, if the previous question was seconded and the main question ordered, it would then be in order to call for a division of the question on the motion of the gentleman from Pennsylvania?

The PRESIDENT replied that, by an express rule of the House of Representatives, it was in order to call for a division of the question either before or after the main question was ordered.

Mr. WALKER, of Alabama, called for a division of the question, so that it should first be taken on the motion to recommit, and then on the instructions.

The previous question was seconded.

Mr. NELMS, of Georgia, rose to a question of privilege. The Convention, by a resolution adopted on Wednesday, decided that in cases where the delegations had not been otherwise instructed by their State Conventions, individual members of such delegations should have the right to vote in opposition to the vote of the majority. The Georgia State Convention had adopted the following resolution:

"*Resolved*, That the delegates from this State to the Charleston Convention be requested to cast the vote of Georgia as a unit."

It would be seen that the resolution was merely a request, appealing to their discretion, and not an instruction. A portion of his delegation had differed with the majority, and he now claimed it as a right that they should be represented in the Convention.

Mr. JONES, of Georgia, in behalf of the majority of that delegation, said that the minority in this case was a minority small in numbers, not only in their delegation here but in the State of Georgia. If the request of this State Convention was a mere appeal to their discretion, where was the necessity of the request? Was it supposed that any portion of the delegation would prove so refractory as to require positive instructions? Requests of sovereignties are the laws of subjects; and when Kings, States, Conventions, and especially Conventions of the Democracy, speak to their constituents by requests, their requests are laws.

The question of order having been raised that no debate was in order,

The PRESIDENT decided that the previous question, having been seconded, no debate was in order at this time. Whenever the question properly arose, it must be decided in some way.

Several further inquiries were propounded, and answered by the President, as to the effect of ordering the main question.

The State of Georgia demanded that the vote on the question before the house should be taken by States.

The vote on the question—"Shall the main question be now put?"—was then taken by States, and the following is the result:—Yeas 302, Nays 1.

Mr. HORN, of Wisconsin, being temporarily in the Chair, announced the result. So the main question was ordered.

The PRESIDENT again took the Chair, and Mr. JOHN COCHRAN, of New York, asked if the vote would not first be on his amendment to the instructions proposed by Mr. Bigler.

Mr. CESSNA, of Pennsylvania, raised the question of order that no amendment offered by Mr. Cochran was pending. The gentleman from Pennsylvania moved to recommit with instructions, and demanded the previous question on the motion. The gentleman from New York rose while the gentleman from Pennsylvania was on the floor, and proposed his amendment, but the gentleman from Pennsylvania being on the floor, it could not have been received.

Mr. COCHRAN stated that the gentleman from Pennsylvania yielded for that purpose.

Mr. BIGLER said he did not yield the floor for that purpose.

Mr. JOHN COCHRAN said he would withdraw his amendment.

Mr. CESSNA demanded a division of the question, so that the vote should first be taken on the motion to recommit, and then upon the instructions.

Mr. COCHRAN raised the question of order, that after the main question had been ordered no division of the question could be entertained. The rule of the House, as recently amended, permits the call for a division of the question either before or after the main question has been seconded, but the rules for the government of the Convention being those in force in the House of Representatives at the time of the Cincinnati Convention, expressly provide that no call for a division can be entertained after the main question has been ordered.

Mr. BIGLER, of Pennsylvania, said the gentleman from New York was right as to his question of order. He, however, had no objection to such a division himself.

The PRESIDENT said that inasmuch as two members of the House had stated with confidence that a division of the main question could not take place after the main question had been ordered, he would simply read the rule of the House of Representatives on the subject:

"53. Any member may call for the division of a question before or after the main question is ordered.—*September* 15 1837."

Mr. WALKER, of Alabama, said he had called for a division of the question before the main question was ordered.

The PRESIDENT replied that he was aware of it, and would entertain the call.

The question being first upon the first branch of the motion of Mr. Bigler to commit the resolutions offered by the Committee on Resolutions, with the amendments, back to the Committee.

Alabama demanded that the vote be by States.

The question was taken, and it was decided in the affirmative. Yeas 152, nays 151, as follows:

	Yeas.	Nays.		Yeas.	Nays		Yeas.	Nays.
Maine	3	5	North Carolina	10	0	Ohio	0	23
New Hampshire	0	5	South Carolina	8	0	Indiana	0	13
Vermont	0	5	Georgia	10	0	Illinois	0	11
Massachusetts	8	5	Florida	3	0	Michigan	0	6
Rhode Island	0	4	Alabama	9	0	Wisconsin	0	5
Connecticut	1½	4½	Louisiana	6	0	Iowa	0	4
New York	0	35	Mississippi	7	0	Minnesota	1	3
New Jersey	4	3	Texas	4	0	California	4	0
Pennsylvania	16	11	Arkansas	4	0	Oregon	3	0
Delaware	3	0	Missouri	5	4			
Maryland	5½	2½	Tennessee	11	1		152	151
Virginia	14	1	Kentucky	12	0			

So the proposed platforms were recommitted.

Mr. PHILLIPS, of Pennsylvania, moved to reconsider the vote by which the resolutions were recommitted, and also moved to lay the motion to reconsider on the table.

The latter motion was agreed to.

The question then recurred on the second branch of Mr. Bigler's motion, which was to require the Committee to report the resolutions proposed by him.

Mr. BISHOP, of Connecticut, asked the Chair whether, if the proposition to instruct was voted down, the Committee would be required to report in one hour ?

The PRESIDENT said the question of instructions and time were distinct and divisible.

Mr. BIGLER proposed to modify his motion, so far as relates to time.

Mr. SAMUELS, of Iowa, objected.

Mr. STUART, of Michigan, asked for a vote on each resolution separately,—first. on the one instructing the affirmation of the Cincinnati platform.

Mr. BAYARD opposed any instructions. Let the whole matter be referred, and the majority and minority each report a platform, and the Convention vote distinctly on them.

Mr. BROOKS, of Alabama, moved to lay the instructions on the table.

Mr. BIGLER, proposed to modify his propositions so as to meet the suggestion of the gentleman from Delaware.

Objection was made.

A DELEGATE raised the question that the motion to lay the instructions on the table would carry the whole subject with it.

The PRESIDENT decided that inasmuch as the report of the Committee, with the amendments, had been recommitted and were now not before the Convention, the motion to lay on the table would simply apply to the instructions, leaving the original matter in the hands of the Committee.

Gov. WINSTON, of Alabama, contended that the previous question not being exhausted, his colleague's motion was not in order.

The PRESIDENT decided the point not well taken.

Mr. SEWARD, of Georgia, again raised the question of privilege relative to the right of individual delegates in the Georgia delegation to cast their own vote.

The PRESIDENT repeated his former decision that the question could not be entertained at this time.

The question was then taken on the motion of Mr. Brooks, and it was decided in the affirmative, yeas 242½, nays 56½, as follows :

	Yeas.	Nays
Maine	8	
New Hampshire	5	
Vermont	5	
Massachusetts	12½	½
Rhode Island	4	
Connecticut	5	1
New York	35	
New Jersey		7
Pennsylvania	8	15
Delaware	3	
Maryland	5½	2½
Virginia	15	
North Carolina	10	
South Carolina	8	
Georgia	10	
Florida	3	
Alabama	9	
Louisiana	6	
Mississippi	7	
Texas	4	
Arkansas	4	
Missouri	4	5
Tennessee		11
Kentucky	5	7
Ohio	23	
Indiana	13	
Illinois	11	
Michigan	6	
Wisconsin	5	
Iowa	4	
Minnesota	4	
California	3½	½
Oregon		3
	242½	56½

So the instructions were laid on the table.

When the State of Georgia was called, the Chairman of that delegation announced the vote of the State in the affirmative.

Mr. SEWARD claimed the right to cast his vote in the negative.

Mr. NELMS, of Georgia, claimed the right to have two votes of the Georgia delegation cast in the negative.

Mr. LAMAR, of Georgia, called for the reading of the resolution adopted by the Convention on the question of allowing individual members of the delegation to vote.

The resolution was read as follows :

"That in any State which has not provided or directed by its State Convention how its vote may be given, the Convention will recognize the right of each delegate to cast his individual vote."

Mr. NELMS, of Georgia, said he had been informed that in the Georgia Convention, the word "instructed" was proposed and rejected.

Mr. JONES, of Georgia, explained that he, as a member of the Georgia Convention, proposed to insert the word "instructed," but did not press the motion, on the statement of the presiding officer that the word "requested" would cover the whole ground.

Mr. NELMS contended that the request of the Georgia delegation to vote as a unit was, he had stated before, simply an appeal to the discretion of the delegation, and the minority were at liberty to cast their individual votes.

Mr. MONTGOMERY moved that in every instance where positive instructions have not been given by the State Conventions, the individual delegates be permitted to cast their votes as they think proper.

Judge MEEK, of Alabama, raised the question that the motion was out of order.

The PRESIDENT decided the motion to be out of order.

Mr. JACKSON, of Georgia, spoke in behalf of allowing the majority to cast the vote of the State as a unit.

The PRESIDENT decided that, under the language of the rule adopted by the Convention, the expression "provided or directed" was one of broader import than merely an instruction. If the word "directed" had been alone used, he would have held that the request of the Georgia Convention would have been sufficient to require the delegation to vote as a unit; but holding the request came within the intent and meaning of the word "provided," as used in the rule of the Convention, he would direct that the vote of the State be received, as given by the Chairman of the delegation, as a unit.

Mr. ISAAC H. WRIGHT, of Massachasetts, moved that the Committee on Platforms be instructed to report at 4 o'clock this afternoon. He moved the previous question.

Hon. WILLARD SAULSBURY, of Delaware, was about to speak against any limitation upon the time when the Committee should report, when he was ruled out of order, the previous question having been moved.

Mr. JONES, of Georgia, moved that the Convention adjourn until 10 o'clock Monday morning.

Mr. PAYNE, of Ohio, asked and obtained leave for the Committee on Resolutions to retire to their Committee room.

Mr. BURROWS, of Arkansas, hoped that the Convention would adjourn.

Mr. MARTIN moved that the vote be taken by States.

The motion to adjourn was withdrawn.

The previous question being seconded and the main question ordered on instructing the Committee on Resolutions to report a 4 o'clock, it was taken and decided in the affirmative.

So the Committee were instructed to report at four o'clock, P. M.

On motion of Mr. Montgomery, of Pennsylvania, the Convention then adjourned till 4 o'clock, P. M.

EVENING SESSION.

The Convention re-assembled at four o'clock P. M., and was called to order by the President.

Mr. AVERY, of North Carolina, from the Committee on Resolutions, said that a majority of the Committee were ready to report, but the minority asked the indulgence of the Committee for a few moments longer.

Mr. GITTINGS, of Maryland, hoped that the Convention would adjourn over until Monday morning at eleven o'clock, and he would make that motion.

Mr. GITTINGS withdrew his motion to adjourn.

Mr. AVERY, of North Carolina. I beg leave, on behalf of the Committee on Resolutions, to make a report. I will state that the Committee understood that this report embodies in substance the Bayard resolutions, and in substance the resolutions of the gentleman from Pennsylvania (Mr. Bigler), and in substance the resolutions offered by the gentleman from New York (Mr. Cochran), being modified in such shape as the Committee think will meet the approbation of the Convention.

Resolved, That the platform adopted by the Democratic party at Cincinnati be affirmed, with the following explanatory resolutions.

1. That the government of a Territory organized by an act of Congress, is provisional and temporary; and, during its existence, all citizens of the United States have an equal right to settle with their property in the Territory without their rights, either of person or property, being destroyed or impaired by Congressional or Territorial legislation.

2. That it is the duty of the Federal Government, in all its departments, to protect, when necessary, the rights of persons and property in the Territories, and wherever else its constitutional authority extends.

3. That when the settlers in a Territory having an adequate population form a State Constitution, the right of sovereignty commences, and, being consummated by admission into the Union, they stand on an equal footing with the people of other States; and the State thus organized ought to be admitted into the Federal Union, whether its Constitution prohibits or recognizes the institution of slavery.

4. That the Democratic party are in favor of the acquisition of the Island of Cuba, on such terms as shall be honorable to ourselves and just to Spain, at the earliest practicable moment.

5. That the enactments of State Legislatures to defeat the faithful execution of the Fugitive Slave Law, are hostile in character, subversive of the Constitution, and revolutionary in their effect.

6. That the Democracy of the United States recognize it as the imperative duty of this Government to protect the naturalized citizen in all his rights, whether at home or in foreign lands, to the same extent as its native-born citizens.

Whereas, one of the greatest necessities of the age, in a political, commercial, postal and military point of view, is a speedy communication between the Atlantic and Pacific coasts; therefore, be it

Resolved, That the Democratic party do hereby pledge themselves to use every means in their power to secure the passage of some bill, to the extent of the constitutional authority of Congress, for the construction of a Pacific Railroad, from the Mississippi River to the Pacific Ocean, at the earliest practicable moment.

Mr. Avery addressed the Convention upon the subject of his report.

Mr. Stevens, of Oregon, desired to present a few thoughts, but

The President decided that he was out of order, and that Mr. Avery had the floor; and Mr. Avery proceeded to address the Convention.

Mr. Samuels, of Iowa, submitted a report from a minority of the Committee, which he offered as a substitute for, and an amendment to, the majority report made by Mr. Avery. The following is the

REPORT OF THE MINORITY OF THE COMMITTEE ON RESOLUTIONS,

As amended and reported back to the Convention, by Mr. Samuels.

1. *Resolved*, That we, the Democracy of the Union in Convention assembled, hereby declare our affirmance of the resolutions unanimously adopted and declared as a platform of principles by the Democratic Convention at Cincinnati, in the year 1856, believing that Democratic principles are unchangeable in their nature, when applied to the same subject matters; and we recommend as the only further resolutions the following:

2. Inasmuch as difference of opinion exists in the Democratic party as to the nature and extent of the powers of a Territorial Legislature, and as to the powers and duties of Congress, under the Constitution of the United States, over the institution of slavery within the Territories,

Resolved, That the Democratic party will abide by the decision of the Supreme Court of the United States upon these questions of Constitutional law.

3. *Resolved*, That it is the duty of the United States to afford ample and complete protection to all its citizens, whether at home or abroad, and whether native or foreign born.

4. *Resolved*, That one of the necessities of the age, in a military, commercial, and postal point of view, is speedy communication between the Atlantic and Pacific States; and the Democratic party pledge such Constitutional Government aid as will insure the construction of a Railroad to the Pacific coast, at the earliest practicable period.

5. *Resolved*, That the Democratic party are in favor of the acquisition of the Island of Cuba on such terms as shall be honorable to ourselves and just to Spain.

6. *Resolved*, That the enactments of the State Legislatures to defeat the faithful execution of the Fugitive Slave Law, are hostile in character, subversive of the Constitution, and revolutionary in their effect.

Mr. SAMUELS addressed the Convention upon the subject of his report.

Mr. BUTLER, of Massachusetts, then submitted a report from a minority of the Committee, which he offered as a substitute for both of the reports already submitted, which report of Mr. Butler is as follows:

Resolved, That we, the Democracy of the Union, in Convention assembled, hereby declare our affirmance of the Democratic resolutions unanimously adopted and declared as a platform of principles at Cincinnati, in the year 1856, without addition or alteration, believing that Democratic principles are unchangeable in their nature, when applied to the same subject matter, and we recommend as the only farther resolution, the following:

Resolved, That it is the duty of the United States to extend its protection alike over all its citizens, whether native or naturalized.

A minority of your Committee have agreed to report the above as the sole resolutions upon the subject of the principles of the party.

In behalf of a minority of the Committee.

B. F. BUTLER, Massachusetts. Mr. CAVANAUGH, Minnesota.
P. C, DUNNING, Indiana. B. WILLIAMSON, N. Jersey.

Mr. BUTLER addressed the Convention on the subject of his report.

Mr. Stevens, of Oregon, Mr. Brent, of Maryland, and Mr. Burrows, of Arkansas, addressed the Convention at length upon the subject of the platform.

Mr. CLAIBORNE, of Missouri, demanded the previous question, and before the demand was seconded, Mr. JACKSON, of Georgia, moved that the Convention adjourn, and called in behalf of the State of Georgia for a vote by States on his motion.

A vote was taken upon the question to adjourn with the following result:

	Yeas.	Nays.		Yeas.	Nays.		Yeas.	Nays.
Maine		8	North Carolina		10	Ohio		23
New Hampshire		5	South Carolina	8		Indiana		13
Vermont		5	Georgia	10		Illinois		11
Massachusetts	6½	6½	Florida	3		Michigan		6
Rhode Island		4	Alabama	9		Wisconsin		5
Connecticut	1	5	Louisiana	6		Iowa		4
New York		35	Mississippi	7		Minnesota		4
New Jersey	4		Texas	4		California	54	
Pennsylvania	14	11	Arkansas	4		Oregon	3	
Delaware	3		Missouri		9			
Maryland	5	3	Tennessee		12			
Virginia	–	15	Kentucky	6	6		97	205½

So the motion to adjourn was lost.

The demand for the previous question was then seconded.

Mr. CLARK, of Mississippi, moved for a division of the first series of resolutions, so that the vote may be taken on the third resolution separately.

Mr. HOWARD, of Tennessee, moved that the Convention adjourn, and called for a vote by States.

A vote was taken on the motion to adjourn, and resulted as follows:

	Yeas.	Nays.		Yeas.	Nays.		Yeas.	Nays.
Maine	0	8	North Carolina	10	0	Ohio	0	23
New Hampshire	0	5	South Carolina	0	8	Indiana	0	13
Vermont	0	5	Georgia	10	0	Illinois	0	11
Massachusetts	5	7½	Florida	3	0	Michigan	0	6
Rhode Island	0	4	Alabama	9	0	Wisconsin	0	5
Connecticut	0	6	Louisiana	6	0	Iowa	0	4
New York	0	35	Mississippi	7	0	Minnesota	0	4
New Jersey	7	0	Texas	4	0	California	4	0
Pennsylvania	13	11	Arkansas	4	9	Oregon	3	0
Delaware	3	0	Missouri	0	9			
Maryland	5½	2½	Tennessee	12	0		139	169
Virginia	14	1	Kentucky	7½	1½			

Mr. SEWARD, of Georgia, moved to reconsider the vote on the question of seconding the demand for the previous question.

The Chair decided Mr. SEWARD's motion to be out of order.

Mr. JACKSON, of Georgia, moved to lay the whole proceedings on the question upon the table, and upon that called for a vote by States.

The vote was taken on laying the whole subject on the table, and it was lost by the following vote:

	Yeas.	Nays.		Yeas.	Nays		Yeas.	Nays.
Maine		8	North Carolina		10	Ohio		23
New Hampshire		5	South Carolina		8	Indiana		13
Vermont		5	Georgia	10		Illinois		11
Massachusetts	4½	8½	Florida	3		Michigan		6
Rhode Island		4	Alabama		9	Wisconsin		5
Connecticut		6	Louisiana		6	Iowa		4
New York		35	Mississippi		7	Minnesota		4
New Jersey		7	Texas		4	California		4
Pennsylvania	3	24	Arkansas		4	Oregon		3
Delaware		3	Missouri		9			
Maryland		8	Tennessee		12		20½	283½
Virginia		15	Kentucky		12			

Mr. GITTINGS, of Maryland, moved to adjourn, and called for a vote by States, which was taken and resulted as follows:

	Yeas.	Nays.		Yeas.	Nays.		Yeas.	Nays.
Maine		8	North Carolina	10		Ohio		23
New Hampshire		5	South Carolina	8		Indiana		13
Vermont		5	Georgia	10		Illinois		11
Massachusetts	5½	7	Florida	8		Michigan		6
Rhode Island		8	Alabama	9		Wisconsin		5
Connecticut	1½	4½	Louisiana	6		Iowa		4
New York		35	Mississippi	7		Minnesota	1	3
New Jersey	4	8	Texas	4		California	4	
Pennsylvania	14	13	Arkansas	4		Oregon	3	
Delaware	3		Missouri	4	5			
Maryland	5½	2½	Tennessee	12			126	178
Virginia		15	Kentucky	11½	½			

Mr. BUTTERWORTH called for a division of the resolutions as reported by the majority.

The PRESIDENT stated that the question now before the house is, "Shall the main question be put?"

Mr. HUNTER, of Louisiana, desired to be heard, and moved that a vote be taken, and that then the Convention adjourn till Monday morning.

Mr. JACKSON, of Georgia, moved to lay the motion on the table.

Mr. MILTON, of Florida, called on the South to do her part in this matter manfully. She had been met fairly in argument, and listened to attentively. She should not now offer factious opposition to the vote.

The question, "Shall the main question be now put?" was voted on, and the State of Georgia called for a vote by States, and the following is the result:

4

	Yeas.	Nays.
Maine	8	
New Hampshire	5	
Vermont	5	
Massachusetts	13	
Rhode Island	4	
Connecticut	6	
New York	35	
New Jersey	7	
Pennsylvania	27	
Delaware	3	
Maryland	8	
Virginia	15	
North Carolina	10	
South Carolina		8
Georgia		10
Florida	3	
Alabama	9	
Louisiana	6	
Mississippi	7	
Texas	4	
Arkansas	4	
Missouri	5	4
Tennessee	3	7
Kentucky	7	2
Ohio	23	
Indiana	13	
Illinois	11	
Michigan	6	
Wisconsin	5	
Iowa	4	
Minnesota	4	
California	4	
Oregon	3	
	272	31

Mr. STUART, of Michigan, moved to reconsider the vote last taken, and to lay that motion on the table, which motion was carried, and then, on motion of Mr. STUART, the Convention adjourned.

SEVENTH DAY.

MONDAY, APRIL 30, 1860.

The Convention was called to order at half-past ten.

Prayer was delivered by Rev. Mr. DANA, of the Central Presbyterian Church.

Mr. PHILLIPS moved the reading of the Journal of Saturday be dispensed with. Agreed to.

The PRESIDENT. The Chair desires to say that on Saturday last, after a warm debate and a protracted session, at the time of the adjournment some little tendency to disorder occurred, which it became necessary for the Chair to check. The Chair is perfectly conscious that in using peremptory language to an assemblage composed of so many high-spirited gentlemen he may have given umbrage, although not designed. His remarks had been rendered necessary by the confusion that prevailed, but he deemed it proper to disclaim any intent to give offense to any member of the Convention.

Mr. PUGH, of Ohio, rose and asked the indulgence of the Convention for a personal explanation.

Mr. BARKSDALE, of Mississippi. As one of the members who have addressed the Convention, in behalf of the Majority Report, I deem it proper to state, in response to the gentleman from Ohio, that I did not understand his remarks to have been used in an offensive sense; and I am gratified that, with his accustomed frankness and courtesy, he has disavowed such an intention.

The PRESIDENT. At the time of the adjournment, the Convention had ordered that the main question be now put. A motion to reconsider and to lay on the table had been adopted. The question then was upon taking the main question, which is a series of resolutions to be voted upon.

The majority of the Committee, through their Chairman, Mr. Avery, reported the resolutions adopted by that majority. Thereupon Mr. Samuels moved to amend those resolutions by substituting the report of the minority. Mr. Butler moved, in behalf of another portion of the minority, to substitute their amendment by the adoption of the amendment of that minority. The first question would be upon the amendment of Mr. Butler, then upon that of Mr. Samuels, then, if both fail, upon the adoption of the majority report.

The question was then taken by States on the amendment of Mr. Butler, and the same was lost by the following vote:

	Yeas.	Nays.
Maine	3	5
New Hampshire		5
Vermont		5
Massachusetts	8	5
Rhode Island		4
Connecticut	2½	3½
New York		35
New Jersey	5	2
Pennsylvania	16½	10½
Delaware	3	
Maryland	5½	2¼
Virginia	12½	2½
North Carolina	10	
South Carolina		8
Georgia	10	
Florida		3
Alabama		9
Louisiana		6
Mississippi		7
Texas		4
Arkansas		4
Missouri	4½	4½
Tennessee	11	1
Kentucky	9	3
Ohio		23
Indiana		13
Illinois		11
Michigan		6
Wisconsin		5
Iowa		4
Minnesota	1½	2½
California		4
Oregon	3	
	105	198

When the State of Georgia was called, Mr. Seward challenged the vote.

Mr. Flournoy, on the State of Arkansas being called, gave notice that he desired to explain the vote of that State at the proper time.

When New Jersey was called, Mr. Williamson, of New Jersey, called attention of the Chair to the fact that a difference existed amongst the Delegates as to how the vote was to be cast. He read the resolutions of the State Convention, on *instructing* the Delegates to vote for William C. Alexander for Vice President, and *recommended* them to cast their other votes as a unit. The decision of the Chair on the Georgia case was held to prevent the individual Delegates of his State from voting as they pleased. He held that the State had not instructed or requested their Delegates to vote as a unit, in the resolutions passed. The difference between the two resolutions showed that no instructions were intended except as related to the vote for Vice President.

Mr. O'Rafferty contended that the resolution was similar to the Georgia resolution, and the Delegates were bound to vote as a unit.

The Chair decided that the same rule applied to both cases, and that the vote of New Jersey must be cast as a unit.

Mr. Williamson appealed from the decision of the Chair.

Mr. Phillips moved to lay the appeal on the table.

Mr. Cochran raised the point of order, that pending an undebatable question, the appeal must be taken without debate.

Michigan demanded the vote by States.

Mr. Irving, of Alabama, raised the point of order that the question was out of order during the calling of the roll.

The President. The question cannot be avoided now, as it affects the vote of the State.

The vote on the motion to lay the appeal on the table was then taken, and it was lost by the following vote:

	Yeas	Nays.		Yeas.	Nays.		Yeas.	Nays.
Maine	3	5	North Carolina	10		Ohio		23
New Hampshire		5	South Carolina	8		Indiana		13
Vermont		5	Georgia	10		Illinois		11
Massachusetts	9	4	Florida	3		Michigan		6
Rhode Island		4	Alabama	9		Wisconsin		5
Connecticut	2½	3½	Louisiana	6		Iowa		4
New York		35	Mississippi	7		Minnesota		4
New Jersey			Texas	4		California	4	
Pennsylvania	17	10	Arkansas	3	1	Oregon	3	
Delaware	3		Missouri	4½	4½		—	—
Maryland	5	3	Tennessee	11	1		146	150
Virginia	14	1	Kentucky	10	2			

The President. The question before the house now is, "Shall the decision of the Chair be sustained?"

The vote was taken, and the result was as follows:

	Yeas.	Nays.		Yeas.	Nays.		Yeas.	Nays.
Maine	3	5	North Carolina	10		Ohio		23
New Hampshire		5	South Carolina	8		Indiana		13
Vermont		5	Georgia	10		Illinois		11
Massachusetts	7½	5½	Florida	3		Michigan		6
Rhode Island		4	Alabama	9		Wisconsin		5
Connecticut	2½	3½	Louisiana	6		Iowa		4
New York		35	Mississippi	7		Minnesota		4
New Jersey			Texas	4		California	4	
Pennsylvania	17	10	Arkansas	3	1	Oregon	3	
Delaware	3		Missouri	4½	4½		—	—
Maryland	5	8	Tennessee	11	1		145	151
Virginia	14	1	Kentucky	10½	1½			

Mr. Stuart moved to re-consider the vote on Mr. Butler's resolutions, and to lay that motion on the table.

A Delegate raised the point of order that while under the operation of the previous question—

Mr. Seward, of Georgia. Is the motion divisible?

The President. It is not.

The PRESIDENT read from the rules to show that the motion to re-consider and lay on the table was in order.

After some further discussion by Messrs. Cochran and Skinner,

Mr. BIGLER rose to speak to the point of order.

Mr. SPINOLA. The question has been decided, and no motion is before the House.

The motion of Mr. Stuart was adopted.

Mr. BUTLER called for a division of the question on the next resolution in order, being the minority report, so that the vote be first taken on that portion re-enacting the Cincinnati Platform.

Mr. PHILLIPS, of Pennsylvania, raised the point that the question was not divisible, being a motion to strike out and insert.

Mr. SPINOLA raised the point of order that the gentleman from Pennsylvania was not in his place.

Mr. PHILLIPS went to his place and renewed his point of order.

The CHAIR referred to the rule that the motion to strike out and insert shall be deemed indivisible, and decided the point well taken.

The question then being on the report of the minority presented by Mr. Samuels—

Mr. B. F. BUTLER desired to make a motion.

The PRESIDENT. The gentleman from Massachusetts has a right to address the Chair.

Mr. BUTLER. I desire to move to lay the whole subject of the Platform on the table, in order to proceed to ballot for a Presidential candidate.

Mr. WINSTON raised the point of order that the House having ordered the previous question to be taken *now*, all motions were out of order until the question has been taken.

Mr. HOOKER, of Mississippi, understood the motion to be to go into the nomination for President. The rule adopted by the Convention prevented the nomination until after the Platform had been adopted. It was, therefore, a reversal of the rule, and out of order.

Mr. BUTLER withdrew his motion to lay on the table.

The question was then upon the adoption of the Minority Report and Resolutions, and a vote was called by States, and the following was the result of the vote:

	Yeas.	Nays.		Yeas.	Nays.		Yeas.	Nays.
Maine	8		North Carolina		10	Ohio	23	
New Hampshire	5		South Carolina		8	Indiana	13	
Vermont	5		Georgia		10	Illinois	11	
Massachusetts	7	6	Florida		3	Michigan	6	
Rhode Island	4		Alabama		9	Wisconsin	5	
Connecticut	6		Louisiana		6	Iowa	4	
New York	35		Mississippi		7	Minnesota	4	
New Jersey	5	2	Texas		4	California		4
Pennsylvania	12	15	Arkansas		4	Oregon		3
Delaware		3	Missouri	4	5			
Maryland	3½	4½	Tennessee	1	11			
Virginia	1	14	Kentucky	2½	9½		165	138

So the Minority Resolutions were adopted.

Mr. STUART moved to re-consider the vote and to lay that motion on the table.

Mr. COCHRAN raised the point of order, that the question could not be put whilst the previous question was before the House.

The PRESIDENT decided that he would receive both motions of Mr. Stuart, but that the question would not then be put, but would be put as soon as the question on the resolutions had been taken.

Mr. ASHE, of North Carolina, made an earnest appeal to the North to pause before consummating this action. It could but lead to a division and ruin, for as a representative of North Carolina he could not remain in the Convention if this Platform was adopted.

The question then being on the adoption of the report as amended, Mr. B. F. Butler, of Massachusetts, moved for a division of the question, so as to take the vote first on the proposition, as follows:

1. *Resolved*, That we, the Democracy of the Union in Convention assembled, hereby declare our affirmance of the resolutions unanimously adopted and declared as a platform of principles by the Democratic Convention at Cincinnati, in the year 1856, believing that Democratic principles are unchangeable in their nature, when applied to the same subject matters.

Mr. SEWARD, of Georgia, raised the point of order that the question was not divisible.

The CHAIR decided that the report having been amended by the insertion of the minority resolutions, the call for a division was in order on any substantive propositions that would make sense when standing alone.

A vote on Mr. Butler's proposition was then ordered, and the State of Michigan demanded a vote by States, which was taken, and the resolution was adopted by the following vote:

	Yeas.	Nays		Yeas.	Nays.		Yeas.	Nays.
Maine	8		North Carolina	10		Ohio	28	
New Hampshire	5		South Carolina		8	Indiana	13	
Vermont	5		Georgia		10	Illinois	11	
Massachusetts	13		Florida		3	Michigan	6	
Rhode Island	4		Alabama		9	Wisconsin	5	
Connecticut	6		Louisiana		6	Iowa	4	
New York	35		Mississippi		7	Minnesota	4	
New Jersey	7		Texas		4	California	½	3½
Pennsylvania	27		Arkansas		4	Oregon		3
Delaware	2	1	Missouri	7½	1½			
Maryland	5	3	Tennessee	10½	1		237½	65
Virginia	14	1	Kentucky	12				

Mr. STUART moved to reconsider the vote just taken, and to lay that motion upon the table.

This motion was received, but not voted upon.

Mr. DRIGGS, of New York, moved to lay the balance of the resolutions upon the table.

Mr. YANCY, of Alabama, rose and made a point of order, that the previous question was before the House, and that the previous question ran through all the propositions before the House, and therefore a motion to lay on the table was not in order.

The PRESIDENT ruled that the motion to lay on the table was in order.

The question upon laying upon the table was then put, and a vote was called for by States. The following was the result:

	Yeas.	Nays.		Yeas.	Nays.		Yeas.	Nays.
Maine		8	North Carolina	9	1	Ohio		23
New Hampshire		5	South Carolina	8		Indiana		13
Vermont		5	Georgia		10	Illinois		11
Massachusetts	8½	4½	Florida		3	Michigan		6
Rhode Island		4	Alabama			Wisconsin		5
Connecticut	2	4	Louisiana		6	Iowa		4
New York		35	Mississippi			Minnesota	1	3
New Jersey	5	2	Texas			California		4
Pennsylvania	16½	10½	Arkansas		1	Oregon		3
Delaware	2	1	Missouri		9			
Maryland		8	Tennessee	10½	1½		81	188
Virginia	11	4	Kentucky	7½	4½			

The States of Florida, Alabama, Mississippi, and three of the votes from Arkansas, after having cast their vote on the last proposition, asked leave to withdraw the vote cast. Leave was granted and the votes of said States were withdrawn.

Mr. EWING, of Tennessee, called for a division of the question, so that a vote might be had on the following preamble and resolution, viz:

2. Inasmuch as differences of opinion exist in the Democratic party as to the nature and extent of the powers of a Territorial Legislature, and as to the powers and duties of Congress, under the Constitution of the United States, over the institution of slavery within the Territories:

Resolved, That the Democratic party will abide by the decision of the Supreme Court of the United States upon these questions of Constitutional law.

Mr. BROWN, of North Carolina, addressed the Convention on the subject.

Mr. RICHARDSON, of Illinois, rose, and was about to address the Convention in response to Mr. Brown, but was called to order by Mr. Meek, and several other gentlemen from Alabama and Mississippi.

Mr. COCHRAN, of New York, believed peace offerings were about to be made, and called on the Convention to hear.

Mr. MEEK insisted on his point of order, and a vote was then had on the preamble and resolution as follows:

	Yeas.	Nays		Yeas.	Nays.		Yeas.	Nays.
Maine		8	North Carolina		10	Ohio		23
New Hampshire	1	4	South Carolina		8	Indiana		13
Vermont		5	Georgia			Illinois		11
Massachusetts		13	Florida			Michigan		6
Rhode Island	4		Alabama			Wisconsin		5
Connecticut		6	Louisiana			Iowa		4
New York		35	Mississippi			Minnesota		4
New Jersey		7	Texas			California		4
Pennsylvania	8	10	Arkansas			Oregon		3
Delaware		2	Missouri	4	5			
Maryland		8	Tennessee		12		21	238
Virginia		15	Kentucky	4	8			

The States of Georgia, Florida, Alabama, Louisiana, Mississippi, Texas, and Arkansas, declined voting.

So the preamble and resolution included in it was lost.

Mr. EWING, of Tennessee, moved to reconsider the vote just taken, and to lay this motion on the table—which motion was received but not voted upon.

Mr. STUART, of Michigan, then called for a division of the remainder of the resolutions, and a vote was demanded by States upon each.

A vote was then had upon the following resolution, viz:

Resolved, That it is the duty of the United States to afford ample and complete protection to all its citizens, whether at home or abroad, and whether native or foreign born. Which resulted as follows:

	Yeas.		Yeas.		Yeas
Maine	8	North Carolina	10	Ohio	23
New Hampshire	5	South Carolina	8	Indiana	13
Vermont	5	Georgia	10	Illinois	11
Massachusetts	13	Florida		Michigan	6
Rhode Island	4	Alabama		Wisconsin	5
Connecticut	6	Louisiana		Iowa	4
New York	35	Mississippi		Minnesota	4
New Jersey	7	Texas		California	4
Pennsylvania	27	Arkansas	4	Oregon	3
Delaware	3	Missouri	9		
Maryland	8	Tennessee	12		274
Virginia	15	Kentucky	12		

The States of Florida, Alabama, Louisiana, Mississippi, and Texas, declined voting.

So the Resolution was unanimously adopted.

A vote was then taken upon the following resolution, viz:

Resolved, That one of the necessities of the age, in a military, commercial, and postal point of view, is speedy communication between the Atlantic and Pacific States; and the Democratic party pledge such Constitutional Government aid as will insure the construction of a Railroad to the Pacific coast, at the earliest practicable period. Which resulted as follows, viz:

	Yeas	Nays.		Yeas.	Nays.		Yeas.	Nays.
Maine	8		North Carolina		10	Ohio	23	
New Hampshire	5		South Carolina	8		Indiana	13	
Vermont	5		Georgia	10		Illinois	11	
Massachusetts	12½		Florida			Michigan	6	
Rhode Island	4		Alabama			Wisconsin	5	
Connecticut	6		Louisiana			Iowa	4	
New York	35		Mississippi			Minnesota	4	
New Jersey	7		Texas			California	4	
Pennsylvania	27		Arkansas	4		Oregon	3	
Delaware		2	Missouri	9				
Maryland	7	1	Tennessee	8½	3½		252	20½
Virginia	11	4	Kentucky	12				

The States of Florida, Alabama, Louisiana, Mississippi, and Texas, declined voting.

So the resolution was adopted.

Mr. McCOOK, of Ohio, moved to reconsider, which motion was received.

A vote was then had on the following resolution, viz :

Resolved, That the Democratic party are in favor of the acquisition of the Island of Cuba, on such terms as shall be honorable to ourselves and just to Spain.

Mr. MEEK, of Alabama, moved that the vote upon the above resolution be taken by acclamation, but a vote by States was insisted upon, and the vote taken by States, and resulted as follows :

	Yeas.		Yeas.		Yeas.
Maine	8	North Carolina	10	Ohio	23
New Hampshire	5	South Carolina	8	Indiana	13
Vermont	5	Georgia	10	Illinois	11
Massachusetts	13	Florida		Michigan	6
Rhode Island	4	Alabama		Wisconsin	5
Connecticut	6	Louisiana		Iowa	4
New York	35	Mississippi		Minnesota	4
New Jersey	7	Texas		California	4
Pennsylvania	27	Arkansas	3	Oregon	3
Delaware	2	Missouri	9		
Maryland	8	Tennessee	12		272
Virginia	15	Kentucky	12		

Florida, Alabama, Louisiana, Mississippi, and Texas, declined voting.

Resolution adopted unanimously.

A vote was then taken on the following resolution, viz :

6. *Resolved,* That the enactments of State Legislatures to defeat the faithful execution of the Fugitive Slave Law, are hostile in character, subversive of the Constitution, and revolutionary in effect.

The result was as follows :

	Yeas		Yeas.		Yeas.
Maine	8	North Carolina	10	Ohio	23
New Hampshire	5	South Carolina	8	Indiana	13
Vermont	5	Georgia	10	Illinois	11
Massachusetts	13	Florida		Michigan	6
Rhode Island	4	Alabama		Wisconsin	5
Connecticut	6	Louisiana		Iowa	4
New York	35	Mississippi		Minnesota	4
New Jersey	7	Texas		California	4
Pennsylvania	27	Arkansas	3	Oregon	3
Delaware	2	Missouri	9		
Maryland	8	Tennessee	12		272
Virginia	15	Kentucky	12		

Florida Alabama, Louisiana, Mississippi, and Texas, refused to vote.

Resolution adopted unanimously.

Mr. STUART, of Michigan, moved to reconsider, and desired to make some remarks.

Mr. MEEK, of Alabama, rose to a point of order, and claimed that Mr. Stuart could not speak to the question till the resolutions had been adopted in a body as a whole.

The CHAIR decided Mr. Stuart to be in order, and Mr. Stuart proceeded to address the Convention, when

Mr. YANCY begged leave to interrupt him for an explanation, which he made.

Several gentlemen rose to points of order, and

Mr. STUART said he would not occupy the attention of the Convention if it was not the desire of the Convention, and moved to lay his motion to reconsider on the table, but gave way to

Mr. WALKER, of Alabama, who presented a written communication to the Convention, under instructions from his Delegation, which communication is as follows, viz :

To the Hon. Caleb Cushing, President of the Democratic National Convention, now in session in the City of Charleston, South Carolina :

The undersigned Delegates, representing the State of Alabama in this Convention, respectfully beg leave to lay before your honorable body, the following statement of facts :

On the eleventh day of January, 1860, the Democratic party of the State of Alabama met in Convention, in the City of Montgomery, and adopted, with singular unanimity, a series of resolutions, herewith submitted.

RESOLUTIONS OF THE DEMOCRATIC STATE CONVENTION.

1. *Resolved by the Democracy of the State of Alabama, in Convention assembled*, That holding all issues and principles upon which they have heretofore affiliated and acted with the National Democratic party to be inferior in dignity and importance to the grea· question of slavery, they content themselves with a general re-affirmance of the Cincinnati Platform as to such issues, and also indorse said Platform as to slavery, together with the following resolutions:

2 *Resolved further*, That we re-affirm so much of the first resolution of the Platform adopted in Convention by the Democracy of this State, on the 8th of January, 1856, as relat s to the subject of slavery, to wit: "The unqualified right of the people of the slave-holding States to the protection of their property in the States, in the Territories, and in the wilderness, in which Territorial Governments are as yet unorganized."

3. *Resolved further*, That in order to meet and clear away all obstacles to a full enjoyment of this right in the Territories, we re-affirm the principle of the 9th resolution of the Platform adopted in Convention by the Democracy of this State, on the 14th of February, 1848, to wit: "That it is the duty of the General Government, by all proper legislation, to secure an entry into those Territories to all the citizens of the United States, together with their property of every description, and that the same should remain protected by the United States while the Territories are under its authority."

4. *Resolved further*, That the Constitution of the United States is a compact between sovereign and co-equal States, united upon the basis of perfect equality of rights and privileges.

5. *Resolved fnrther*, That the Territories of the United States are common property, in which the States have equal rights, and to which the citizens of every State may rightfully emigrate wiih their slaves or other property recognized as such, in any of the States of the Union, or by the Constitution of the United States.

6. *Resolved further*, That the Congress of the United States has no power to abolish slavery in the Territories, or to prohibit its introduction into any of them.

7. *Resolved further*, That the Territorial Legislatures, created by the legislation of Congress, have no power to abolish slavery, or to prohibit the introduction of the same, or to impair by unfriendly legislation, the security and full enjoyment of the same within the Territories, and such constitutional power certainly does not belong to the people of the Territories in any capacity, before, in the exercise of a lawful authority, they form a Constitution preparatory to admission as a State into the Union; and their action in the exercise of such lawful authority, certainly cannot operate or take effect before their actual admission as a State into the Union.

8. *Resolved further*, That the principles enunciated by Chief Justice Taney, in his opinion in the Dred Scott case, deny to the Territorial Legislature the power to destroy or impair by any legislation whatever, the right of property in slaves, and maintain it to be the duty of the Federal Government, in *all* of its departments, to protect the rights of the owner of such property in the Territories; and the principles so declared are hereby asserted to be the rights of the South, and the South should maintain them.

9. *Resolved further*, That we hold all of the foregoing propositions to contain *cardinal principles*—true in themselves—and just and proper, and necessary for the safety of all that is dear to us, and we do hereby instruct our

Delegates to the Charleston Convention, to present them for the calm consideration and approval of that body—from whose justice and patriotism we anticipate their adoption.

10. *Resolved further,* That our Delegates to the Charleston Convention are hereby expressly instructed to insist that said Convention shall adopt a platform of principles, recognizing distinctly the rights of the South as asserted in the foregoing resolutions; and if the said National Convention shall refuse to adopt, in substance, the propositions embraced in the preceding resolutions, prior to nominating candidates, our Delegates to said Convention are hereby positively instructed to withdraw therefrom.

11. *Resolved further,* That our Delegates to the Charleston Convention shall cast the vote of Alabama as a unit, and a majority of our Delegates shall determine how the vote of this State shall be given.

12. *Resolved further,* That an Executive Committee, to consist of one from each Congressional District, be appointed, whose duty it shall be, in the event that our Delegates withdraw from the Charleston Convention, in obedience to the 10th resolution, to call a Convention of the Democracy of Alabama, to meet at an early day to consider what is best to be done.

Under these resolutions, the undersigned received their appointment, and participated in the action of this Convention.

By the resolution of instruction—the tenth in the series—we were directed to insist that the Platform adopted by this Convention should embody, "in substance," the propositions embraced in the preceding resolutions, prior to nominating candidates.

Auxious, if possible, to continue our relations with this Convention, and thus to maintain the nationality of the Democratic party, we agreed to accept, as the substance of the Alabama Platform, either of the two reports submitted to this Convention by the majority of the Committee on Resolutions—this majority representing not only a majority of the States of the Union, but also the *only* States at all likely to be carried by the Democratic party in the Presidential election.

We beg to make these Reports parts of this communication:

PLATFORM—FIRST MAJORITY REPORT.

Resolved, That the Platform adopted at Cincinnati be affirmed, with the following resolutions:

1. That the National Democracy of the United States hold these cardinal principles on the subject of slavery in the Territories: First, That Congress has no power to abolish slavery in the Territories. Second, That the Territorial Legislature has no power to abolish slavery in any Territory, nor to prohibit the introduction of slaves therein; nor any power to exclude slavery therefrom, nor any power to destroy or impair the right of property in slaves by any legislation whatever.

2. *Resolved,* That the enactments of State Legislatures to defeat the faithful execution of the Fugitive Slave Law are hostile in character, subversive of the Constitution, and revolutionary in their effect.

3. *Resolved,* That it is the duty of the Federal Government to protect, when necessary, the rights of persons and property on the high seas, in the Territories, or wherever else its constitutional authority extends.

4. *Resolved,* That the Democracy of the Nation recognize it as the imperative duty of this Government to protect the naturalized citizen in all his rights, whether at home or in foreign lands, to the same extent as its native-born citizens.

5. *Resolved,* That the National Democracy earnestly recommend the acquisition of the Island of Cuba at the earliest practicable period.

Whereas, That one of the greatest necessities of the age, in a political, commercial, postal, and military point of view, is a speedy communication between the Pacific and Atlantic coasts. Therefore, be it

Resolved, That the National Democratic party do hereby pledge themselves to use every means in their power to secure the passage of some bill for the construction of a Pacific Railroad, from the Mississippi River to the Pacific Ocean, at the earliest practicable moment.

SECOND MAJORITY REPORT.

Resolved, That the Platform adopted by the Democratic party at Cincinnati be affirmed, with the following explanatory resolutions:

1. That the Government of a Territory organized by an act of Congress is provisional and temporary, and during its existence all citizens of the United States have an equal right to settle with their property in the Territory, without their rights, either of person or property, being destroyed or impaired by Congressional or Territorial legislation.

2. That it is the duty of the Federal Government, in all its departments, to protect, when necessary, the rights of persons and property in the Territories, and wherever else its constitutional authority extends.

3. That when the settlers in a Territory having an adequate population, form a State Constitution, the right of sovereignty commences, and being consummated by admission into the Union, they stand on an equal footing with the people of other States, and the State thus organized ought to be admitted into the Federal Union, whether its Constitution prohibits or recognizes the institution of slavery.

Resolved, That the Democratic party are in favor of the acquisition of the Island of Cuba, on such terms as shall be honorable to ourselves and just to Spain, at the earliest practicable moment.

Resolved, That the enactments of State Legislatures to defeat the faithful execution of the Fugitive Slave Law, are hostile in character, subversive of the Constitution, and revolutionary in their effect.

Resolved, That the Democracy of the United States recognize it as the imperative duty of this Government to protect the naturalized citizen in all his rights, whether at home or in foreign lands, to the same extent as its native-born citizens.

WHEREAS, One of the greatest necessities of the age, in a political, commercial, postal and military point of view, is a speedy communication between the Pacific and Atlantic coasts. Therefore, be it

Resolved, That the National Democratic party do hereby pledge themselves to use every means in their power to secure the passage of some bill, to the extent of the constitutional authority of Congress, for the construction of a Pacific Railroad from the Mississippi River to the Pacific Ocean, at the earliest practicable moment.

These reports received the indorsement, in the Committee on Resolutions, of every Southern State, and had either of them been adopted as the Platform of principles of the Democratic party, although, possibly, in some respects, subject to criticism, we should not have felt ourselves in duty bound to withhold our acquiescence.

But it has been the pleasure of this Convention, by an almost exclusive sectional vote, not representing a majority of the States, nor a majority of the Democratic electoral votes, to adopt a Platform which does not, in our opinion, nor in the opinion of those who urge it, embody in substance the principles of the Alabama resolutions.

That Platform is as follows:

Resolved, That we, the Democracy of the Union in Convention assembled, hereby declare our affirmance of the resolutions unanimously adopted and declared as a platform of principles by the Democratic Convention at

Cincinnati, in the year 1856, believing that Democratic principles are unchangeable in their nature, when applied to the same subject matters.

Resolved, That it is the duty of the United States to afford ample and complete protection to all its citizens, whether at home or abroad, and whether native or foreign born.

Resolved, That one of the necessities of the age, in a military, commercial, and postal point of view, is speedy communication between the Atlantic and Pacific States; and the Democratic party pledge such Constitutional Government aid as will insure the construction of a railroad to the Pacific coast at the earliest practicable period.

Resolved, That the Democratic party are in favor of the acquisition of the Island of Cuba, on such terms as shall be honorable to ourselves and just to Spain.

Resolved, That the enactments of State Legislatures to defeat the faithful execution of the Fugitive Slave Law, are hostile in character, subversive of the Constitution, and revolutionary in their effect.

The points of difference between the Northern and Southern Democracy are:

1st. As regards the *status* of slavery as a political institution in the Territories, whilst they remain in the Territories, and the power of the people of a Territory to exclude it by unfriendly legislation.

And 2d. As regards the duty of the Federal Government to protect the owner of slaves in the enjoyment of his property in the Territories, so long as they remain such.

This Convention has refused, by the platform adopted, to settle either of these propositions in favor of the South. We deny to the people of a Territory any power to legislate against the institution of slavery, and we assert that it is the duty of the Federal Government, in all its departments, to protect the owner of slaves in the enjoyment of his property in the Territories. These principles, as we state them, are embodied in the Alabama Platform.

Here, then, is a plain, explicit and direct issue between this Convention and the constituency which we have the honor to represent in this body.

Instructed, as we are, not to waive this issue, the contingency therefore, has arisen when, in our opinion, it becomes our duty to withdraw from this Convention.

We beg, sir, to communicate this fact through you, and to assure the Convention that we do so in no spirit of anger, but under a sense of imperative obligation—properly appreciating its responsibilities, and cheerfully submitting to its consequences.

L. P. WALKER, Chairman.
F. S. LYON
JOHN A. WINSTON,
H. D. SMITH,
JOHN ERWIN,
W. L. YANCY,
D. W. BAINE,
N. H. R. DAWSON,
R. M. PATTON,
W. C. McIVER,
P. O. HARPER,
LEWIS L. CATO,
JOHN W. PORTIS,
ROBERT G SCOTT,
A. B. MEEK,
J. R BREARE,
A. W. DILLARD,

F. G. NORMAN,
J. C. GUILD,
JULIUS C. B. MITCHELL.
W. C. SHERROD,
G. G. GRIFFIN,
J. T. BRADFORD,
T. J BURNETT,
A G. HENRY,
WILLIAM M. BROOKS,
R. CHAPMAN,
[Delegate appointed though not participating in the Convention.]

THOS. B COOPER,
PEYTON G. KING,
W. G. GARRETT,
M. J. BOLGER,

Judge Meek offered the following resolution, which was unanimously adopted:

Resolved, That in the event the Alabama delegation should withdraw from the Convention, no delegate or any other person shall thenceforward have any authority to represent Alabama upon the floor of the Convention, or to cast the vote of Alabama therein ; and that our Chairman be instructed so to inform said Convention.

And thereupon the delegation from Alabama withdrew from the Convention.

Mr. BARRY, of Mississippi, rose and stated that they would retire from the Convention with the delegation from Alabama, and would have no further connection with the Convention. That they had prepared a protest, but were not in readiness to present it to the Convention. They protested against any other persons being allowed to represent the State of Mississippi in the Convention.

Mr. MOUTON, of Louisiana, rose in behalf of the delegation from that State, and stated that the majority of the delegation would no longer take a part in the proceedings of the Convention. That two delegates still determined to remain in the Convention.

Mr. SIMMONS, of South Carolina, presented to the Convention a statement in writing, as follows ;

To the Hon. Caleb Cushing, President of the Charleston Convention:

We, the undersigned, delegates appointed by the Democratic State Convention of South Carolina, beg leave respectfully to state, that according to the principles enunciated in their platform at Columbia, the power, either of the Federal Government, or of its agent, the Territorial Government, to abolish or legislate against property in slaves, by either direct or indirect legislation, is explicitly denied; and as the platform adopted by this Convention palpably and intentionally pretermits any expression affirming the incapacity of the Territorial Government so to legislate, they do not believe they would be acting in good faith to their principles, or in accordance with the wishes of their constituents, longer to remain in this Convention; and they hereby therefrom respectfully announce their withdrawal.

JAMES SIMMONS,
S. McGOWAN,
B. H. WILSON,
R. B. BOYLSTON,
Delegates from the State at large.
JAS. H. WITHERSPOON,
E. W. CHARLES,
Delegates from 1st Congressional District.
G. N. REYNOLDS, JR.,
THOS. Y. SIMONS,
Delegates from 2d Congressional District.
JAMES PATTERSON,
B. H. BROWN,
Delegates from 3d Congressional District.
J. A. METTS,
Delegate from 4th Congressional District.
JOHN S. PRESTON,
FRANKLIN GAILLARD,
Delegates from 6th Congressional District.

And which he stated was signed by all the delegates but three.

Mr. GLENN, of Mississippi, addressed the Convention, and read a communication which is as follows :

To the President of the Democratic Convention :

SIR—As Chairman of the Delegation which has the honor to represent the State of Mississippi on this floor, I desire to be heard by you and by the Convention.

In common consultation we have met here, the representatives of sister States, to resolve the principles of a great party. While maintaining principles, we profess no spirit, save that of harmony, conciliation, the success of our party, and the safety of our organization. But to the former the latter must yield, for no organization is valuable without it, and no success is honorable which does not crown it.

We came here simply asking a recognition of the equal rights of our State under the laws and Constitution of our common Government; that our right to property should be asserted, and the protection of that property, when necessary, should be yielded by the Government, which claims our allegiance. We had regarded Government and protection as co-relative ideas, and that so long as the one was maintained the other still endured.

After a deliberation of many days, it has been announced to us by a controlling majority of Representatives of nearly one-half the States of this Union, and that, too, in the most solemn and impressive manner, that our demand cannot be met, and our rights cannot be recognized. While it is granted that the capacity of the Federal Government is ample to protect all other property within its jurisdiction, it is claimed to be impotent when called upon to act in favor of a species of property recognized in fifteen sovereign States. Within those States even Black Republicans admit it to be guaranteed by the Constitution, and to be only assailed by a Higher Law; without them they claim the right to prohibit or destroy it. The controlling majority of Northern Representatives on this floor, while they deny all power to destroy, equally deny all power to protect; and this, they assure us, is and must, and shall be the condition of our co-operation in the next Presidential election.

In this state of affairs our duty is plain and obvious. The State which sent us here, announced to us her principles. In common with seventeen of her sister States, she has asked a recognition of her Constitutional rights. These have been plainly and explicitly denied to her. We have offered to yield everything except an abandonment of her rights—everything except her honor—and it has availed us nothing.

As the representatives of Mississippi, knowing her wishes—as honorable men, regarding her commands, we withdraw from the Convention, and, as far as our action is concerned, absolve her from all connection with this body, and all responsibility for its action.

To you, sir, as presiding officer of the Convention while it has existed in its integrity, we desire, collectively as a delegation, and individually as men, to tender the highest assurances of our profound respect and consideration.

(Signed) D. C. GLENN,
Chairman of the Mississippi Delegation.
GEORGE H. GORDON,
JAMES DRANE,
BEVERLY MATHEWS,
J. T. SIMMS,
JOS. R. DAVIS,
W. S. WILSON,
ISAAC ENLOE,
CHAS. EDWARD HOOKER,
W. H. H TYSON,
ETHELBERT BARKSDALE,
W. S BARRY,
J. M. THOMPSON.

Mr. MILTON, of Florida, addresssd the Convention, and presented a communication, as follows:

To the Hon. Caleb Cushing, President of the Democratic National Convention:

The undersigned, Democratic Delegates from the State of Florida, enter this, their solemn protest, against the action of the Convention in voting down the platform of the majority.

Florida, with her Southern sisters, is entitled to a clear and unambiguous recognition of her rights in the Territories, and this being refused by the rejection of the majority report, we protest against receiving the Cincinnati Platform with the interpretation that it favors the doctrine of Squatter Sovereignty in the Territories, which doctrine, in the name of the people represented by us, we repudiate.

T. J. EPPES,
B. F. WARDLAW,
JOHN MILTON,
J B. OWENS,
C. F. DYKE.
Delegates from Florida.

The delegates from Florida, before retiring, have adopted the following resolution:

Resolved, That no person not a regularly appointed delegate has a right to cast the vote of the State of Florida in this Convention.

JOHN MILTON, Chairman Delegation.

Mr. BRYAN, of Texas, addressed the Convention, and presented a protest, in writing, as follows:

Hon. Caleb Cushing, President of the Democratic National Convention:

The undersigned, Delegates from the State of Texas, would respectfully protest against the late action of this Convention, in refusing to adopt the report of the majority of the Committee on Resolutions, which operates as the virtual adoption of principles affirming doctrines in opposition to the decision of the Supreme Court in the Dred Scott case, and in conflict with the Federal Constitution, and especially opposed to the Platform of the Democratic party of Texas, which declares:

1st. That the Democratic party of the State of Texas re-affirm, and concur in the principles contained in the Platform of the National Democratic Convention, held at Cincinnati in June, 1856, as a true expression of political faith and opinion, and herewith re-assert and set forth the principles therein contained, as embracing the only doctrine which can preserve the integrity of the Union and the equal rights of the States, "*expressly rejecting any interpretation thereof favoring the doetrine known as Squatter Sovereignty,*" and that we will continue to adhere to and abide by the principles ard doctrines of the Virginia and Kentucky resolutions of 1798 and 1799, and Mr. Madison's report relative thereto.

2d. That it is the right of every citizen to take his property of any kind, including slaves, into the common territory belonging equally to all the States of the Confederacy, and to have it protected there under the Federal Constitution. Neither Congress nor a Territorial Legislature, nor any human power, has any authority, either directly or indirectly, to impair these sacred rights; and they, having been affirmed by the Supreme Court in the decision of the Dred Scott case, we declare that it is the duty of the Federai Government, the common agent of all the States, to establish such government and enact such laws for the Territories, and so change the same from time to time as may be necessary to insure protection and preservation of these rights, and prevent every infringement of the same. The affirmation of this principle of the duty of Congress to simply protect the right of property, is nowise in conflict with the heretofore established and well recognized principles of the Democratic party, that Congress does not possess the power to legislate slavery into the Territories, or to exclude it therefrom.

Recognizing these declarations of principles as instructions to us for our government in the National Convention, and believing that a repudiation of them by all of the Northern States except the noble States of Oregon and California, the whole vote of which is more than doubtful in the ensuing Presidential election, demand from us our unqualified disapproval.

The undersigned do not deem this the place or time to discuss the practical illustration that has been given of the irrepressible conflict between the Northern and Southern States, that has prevailed in this Convention for the last week.

It is sufficient to say, that if the principles of the Northern Democracy are properly represented, by the opinion and action of the majority of the delegates from that section on this floor, we do not hesitate to declare that their principles are not only not ours, but, if adhered to and enforced by them, will destroy this Union.

In consideration of the foregoing facts, we cannot remain in the Convention. We consequently respectfully withdraw, leaving no one authorized to cast the vote of the State of Texas.

GUY M. BRYAN, Chairman.	H. R. RUNNELS.	WM. H. PARSONS.
F. R. LUBBOCK.	WM. P. OCHILTREE.	R WARD.
F. S. STOCKDALE.	M. W. COVEY.	J. F. CROSBY.
E. GREER.		

Mr. BURROWS, of Arkansas, rose and addressed the Convention, and presented a communication, as follows :

Hon. Caleb Cushing, President of Charlestion Convention :

The undersigned Delegates, accredited by the Democracy of Arkansas to represent said Democracy in the Convention of the Democracy of the United

States, assembled on the 23d of April, 1860, beg leave to submit the following protest against certain actions of this Convention, and statement of the causes which, in their opinion, require them to retire from this Convention.

1st. The Convention of the Democracy of the State of Arkansas, convened at Little Rock on the 2d day of April, 1860, passed, among other things, the following resolutions, viz :

1st. *Resolved*, We, the Democracy of Arkansas, through our representatives in Convention assembled, proclaim our confidence in the virtue and intelligence of the people, and unabated faith in the principles of the Democracy.

2d. We re-affirm the political principles enunciated in the Cincinnati Platform by the Democracy of the United States in June, 1856, and assert as illustrative thereof, that neither Congress nor a Territorial Legislature, whether by direct legislation or by legislation of an indirect and unfriendly character, possesses the power to annul or impair the Constitutional rights of any citizen of the United States to take his slave property into the common Territories, and there hold and enjoy the same, and that if experience should at any time prove that the judiciary and executive power do not possess the means to insure protection to Constitutional rights in a Territory, and if the Territorial Government should fail or refuse to provide the necessary remedies for that purpose, it will be the duty of Congress to supply the deficiency.

3d. That the representatives of the Democracy of Arkansas, in the Charleston Convention, be instructed to insist upon the recognition by said Convention of the purpose hereinbefore declared, prior to balloting for any candidate for the Presidency, and if said Convention refuse to recognize the rights of the South in the Territories of the United States, the representatives of the Democracy of Arkansas be instructed to retire from said Convention, and refuse to aid in the selection of any candidate whomsoever by said Convention.

4th. That the unity of the Democratic party and the safety of the South demands the adoption of the two-thirds rule by the Charleston Convention of the Democracy of the United States, and that our delegates to said Convention be required to insist upon and maintain the adoption thereof as an indispensable necessity.

In accordance with the instructions contained in resolution 3d, above, one of the undersigned had the honor, on the second day of the session of this Convention, to offer to the consideration of this Convention the following resolution, viz: "*Resolved*, That the Convention will not proceed to nominate a candidate for the Presidency until the platform shall have been made," which said resolution was passed by the Convention by great unanimity. Subsequently the Committee on Resolutions and Platform, appointed by the Convention, in accordance with the usages and custom of the Democratic party of the United States, agreed upon and reported to this Convention a platform of principles, recognizing the principle contained in the resolutions of the Democracy of Arkansas, above cited, and fully asserting the equal rights of the Southern States in the common Territories of the United States, and the duty of the Federal Government to protect those rights when necessary, according to the usages and customs of the Democracy of the United States, as developed by the practice of said Democracy, assembled in Conventions on former occasions, and in strict accordance, as is believed by the undersigned, with the compact and agreement made by and between the Democrats of the several States, upon which the Conventions of the Democracy of the United States were agreed first to be founded, and assented to by the several Southern States. The report and determination of the Committee on Platform became and was henceforward as the platform of the Democracy of the United States, and this Convention had no duty to perform in relation thereto, but to receive, confirm and publish the same, and cause it to be carried into effect wherever in the respective States the Democracy were able to enforce their decrees at the ballot box.

The undersigned are confirmed in this opinion by reference not only to the history of the past, which shows that in all instances the sovereignty of the States, and not the electoral votes of the States, has uniformly been represented in the Committee on Platform, and that the report of the Committee has invariably been registered as the supreme law of the Democratic party by unanimous consent of the entire Conventions, without changing or in any manner altering any part or portion thereof. It is asserted as a part of our traditional learning, and confidently believed, that the Democracy of the United States, by a peculiar system of checks and balances, formed after the fashion of the Federal Government, were contracted and bound themselves to fully recognize the sovereignty of the States in making the Platform, and the population or masses of the States, in naming the candidate to be placed on the Platform. That many States have been uniformly allowed to vote the full strength of their electoral college in these Conventions, when it was well known that said States had never heretofore, and probably would never hereafter, give a single electoral vote at the polls to the candidate which they had so large a share in nominating, cannot be accounted for on any other principle than that it was intended only as a recognition of the sovereignty and equality of said States.

Would it be right at this time for the numerical majority to deprive all the Black Republican States represented on this floor by their representatives, which by custom they have so long enjoyed, simply because it is now evident that they are or will be unable to vote the Democratic ticket in the next Presidential election ?

By common consent we say that a reckless numerical majority should not be thus allowed to tread under foot the vested rights of those States, and the well established usages and customs of the party.

If thus it be wrong for the numerical majority to deprive the Black Republican States of this long vested right, how much more unjust is it for the numerical majority to deprive *all* the States of their vested right to make and declare the Platform in the usual and customary manner ? And when we call to mind that the numerical majority resides chiefly in the Black Republican States, to whom the South has uniformly accorded so large a privilege, in naming candidates who were alone to be elected by Southern votes, we have much reason to believe that he to whom you gave an inch seems emboldened thereby to demand an ell.

The undersigned beg leave to state that many patriotic States, Right Democrats, in the South, have long contended that these Conventions of the Democracy, representing in fact the whole consolidated strength of the Union, acting through party sympathy upon the individual members of society, would ultimate in a despotic, colossal centralism, possessed of power to override and destroy at its will and pleasure the Constitutions and reserved rights of any and all the States. The South, however, has heretofore felt safe, because of the checks and balances imposed upon the machinery of the Conventions. The South felt that where she retained an equal power to write the creed of faith, she could trust her Northern sisters, with their immense populations, to name the candidate ; and all would alike support the creed and the candidate.

The undersigned, well knowing the hostility of the Northern masses towards the "peculiar institutions" of the South, and calling to mind the relative numbers of the Northern and Southern States, assert with confidence that no Southern State in the Union would ever have consented to surrender so abjectly and hopelessly, all their fortunes to the numerical majority who have just now voted to set aside the Platform, unless upon the full assurance that the States were entitled by agreement to make and establish the creed of faith and prescribe the rule of action. This violation of plighted faith on the part of the numerical majority—this violation of the well established usage and custom of the party—drive us to the conclusion that we cannot longer trust the fortunes of the slaveholding States to the chances of a numerical majority in a Convention, where all the Black Republicans of the Union, the immense populations of Massachusetts, New York, Pennsylvania and Ohio, and other Northern States, are fully represented, on the one side, against the small populations from the slave States on the other—had these populations adhered strictly to the usages and customs of the party, longer associations might have been practicable ; but annihilation is staring us in the face, and we are admonished of our duty to stand upon our reserved rights.

We declare, therefore, that we believe our mission in this Convention at an end :

1st. Because the numerical majority have usurped the prerogatives of the States in setting aside the platform made by the States, and have thus unsettled the basis of the Convention, and thereby permanently disorganized its Constitution. Its decrees, therefore, become null and void.

2d. Because we were positively instructed by the Democracy of Arkansas to insist on the recognition of the equal rights of the South in common Territories, and protection in those rights by the Federal Government prior to any nomination of a candidate, and as this Convention has refused to recognize the principle required by the State of Arkansas, in her popular Convention first, and twice subsequently re-asserted by Arkansas, together with all her Southern sisters in the report of Platform to this Convention, and as we cannot serve two masters, we are determined first to serve the Lord our God, we cannot ballot for any candidate whatever.

3d. In retiring, we deny to any person or persons any right whatever to cast hereafter, in this Convention, either our vote or the vote of Arkansas on any propositions which may or can possibly come up for consideration. The delegates of Arkansas cannot take any part in placing a sound candidate on an unsound platform, because it would disgrace any sound Southern man who would consent to stand on such a platform ; and as a Squatter Sovereignty platform has been adopted, we believe that good faith and honor requires that the Chief of Squatter Sovereignty should be placed on it; we wish no part or lot in such misfortune, nor do we believe that we can safely linger under the shade of the upas tree this day planted certainly.

P. JORDAN,
N. B. BURROWS,
VAN H. MANNING.

Mr. BENNING, of Georgia, asked leave of the Convention to withdraw for consultation, and leave was granted.

Mr. RUSSELL, of Virginia, addressed the Convention.

Mr. BAYARD, of Delaware, addressed the Convention, and stated that he and his colleagues would withdraw from the Convention.

Mr. SAULSBURY, of Delaware, also addressed the Convention.

Mr. MERRICK, of Illinois, addressed the Convention.

Mr. COCHRAN, of New York, moved that the Convention adjourn till 10 o'clock to-morrow, which motion prevailed, and the Convention adjourned.

EIGHTH DAY.

TUESDAY, MAY 1, 1860.

The Convention was called to order soon after 10 o'clock.

Prayer by Rev. Mr. INGERSOLL.

On motion, the reading of the Journal was dispensed with.

The PRESIDENT stated the regular order of business to be, the motions to reconsider, and the motions to lay the motions to reconsider on the table, by which the various resolutions constituting the platform were adopted. Pending the determination of these questions, yesterday evening, the Chairmen of several of the delegations rose to questions of privilege, under which their delegations retired from the hall. When the Convention adjourned the gentleman from Illinois (Mr, Merrick) was upon the floor.

Mr. BENNING, of Georgia, rose to a question of privilege, and stated that after retiring yesterday, the delegation from Georgia came to the conclusion to present to the Convention two resolutions, which are as follows :

Resolved, That upon the opening of the Convention this morning, our Chairman be requested to state to the President that the Georgia delegation, after a mature deliberation, have felt it to be their duty, under existing circumstances, not to participate further in the deliberations of the Convention, and that therefore the delegation withdraw.

Resolved, That all who acquiesce in the foregoing resolution sign the same, and request the Convention to enter it on their records.

(Signed) JUNIUS WINGFIELD, HENRY L. BENNING,
HENRY R. JACKSON, P. TRACY,
J. M. CLARK, JEFFERSON N. LAMAR,
WM. M. SLAUGHTER, EDMOND J. McGEHEE,
JOHN A. JONES, GEORGE HILLYER,
DAVID C. BARROW, MARK JOHNSTON,
JAS. J. DIMOND, EDWARD R. HARDEN,
A. FRANKLIN HILL, JOHN H. LUMPKIN,
EDW. L. STROECKER, G. G. FAIN,
O. C. GIBSON, JAMES HOGE,
HENRY O. THOMAS, W. J. JOHNSON.

The undersigned, delegates from Georgia, having voted in the meeting of the delegation against withdrawing from the Convention, yet believe, under the instructions contained in the resolution of the Georgia Convention, that the vote of the majority should control our action, and we therefore withdraw with the majority.

ISAIAH T. IRWIN, JULIAN HARTRIDGE,
WILLIAM H. HULL, L. H. BRISCOE.

This paper is signed by twenty-six out of the thirty-six delegates in that Convention from the State of Georgia.

I have now, Mr. President, discharged the duty which has been entrusted to me by my delegation.

The majority of the Georgia delegation then retired from the hall.

Mr. JOHNSON, of Arkansas, addressed the Convention.

Mr. TERRY, of Arkansas, then read the following paper to the Convention :

To the Hon. Caleb Cushing, President:

The undersigned, delegates from Arkansas, ask permission to make the following statement :

We have, thus far, abstained from taking any active part in the measures which were consummated on yesterday, in this Convention, by the withdrawal, in whole or in part, of several Southern States. We have counseled our Southern friends to patience and forbearance ; and, while we were conscious of causes sufficient to induce them to this step, yet we still hoped that some more auspicious event would transpire that would avert its necessity. Nothing has occurred to palliate these causes. Hence we cannot hesitate in our course, and therefore ask permission to withdraw and surrender to our State the high trust reposed in us. To you, sir, who have with so much ability presided over our deliberations, and meted out justice with an even hand, we part with sorrow. Hoping that the cloud which now hangs over our beloved country may be dispelled, and her counsels directed by some statesman like yourself—able, honest, just, and true.

FRANCIS TERRY, Vice President.
J. P. JOHNSON, Chairman of Delegation.
Charleston, May 1, 1860. F. W. HOADLEY, Secretary.

The Tennessee delegation asked and obtained leave to retire for consultation.

Mr. GLASS, of Virginia, asked leave of the Convention for the Virginia delegation to retire for consultation, and leave was granted.

A portion of the delegations from Kentucky, from North Carolina, and from Maryland, also had leave to retire for consultation.

Mr. COHEN, of Georgia, addressed the Convention.

Mr. FLOURNOY, of Arkansas, addressed the Convention.

Mr. GOULDEN, of Georgia, addressed the Convention, and stated his reasons for remaining in it.

Mr. McCOOK, of Ohio. I move the adoption of the following resolution :

Resolved, That at 2 o'clock P. M. of this day, the Convention will proceed by a call of the States to nominate a candidate for the Presidency, and immediately thereafter a candidate for the Vice Presidency.

The time given by this resolution will afford the State which asks the longest time the period they request for her deliberations, and upon the motion which I now submit I ask the previous question.

VOICES. Say 4 o'clock.

Mr. PUGH, of Ohio, suggested to his colleague that several States had had leave to retire, and it seemed to him that they ought not to ask a vote on this resolution till they returned.

Mr. VAN ARSDALE, of New Jersey, submitted a protest against the decision of the Convention yesterday that the delegation from New Jersey should not be required to give the vote of that State as a unit. The protest was as follows :

The undersigned, delegates from the State of New Jersey to the Democratic National Convention at Charleston, and representing a large majority of the Democracy of that State, in view of the decision made by the said Convention on the morning of the 30th April, 1860, denying to the majority of said delegates the right of representing their State in the manner provided by their State Convention, held on the 28th of March, 1860, in the following words, to wit :

"*Resolved*, That we recommend to the representatives of this State to the Charleston Convention to cast on all occasions that may arise in the Convention a united vote"—do hereby solemnly and earnestly protest against such decision, for the following reasons :

1st. Because it is the duty of the representatives to obey the will and carry out the wishes of their constituents.

2d. Because a rule of the National Convention, depriving all delegations whose manner of voting may have been *provided* for by their respective State Conventions from casting individual votes.

3d. Because, under the above rule, and in obedience to its requirement, the delegates of the State of Georgia, by the unquestioned ruling of the President of the Convention, were deprived of the privilege of voting according to their individual judgment.

4th. Because the consistent ruling of the President of the Convention was overruled by a majority of the votes of delegations who were themselves under the constraint of provisions made by their respective State Conventions.

Therefore, the undersigned hold that the rights of the sovereign State of New Jersey have been infringed to its great wrong and detriment, and solemnly protest against the same.

Done at Charleston this first day of May, in the year one thousand eight hundred and sixty.

J. VAN ARSDALE,
For 5th Congressional District.
WM. WRIGHT,
JOHN C. RAFFERTY,
A. R. SPEER,
JOHN HUYLER,
DAVID NAAR,
S. DOUGHTY,
SAMUEL HANNA.

Mr. COCHRAN, of New York, moved to amend the resolution of the gentleman from Ohio (Mr. McCook) by inserting four o'clock instead of "two." He said that several States were now in consultation, and he wished to give them time.

Mr. PUGH inquired if it would be in order to take the vote now upon Mr. McCook's resolution, during the absence of those delegations who had obtained leave of the Convention to retire?

The PRESIDENT stated that in his construction of the rules, the Convention having given unanimous consent to the temporary retirement of the delegations of the several States for the purpose of consultation, it had, by that very act, decided that it would not divide upon any material questions until those delegations had had notice to return.

Mr. RICHARDSON, of Illinois. Suppose the Convention should give leave to a delegation to retire, and it should not return, were the Convention then not to proceed?

The PRESIDENT said he could make no decision upon that question until it should arise. He only decided upon the question as to the several delegations who had express leave of the Convention to retire for the purpose of deliberation.

Mr. RICHARDSON was not in favor of proceeding into any important business during the absence of any of the delegations.

Mr. McCOOK withdrew the demand for the previous question.

Mr. BIDWELL read resolutions of California concerning the slavery question, and explained his vote on the minority platform, taking what was good and rejecting what was bad. The California resolutions were as follows:

1. *Resolved,* That the platform adopted by the Cincinnati Convention in 1856 is hereby affirmed.

2. *Resolved,* That to entitle a Territory to form a Constitution for admission into the Union as a sovereign State, it should contain a reasonable number of inhabitants, which should not be less than the number required for a representative in Congress.

3. *Resolved,* That the true interpretation of the Cincinnati Platform is hereby declared to be that the right to hold slaves in a Territory rests upon the same ground, and is entitled to the same protection, as other property.

4. *Resolved,* That any infraction of the rights of property in a Territory would be a judicial question, and that it is the duty of Congress to pass such laws as may be necessary to secure the faithful execution of the mandates of the Courts.

5. *Resolved,* That Congress has the power at any time to change or repeal any Territorial organic act, and to revise or annul any Territorial law conflicting therewith.

He concluded by moving the previous question on behalf of Mr. McCook.

Mr. McCook again withdrew his call for the previous question.

Messrs. Krum, of Missouri, Seward, of Georgia, Holden, of North Carolina, Richardson, of Illinois, Perry, of South Carolina, Howard, of Tennessee, and Caldwell, of Kentucky, addressed the Convention.

Mr. McCook renewed his demand for the previous question.

Mr. Caldwell, of Kentucky, moved that the Convention do now adjourn, and a vote by States was demanded, and resulted as follows :

	Yeas.	Nays.		Yeas.	Nays.		Yeas.	Nays.
Maine	2	6	North Carolina	8½	1½	Ohio		23
New Hampshire		5	South Carolina	1		Indiana		13
Vermont		5	Georgia			Illinois		11
Massachusetts	8	5	Florida			Michigan		6
Rhode Island		4	Alabama			Wisconsin		5
Connecticut	2	4	Louisiana			Iowa		4
New York		35	Mississippi			Minnesota	1½	2½
New Jersey	5	2	Texas			California	3	1
Pennsylvania	12	13	Arkansas		1	Oregon	3	
Delaware	2		Missouri	4½	4½			
Maryland	4	4	Tennessee	9	3		92	159
Virginia	15		Kentucky	11½	½			

The States of Florida, Alabama, Louisiana, Mississippi, and Texas, declined voting.

And the motion to adjourn was lost.

When the State of Georgia offered to vote on the last question,

Mr. Horn, of Wisconsin, objected to the vote of Georgia being cast by the portion present, the State having withdrawn.

Mr. Cohen, of Georgia, explained that Georgia was represented here by ten delegates who refused to withdraw. The delegates were requested by their State to cast their votes *in Convention* as a unit. The act of withdrawal had been done by the majority *out* of the Convention, not *in* it. He claimed the right of the remaining delegates to cast the vote of the State.

The President decided, that as the State had ordered the majority of the delegates to vote, and as that majority had officially represented to the Convention that they had concluded to withdraw, the minority had no right to represent the State.

Mr. Holden, of Georgia, appealed from the decision of the Chair. He said : Whom the Gods would destroy they first make mad. The decision of the Chair is most suicidal and destructive. It destroyed the rights of the State. He came here to represent the Democracy of his District. He held that the bolters and seceders did not represent she Democracy of the State; that they did not follow their duty to their State. They came here with instructions to vote, not to bolt. Those who remain, remain to vote—remain with, and act with the Democratic Convention, and they called upon its members to sustain them.

Mr. King, of Missouri, took the floor.

The President. The Chair begs to remind the gentleman that the question is not debateable, and that the Chair only allowed discussion on the part of the gentleman from Georgia as an act of courtesy.

Mr. King. If I am not in order I do not desire to occupy the floor.

Mr Samuels. I desire to know whether the decision of Chair is that the majority of the delegation from Georgia having withdrawn, therefore, the remaining delegates have no right to represent the State.

The President. And for the further reason that the delegation have reported to the Convention that a majority have given notice that the delegates have decided to withdraw.

After further debate, the decision of the Chair was sustained by 148 ayes to 100 nays.

Mr. Seward, of Georgia, protested against the act of injustice to the State, and withdrew from the Convention.

The previous question on the motion of Mr. Howard was then seconded.

The CHAIR declared the former motion for adjournment lost.

Mr. OWEN, of Maine, moved to adjourn till 5 o'clock, and Mr. Randall till the usual hour to-morrow.

Mr. COCHRAN discussed the point of order, as to which motion had precedence.

The Convention adjourned to meet at five o'clock P. M.

AFTERNOON SESSION.

The PRESIDENT asked to lay before the Convention a written communication which had been handed to him.

It was a communication from the Delegation of the State of Louisiana, and is as follows:

CHARLESTON, April 30, 1860.

To the Hon. Caleb Cushnig, President of the Democratic Convention:

SIR: The undersigned, delegates from the State of Louisiana, in withdrawing from the Convention, beg leave to make the following statement of facts:

On the 5th day of March, 1860, the Democracy of Louisiana assembled in State Convention at Baton Rouge, and unanimously adopted the following declaration of their principles:

Resolved, That the Territories of the United States belong to the several States as their common property, and not to individual citizens thereof; that the Federal Constitution recognizes property in slaves; and as such, the owner thereof is entitled to carry his slaves into any Territory in the United States; to hold them there as property; and in case the people of the Territories, by inaction, unfriendly legislation or otherwise, should endanger the tenure of such property, or discriminate against it by withholding that protection given to other species of property in the Territories, it is the duty of the General Government to interpose, by the active exertion of its constitutional power, to secure the rights of the slaveholder.

The principles enunciated in the foregoing resolution are guaranteed to us by the Constitution of the United States, and their unequivocal recognition by the Democracy of the Union we regard as essential, not only to the integrity of the party, but to the safety of the States whose interests are directly involved. They have been embodied in both of the series of resolutions presented to the Convention by a majority of the States of the Union, and have been rejected by a numerical vote of the delegates.

The Convention has, by this vote, refused to recognize the fundamental principles of the Democracy of the State we have the honor to represent, and we feel constrained, in obedience to a high sense of duty, to withdraw from its deliberations, and unanimously to enter our solemn protest against its action.

We ask that the communication may be spread upon the minutes of the Convention, and beg leave to express our appreciation of the justice and dignity which have characterized your action as its presiding officer.

(Signed)	A. MOUTON,	JOHN TARLTON,
	RICHARD TAYLOR,	EMILE LASERE,
	F. H. HATCH,	E. LAWRENCE,
	A. TALBOT,	B. W. PEARCE,
	R. A. HUNTER,	D. D. WITHERS.

The undersigned, in explanation of their position, beg leave to annex the following statement, viz:

Whilst we took the same view with our colleagues, that the platform of principles, as adopted by this Convention, was not what was expected by Louisiana, and desired by ourselves, as sufficient to guard the rights of that State, and of the whole South, under the Constitution, are now unwilling precipitately to retire from the Convention, until all hope of accommodation shall have been exhausted, and until the last moment had arrived, at which, in justice to our own honor, and the interest and dignity of our State, we would be forced to retire. *We, therefore, were opposed to the retirement of the delegation at the time it was made;* but believing that the other members of the delegation were actuated by the same high motives which governed our own opinions, and desiring our State to present a firm, undivided front, we being in the minority of the delegation, were willing to yield, and did yield, our opinions to the judgment of the majority.

J. A. McHATTON,
CHARLES JONES.

CHARLESTON, S. C., May 1, 1860.

Mr. HOWARD, of Tennessee, asked to state a question of privilege, and offered a resolution, which is as follows, viz:

Resolved, That the President of the Convention be and is hereby directed not to declare any person nominated for the office of President or Vice President unless he shall have received a number of votes equal to two-thirds of the votes of all the Electoral Colleges.

Mr. McCOOK, of Ohio, called up his resolution, the previous question having been seconded, that the main question should now be put.

The PRESIDENT stated that it was his duty now to call on the House to determine whether the main question must now be put.

Mr. HOWARD raised a point of order, viz: that the time fixed in Mr. McCook's resolution had passed.

The PRESIDENT. The time named in the resolution cannot affect its passage, and if adopted the effect would be to take the House to a vote instanter.

Mr. RUSSELL, of Virginia, called for a vote by States.

And the question was then put,—"Shall the main question now be put?" and the vote on such question was as follows, viz:

	Yeas.	Nays
Maine	5	3
New Hampshire	5	
Vermont	5	
Massachusetts	6	7
Rhode Island		4
Connecticut	3½	2
New York	35	
New Jersey	7	
Pennsylvania	10½	16½
Delaware		2
Maryland	3	5
Virginia		15
North Carolina		10
South Carolina		
Georgia		
Florida		
Alabama		
Louisiana		
Mississippi		
Texas		
Arkansas	1	
Missouri	4½	4½
Tennessee	1	11
Kentucky		12
Ohio	23	
Indiana	13	
Illinois	11	
Michigan	6	
Wisconsin	5	
Iowa	4	
Minnesota	2½	1½
California		4
Oregon		3
	149	102

So the question was decided in the affirmative.

The main question was then put, and Mr. McCook's resolution was adopted.

Mr. STUART moved to reconsider the vote by which the resolution was agreed to, and to lay the motion on the table.

The PRESIDENT. The motion would be entered.

Mr. HOWARD called up his resolution, and the Chair decided it to be in order.

Mr. RICHARDSON, of Illinois, moved to lay the resolution of Mr. Howard on the table; and upon this motion,

Mr. RUSSELL, of Virginia, called for a vote by States.

The vote on Mr. Richardson's resolution to lay on the table was as follows:

	Yeas	Nays
Maine	5	3
New Hampshire	5	
Vermont	5	
Massachusetts	4½	8¼
Rhode Island	4	
Connecticut	3½	2½
New York		35
New Jersey	1½	5½
Pennsylvania	10	16½
Delaware		2
Maryland	2	6
Virginia		15
North Carolina		10
South Carolina		
Georgia		
Florida		
Alabama		
Louisiana		
Mississippi		
Texas		
Arkansas		1
Missouri	4½	4½
Tennessee	1	11
Kentucky		12
Ohio	23	
Indiana	13	
Illinois	11	
Michigan	6	
Wisconsin	5	
Iowa	4	
Minnesota	2½	1½
California		4
Oregon		3
	111½	141

So the motion to lay on the table was lost.

Mr. STUART, of Michigan, contended that the resolution was not in order. The effect of it was to change the rules of this Convention, and it must therefore lie over for one day. He would read the rule of the Convention upon this subject:

"*Resolved*, That two-thirds of the whole number of votes given shall be necessary to a nomination of a candidate for President and Vice President by this Convention." There was the rule, that two-thirds of the votes given shall be necessary.

Was there a gentleman here prepared to admit the doctrine that at any future Convention a minority of the voters, by merely refusing to vote, could break up their deliberations? The mere statement of the question itself was its own best answer. The language of the rule was—"two-thirds of the votes given." Given for what? Why, given for a candidate for President of the United States.

Mr. STUART would not detain the Convention further with the discussion of this question of order. He asked whether gentlemen were prepared to set a new precedent, which would in future times enable one-third of the gentlemen attending a National Convention to break it up by refusing to vote?

Mr. PHILLIPS, of Pennsylvania, submitted the question of order, that the gentleman from Michigan (Mr. Stuart) was too late in making his point. The resolution of the gentleman from Tennesee had been introduced by unanimous consent, and was in the full possession of the Convention. He would submit that, according to all parliamentary rules, the gentleman from Michigan was too late in making his point of order.

The PRESIDENT. The gentleman from Michigan has raised the point of order, that the motion of the gentleman from Tennessee will constitute a change of the rule of the Convention, as adopted at its present session, in accordance with the rule of the Convention of 1852. The gentleman from Pennsylvania (Mr. Phillips) objects that it is too late to make this question of order. As the Chair entertains a different opinion upon the question, he desires to state that opinion. The resolution of the Convention of 1852 is in substance, as the gentleman from Michigan has stated it, that two-thirds of the whole number of votes given shall be necessary to a nomination of candidates for President and Vice President. Now, it is true that, in a rigorous construction of this order, it applies to a nomination of candidates for President and Vice President by this Convention.

Thus far the Chair concurs with the gentleman from Michigan. The Chair is not prepared to determine what is the force of the words "votes given." A *prima facia* impression of the words might be "votes cast" in a ballot in the Convention, but the rule does not say so. It uses the absolute independent phrase "votes given." The gentleman from Michigan objects to that construction on the ground of alleged inconvenience, that of having the nomination of a Convention prevented by the secession of one-third of the States in that Convention. The Chair can see that the argument of inconvenience is sufficiently strong, if not stronger upon the other side. A Convention of this sort has no legal authority. Its sole authority is its moral authority, as the representative of the opinion of the party whose members constitute its party. It seems to the Chair that the inconvenience of assuming that the nomination by a fractional party of the Convention, although it may be that of two-thirds, constitutes a binding nomination upon the people of the United States, is a vastly greater inconvenience than that which would arise from the fact that a secession of one-third of the members would prevent a nomination. A nomination to be made by the Convention is a constitutional necessity. It is a formal recommendation to the constituents of the Convention. That recommendation, in order that it should have moral authority with the persons to whom it is addressed, should be the act of all the States of the Union. (Applause.) The Chair, therefore, is not prepared to adopt the construction of the gentleman from Michigan of the rule of 1852; and, therefore, the Chair is of the opinion that the resolution of the gentleman from Tennessee (Mr. Howard) does not constitute such a modification of the standing rules of the Convention as shall require it to lie over for one day.

Mr. STUART. I trust it is not necessary for me to say that, in taking an appeal from the decision of the Chair, it is in consequence of no want of respect for the occupant of the Chair. I contend that the construction given by the Chair to the words "votes given," as relating to the place where given, can never receive the sanction of logic. Can this Convention give a vote anywhere else than here?

"*Resolved*, That two thirds of the votes given here"——is not that supererogation? All votes are given here, and they can be given nowhere else. The rule, therefore, is plain and palpable. Two-thirds of the votes given on a question. I beg gentlemen to remember that the nomination of a candidate for President and Vice President is the only question we can make before this body; that, in its business, requires a two-third vote. Now, I say with the utmost respect for the presiding officer, that the construction of these words to the place where given cannot bear the test of investigation, for we can give a vote nowhere else unless we adjourn somewhere else. It is of the utmost importance that this Convention should decide rightly. Let us meet every question upon the broad principles of right—do not let us compromit our honor in doing a thing we do not believe to be right.

The PRESIDENT. The question now is, "Shall the decision of the Chair stand as the judgment of the Convention?"

Michigan demanded a vote by States.

The question was then taken with the following result:

	Yeas.	Nays.		Yeas.	Nays.		Yeas.	Nays.
Maine	3	5	North Carolina	10		Ohio		23
New Hampshire	1	4	South Carolina	1		Indiana		13
Vermont		5	Georgia			Illinois		11
Massachusetts	5½	3½	Florida			Michigan		6
Rhode Island		4	Alabama			Wisconsin		5
Connecticut	2½	3	Louisiana			Iowa		4
New York	35		Mississippi			Minnesota	1	2½
New Jersey	5½	1½	Texas			California	4	
Pennsylvania	17½	9½	Arkansas			Oregon	3	
Delaware	2		Missouri	4½	4½			
Maryland	6	2	Tennessee	11	1		144	108
Virginia	15		Kentucky	11½	½			

So the decision of the Chair was sustained.

Mr. STUART, of Michigan, offered the following amendment to the resolution:

"And that every delegate voting for a candidate will be bound to abide by the result of the nomination."

Mr. HOWARD, of Tennessee, simply desired to know who had invested the gentleman from Michigan with the power to bind the consciences of those who were his peers.

Mr. BUTLER, of Massachusetts, inquired if the amendment was germane to the principal question.

Mr. RUSSELL, of Virginia, desired to say that as long as the delegation from Virginia continued in this Convention and participated in its proceedings, she expected to be bound by every nomination, by every act that was done.

Mr. STUART said that the suggestion he wished to make was this: that the resolution of the gentleman from Tennessee, instructing the Chair not to declare any man nominated unless he had received two-thirds of the votes which constituted this body. What he proposed to add was that the result, when declared, should be binding upon every gentleman who participated in the proceedings of the body.

The PRESIDENT decided the amendment of the gentleman from Michigan not to be in order.

The previous question upon the adoption of the resolution was moved, seconded, and the main question ordered.

Ohio demanded a vote by States.

The question was then taken upon Mr. Howard's resolution with the following result :

	Yeas.	Nays.		Yeas.	Nays.		Yeas.	Nays.
Maine	3	5	North Carolina	10	0	Ohio	0	23
New Hampshire	0	5	South Carolina	1	0	Indiana	0	13
Vermont	0	5	Georgia	0	0	Illinois	0	11
Massachusetts	8½	4½	Florida	0	0	Michigan	0	6
Rhode Island	0	4	Alabama	0	0	Wisconsin	0	5
Connecticut	2½	3½	Louisiana	0	0	Iowa	0	4
New York	35	0	Mississippi	0	0	Minnesota	1½	2½
New Jersey	5½	1½	Texas	0	0	California	4	0
Pennsylvania	17½	9½	Arkansas	0	1	Oregon	3	0
Delaware	2	0	Missouri	2½	2½			
Maryland	6	2	Tennessee	11	1		141	112
Virginia	15	0	Kentucky	11	1			

And the resolution of Mr. HOWARD was declared to be adopted.

Mr. BIGLER, of Pennsylvania, moved to reconsider the vote just taken, and to lay that motion on the table, and Mr. Bigler's motion was adopted.

Mr. McCOOK, of Ohio, now demanded that the Convention now proceed to vote by States for President of the United States.

Mr. KING, of Missouri. Do I understand that nominations are now in order ?

The PRESIDENT. The Chair understands it now to be in order to call on the several States to vote.

Mr KING. I put in nomination, before this Convention, as a candidate for the office of President of the United States, STEPHEN A. DOUGLAS. (Applause.)

Mr. CALDWELL, of Kentucky. I am instructed by the delegation from Kentucky unanimously to nominate for the office of President, Kentucky's favorite son and incorruptible statesman, JAMES GUTHRIE. (Applause.)

Mr. BIDWELL, of California. I desire to put in nomination DANIEL S. DICKINSON, of New York, "the noblest Roman of them all." (Applause.)

Mr. RUSSELL, of Virginia. By the unanimous direction of the delegation from Virginia, I offer to this Convention the name of ROBERT M. T. HUNTER, of that State. (Applause.)

Mr. EWING, of Tennessee. I put in nomination the name of the Hon. ANDREW JOHNSON, of Tennessee. (Applause.)

Mr. STOUT, of Oregon. I desire to place in nomination General JOSEPH LANE, of Oregon. (Applause.)

The Convention then proceeded in the execution of its order to vote by States for a candidate for the Presidency.

FIRST VOTE FOR PRESIDENT.

Maine—Douglas 5, Guthrie 3.
New Hampshire—Douglas 5.
Vermont—Douglas 5.
Massachusetts—Douglas 5½, Hunter 6, Davis 1½.
Rhode Island—Douglas 4.
Connecticut—Douglas 3½, Toucey 2½.
New York—Douglas 35.
New Jersey—Guthrie 7.
Pennsylvania—Douglas 9, Guthrie 9, Dickinson 2, Hunter 3, Lane 3, Pearce 1.
Delawara—Hunter 2.
Maryland—Douglas 2, Dickinson 1, Hunter 5.
Virginia—Hunter 15.
North Carolina—Douglas 1, Hunter 9.
South Carolina—Hunter 1.
Arkansas—Hunter 1.
Missouri—Douglas 4½, Guthrie 4½.
Tennessee—Johnson 12,
Kentucky—Guthrie 12.
Ohio—Douglas 23.
Indiana—Douglas 13.
Illinois—Douglas 11.
Michigan—Douglas 6.
Wisconsin—Douglas 5.
Iowa—Douglas 4.
Minnesota—Douglas 4.
California—Dickinson 4.
Oregon—Lane 3.

Whole number of electoral votes, 303—Necessary to a choice, under the decision of the Chair, 202. Douglas 145½, Guthrie 35, Dickinson 7, Hunter 42, Johnson 12, Lane 6, Davis 1½, Toucey 2½, Pearce 1.

The Chair decided there was no choice, and the Convention proceeded to a

SECOND VOTE FOR PRESIDENT.

Maine—Douglas 5, Guthrie 3.
New Hampshire—Douglas 5.
Vermont—Douglas 5.
Massachusetts—Douglas 6½, Hunter 5½.
Rhode Island—Douglas 4.
Connecticut—Douglas 3½, Toucey 2½.
New York—Douglas 35.
Pennsylvania—Douglas 9½, Guthrie 10, Hunter 3, Dickinson 1½, Lane 3.
Delaware—Hunter 2.
Maryland—Douglas 2 Hunter 5, Dickinson 1.
Virginia—Hunter 15.
North Carolina—Douglas 1, Hunter 9.
South Carolina—Hunter 1.
Arkansas—Hunter 1
Missouri—Douglas 4½, Guthrie 4½.
Tennessee—Johnson 12.
Kentucky—Guthrie 12.
Ohio—Douglas 23.
Indiana—Douglas 13.
Illinois—Douglas 11.
Michigan—Douglas 6.
Wisconsin—Douglas 5.
Iowa—Douglas 4.
Minnesota—Douglas 4.
California—Dickinson 4.
Oregon—Lane 3.

Whole number of votes, 303—Necessary to a choice under the ruling of the Chair, 202. Douglas 147, Guthrie 36½, Hunter 41½, Davis 1. Toucey 2½, Dickinson 6½, Johnson 12, Lane 6.

The Chair decided that no choice had been made, and the Convention proceeded to a

THIRD VOTE FOR PRESIDENT.

Maine—Douglas 5, Guthrie 3.
New Hampshire—Douglas 5.
Vermont—Douglas 5.
Massachusetts—Douglas 6½, Hunter 5½. Davis 1.
Rhode Island—Douglas 4.
Connecticut—Douglas 3½, Guthrie 2½.
New York—Douglas 35.
New Jersey—Douglas 1 1-2, Guthrie 5 1-2.
Pennsylvania—Douglas 9 1-2, Guthrie 9 1-2, Dickinson 1 1-2, Hunter 3 1-2, Lane 3.
Delaware—Hunter 2.
Maryland—Guthrie 2, Dickinson 1, Hunter 5.
Virginia—Hunter 15.
North Carolina—Guthrie 1, Hunter 9
Arkansas—Dickinson 1.
Missouri—Douglas 4 1-2, Guthrie 4 1-2.
Tennesee—Johnson 12.
Kentucky—Guthrie 12.
Ohio—Douglas 23.
Indiana—Douglas 13.
Illinois—Douglas 11.
Michigan—Douglas 6.
Wisconsin—Douglas 5.
Iowa—Douglas 4.
Minnesota—Douglas 4.
California—Dickinson 4.
Oregon—Lane 3.

Whole number of electoral votes, 303—Necessary to a choice, under the ruling of the Chair 202 Douglas 148 1-2, Guthrie 42. Dickinson 6 1-2, Hunter 36, Johnson 12, Lane 6, Davis 1.

Under such ruling there being no choice, the Convention proceeded to a

FOURTH VOTE FOR PRESIDENT.

Maine—Douglas 5, Guthrie 3,
New Hampshire—Douglas 5.
Vermont—Douglas 5
Massachusetts—Douglas 7, Hunter 5. Davis 1.
Rhode Island—Douglas 4.
Connecticut—Douglas 3 1-2, Guthrie 2 1-2.
New York—Douglas 35.
New Jersey—Douglas 1 1-2; Guthrie 5 1-2.
Pennsylvania—Douglas 9 1-2; Guthrie 9 1-2, Hunter 4 1-2, Lane 3, Dickinson 1-2.
Delaware—Hunter 2.
Maryland—Douglas 2, Guthrie 1-2, Hunter 5, Dickinson 1-2.
Virginia—Hunter 15.
North Carolina—Douglas 1, Hunter 9.
Arkansas—Hunter 1.
Missouri—Douglas 4 1-2, Guthrie 4 1-2.
Tennessee—Johnson 12.
Kentucky—Guthrie 12.
Ohio—Douglas 23.
Indiana—Douglas 13.
Illinois—Douglas 11.
Michigan—Douglas 6.
Wisconsin—Douglas 5.
Iowa—Douglas 4.
Minnesota—Douglas 4.
California—Dickinson 4.
Oregon—Lane 3.

Whole number of votes cast, 252—Necessary to a choice, under the ruling of the Chair 202. Douglas 149, Guthrie 37 1-2, Hunter 41 1-2, Davis 1, Lane 6, Dickinson 5, Johnson 12.

There being no eliction, the Convention proceeded to a

FIFTH VOTE FOR PRESIDENT.

Maine—Douglas 5, Guthrie 3.
New Hampshire—Douglas 5.
Vermont—Douglas 5.
Massachusetts—Douglas 7, Hunter 5, Davis 1.
Rhode Island—Douglas 4.
Connecticut—Douglas 3 1-2 Guthrie 2 1-2.
New York—Douglas 35.
New Jersey—Douglas 1 1-2, Guthrie 5 1-2.
Pennsylvania—Douglas 9 1-2, Guthrie 9 1-2, Dickinson 1, Hunter 4, Lane 3.
Delaware—Hunter 2.
Maryland—Douglas 2 1-2, Guthrie 1-2, Hunter 5.
Virginia—Hunter 15
North Carolina—Guthrie 1, Hunter 9.
Arkansas—Hunter 1.
Missouri—Douglas, 4 1-2, Guthrie 4 1-2.
Tennessee—Johnson 12.
Kentucky—Guthrie 12.
Ohio—Douglas 23.
Indiana—Douglas 13.
Illinois—Douglas 11.
Michigan—Douglas 6.
Wisconsin—Douglas 5.
Iowa—Douglas 4.
Minnesota—Douglas 4.
California—Dickinson 4.
Oregon—Lane 3.

Whole number of votes cast, 252—Necessary to a choice under the ruling of the Chair 202. Douglas 149 1-2, Guthrie 37 1-2, Dickinson 5, Hunter 41, Johnson 12, Lane 6, Davis 1.

There being no election, the Convention proceeded to a

SIXTH VOTE FOR PRESIDENT.

Maine—Douglas 5, Guthrie 3.
New Hampshire—Douglas 5.
Vermont—Douglas 5.
Massachusetts—Douglas 7, Hunter 5, Lane 1.
Rhode Island—Douglas 4.
Connecticut—Douglas 3 1-2, Guthrie 2 1-2.
New York—Douglas 35.
New Jersey—Douglas 1 1-2, Guthrie 5 1 2.
Pennsylvania—Douglas 9 1-2, Guthrie 9 1 2, Dickinson 1, Hunter 4, Lane 3.
Delaware—Hunter 2.
Maryland—Douglas 2 1 2, Guthrie 1-2, Hunter 5.
Virginia—Hunter 15.
North Carolina—Douglas 1. Hunter 9.
Arkansas—Hunter 1.
Missouri - Douglas 4 1-2, Guthrie 4 1-2,
Tennessee—Johnson 12.

Kentucky—Guthrie 12.
Ohio—Douglas 23.
Indiana—Douglas 13.
Illinois—Douglas 11.
Michigan—Douglas 6.
Wisconsin--Douglas 5.
Iowa—Douglas 4.
Minnesota—Douglas 4.
California—Guthrie 2, Dickinson 2.
Oregon--Lane 3.

Whole number of votes cast 252—Necessary to a choice, under the ruling of the Chair, 202. Douglas 149 1-2 Guthrie 39 1-2, Dickinson 3, Hunter 41, Johnson 12, Lane 7.

There being no election, the Convention proceeded to a

SEVENTH VOTE FOR PRESIDENT.

Maine—Douglas 5. Guthrie 3.
New Hampshire—Douglas 5.
Vermont—Douglas 5.
Massachusetts—Douglas 7, Hunter 5, Davis 1.
Rhode Island—Douglas 4.
Connecticut--Douglas 3 1-2, Guthrie 2 1-2.
New York—Douglas 35.
New Jersey--Douglas 1 1-2, Guthrie 5 1-2.
Pennsylvania---Douglas 9 1-2, Guthrie 10 1-, Hunter 4. Lane 3.
Delaware---Hunter 2.
Maryland---Douglas 2 1-2, Guthrie 1-2, Hunter 5.
Virginia--Hunter 15.
North Carolina---Douglas 1, Hunter 9.
Arkansas---Hunter 1.
Missouri—Douglas 4 1-2, Guthrie 4 1-2.
Tennessee--Douglas 1, Johnson 11.
Kentucky---Guthrie 12.
Ohio---Douglas 23.
Indiana---Douglas 13.
Illinois--Douglas 11.
Michigan---Douglas 6.
Wisconsin---Douglas 5.
Iowa---Douglas 4.
Minnesota---Douglas 4.
California---Dickinson 4.
Oregon---Lane 3.

Whole number of votes 252. Douglas 150 1-2, Guthrie 38 1 2, Dickinson 4, Hunter 41, Johnson 11, Lane 6, Davis 1.

And under the ruling of the Chair, there being no choice, the Convention proceeded to an

EIGHTH VOTE FOR PRESIDENT.

Maine......Douglas 5, Guthrie 3.
New Hampshire..... Douglas 5.
Vermont......Douglas 5.
Massachusetts......Douglas 7 1-2, Hunter 4 1-2, Davis 1.
Rhode Island......Douglas 4.
Connecticut......Douglas 3 1-2, Guthrie 2 1-2.
New York......Douglas 35.
New Jersey......Douglas 1 1-2. Guthrie 5 1-2.
Pennsylvania..... Douglas 9 1-2, Guthrie 10 1-2, Hunter 4, Lane 3
Delaware......Hunter 2.
Maryland......Douglas 2, Guthrie 1-2, Dickinson 1-2, Hunter 5
Virginia......Hunter 15.
North Carolina......Douglas 1, Hunter 9.
Arkansas......Hunter 1.
Missouri......Douglas 4 1-2, Guthrie 4 1-2.
Tennessee......Douglas 1. Johnson 11.
Kentucky......Guthrie 12.
Ohio......Douglas 23.
Indiana......Douglas 13.
Illinois..... Douglas 11.
Michigan......Douglas 6
Wisconsin......Douglas 5.
Iowa......Douglas 4
Minnesota......Douglas 4
California......Dickinson 4.
Oregon......Lane 3.

Whole number of votes 252. Douglas 150 1-2, Guthrie 38 1-2, Dickinson 4 1-2, Hunter 40 1-2, Johnson 11, Lane 6, Davis 1.

Before the annoncement of the result of the eighth vote,

Mr. STEVENS, of Massachusetts, arose and stated that one of the delegates from Massachusetts having been ill, had substituted his alternate to cast his vote, and had instructed him to vote for STEPHEN A. DOUGLAS. That he had violated his instructions, and that the principal had been brought into the Convention and desired to cast his own vote, and wanted the vote of Massachusetts changed one-half vote.

The PRESIDENT decided that the principal had the right at any time before the vote was announced, to control his vote, and the vote of Massachusetts would be changed according to the wishes of the gentleman, and was so changed before the announcement of the vote.

Under the ruling of the Chair, there being no choice, the Convention proceeded to a

NINTH VOTE FOR PRESIDENT.

Maine......Douglas 5, Guthrie 3.
New Hampshire......Douglas 5.
Vermont......Douglas 5.
Massachustts......Douglas 7, Hunter 4, Davis 1 1-2
Rhode Island......Douglas 4
Connecticut......Douglas 3 1-2, Guthrie 2 1-2.
New York......Douglas 35.
New Jersey......Douglas 1 1-2, Guthrie 5 1 2.
Pennsylvania......Douglas 9 1-2, Guthrie 10 1-2, Hunter 4, Lane 3.
Delaware......Hunter 2.
Maryland......Douglas 2 1 2, Guthrie 1-2, Hunter 4
Virginia......Hunter 15.
North Carolina......Douglas 1, Hunter 9.
Arkansas......Hunter 1.
Missouri......Douglas 4 1-2, Guthrie 4 1-2.
Tennessee..... Douglas 1, Johnson 11.
Kentucky......Guthrie 12.
Ohio......Douglas 23
Indiana......Douglas 13.
Illinois......Douglas 11.
Michigan......Douglas 6.
Wisconsin......Douglas 5.
Iowa......Douglas 4.
Minnesota......Douglas 3, Johnson 1.
California......Guthrie 3, Dickinson 1.
Oregon......Lane 3.

Whole number of votes 252. Douglas 150 1-2, Guthrie 41, Dickinson 1, Hunter 39 1-2, Johnson 12, Lane 6, Davis 1.

Before the 9th vote was announced,

Mr. EDGERTON, of Minnesota, arose and desired to make a change of one vote from Minnesota, taking it from Mr. Douglas and giving it to Mr. Johnson.

Mr. GORMAN objected, stating that a resolution had been adopted in their delegation directing him, as chairman, to cast the whole vote of Minnesota for STEPHEN A. DOUGLAS, so long as he should consider it of advantage to Mr. Douglas.

Mr. SAMUELS, of Iowa, arose to a point of order: that the State Convention of Minnesota had passed resolutions, which, according to the decision of the President of this Convention, would be considered instructions, and that the delegation was bound to vote according to those instructions.

The PRESIDENT decided that the delegates of Minnesota had the right to cast their votes as their consciences should dictate to them, and that the resolution of the Minnesota State Convention did not go so far as to amount to instructions, and that the vote of Minnesota could be changed, and was accordingly changed before the 9th vote was announced, Mr. Edgerton and Mr. Fridley voting for Mr. Johnson.

Under the decision of the Chair, there being no choice, the Convention proceeded to a

TENTH VOTE FOR PRESIDENT

Maine—Douglas 5, Guthrie 3.
New Hampshire—Douglas 5.
Vermont—Douglas 5.
Massachusetts—Douglas 7, Hunter 4 1-2, Davis 1½.
Rhode Island—Douglas 4.
Connecticut—Douglas 3 1-2, Guthrie 2 1-2.
New York—Douglas 35.
New Jersey—Douglas 1 1-2, Guthrie 5 1-2.
Pennsylvania—Douglas 9 1-2, Guthrie 11 1-2, Hunter 3 1-2, Lane 2 1-2.
Delaware—Hunter 2.
Maryland—Douglas 3 1-2, Guthrie 1-2, Hunter 4.
Virginia—Hunter 15
North Carolina—Douglas 1, Hunter 9.
Arkansas—Hunter 1.
Missouri—Douglas 4 1-2, Guthrie 4 1-2.
Tennessee—Douglas 1, Johnson 11.
Kentucky—Guthrie 12.
Ohio—Douglas 23.
Indiana—Douglas 13.
Illinois—Douglas 11.
Michigan—Douglas 6.
Wisconsin—Douglas 5.
Iowa—Douglas 4.
Minnesota -Douglas 3, Johnson 1
California—Dickinson 4.
Oregon—Lane 3.

Whole number of votes, 252—Douglas 150 1-2 Guthrie 39 1-2, Dickinson 4, Hunter 39, Johnson 12, Lane 5 1-2, Davis 1 1-2.

Under the ruling of the Chair there being no choice, the Convention proceeded to a

ELEVENTH VOTE FOR PRESIDENT.

Maine—Douglas 5, Guthrie 3.
New Hampshire—Douglas 5.
Vermont—Douglas 5.
Massachusetts—Douglas 7, Hunter 4 1-2, Davis 1 1-2.
Rhode Island—Douglas 4.
Connecticut—Douglas 3 1-2, Guthrie 2 1-2.
New York—Douglas 35.
New Jersey—Douglas 1 1-2, Guthrie 5 1-2.
Pennsylvania—Douglas 9 1-2, Guthrie 11 1-2, Hunter 3 1-2. Lane 2 1-2.
Delaware—Hunter 2.
Maryland—Douglas 3 1-2, Guthrie 1-2, Hunter 4.
Virginia—Hunter 15.
North Carolina—Douglas 1, Hunter 9.
Arkansas—Lane 1.
Missouri—Douglas 4 1-2, Guthrie 4 1-2.
Tennessee—Douglas 1, Johnson 11.
Kentucky—Guthrie 12.
Ohio—Douglas 23.
Indiana—Douglas 13.
Illinois—Douglas 11.
Michigan—Douglas 6.
Wisconsin—Douglas 5.
Iowa—Douglas 4.
Minnesota—Douglas 8, Johnson 1.
California—Dickinson 4.
Oregon—Lane 8.

Whole number of votes, 252—Douglas 150 1-2, Guthrie 39 1-2, Dickinson 4, Hunter 38, Johnson, 12, Lane 6 1-2, Davis 1 1-2.

After the announcement of the Eleventh Vote, a motion was made to adjourn, and was put and lost.

There being no choice, the Convention proceeded to a

TWELFTH VOTE FOR PRESIDENT.

Maine—Douglas 5, Guthrie 3.
New Hampshire—Douglas 5.
Vermont—Douglas 5.
Massachusetts—Douglas 7, Hunter 4 1-2, Davis 1 1-2.
Rhode Island—Douglas 4.
Connecticut—Douglas 3 1-2, Guthrie 2 1-2.
New York—Douglas 35.
New Jersey—Douglas 1 1-2, Guthrie 5 1-2.
Pennsylvania—Douglas 9 1-2, Guthrie 11 1-2, Hunter 3 1-2, Lane 2 1-2
Delaware—Hunter 2.
Maryland—Douglas 3 1-2, Guthrie 1-2, Hunter, 4.
Virginia—Hunter 15.
North Carolina—Douglas 1, Hunter 9.
Arkansas—Lane 1.
Missouri—Douglas 4 1-2, Guthrie 4 1-2.
Tennessee—Douglas 1, Johnson 11.
Kentucky—Guthrie 12.
Ohio—Douglas 23.
Indiana—Douglas 13.
Illinois—Douglas 11.
Michigan—Douglas 6.
Wisconsin—Douglas 5.
Iowa—Douglas 4.
Minnesota—Douglas 3, Johnson 1.
California—Dickinson 4.
Oregon—Lane 3.

Total number of votes, 252. Douglas, 150 1 2 Guthrie 39 1-2, Dickinson 4, Hunter 38, Johnson 12, Lane 6 1-2, Davis 1 1-2.

The Chair decided that there had been no choice made, and on motion of Mr. Richardson, of Illinois, the Convention adjourned until ten o'clock to-morrow morning.

NINTH DAY.

WEDNESDAY, MAY 2, 1860.

The Convention, after having been entertained by Gilmore's Brass Band, of Boston, was called to order by the PRESIDENT at half-past 10 A. M.

The proceedings were opened with prayer by the Rev. Mr. KENDRICK.

On motion of Mr. ATKINS, of Tennessee, the reading of the Journal of yesterday was dispensed with.

The Convention then resumed the execution of its order to vote for a candidate for the office of President.

THIRTEENTH VOTE FOR PRESIDENT.

Maine--Douglas 5, Guthrie 3.
New Hampshire---Douglas 5.
Vermont---Douglas 5.
Massachusetts---Douglas 7, Hunter 4 1-2, Davis, 1 1-2.
Rhode Island---Douglas 4
Connecticut---Douglas 3 1-2, Guthrie 2 1-2.
New York---Douglas 35.
New Jersey---Douglas 1 1-2, Guthrie 5, Lane 1-2.
Pennsylvania---Douglas 9 1-2, Guthrie 12, Hunter 3, Lane 2 1-2.
Delaware --Hunter 2.
Maryland---Douglas 3 1-2, Guthrie 1-2, Hunter 4.
Virginia---Hunter 15.
North Carolina---Lane 10.
Arkansas---Lane 1.
Missouri---Douglas 4 1-2, Guthrie 4 1-2.
Tennessee---Douglas 1, Johnson 11.
Kentucky---Guthrie 12.
Ohio--Douglas 23.
Indiana---Douglas 13.
Illinois---Douglas 11.
Michigan---Douglas 6.
Wisconsin---Douglas 5.
Iowa---Douglas 4
Minnesota---Douglas 3, Johnson 1.
California---Dickinson 1, Lane 3.
Oregon---Lane 3.

Whole number of votes, 252--Douglas 149 1-2. Guthrie 39 1-2, Dickinson 1. Hunter 28 1-2, Johnson 12, Lane 20, Davis 1 1-2, and under the ruling of the Chair there was no choice, and the Convention proceeded to the

FOURTEENTH VOTE FOR PRESIDENT.

Maine—Douglas 5, Guthrie 3.
New Hampshire—Douglas 5.
Vermont—Douglas 5.
Massachusetts—Douglas 7, Guthrie 2, Hunter 3, Davis 1.
Rhode Island—Douglas 4.
Connecticut—Douglas 3½, Guthrie 2½.
New York—Douglas 35.
New Jersey—Douglas 2, Guthrie 4½, Lane ½.
Pennsylvania—Douglas 9½, Guthrie 12, Hunter 3, Lane 2½.
Delaware—Hunter 2.
Maryland—Douglas 3½, Guthrie ½. Hunter 4.
Virginia—Hunter 15.
North Carolina—Lane 10.
Arkansas—Lane 1.
Missouri—Douglas 4½, Guthrie 4½.
Tennessee—Douglas 1, Johnson 11.
Kentucky—Guthrie 12.
Ohio—Douglas 23.
Indiana—Douglas 13.
Illinois—Douglas 11.
Michigan—Douglas 6.
Wisconsin—Douglas 5.
Iowa—Douglas 4.
Minnesota—Douglas 3, Johnson 1.
California—Dickinson ½, Lane 3½.
Oregon—Lane 3.

Whole No. of votes 252—Douglas 150, Guthrie 41, Dickinson ½. Hunter 27, Johnson 12, Lane 20½ Davis 1.

There being no choice, the Convention proceeded to the

FIFTEENTH VOTE FOR PRESIDENT.

Maine—Douglas 5, Guthrie 3.
New Hampshire—Douglas 5.
Vermont—Douglas 5.
Massachusetts—Douglas 7. Guthrie 2½. Hunter 2½, Davis 1
Rhode Island—Douglas 4.
Connecticut—Douglas 3½, Guthrie 2½.
New York—Douglas 35.
New Jersey—Douglas 2. Guthrie 4½, Lane ½.
Pennsylvania—Douglas 9½, Guthrie 12, Hunter 3, Lane 2½.
Delaware—Hunter 2.
Maryland—Douglas 3½, Guthrie ½, Hunter 4.
Virginia—Hunter 15.
North Carolina—Lane 10.
Arkansas—Lane 1.
Missouri—Douglas 4½, Guthrie 4½.
Tennessee—Douglas 1, Johnson 11.
Kentucky—Guthrie 12.
Ohio—Douglas 23.
Indiana—Douglas 13.
Illinois—Douglas 11.
Michigan—Douglas 6.
Wisconsin—Douglas 5.
Iowa—Douglas 4.
Minnesota—Douglas 3, Johnson 1.
California—Dickinson ½, Lane 3½.
Oregon—Lane 3.

Whole number of votes 252—Douglas 150, Guthrie 41½, Dickinson ½, Hunter 26½. Johnson 12, Lane 20½, Davis 1. Necessary to a choice under the decision of the Chair, 202. There being no choice, the Convention proceeded to the

SIXTEENTH VOTE FOR PRESIDENT.

Maine—Douglas 5, Guthrie 3.
New Hampshire—Douglas 5.
Vermont—Douglas 5.
Massachusetts—Douglas 7, Guthrie 2½, Hunter 2½, Davis 1.
Rhode Island—Douglas 4.
Connecticut—Douglas 3, Guthrie 2½.
New York—Douglas 35.
New Jersey—Douglas 2, Guthrie 4½, Lane ½.
Pennsylvania—Douglas 9½, Guthrie 12½, Hunter 2½, Lane 2½.
Delaware—Hunter 2.
Maryland—Douglas 3½, Guthrie ½ Hunter 4.
Virginia—Hunter 15.
North Carolina—Lane 10.
Arkansas—Lane 1.
Missouri—Douglas 4½, Guthrie 4½.
Tennessee—Douglas 1, Johnson 11.
Kentucky—Guthrie 12.
Ohio—Douglas 23.
Indiana—Douglas 13.
Illinois—Douglas 11.
Michigan—Douglas 6.
Wisconsin—Douglas 5.
Iowa—Douglas 4.
Minnesota—Douglas 3, Johnson 1.
California—Dickinson ½, Lane 3½.
Oregon—Lane 3.

Whole No. of votes 252—Douglas 150, Guthrie 42, Dickinson ½, Hunter 26, Johnson 12, Lane 20½, Davis 1. Necessary to a choice, under the decision of the Chair, 202. There being no choice, the Convention proceeded to the

SEVENTEENTH VOTE FOR PRESIDENT.

Maine—Douglas 5, Guthrie 3.
New Hampshire—Douglas 5.
Vermont—Douglas 5.
Massachusetts—Douglas 7, Guthrie 2½, Hunter 2½, Davis 1.
Rhode Island—Douglas 4.
Connecticut—Douglas 3½, Guthrie 2½.
New York—Douglas 35.
New Jersey—Douglas 2, Guthrie 4½, Lane ½.
Pennsylvania—Douglas 9½, Guthrie 12½, Hunter 2 1-2, Lane 2 1-2.
Delaware—Hunter 2.
Maryland—Douglas 3 1-2, Guthrie, 1-2, Hunter 4.
Virginia—Hunter 15.
North Carolina—Lane 10.
Arkansas—Lane 1.
Missouri—Douglas 4 1-2, Guthrie 4 1-2.
Tennesee—Douglas 1, Johnson 11.
Kentucky—Guthrie 12.
Ohio—Douglas 23.
Indiana—Douglas 13.
Illinois—Douglas 11.
Michigan—Douglas 6.
Wisconsin—Douglas 5.
Iowa—Douglas 4.
Minnesota—Douglas 3, Johnson 1.
California—Dickinson 1-2, Lane 3 1-2.
Oregon—Lane 3.

Whole No. of votes 252—Douglas 150, Guthrie 42, Dickinson 1-2, Hunter 26, Johnson 12, Lane 20 1-2, Davis 1. Necessary to a choice 202. No election, and the Convention proceeded to the

EIGHTEENTH VOTE FOR PRESIDENT.

Maine—Douglas 5, Guthrie 3.
New Hampshire—Douglas 5.
Vermont—Douglas 5.
Massachusetts—Douglas 7, Guthrie 2 1-2, Hunter 2 1-2, Davis 1.
Rhode Island—Douglas 4.
Connecticut—Douglas 3 1-2, Guthrie 2 1-2.
New York—Douglas 35.
New Jersey—Douglas 2, Guthrie 4 1-2, Lane 1-2.
Pennsylvania—Douglas 9 1-2, Guthrie 12, Dickinson 1-2, Hunter 2 1-2, Lane 2 1-2.
Delaware—Hunter 2.
Maryland—Douglas 3 1-2, Guthrie 1-2, Hunter 4.
Virginia—Hunter 15.
North Carolina—Lane 10.
Arkansas—Lane 1.
Missouri—Douglas 4 1-2, Guthrie 4 1-2.
Tennessee—Douglas 1, Johnson 11.
Kentucky—Guthrie 12.
Ohio—Douglas 23.
Indiana—Douglas 13.
Illinois—Douglas 11.
Michigan—Douglas 6.
Wisconsin—Douglas 5.
Iowa—Douglas 4.
Minnesota—Douglas 3, Johnson 1.
California—Dickinson ½, Lane 3½.
Oregon—Lane 3.

Whole No. of votes 252—Douglas 150, Guthrie 41½, Dickinson 1, Hunter 26, Johnson 12, Lane 20 1-2, Davis 1. Required for an election. 202. No choice, and the President directed the Convention to proceed to the

NINETEENTH VOTE FOR PRESIDENT.

Maine—Douglas 5, Guthrie 3.
New Hampshire—Douglas 5.
Vermont—Douglas 5.
Massachusetts—Douglas 7, Guthrie 2½, Hunter 2½, Davis 1.
Rhode Island—Douglas 4.
Connecticut—Douglas 3½, Guthrie 2½.
New York—Douglas 35.
New Jersey—Douglas 2, Guthrie 4½, Lane ½.
Pennsylvania—Douglas 9½, Guthrie 12, Dickinson ½, Hunter 2½, Lane 2½.
Delaware—Hunter 2.
Maryland—Douglas 3½, Guthrie ½, Hunter 4.
Virginia—Hunter 15.
North Carolina—Lane 10.
Arkansas—Lane 1.
Missouri—Douglas 4½, Guthrie 4½.
Tennessee—Douglas 1, Johnson 11.
Kentucky—Guthrie 12.
Ohio—Douglas 23.
Indiana—Douglas 13.
Illinois—Douglas 11.
Michigan—Douglas 6.
Wisconsin—Douglas 5.
Iowa—Douglas 4.
Minnesota—Douglas 3, Johnson 1.
California—Dickinson ½ Lane 3½.
Oregon—Lane 3.

Whole No. of votes cast, 252—Douglas 150, Guthrie 41½, Dickinson 1, Hunter 26, Johnson 12, Lane 20½, Davis 1. No choice having been made, the Convention proceeded to the

TWENTIETH BALLOT FOR PRESIDENT.

Maine—Douglas 5, Guthrie 3.
New Hampshire—Douglas 5.
Vermont—Douglas 5.
Massachusetts—Douglas 7, Guthrie 2½, Hunter 2½, Davis 1.
Rhode Island—Douglas 4.
Connecticut—Douglas 3½, Guthrie 2½.
New York—Douglas 35.
New Jersey—Douglas 2, Guthrie 4½, Lane ½.
Pennsylvania—Douglas 9½, Guthrie 12½, Hunter 2½, Lane 2½.
Delaware—Hunter 2.
Maryland—Douglas 3½, Guthrie ½, Hunter 4.
Virginia—Hunter 15.
North Carolina—Lane 10.
Arkansas—Lane 1.
Missouri—Douglas 4½, Guthrie 4½.
Tennessee—Douglas 1, Johnson 11.
Kentucky—Guthrie 12.
Ohio—Douglas 23.
Indiana—Douglas 13.
Illinois—Douglas 11.
Michigan—Douglas 6.
Wisconsin—Douglas 5.
Iowa—Douglas 4.
Minnesota—Douglas 3, Johnson 1.
California—Dickinson ½, Lane 3½.
Oregon—Lane 3.

Whole number of votes cast, 252—Douglas 150, Guthrie 42, Dickinson ½, Hunter 26, Johnson 12, Lane 20½, Davis 1. There being no choice, the Convention proceeded to the

TWENTY-FIRST VOTE FOR PRESIDENT.

Maine......Douglas 5, Guthrie 3,
New Hampshire......Douglas 5.
Vermont......Douglas 5.
Massachusetts......Douglas 7, Guthrie 2 1-2, Hunter 2 1-2; Davis 1.
Rhode Island......Douglas 4.
Connecticut......Douglas 3 1-2, Guthrie 2 1-2.
New York......Douglas 35.
New Jersey......Douglas 2, Guthrie 4 1-2, Lane 1-2
Pennsylvania......Douglas 9 1-2, Guthrie 12 1-2, Hunter 2 1-2, Lane 2 1-2.
Delaware......Hunter 2.
Maryland......Douglas 4, Hunter 4.
Virginia......Hunter 15.
North Carolina..... Lane 10.
Arkansas......Lane 1.
Missouri......Douglas 4 1-2, Guthrie 4 1-2.
Tennessee......Douglas 1. Johnson 11.
Kentucky......Guthrie 12,
Ohio......Douglas 23.
Indiana......Douglas 13.
Illinois......Douglas 11.
Michigan......Douglas 6.
Wisconsin......Douglas 4.
Iowa......Douglas 4.
Minnesota .....Douglas 3, Johnson 1.
California......Dickinson 1-2, Lane 3 1-2.
Oregon .....Lane 3.

Douglas 150 1-2, Guthrie 41 1-2, Dickinson 1-2, Hunter 26, Johnson 12, Lane 20 1-2, Davis 1.

Whole number of votes 252. Necessary to a choice, under the decision of the Chair 202. No choice having been made, the Convention went into the

TWENTY-SECOND VOTE FOR PRESIDENT.

Maine .. .Douglas 5, Guthrie 3.
New Hampshire......Douglas 5.
Vermont..... Douglas 5.

Massachusetts......Douglas 7; Guthrie 2 1-2, Hunter 2 1-2, Davis 1.
Rhode Island......Douglas 4.
Connecticut......Douglas 3 1-2, Guthrie 2 1-2.
New York......Douglas 35.
New Jersey......Douglas 2, Guthrie 4 1-2, Lane 1-2.
Pennsylvania......Douglas 9 1-2, Guthrie 12 1-2, Hunter 2 1-2, Lane 2 1-2.
Delaware......Hunter 2.
Maryland......Doulgas 4, Hunter 4.
Virginia......Hunter 15.
North Carolina......Lane 10.
Arkansas......Lane 1.
Missouri......Douglas 4 1-2, Guthrie 4 1-2.
Tennesee..... Douglas 1, Johnson 11.
Kentucky......Guthrie 12.
Ohio..... Douglas 23
Indiana......Douglas 13.
Illinois......Douglas 11.
Michigan......Douglas 6.
Wisconsin......Douglas 5.
Iowa......Douglas 4.
Minnesota......Douglas 3, Johnson 1.
California......Dickinson 1-2, Lane 3 1-2.
Oregon......Lane 3.
Douglas 150 1-2, Guthrie 41 1-2, Dickinson 1-2, Hunter 26, Johnson 12, Lane 20 1-2, Davis 1.
Whole number of votes 252. No choice.

The Convention then proceeded to the 23d vote for President.

When Virginia was called upon to vote, Mr. RUSSELL, Chairman of the Virginia delegation, rose to a question of privilege, asking the instruction of the Chair as to his duty in announcing the vote of Virginia. The practice of the Virginia delegation of casting their vote as a unit in National Democratic Conventions had been continued so long that it had become common law for that delegation. He understood that a resolution was introduced into the Virginia State Convention instructing the delegation from that State to vote as a unit in this body, but was withdrawn on the statement that the practice had become so thoroughly established that there was no need of any instruction to that effect. The delegates were not elected by the State Convention, but in the Congressional Districts from which they came.

After meeting here the delegation unanimously voted to cast the vote of the State as a unit upon the nominations. Two gentlemen, however, stated at the time that they would not hold themselves bound so to vote whenever, in their judgment, the interests of the party required them to cast a different vote. He, however, had stated at the same time that whenever they sought to vote differently he should bring the matter before the Convention. These gentlemen now having the right to cast one vote, desired to cast that vote for a candidate not recommended by the majority of the delegation from Virginia. In his opinion, under the circumstances, they had no right to separate their vote.

Mr. MOFFITT, of Virginia, said this was not the first time the vote of the State has not been cast as a unit. They had divided on other questions as important as the present since the meeting of this Convention. He represented the Tenth Legion of Virginia, which would hold him accountable to them, and he intended to redeem the pledges he had made to his people, who were entitled to be heard through him.

Mr. RUSSELL said that, under the rules of this Convention and the common law of the Democratic party of Virginia, the majority of the delegation were entitled to cast the vote of that State. In 1852, the National Convention refused to allow the minority to separate their vote from that of the majority.

Mr. MOFFITT replied that this Convention had established a rule on the subject for its own guidance.

Mr. YOST, of Virginia, had cast his vote for Mr. Hunter as long as he could do so with any advantage to him; he was now disposed to vote as his constituents desired, for Stephen A. Douglas.

The PRESIDENT decided that unless instructions had been given by a State, each individual delegate had a right to cast his own vote.

The result of the vote was then announced as follows:

TWENTY-THIRD VOTE FOR PRESIDENT.

Maine......Douglas 5, Guthrie 3.
New Hampshire......Douglas 5.
Vermont......Douglas 5.
Massachusetts—Douglas 7, Guthrie 2 1-2, Hunter 2 1-2, Davis 1.
Rhode Island......Douglas 4.
Connecticut......Douglas 3 1-2, Guthrie 2 1-2.
New York......Douglas 35.
New Jersey......Douglas 2, Guthrie 4 1-2, Lane 1-2
Pennsylvania......Douglas 9 1-2, Guthrie 12 1-2, Hunter 2, Lane 2 1-2.
Delaware......Hunter 2.
Maryland......Douglas 4, Hunter 4.
Virginia......Douglas 1, Hunter 14.
North Carolina......Douglas 1, Lane 9.

Arkansas......Lane 1.
Missouri......Douglas 4 1-2, Guthrie 4 1-2.
Tennessee......Douglas 1. Johnson 11.
Kentucky......Guthrie 12.
Ohio......Douglas 23.
Indiana......Douglas 13.
Illinois......Douglas 11.
Michigan......Douglas 6.
Wisconsin......Douglas 5.
Iowa......Douglas 4
Minnesota......Douglas 3. Johnson 1.
California......Dickinson 1-2, Lane 3 1-2.
Oregon......Lane 3.

Douglas 152 1-2. Guthrie 41 1-2, Dickinson 1-2, Hunter 25, Johnson 12, Lane 19 1-2, Davis 1.

Whole vote 252. No choice, and the Convention proceeded to the

TWENTY-FOURTH VOTE FOR PRESIDENT.

Maine......Douglas 5, Guthrie 3
New Hampshire......Douglas 5.
Vermont......Douglas 5.
Massachusetts......Douglas 7, Guthrie 2 1-2, Hunter 2 1-2, Davis 1.
Rhode Island......Douglas 4.
Connecticut......Douglas 3 1-2, Guthrie 2 1-2.
New York......Douglas 35.
New Jersey......Douglas 2, Guthrie 4 1-2, Lane 1-2
Pennsylvania..... Douglas 9 1-2, Guthrie 12 1-2, Hunter 2 1-2, Lane 2 1-2.
Delaware......Hunter 2.
Maryland......Douglas 4, Hunter 4.
Virginia......Douglas 1, Hunter 14.
North Carolina......Lane 10
Arkansas......Dickinson 1.
Missouri...... Douglas 4 1-2, Guthrie 4 1-2.
Tennesee......Douglas 1, Johnson 11.
Kentucky......Guthrie 12.
Ohio......Douglas 23.
Indiana......Douglas 13.
Illinois......Douglas 11.
Michigan......Douglas 6.
Wisconsin......Douglas 5.
Iowa......Douglas 4.
Minnesota......Douglas 3, Johnson 1.
California......Dickinson 1-2, Lane 3 1-2.
Oregon..... Lane 3.

Douglas 151 1 2, Guthrie 41 1-2, Dickinson 1 1-2 Hunter 25, Johnson 12, Lane 19 1-2, Davis 1.

Whole vote 252. No choice being made, the Convention proceeded to a

TWENTY-FIFTH VOTE FOR PRESIDENT.

Maine......Douglas 5, Guthrie 3.
New Hampshire......Douglas 5.
Vermont......Douglas 5.
Massachusetts......Douglas 7, Guthrie 2 1-2, Hunter 2 1-2, Davis 1.
Rhode Island......Douglas 4.
Connecticut......Douglas 3 1-2, Guthrie 2 1-2.
New York......Douglas 35.
New Jersey......Douglas 2, Guthrie 4 1-2, Lane 1-2
Pennsylvania......Douglas 9 1-2, Guthrie 12 1-2, Hunter 2 1-2, Lane 2 1-2,
Delaware......Hunter 2.
Maryland......Douglas 4, Hunter 4.
Virginia......Douglas 1, Hunter 14.
North Carolina..... Hunter 10.
Arkansas......Dickinson 1.
Missouri......Douglas 4 1-2. Guthrie 4 1-2.
Tennessee......Douglas 1, Johnson 11.
Kentucky......Guthrie 12.
Ohio......Douglas 23.
Indiana......Douglas 13.
Illinois......Douglas 11.
Michigan......Douglas 6.
Wisconsin......Douglas 5.
Iowa......Douglas 4.
Minnesota......Douglas 3, Johnson 1.

California......Dickinson 1-2, Lane 3 1-2.
Oregon......Lane 3.

Douglas 151 1-2, Guthrie 41 1-2, Dickinson 1 1-2, Hunter 35. Johnson 12, Lane 9 1-2, Davis 1.

Whole number of votes 252. No choice being made, the Convention proceeded to the

TWENTY-SIXTH VOTE FOR PRESIDENT.

Maine—Douglas 5, Guthrie 3.
New Hampshire—Douglas 5.
Vermont—Douglas 5.
Massachusetts—Douglas 7, Guthrie 2½, Hunter 2½, Davis 1.
Rhode Island—Douglas 4.
Connecticut—Douglas 3½, Guthrie 2½.
New York—Douglas 35.
New Jersey—Douglas 2, Guthrie 4½, Lane ½.
Pennsylvania—Douglas 9½, Guthrie 12½, Hunter 2½, Lane 2½.
Delaware—Hunter 2.
Maryland—Douglas 4, Hunter 4, Lane 1.
Virginia—Hunter 14.
North Carolina—Dickinson 10.
Arkansas—Dickinson 1.
Missouri—Douglas 4½, Guthrie 4½.
Tennessee—Douglas 1, Johnson 11.
Kentucky—Guthrie 12.
Ohio—Douglas 23.
Indiana—Douglas 13.
Illinois—Douglas 11.
Michigan—Douglas 6.
Wisconsin—Douglas 5.
Iowa—Douglas 4.
Minnesota—Douglas 3, Lane 1.
California—Dickinson 1, Lane 3.
Oregon—Lane 3.

Total number of votes cast, 252—Douglas 151½, Guthrie 41½, Dickinson 12, Hunter 25, Johnson 12, Lane 9, Davis 1. So there was no choice.

Mr. Brown, of North Carolina, in casting the vote of North Carolina on this ballot, said she would vote for that distinguished statesman, incorruptible patriot, and National Democrat, Daniel S. Dickinson, of New York.

The Convention then proceeded to take the

TWENTY-SEVENTH VOTE FOR PRESIDENT.

Maine—Douglas 5, Guthrie 3.
New Hampshire—Douglas 5.
Vermont—Douglas 5.
Massachusetts—Douglas 7, Guthrie 2½, Hunter 2½, Davis 1.
Rhode Island—Douglas 4.
Connecticut—Douglas 3½, Guthrie 2½.
New York—Douglas 35.
New Jersey—Douglas 2, Guthrie 4½, Lane ½.
Pennsylvania—Douglas 9½, Guthrie 12½, Hunter 2½, Lane 2½.
Delaware—Hunter 2.
Maryland—Douglas 4, Hunter 4.
Virginia—Douglas 1, Hunter 14.
North Carolina—Dickinson 10.
Arkansas—Dickinson 1.
Missouri—Douglas 4½, Guthrie 4½.
Tennessee—Douglas 1, Johnson 11.
Kentucky—Guthrie 12.
Ohio—Douglas 23.
Indiana—Douglas 13.
Illinois—Douglas 11.
Michigan—Douglas 6.
Wisconsin—Douglas 5.
Iowa—Douglas 4.
Minnesota—Douglas 3, Johnson 1.
California—Guthrie 1, Dickinson 1, Lane 2.
Oregon—Lane 3.

Total vote 252—Douglas 151½, Guthrie 42½, Dickinson 12, Hunter 25, Johnson 12, Lane 8, Davis 1. No choice, and the Convention proceeded to the

TWENTY-EIGHTH VOTE FOR PRESIDENT.

Maine—Douglas 5, Guthrie 3.
New Hampshire—Douglas 5.
Vermont—Douglas 5.
Massachusetts—Douglas 7, Guthrie 2½, Hunter 2½, Davis 1.
Rhode Island—Douglas 4.
Connecticut—Douglas 3½, Guthrie 2½.
New York—Douglas 35.
New Jersey—Douglas 2, Guthrie 4½, Lane ½.
Pennsylvania—Douglas 9½, Guthrie 13, Hunter 2½ Lane 2.
Delaware—Hunter 2.

Maryland—Douglas 4, Hunter 4.
Virginia—Douglas 1, Hunter 14.
North Carolina—Dickinson 10.
Arkansas—Dickinson 1.
Missouri—Douglas 4½, Guthrie 4½.
Tennessee—Douglas 1, Johnson 11.
Kentucky—Guthrie 12.
Ohio—Douglas 23.
Indiana—Douglas 13.
Illinois—Douglas 11.
Michigan—Douglas 6.
Wisconsin—Douglas 5.
Iowa—Douglas 4.
Minnesota—Douglas 3, Johnson 1.
California—Dickinson 1½, Lane 2½.
Oregon—Lane 3.

Total vote 252—Douglas 151½, Guthrie 42, Dickinson 12½, Hunter 25, Johnson 12, Lane 8, Davis 1. No choice, and the Convention proceeded to the

TWENTY-NINTH VOTE FOR PRESIDENT.

Maine......Douglas 5, Guthrie 3.
New Hampshire......Douglas 5.
Vermont......Douglas 5.
Massachusetts......Douglas 7, Guthrie 2 1-2, Hunter 2 1-2, Davis 1.
Rhode Island......Douglas 4.
Connecticut......Douglas 3 1-2, Guthrie 2 1-2.
N. w York......Douglas 35.
New Jersey......Douglas 2, Guthrie 4 1-2, Lane 1-2.
Pennsylvania......Douglas 9 1-2, Guthrie 13, Hunter 2 1-2, Lane 2.
Delaware......Hunter 2.
Maryland......Douglas 4, Hunter 4.
Virginia......Douglas 1, Hunter 14.
North Carolina......Dickinson 10.
Arkansas......Dickinson 1.
Missouri......Douglas 4 1-2, Guthrie 4 1-2.
Tennessee......Douglas 1, Johnson 11.
Kentucky......Guthrie 12.
Ohio......Douglas 28.
Indiana......Douglas 13.
Illinois......Douglas 11.
Michigan......Douglas 6.
Wisconsin......Douglas 5.
Iowa......Douglas 4.
Minnesota......Douglas 3, Johnson 1.
California......Dickinson 2, Lane 2.
Oregon..... Lane 3.

Douglas 151 1-2, Guthrie 42, Dickinson 13, Hunter 25, Johnson 12, Lane 7 1-2, Davis 1.
Total vote 252. No choice, and the Convention proceeded to the

THIRTIETH VOTE FOR PRESIDENT.

Maine..... Douglas 5, Guthrie 3.
New Hampshire......Douglas 5.
Vermont......Douglas 5.
Massachusetts......Douglas 7, Guthrie 2 1-2, Hunter 2 1-2, Davis 1.
Rhode Island......Douglas 4.
Connecticut......Douglas 3 1-2, Guthrie 2 1-2.
New York......Douglas 35.
New Jersey......Douglas 2, Guthrie 4 1-2, Lane 1-2.
Pennsylvania......Douglas 9 1-2, Guthrie 15, Hunter 2 1-2.
Delaware......Hunter 2.
Maryland......Douglas 4, Hunter 4.
Virginia......Douglas 1, Hunter 14.
North Carolina .....Dickinson 10.
Arkansas......Dickinson 1.
Missouri......Douglas 4 1-2, Guthrie 4 1-2.
Tennessee......Douglas 1, Guthrie 1, Johnson 10.
Kentucky......Guthrie 12.
Ohio......Douglas 23.
Indiana......Douglas 13.
Illinois......Douglas 11.
Michigan......Douglas 6.
Wisconsin......Douglas 5.
Iowa......Douglas 4.
Minnesota......Douglas 3, Johnson 1.
California..... Dickinson 2, Lane 2.
Oregon......Lane 3.

Douglas 151 1-2, Guthrie 45, Dickinson 13, Hunter 25, Johnson 11, Lane 5 1-2, Davis 1.
Total vote 252. No choice, and the Convention proceeded to the

THIRTY FIRST VOTE FOR PRESIDENT.

Maine......Douglas 5, Guthrie 3.
New Hampshire......Douglas 5.
Vermont......Douglas 5.
Massachusetts......Douglas 7, Guthrie 2 1-2, Hunter 2 1-2, Davis 1.
Rhode Island......Douglas 4.
Connecticut......Douglas 3 1-2, Guthrie 2 1-2.
New York .... Douglas 35.
New Jersey......Douglas 2, Guthrie 4 1-2, Lane 1-2.
Pennsylvania......Douglas 9 1-2, Guthrie 17 1-2.
Delaware......Hunter 2.
Maryland......Douglas 4, Hunter 4.
Virginia......Douglas 1, Hunter 14.
North Carolina......Hunter 10.
Arkansas......Dickinson 1.
Missouri......Douglas 4 1-2, Guthrie 4 1-2.
Tennessee......Douglas 1, Guthrie 1, Johnson 10.
Kentucky......Guthrie 12.
Ohio .....Douglas 23
Indiana......Douglas 13.
Illinois......Douglas 11.
Michigan......Douglas 6.
Wisconsin......Douglas 5.
Iowa......Douglas 4.
Minnesota .....Douglas 3, Johnson 1.
California......Dickinson 2, Lane 2.
Oregon......Lane 3,

Douglas 151 1-2, Guthrie 47 1-2, Dickinson 3, Hunter 32 1-2, Johnson 11, Lane 5 1-2, Davis 1.
Total vote 252. No choice, and the Convention proceeded to the

THIRTY-SECOND VOTE FOR PRESIDENT.

Maine......Douglas 5, Guthrie 3.
New Hampshire......Douglas 5.
Vermont......Douglas 5.
Massachusetts......Douglas 7, Guthrie 2½, Hunter 2½, Davis 1.
Rhode Island......Douglas 4.
Connecticut......Douglas 3½. Guthrie 2½.
New York......Douglas 35.
New Jersey.... Douglas 2, Guthrie 4½, Lane ½.
Pennsylvania......Douglas 9½, Guthrie 17½.
Delaware..... Hunter 2.
Maryland......Douglas 4, Hunter 4.
Virginia......Douglas 1, Hunter 14.
North Carolina......Douglas 1, Lane 9.
Arkansas......Dickinson 1.
Missouri .....Douglas 4½, Guthrie 4½.
Tennessee......Douglas 1, Guthrie 1, Johnson 10.
Kentucky......Guthrie 12.
Ohio......Douglas 23.
Indiana .....Douglas 13.
Illinois......Douglas 11.
Michigan......Douglas 6.
Wisconsin......Douglas 5.
Iowa... ..Douglas 4.
Minnesota......Douglas 3, Johnson 1.
California......Dickinson 2, Lane 2.
Oregon......Lane 3.

Douglas 152½, Guthrie 47½, Dickinson 3, Hunter 22½, Johnson 11, Lane 14½, Davis 1.
Total vote 252. No choice, and the Convention proceeded to the

THIRTY-THIRD VOTE FOR PRESIDENT.

Maine......Douglas 5, Guthrie 3.
New Hampshire......Douglas 5.
Vermont......Douglas 5.
Massachusetts......Douglas 7, uGthrie 2½, Hunter 2½, Davis 1.

Rhode Island......Douglas 4.
Connecticut......Douglas 3½, Guthrie 2½.
New York......Douglas 35.
New Jersey......Douglas 2, Guthrie 4½, Lane ½.
Pennsylvania......Douglas 9 1-2, Guthrie 17 1-2.
Delaware......Hunter 2.
Maryland......Douglas 4, Hunter 4.
Virginia......Douglas 1, Hunter 14.
North Carolina......Douglas 1, Lane 9.
Arkansas......Dickinson 1.
Missouri......Douglas 4 1-2, Guthrie 4 1-2.
Tennessee......Douglas 1, Guthrie 1, Johnson 10.
Kentucky......Guthrie 12.
Ohio......Douglas 23.
Indiana......Douglas 13.
Illinois......Douglas 11
Michigan......Douglas 6.
Wisconsin......Douglas 5,
Iowa......Douglas 4.
Minnesota......Douglas 3, Johnson 1.
California......Dickinson 2, Lane 2.
Oregon......Lane 3.

Douglas 152 1-2, Guthrie 47 1-2, Dickinson 3, Hunter 22 1-2, Johnson 11, Lane 14½, Davis 1.

Total vote 252. No choice, and the Convention proceeded to the

THIRTY-FOURTH VOTE FOR PRESIDENT.

Maine......Douglas 5, Guthrie 3.
New Hampshire......Douglas 5.
Vermont......Douglas 5.
Massachusetts......Douglas 7, Guthrie 2½, Hunter 2½, Davis 1.
Rhode Island......Douglas 4.
Connecticut......Douglas 3½, Guthrie 2½.
New York......Douglas 35.
New Jersey......Douglas 2, Guthrie 4½, Lane ½.
Pennsylvania......Douglas 9½, Guthrie 17½.
Delaware......Hunter 2.
Maryland....Douglas 4. Hunter 4.
Virginia......Douglas 1, Hunter 14.
North Carolina......Douglas 1, Lane 9.
Arkansas....Dickinson 1.
Missouri......Douglas 4½, Guthrie 4½.
Tennessee......Douglas 1, Guthrie 1, Johnson 10.
Kentucky......Guthrie 12.
Ohio......Douglas 23.
Indiana......Douglas 13.
Illinois......Douglas 11.
Michigan......Douglas 6.
Wisconsin...... Douglas 5.
Iowa......Douglas 4.
Minnesota......Douglas 3, Johnson 1.
California......Dickinson 4.
Oregon......Lane 3.

Douglas 152½, Guthrie 47½, Dickinson 5, Hunter 22½, Johnson 11, Lane 12½, Davis 1.

Total number no votes 252. No choice.

Mr. KRUM, of Missouri. Mr. President, I rise to a privileged question. My attention has been called to the proceedings of the City Council of Charleston in respect to the Hall occupied by this Convention. The very magnanimous and liberal action of the Council seems to render it proper that it should meet with an appropriate response from this Convention. I, therefore, move the adoption of the following resolution:

Resolved, That the thanks of the Convention be returned to the City Council of Charleston for the liberal appropriation made by said Council to defray the expense of the Hall of the South Carolina Institute, in which the sessions of this Convention have been held.

The resolution was unanimously adopted.

On motion of Mr. ASHE, of North Carolina, the Convention then took a recess till 5 o'clock P. M.

AFTERNOON SESSION.

The Convention re-assembled at 5 o'clock, and the roll of States was at once called for the thirty-fifth ballot, with the following result:

THIRTY-FIFTH VOTE FOR PRESIDENT.

Maine—Douglas 5, Guthrie 3.
New Hampshire—Douglas 5.
Vermont—Douglas 5.
Massachusetts—Douglas 6½, Guthrie 3½, Hunter 2, Davis 1.
Rhode Island—Douglas 4.
Connecticut—Douglas 3½, Guthrie 2½.
New York—Douglas 35.
New Jersey—Douglas 2, Guthrie 4½, Lane ½.
Pennsylvania—Douglas 9½, Guthrie 17½.
Delaware—Hunter 2.
Maryland—Douglas 4, Hunter 4.
Virginia—Douglas 1, Hunter 14.
North Carolina—Douglas 1, Lane 9.
Arkansas—Dickinson 1.
Missouri—Douglas 4 1-2, Guthrie 4 1-2.
Tennesee—Douglas 1, Johnson 11.
Kentucky—Guthrie 12.
Ohio—Douglas 23.
Indiana—Douglas 13.
Illinois—Douglas 11.
Michigan—Douglas 6.
Wisconsin—Douglas 5.
Iowa—Douglas 4.
Minnesota—Douglas 3, Johnson 1.
California—Dickinson 3 1-2. Lane 1-2,
Oregon—Lane 3.

Whole No. of votes 252—Douglas 152, Guthrie 47½, Dickinson 4½, Hunter 22, Johnson 12, Lane 13, Davis 1. No election.

Mr. GITTINGS, of Maryland, moved that after next ballot, the Convention adjourn to meet in the city of Baltimore on the first Monday of June next.

Mr. LUDLOW, of New York, raised the question of order, that the motion was not in order while the Convention was in the execution of its order, adopted under the previous question.

Mr. RANDALL, of Pennsylvania, wanted to address the Convention, but was decided to be out of order.

The PRESIDENT decided that a motion to name a time and place of meeting was, by the rules and practice of the House of Representatives, always in order.

Mr. JOHN COCHRAN, of New York, said the motion to fix the time of adjournment was a privileged question, but when the matter of place was added, the question became one not of privilege.

Mr. GITTINGS said, at the suggestion of gentlemen around him, he would withdraw the motion, to renew it at some subsequent time.

The thirty-sixth vote was then taken and announced as follows:

THIRTY-SIXTH VOTE FOR PRESIDENT.

Maine—Douglas 5, Guthrie 3.
New Hampshire—Douglas 5.
Vermont—Douglas 5.
Massachusetts—Douglas 6, Guthrie 4, Hunter 2, Davis 1.
Rhode Island—Douglas 4.
Connecticut—Douglas 3 1-2, Guthrie 2 1-2.
New York—Douglas 35.
New Jersey—Douglas 2, Guthrie 4 1-2, Lane 1-2.
Pennsylvania—Douglas 9 1-2, Guthrie 17½.
Delaware—Hunter 2.
Maryland—Douglas 4, Hunter 4.
Virginia—Douglas 1, Hunter 14.
North Carolina—Douglas 1, Lane 9.
Arkansas—Dickinson 1.
Missouri—Douglas 4 1-2, Guthrie 4 1-2.
Tennessee—Douglas 1, Johnson 11.
Kentucky—Guthrie 12.
Ohio—Douglas 23.
Indiana—Douglas 13.
Illinois—Douglas 11.
Michigan—Douglas 6.
Wisconsin—Douglas 5.
Iowa—Douglas 4.
Minnesota—Douglas 3, Johnson 1.
California—Dickinson 3½, Lane ½.
Oregon—Lane 3.

Whole No. of votes 252—Douglas 151½, Guthrie 48, Dickinson 4¼, Hunter 22, Johnson 12, Lane 13, Davis 1. Required for an election, 252. No choice.

On the above vote Arkansas cast one vote for Breckinridge.

Mr. BECK, of Kentucky, appealed to the gentleman to withdraw that vote. He assured him it was not the wish of Mr. Breckinridge to appear here as a candidate in opposition to the distinguished gentleman from Kentucky, whose name had been before the Convention from the first.

The vote was accordingly withdrawn and cast for Dickinson.

Mr. EWING, of Tennessee, said the delegation from the State of Tennessee had, with one exception, cast their vote steadily for a gifted son of that State. Without communication with their candidate, however, a majority of the delegation had come to the conclusion to withdraw their vote from him, and they hoped a nomination would now be made.

The Convention then proceeded to a 37th vote with the following result:

THIRTY-SEVENTH VOTE FOR PRESIDENT.

Maine—Douglas 5, Guthrie 3.
New Hampshire—Douglas 5.
Vermont—Douglas 5.
Massachusetts—Douglas 6, Guthrie 6, Davis 1.
Rhode Island—Douglas 4.
Connecticut—Douglas 3½, Guthrie 2½.
New York—Douglas 35.
New Jersey—Douglas 2, Guthrie 4½, Lane ½.
Pennsylvania—Douglas 9½, Guthrie 17½.
Delaware—Hunter 2.
Maryland—Douglas 4, Guthrie 4.
Virginia—Douglas 1, Hunter 14.
North Carolina—Douglas 1, Lane 9.
Arkansas—Dickinson 1.
Missouri—Douglas 4½, Guthrie 4½.
Tennessee—Douglas 1, Guthrie 10½, Johnson ¼.
Kentucky—Guthrie 12.
Ohio—Douglas 23.
Indiana—Douglas 13.
Illinois—Douglas 11.
Michigan—Douglas 6.
Wisconsin—Douglas 5.
Iowa—Douglas 4.
Minnesota—Douglas 3, Dickinson 1.
California—Dickinson 3½. Davis ½.
Oregon—Lane 3.

Whole No. of votes cast, 252—Douglas 151½, Guthrie 64½, Dickinson 5½, Hunter 16. Johnson ½, Lane 12½, Davis 1½. No choice.

THIRTY-EIGHTH VOTE FOR PRESIDENT.

Maine—Douglas 5, Guthrie 3.
New Hampshire—Douglas 5.
Vermont—Douglas 5.
Massachusetts—Douglas 6, Guthrie 7.
Rhode Island—Douglas 4.
Connecticut—Douglas 3½, Guthrie 2½.
New York—Douglas 35.
New Jersey—Douglas 2, Guthrie 4½, Lane ½.
Pennsylvania—Douglas 9½, Guthrie 17½.
Delaware—Hunter 2.
Maryland—Douglas 4, Guthrie 4.
Virginia—Douglas 1, Hunter 14.
North Carolina—Douglas 1, Lane 9.
Arkansas—Dickinson 1.
Missouri—Douglas 4½, Guthrie 4½.
Tennessee—Douglas 1, Guthrie 11.
Kentucky—Guthrie 12.
Ohio—Douglas 23.
Indiana—Douglas 13.
Illinois—Douglas 11.
Michigan—Douglas 6.
Wisconsin—Douglas 5.
Iowa—Douglas 4.
Minnesota—Douglas 3, Dichinson 1.
California—Dickinson 3½, Lane ½.
Oregon—Lane 3.

Whole number of votes cast, 252—Douglas 151½, Guthrie 66, Dickinson 5½, Hunter 16, Johnson 0, Lane 13. No choice.

Mr. GITTINGS, of Maryland, then desired to renew his motion, that when the Convention adjourns, it adjourn to meet in Baltimore on the first Monday in June.

The PRESIDENT decided the motion out of order, on the ground suggested by Mr. Cochran, when the motion was before made. The motion could be made that when the Convention adjourns, it adjourn to meet on the first

Monday of next June, and the place of meeting could be fixed at some subsequent time.

Mr. Gittings said he would submit his motion in that form; the only object he had in making the motion was to enable him to go home to his family.

Mr. Stuart, of Michigan, moved to lay Mr. Gittings' motion to adjourn on the table, which motion carried, and Mr. Gittings' resolution was laid upon the table.

The Convention then proceeded to take the 39th vote for President, and the following was the result:

THIRTY-NINTH VOTE FOR PRESIDENT.

Maine—Douglas 5, Guthrie 3.
New Hampshire—Douglas 5.
Vermont—Douglas 5.
Massachusetts—Douglas 6, Guthrie 7.
Rhode Island—Douglas 4.
Connecticut—Douglas 3½, Guthrie 2½.
New York—Douglas 35.
New Jersey—Douglas 2, Guthrie 5.
Pennsylvania—Douglas 9½, Guthrie 17½.
Delaware—Hunter 2.
Maryland—Douglas 4, Guthrie 4.
Virginia—Douglas 1, Hunter 14.
North Carolina—Douglas 1, Lane 9.
Arkansas—Dickinson 1.
Missouri—Douglas 4½, Guthrie 4½.
Tennessee—Douglas 1, Guthrie 11.
Kentucky—Guthrie 12.
Ohio—Douglas 23.
Indiana—Douglas 13.
Illinois—Douglas 11.
Michigan—Douglas 6.
Wisconsin—Douglas 5.
Iowa—Douglas 4.
Minnesota—Douglas 3, Dickinson 1.
California—Dickinson 3½, Lane ½.
Oregon—Lane 3.

Whole No of votes 252—Douglas 151½, Guthrie 66½, Dickinson 5½, Hunter 16, Lane 12½.

No choice.

FORTIETH VOTE FOR PRESIDENT.

Maine—Douglas 5, Guthrie 3.
New Hampshire—Douglas 5.
Vermont—Douglas 5.
Massachusetts—Douglas 6, Guthrie 7.
Rhode Island—Douglas 4.
Connecticut—Douglas 3½, Guthrie 2½.
New York—Douglas 35.
New Jersey—Douglas 2, Guthrie 5.
Pennsylvania—Douglas 9½, Guthrie 17½.
Delaware—Hunter 2.
Maryland—Douglas 4, Guthrie 4.
Virginia—Douglas 1 Hunter 14.
North Carolina—Douglas 1, Lane 9.
Arkansas—Dickinson 1.
Missouri—Douglas 4½, Guthrie 4½.
Tennessee—Douglas 1, Guthrie 11.
Kentucky—Guthrie 12.
Ohio—Douglas 23.
Indiana—Douglas 13.
Illinois—Douglas 11.
Michigan—Douglas 6.
Wisconsin—Douglas 5.
Iowa—Douglas 4.
Minnesota—Douglas 3, Dickinson 1.
California—Dickinson 3½, Lane ½.
Oregon—Lane 3.

Whole number of votes 252—Douglas 151½, Guthrie 66½, Dickinson 5½, Hunter 16, Lane 12½.

No choice.

FORTY-FIRST VOTE FOR PRESIDENT.

Maine—Douglas 5, Guthrie 3.
New Hampshire—Douglas 5.
Vermont—Douglas 5.
Massachusetts—Douglas 6, Guthrie 7.
Rhode Island—Douglas 4.
Connecticut—Douglas 3½, Guthrie 2½.
New York—Douglas 35.
New Jersey—Douglas 2, Guthrie 5.
Pennsylvania—Douglas 9½, Guthrie 17½.
Delaware—Hunter 2.
Maryland—Douglas 4, Guthrie 4.
Virginia—Douglas 1, Hunter 14.
North Carolina—Douglas 1, Lane 9.
Arkansas—Dickinson 1.
Missouri—Douglas 4½, Guthrie 4½.
Tennessee—Douglas 1, Guthrie 11.
Kentucky—Guthrie 12.
Ohio—Douglas 23.
Indiana—Douglas 13.
Illinois—Douglas 11.
Michigan—Douglas 6.
Wisconsin—Douglas 5.
Iowa—Douglas 4.
Minnesota—Douglas 3, Dickinson 1.
California—Dickinson 3, Lane 1.
Oregon—Lane 3.

Whole No. of votes 252—Douglas 151½, Guthrie 66½, Dickinson 5, Hunter 16, Lane 13.

No choice.

FORTY-SECOND VOTE FOR PRESIDENT.

Maine-- Douglas 5, Guthrie 3.
New Hampshire---Douglas 5.
Vermont---Douglas 5.
Massachusetts---Douglas 6, Guthrie 7.
Rhode Island---Douglas 4
Connecticut---Douglas 3 1-2, Guthrie 2 1-2.
New York---Douglas 35.
New Jersey---Douglas 2, Guthrie 5
Pennsylvania---Douglas 9 1-2, Guthrie 17 1-2.
Delaware --Hunter 2.
Maryland---Douglas 4, Guthrie 4.
Virginia---Douglas 1, Hunter 14.
North Carolina---Douglas 1 Lane 9.
Arkansas---Dickinson 1.
Missouri---Douglas 4 1-2, Guthrie 4 1-2.
Tennessee---Douglas 1, Guthrie 11.
Kentucky---Guthrie 12.
Ohio---Douglas 23.
Indiana---Douglas 13.
Illinois---Douglas 11.
Michigan—Douglas 6.
Wisconsin---Douglas 5.
Iowa---Douglas 4
Minnesota---Douglas 3, Dickinson 1.
California---Dickinson 3, Lane 1.
Oregon---Lane 3.

Whole number of votes, 252 - Douglas 151 1-2, Guthrie 66 1-2, Dickinson 5, Hunter 16, Lane 13.

No choice.

FORTY-THIRD VOTE FOR PRESIDENT.

Maine......Douglas 5, Guthrie 3,
New Hampshire......Douglas 5.
Vermont..... Douglas 5.
Massachusetts......Douglas 6, Guthrie 6, Davis 1.
Rhode Island......Douglas 4.
Connecticut......Douglas 3 1-2, Guthrie 2 1-2.
New York......Douglas 35.
New Jersey..... .Douglas 2, Guthrie 5.
Pennsylvania......Douglas 9 1-2, Guthrie 17 1-2.
Delaware......Hunter 2.
Maryland......Douglas 4, Hunter 4.
Virginia...... Douglas 1, Hunter 14.
North Carolina..... Douglas 1, Lane 9.
Arkansas......Dickinson 1.
Missouri......Douglas 4 1-2, Guthrie 4 1-2.
Tennessee......Douglas 1. Guthrie 11.
Kentucky......Guthrie 12.
Ohio......Douglas 23.
Indiana......Douglas 13.
Illinois......Douglas 11.

Michigan......Douglas 6.
Wisconsin......Douglas 5.
Iowa......Douglas 4.
Minnesota .....Douglas 3. Dickinson 1.
California......Dickinson 3, Lane 1.
Oregon ....Lane 3.

Douglas 151 1-2, Guthrie 65 1-2, Dickinson 5, Hunter 16, Lane 13, Davis 1.

Whole number of votes 252. No choice.

FORTY-FOURTH VOTE FOR PRESIDENT.

Maine .. .Douglas 5, Guthrie 3.
New Hampshire......Douglas 5.
Vermont......Douglas 5.
Massachusetts......Douglas 6. Guthrie 6, Davis 1.
Rhode Island......Douglas 4.
Connecticut......Douglas 3 1-2, Guthrie 2 1-2.
New York......Douglas 35.
New Jersey......Douglas 2, Guthrie 5.
Pennsylvania......Douglas 9 1-2, Guthrie 17 1-2.
Delaware......Hunter 2.
Maryland......Doulgas 4, Guthrie 4.
Virginia......Douglas 1, Hunter 14.
North Carolina......Douglas 1, Lane 9.
Arkansas......Dickinson 1.
Missouri......Douglas 4 1-2. Guthrie 4 1-2.
Tennesee..... Douglas 1, Guthrie 11.
Kentucky......Guthrie 12.
Ohio..... Douglas 23.
Indiana......Douglas 13.
Illinois......Douglas 11.
Michigan......Douglas 6.
Wisconsin......Douglas 5.
Iowa......Douglas 4.
Minnesota......Douglas 3, Dickinson 1.
California......Dickinson 3, Lane 1.
Oregon......Lane 3.

Douglas 151 1-2, Guthrie 65 1-2, Dickinson 5, Hunter 16, Lane 13, Davis 1.

Whole number of votes 252. No choice, and 45th vote ordered.

FORTY-FIFTH VOTE FOR PRESIDENT.

Maine—Douglas 5, Guthrie 3.
New Hampshire—Douglas 5.
Vermont—Douglas 5.
Massachusetts—Douglas 6, Guthrie 6, Davis 1
Rhode Island—Douglas 4.
Connecticut—Douglas 3½, Guthrie 2½.
New York—Douglas 35.
New Jersey—Douglas 2, Guthrie 5.
Pennsylvania—Douglas 9 1-2, Guthrie 17 1-2.
Delawara—Hunter 2.
Maryland—Douglas 4, Guthrie 4.
Virginia—Douglas 1, Hunter 14.
North Carolina—Douglas 1, Lane 9.
Arkansas—Dickinson 1
Missouri—Douglas 4½, Guthrie 4½.
Tennessee—Douglas 1, Guthrie 11.
Kentucky—Guthrie 12.
Ohio—Douglas 23.
Indiana—Douglas 13.
Illinois—Douglas 11.
Michigan—Douglas 6.
Wisconsin—Douglas 5.
Iowa—Douglas 4.
Minnesota—Douglas 3, Dickinson 1.
California—Dickinson 3, Lane 1.
Oregon—Lane 3.

Douglas 151½, Guthrie 65½, Dickinson 5, Hunter 16, Lane 13, Davis 1

Total vote, 252. No choice, and 46th vote ordered.

FORTY-SIXTH VOTE FOR PRESIDENT.

Maine......Douglas 5, Guthrie 3.
New Hampshire......Douglas 5.
Vermont......Douglas 5.
Massachustts......Douglas 6, Guthrie 6, Davis 1.
Rhode Island......Douglas 4
Connecticut......Douglas 3 1-2, Guthrie 2 1-2.
New York......Douglas 35.
New Jersey......Douglas 2, Guthrie 5
Pennsylvania......Douglas 9 1-2, Guthrie 17 1-2.
Delaware......Hunter 2.
Maryland......Douglas 4, Guthrie 4.
Virginia......Douglas 1, Hunter 14.
North Carolina......Douglas 1, Lane 9.
Arkansas......Dickinson 1.
Missouri......Douglas 4 1-2, Guthrie 4 1-2.
Tennessee..... Douglas 1, Guthrie 11.
Kentucky......Guthrie 12.
Ohio......Douglas 23
Indiana......Douglas 13.
Illinois......Douglas 11.
Michigan......Douglas 6.
Wisconsin......Douglas 5.
Iowa......Douglas 4.
Minnesota......Douglas 3, Dickinson 1.
California......Dickinson 3, Lane 1.
Oregon......Lane 3

Douglas 151 ½, Guthrie 65½, Dickinson 5, Hunter 16, Lane 13, Davis 1.

Whole number of votes 252. No choice, and 47th vote ordered.

FORTY-SEVENTH VOTE FOR PRESIDENT.

Maine......Douglas 5, Guthrie 3.
New Hampshire...... Douglas 5.
Vermont......Douglas 5.
Massachusetts......Douglas 6, Guthrie 6, Davis 1.
Rhode Island......Douglas 4.
Connecticut......Douglas 3 1-2, Guthrie 2 1-2.
New York......Douglas 35.
New Jersey......Douglas 2, Guthrie 5.
Pennsylvania......Douglas 9 1-2, Guthrie 17 1-2.
Delaware......Hunter 2.
Maryland......Douglas 4, Guthrie 4.
Virginia......Douglas 1, Hunter 14.
North Carolina......Douglas 1, Lane 9.
Arkansas......Dickinson 1.
Missouri......Douglas 4 1-2, Guthrie 4 1-2.
Tennessee......Douglas 1, Guthrie 11.
Kentucky......Guthrie 12.
Ohio......Douglas 23.
Indiana......Douglas 13.
Illinois......Douglas 11.
Michigan .....Douglas 6,
Wisconsin .....Douglas 5.
Iowa......Douglas 4.
Minnesota......Douglas 3, Dickinson 1.
California......Dickinson 3, Lane 1.
Oregon......Lane 3.

Douglas 151 1-2. Guthrie 65 1-2, Dickinson 5, Hunter 16. Lane 13, Davis 1.

Whole number of votes, 252. No choice, and 48th vote ordered.

FORTY-EIGHTH VOTE FOR PRESIDENT

Maine—Douglas 5, Guthrie 3.
New Hampshire—Douglas 5.
Vermont—Douglas 5.
Massachusetts—Douglas 6, Guthrie 6, Davis 1.
Rhode Island—Douglas 4.
Connecticut—Douglas 3 1-2, Guthrie 2 1-2.
New York—Douglas 35.
New Jersey—Douglas 2, Guthrie 5.
Pennsylvania—Douglas 9 1-2, Guthrie 17 1-2.
Delaware—Hunter 2
Maryland—Douglas 4. Guthrie 4.
Virginia—Dou6las 1, Hunter 14
North Carolina—Douglas 1. Lane 9.
Arkansas—Dickinson 1.
Missouri—Douglas 4 1-2. Guthrie 4 1-2.
Tennessee—Douglas 1, Guthrie 11.
Kentucky—Guthrie 12.
Ohio—Douglas 23.
Indiana—Douglas 13.
Illinois—Douglas 11.
Michigan—Douglas 6.
Wisconsin—Douglas 5.
Iowa—Douglas 4.

Minnesota—Douglas 3, Dickinson 1.
California—Dickinson 3, Lane 1.
Oregon—Lane 3.

Whole number of votes, 252—Douglas 151 1-2 Guthrie 65 1-2, Dickinson 5, Hunter 16, Lane 13. Davis 1.

No choice, and 49th vote ordered.

FORTY-NINTH VOTE FOR PRESIDENT.

Maine—Douglas 5, Guthrie 3.
New Hampshire—Douglas 5.
Vermont—Douglas 5
Massachusetts—Douglas 6 Guthrie 6 Davis 1.
Rhode Island—Douglas 4
Connecticut—Douglas 3 1-2. Guthrie 2 1-2.
New York—Douglas 35.
New Jersey—Douglas 2, Guthrie 5
Pennsylvania—Douglas 9 1-2 ; Guthrie 17 1-2.
Delaware—Hunter 2.
Maryland—Douglas 4. Guthrie 4.
Virginia—Douglas 1. Hunter 14.
North Carolina—Douglas 1, Lane 9.
Arkansas—Lane 1.
Missouri—Douglas 4 1-2. Guthrie 4 1-2.
Tennessee—Douglas 1. Guthrie 11.
Kentucky—Guthrie 12.
Ohio—Douglas 23.
Indiana—Douglas 13.
Illinois—Douglas 11.
Michigan—Douglas 6.
Wisconsin—Douglas 5.
Iowa—Douglas 4.
Minnesota—Douglas 3, Dickinson 1
California—Dickinson 3, Lane 1.
Oregon—Lane 3.

Whole number of votes cast, 252—Douglas 151½. Guthrie 65 1-2. Dickinson 4, Hunter 16, Lane 14, Davis 1. No choice.

A Delegate, from North Carolina, moved that the Convention adjourn, which motion was put and lost.

The Convention then proceeded to take the 50th vote for President, with the following result :

FIFTIETH VOTE FOR PRESIDENT.

Maine—Douglas 5, Guthrie 3.
New Hampshire—Douglas 5.
Vermont—Douglas 5.
Massachusetts—Douglas 6, Guthrie 6, Davis 1.
Rhode Island—Douglas 4.
Connecticut—Douglas 3 1-2, Guthrie 2 1-2.
New York—Douglas 35.
New Jersey—Douglas 2, Guthrie 5.
Pennsylvania—Douglas 9 1-2, Guthrie 17 1-2.
Delaware—Hunter 2.
Maryland—Douglas 4. Guthrie 4.
Virginia—Douglas 1, Hunter 14
North Carolina—Douglas 1, Lane 9.
Arkansas—Lane 1
Missouri—Douglas 4 1-2, Guthrie 4 1-2.
Tennessee—Douglas 1, Guthrie 11.
Kentucky—Guthrie 12.
Ohio—Douglas 23.
Indiana—Douglas 13.
Illinois—Douglas 11.
Michigan—Douglas 6.
Wisconsin—Douglas 5.
Iowa—Douglas 4.
Minnesota—Douglas 3, Dickinson 1.
California—Dickinson 3, Lane 1.
Oregon—Lane 3.

Whole number of votes, 252—Douglas 151 1-2, Guthrie 65 1-2, Dickinson 4, Hunter 16, Lane 14, Davis 1. No choice

FIFTY-FIRST VOTE FOR PRESIDENT.

Maine—Douglas 5. Guthrie 3.
New Hampshire—Douglas 5.
Vermont—Douglas 5.
Massachusetts—Douglas 6, Guthrie 6, Davis 1.
Rhode Island—Douglas 4.
Connecticut—Douglas 3 1-2, Guthrie 2 1-2.
New York—Douglas 35.
New Jersey—Douglas 2, Guthrie 5
Pennsylvania—Douglas 9 1-2, Guthrie 17 1-2.
Delaware—Hunter 2.
Maryland—Douglas 4, Guthrie 4.
Virginia—Douglas 1, Hunter 14.
North Carolina—Douglas 1, Lane 9.
Arkansas—Lane 1.
Missouri—Douglas 4 1-2. Guthrie 4 1-2.
Tennessee—Douglas 1, Guthrie 11.
Kentucky—Guthrie 12.
Ohio—Douglas 23.
Indiana—Douglas 13.
Illinois—Douglas 11.
Michigan—Douglas 6.
Wisconsin—Douglas 5.
Iowa—Douglas 4.
Minnesota—Douglas 3, Dickinson 1.
California—Dickinson 3, Lane 1
Oregon—Lane 3

Total number of votes, 252, Douglas, 151 1-2, Guthrie 16 1-2. Dickinson 4, Hunter 16, Lane 14, Davis 1. No choice.

FIFTY-SECOND VOTE FOR PRESIDENT.

Maine—Douglas 5, Guthrie 3.
New Hampshire—Douglas 5.
Vermont—Douglas 5.
Massachusetts—Douglas 6, Hunter 6, Davis 1.
Rhode Island—Douglas 4.
Connecticut—Douglas 3½, Guthrie 2½.
New York—Douglas 35.
Pennsylvania—Douglas 9½, Guthrie 17½.
Delaware—Hunter 2.
Maryland—Douglas 4 Guthrie 4.
Virginia—Douglas 1, Hunter 14.
North Carolina—Douglas 1, Lane 9.
Arkansas—Lane 1.
Missouri—Douglas 4½, Guthrie 4½.
Tennessee—Douglas 1, Guthrie 11.
Kentucky—Guthrie 12.
Ohio—Douglas 23.
Indiana—Douglas 13.
Illinois—Douglas 11.
Michigan—Douglas 6.
Wisconsin—Douglas 5.
Iowa—Douglas 4.
Minnesota—Douglas 3, Dickinson 1.
California—Dickinson 3, Lane 1.
Oregon—Lane 3.

Whole number of votes, 252. Douglas 151½, Guthrie 65½, Dickinson 4, Hunter 16, Lane 14, Davis 1. No choice.

FIFTY-THIRD VOTE FOR PRESIDENT.

Maine—Douglas 5, Guthrie 3.
New Hampshire—Douglas 5.
Vermont—Douglas 5.
Massachusetts—Douglas 6, Hunter 6. Davis 1.
Rhode Island—Douglas 4.
Connecticut—Douglas 3½, Guthrie 2½.
New York—Douglas 35.
New Jersey—Douglas 2. Guthrie 5.
Pennsylvania—Douglas 9 1-2, Guthrie 17 1-2.
Delaware—Hunter 2.
Maryland—Douglas 4, Guthrie 4.
Virginia—Douglas 1, Hunter 14.
North Carolina—Douglas 1, Lane 9.
Arkansas—Lane 1.
Missouri—Douglas 4 1-2, Guthrie 4 1-2.
Tennesee—Douglas 1, Guthrie 11.

Kentucky—Guthrie 12.
Ohio—Douglas 23.
Indiana—Douglas 13.
Illinois—Douglas 11.
Michigan—Douglas 6.
Wisconsin—Douglas 5.
Iowa—Douglas 4.
Minnesota—Douglas 3, Dickinson 1.
California—Dickinson 3, Lane 1.
Oregon—Lane 3.

Total vote 252. Douglas 151 1-2. Guthrie 65½. Dickinson 4, Hunter 16 Lane 14, Davis 1. No choice.

FIFTY-FOURTH VOTE FOR PRESIDENT.

Maine—Douglas 5, Guthrie 3.
New Hampshire—Douglas 5.
Vermont—Douglas 5.
Massachusetts—Douglas 6. Hunter 6, Davis 1.
Rhode Island—Douglas 4.
Connecticut—Douglas 3 1-2 Guthrie 2 1-2.
New York—Douglas 35.
New Jersey—Douglas 2, Guthrie 5.
Pennsylvania—Douglas 9 1-2, Guthrie 17 1-2.
Delaware—Hunter 2.
Maryland—Douglas 4, Guthrie 4.
Virginia—Douglas 1, Hunter 14.
North Carolina—Douglas 1, Lane 9.
Arkansas—Lane 1.
Missouri—Douglas, 4 1-2, Hunter 4 1-2.
Tennessee—Douglas 1. Guthrie 11.
Kentucky—Guthrie 12.
Ohio—Douglas 23.
Indiana—Douglas 13.
Illinois—Douglas 11.
Michigan—Douglas 6.
Wisconsin—Douglas 5.
Iowa—Douglas 4.
Minnesota—Douglas 3, Dickinson 1.
California—Dickinson 1, Lane 3.
Oregon—Lane 3.

Whole number of votes cast, 252—Douglas 151 1-2, Guthrie 61, Dickinson 2, Hunter 20,½ Lane 16 Davis 1. No choice.

Mr. GREEN, of North Carolina, moved that the Convention adjourn. The question was taken, and the motion did not prevail.

The Convention then proceeded to the 55th ballot for President, with the following result:

FIFTY-FIFTH VOTE FOR PRESIDENT.

Maine—Douglas 5, Guthrie 3.
New Hampshire—Douglas 5.
Vermont—Douglas 5
Massachusetts—Douglas 6, Guthrie 6, Davis 1.
Rhode Island—Douglas 4.
Connecticut—Douglas 3 1-2, Guthrie 2 1-2.
New York—Douglas 35.
New Jersey—Douglas 2, Guthrie 5.
Pennsylvania—Douglas 9 1-2, Guthrie 17 1-2.
Delaware—Hunter 2.
Maryland—Douglas 4. Guthrie 4.
Virginia—Douglas 1, Hunter 14.
North Carolina—Douglas 1, Lane 9.
Arkansas—Lane 1.
Missouri - Douglas 4 1-2, Guthrie 4 1-2.
Tennessee—Douglas 1, Guthrie 11.
Kentucky—Guthrie 12.
Ohio—Douglas 23
Indiana—Douglas 13.
Illinois—Douglas 11.
Michigan—Douglas 6.
Wisconsin—Douglas 5.
Iowa—Douglas 4.
Minnesota—Douglas 3, Dickinson 1.
California—Dickinson 3, Lane 1.
Oregon—Lane 3.

Whole number of votes cast. 252—Douglas 151½, Guthrie 65 1-2, Dickinson 4, Hunter 16, Lane 14, Davis 1. No choice.

FIFTY-SIXTH VOTE FOR PRESIDENT.

Maine—Douglas 5, Guthrie 3.
New Hampshire—Douglas 5.
Vermont—Douglas 5.
Massachusetts—Douglas 6, Guthrie 6, Davis 1.
Rhode Island—Douglas 4.
Connecticut—Douglas 3 1-2, Guthrie 2 1-2.
New York—Douglas 35.
New Jersey—Douglas 2, Guthrie 5.
Pennsylvania—Douglas 9 1-2, Guthrie 17 1-2.
Delaware—Hunter 2
Maryland—Douglas 4, Guthrie 4.
Virginia—Douglas 1, Hunter 14.
North Carolina—Douglas 1, Lane 9.
Arkansas—Lane 1.
Missouri—Douglas 4 1-2, Guthrie 4 1-2.
Tennessee—Douglas 1, Guthrie 11.
Kentucky—Guthrie 12.
Ohio—Douglas 23.
Indiana—Douglas 13.
Illinois—Douglas 11.
Michigan—Douglas 6.
Wisconsin—Douglas 5.
Iowa—Douglas 4.
Minnesota—Douglas 3, Dickinson 1.
California—Dickinson [illegible], Lane 1.
Oregon—Lane 3.

Whole number of votes 252. Douglas 151 1-2, Guthrie 65 1-2, Dickinson 4, Hunter 16, Lane 14, Davis 1. No choice.

FIFTY-SEVENTH VOTE FOR PRESIDENT.

Maine......Douglas 5. Guthrie 3.
New Hampshire..... Douglas 5.
Vermont......Douglas 5.
Massachusetts......Douglas 6, Guthrie 6, Davis 1.
Rhode Island......Douglas 4.
Connecticut......Douglas 3 1-2, Guthrie 2 1-2.
New York......Douglas 35.
New Jersey......Douglas 2, Guthrie 5.
Pennsylvania..... Douglas 9 1-2, Guthrie 17 1-2.
Delaware......Hunter 2.
Maryland......Douglas 4. Guthrie 4.
Virginia......Douglas 1, Hunter 14.
North Carolina......Douglas 1, Lane 9.
Arkansas......Lane 1.
Missouri......Douglas 4 1-2, Guthrie 4 1-2.
Tennessee......Douglas 1, Guthrie 11.
Kentucky......Guthrie 12.
Ohio......Douglas 23.
Indiana......Douglas 13.
Illinois..... Douglas 11.
Michigan......Douglas 6
Wisconsin......Douglas 5.
Iowa......Douglas 4
Minnesota......Douglas 3, Dickinson 1.
California......Dickinson 3, Lane 1.
Oregon...... Lane 3.

Douglas 151 1-2, Guthrie 65 1-2, Dickinson 4, Hunter 16, Lane 14, Davis 1.

Whole number of votes 252. Necessary to a choice, under the decision of the Convention, 202. No choice having been made,

Mr. ASHE, of North Carolina, moved that the Convention adjourn, and upon that motion he called for a vote by States.

Mr. GITTINGS, of Maryland, moved that when they adjourn, it be to meet at Baltimore, the first day of June next, and he called for a vote by States.

On motion of Mr. MONTGOMERY, the motion of Mr. Gittings was laid upon the table.

The question was then taken on Mr. ASHE's motion to adjourn, and it resulted as follows:—Yeas 148, nays 100.

The Convention then adjourned till Thursday morning at 10 o'clock.

TENTH DAY.

THURSDAY, MAY 3, 1860.

The Convention was called to order by the PRESIDENT at 10 o'clock, A. M.

Prayer was offered by the Rev. Mr. MICKLER.

On motion, the reading of yesterday's Journal was dispensed with.

Mr. RUSSELL, of Virginia, rose in his place and offered the following resolution, viz :

Resolved, That when this Convention adjourn to-day, it be adjourned to re-assemble at Baltimore, Maryland, on Monday, the 18th day of June next, and that it be respectfully recommended to the Democratic party of the several States to make provision for supplying all vacancies in their respective delegations to this Convention when it shall re-assemble.

Mr. ATKINS, of Tennessee, moved to amend the resolution by striking out "Baltimore," and inserting Philadelphia.

Mr. MASON, of Kentucky, raised a point of order, that the preceding question was the nomination of President and Vice President of the United States.

Mr. RUSSELL then moved that the pending question be laid upon the table. And upon this motion,

Mr. MASON called for a vote by States.

The vote to lay on the table was then had, and the following is the result:

	Yeas.	Nays.		Yeas.	Nays		Yeas.	Nays.
Maine	5	3	North Carolina	4	6	Ohio	23	0
New Hampshire	5	0	South Carolina	0	0	Indiana	13	0
Vermont	5	0	Georgia	0	0	Illinois	11	0
Massachusetts	7½	5½	Florida	0	0	Michigan	6	0
Rhode Island	4	0	Alabama	0	0	Wisconsin	5	0
Connecticut	6		Louisiana	0	0	Iowa	4	0
New York	35	0	Mississippi	0	0	Minnesota	3	1
New Jersey	7		Texas	0	0	California	0	4
Pennsylvania	27		Arkansas	1	0	Oregon	0	3
Delaware	0	0	Missouri	4½	4½			
Maryland	4	4	Tennessee	4½	7½		199	51
Virginia	14½	½	Kentucky		12			

So the motion to lay on the table was carried.

Mr. RUSSELL's resolution to adjourn was then called up and the reading commenced, when several gentlemen endeavored to get the floor.

Mr. PECK, of Michigan, raised a point of order, that nothing would be now in order until the reading of the resolution was completed.

The reading of the resolution was completed, and Hon. D. L. SEYMOUR, of New York, offered an amendment that the word New York be substituted for Baltimore.

Mr. RANDALL, of Pennsylvania, raised a point of order, and the President deemed Mr. Randall out of order in raising the point.

Several members then raised points of order.

Mr. RANDALL, of Pennsylvania, moved to amend the resolution by striking out the time and place, and inserting the 4th day of July, at Independence Hall, Philadelphia.

Mr. LUDLOW, of New York, called for the previous question.

The demand for the previous question was seconded.

The PRESIDENT then stated the question then before the Convention.

The first question, being on Mr. Seymour's amendment, was taken, and the amendment was lost.

The next question in order was the amendment offered by Mr. Atkins, of Tennessee, and a vote was called for by States.

The roll of States was called, and the following is the result of the vote: Ayes 86½, nays 166.

So the amendment was lost.

And the question then was upon the original Virginia resolution to adjourn to meet at Baltimore on the 18th day of June, 1860, and the State of New York called for a vote by States.

The roll of States was called, and the following is the result of the vote:

	Yeas.	Nays.		Yeas.	Nays.		Yeas.	Nays.
Maine	5	3	North Carolina		10	Ohio	23	
New Hampshire	5		South Carolina			Indiana	13	
Vermont	5		Georgia			Illinois	11	
Massachusetts	10	3	Florida			Michigan	6	
Rhode Island	4		Alabama			Wisconsin	5	
Connecticut	6		Louisiana			Iowa	4	
New York	35		Mississippi			Minnesota	3½	½
New Jersey	2	5	Texas			California		4
Pennsylvania	23½	3½	Arkansas	1		Oregon		3
Delaware			Missouri	6	3			
Maryland	5	3	Tennessee	7	5		194½	55
Virginia	14½	½	Kentucky		12			

So the Virginia resolution was adopted.

Mr. Stuart, of Michigan, moved that the Convention do now adjourn.

Mr. Miles, of Maryland, hoped that arrangements would be made for printing the official proceedings of the Convention.

The President asked permission, before putting the motion to adjourn, to address a few words to the Convention, and he proceeded as follows:

I desire first to say, and in saying it to bear testimony to your constituents and to the people of the United States, that considering the numerousness of this assembly, and the important interests involved in deliberations and the emotions thus naturally awakened in your bosoms,—considering all this, I say your sessions have been distinguished by order, by freedom from personalities, by decorum, and by an observance of parliamentary method and law. In competition for the floor, and in the zeal of gentlemen to promote their respective opinions by motions or objections to motions, in the lassitude of protracted sittings, occasions have occurred of apparent, but only apparent confusion. But there has been no real confusion, no deliberate violation of order. I am better able than any other person to speak knowingly on this point, and to speak impartially, and I say it with pride and pleasure, one thing especially proper for me to say from the Chair. I desire further to say, for and in behalf of myself, that I also know by knowledge of my own heart and conscience, that in the midst of circumstances always arduous, and in some respects peculiar embarrassments, it has been my steady purpose and constant endeavor to discharge impartially the duties of the Chair. If, in the execution of the duties, it shall have happened to me to address any gentleman abruptly, or not to have duly recognized him, I beg pardon of him and of the Convention. Finally, permit me to remind you, gentlemen, that not merely the fortunes of the great constitutional party which you represent, but the fortunes of the Constitution also are at stake on the acts of this Convention. During a period now of eighty-four years, we, the States of this Union, have been associated together, in one form or another, for objects of domestic order and foreign security. We have traversed side by side the wars of the Revolution and other and later wars,—through peace and war, through sunshine and storm. We have held our way manfully on until we have come to be a great Republic. Shall we cease to be such? I will not believe it. I will not believe that the noble work of our fathers is to be shattered—that this great Republic is to be but a name, but a history of a mighty people once existing, but existing no longer save as a shadowy memory or a monumental ruin by the side of the pathway of time. I fondly trust that we shall continue to march on forever, the hope of nations, as well in the old world as in the new, like the bright orbs of the firmament which roll on without rest, because bound for eternity—without haste, because predestined for eternity. So may it be with this glorious Confederacy of States. I pray you, therefore, gentlemen, in your return to your constituents, and to the bosoms of your families, to take with you as your guiding thought the sentiment of the Constitution and the Union, and with this I cordially bid you farewell until the prescribed re-assembling of the Convention.

Mr. Brent, in behalf of the city of Baltimore, tendered the hospitalities of that city to the members of the Convention.

The motion of Mr. Stuart to adjourn was then put, and the Convention adjourned to meet in the city of Baltimore, on the 18th day of June, 1860.

Democratic National Convention,

1860,

AT CHARLESTON AND BALTIMORE.

PROCEEDINGS AT BALTIMORE.

JUNE 18---23.

FIRST DAY.

MONDAY, JUNE 18, 1860.

THE National Democratic Convention, in accordance with the order of adjournment adopted at Charleston, re-assembled in the city of Baltimore, on the 18th day of June, 1860.

The Convention assembled at the Front Street Theater, the place selected for the holding thereof, at 10 o'clock A. M.

The President, Hon. CALEB CUSHING, directed the Secretary to call the roll of States, in order to ascertain if the delegates were present.

On the calling of the roll, the following States were found to be fully represented, viz: Maine, New Hampshire, Vermont, Massachusetts, Rhode Island, New York, New Jersey, Maryland, Virginia, North Carolina, Missouri, Ohio, Indiana, Illinois, Michigan, Wisconsin, Iowa, Minnesota, California, Oregon.

Connecticut was represented in part, there being some misunderstanding as to the hour of meeting. The Chairman of the delegation stated that the delegation would all be here by 12 o'clock.

Pennsylvania was represented with but two exceptions.

Two delegates were present from Delaware.

When the State of South Carolina was called, the Chair directed that only those States be called which were present at the adjournment of the Convention at Charleston; consequently, South Carolina, Georgia, Florida, Alabama, Louisiana, Mississippi, and Texas, were not called.

Subsequently, on a call of the States that were not represented in full, Connecticut and Kentucky were found to be fully represented.

At eleven o'clock A. M., the PRESIDENT said:

GENTLEMEN OF THE CONVENTION—The standing hour of adjournment has already passed. The Chair has been informed, however, that some misapprehension existed upon that point, and that some gentlemen supposed the hour of adjournment to be noon, whereas, in fact, it was ten o'clock A. M. In view of that uncertainty as to the understanding of members, the Chair will, in the first place, direct the Secretary to call the roll of States, in order to ascertain whether delegates are present, and after that, if they are present, will proceed to call the Convention to order for the purposes of business. Each Chairman, as his State is called, will be good enough to respond upon the question of fact whether his delegation be or be not present.

Mr. SAULSBURY, of Delaware. I understand that a portion of our delegation are unable to gain admission to the hall, from the fact that they have no tickets. I do not know what has been the order of this adjourned Convention in reference to issuing tickets, but I understand that some of the members are outside wishing admission who cannot get in, being refused by the doorkeeper. They cannot obtain tickets. I do not understand who issues tickets to this Convention. I would like the Chair to indicate by what authority tickets are issued, and how delegates may gain admission to the floor.

The PRESIDENT. The Chair will inform the gentleman from Delaware (Mr. Saulsbury) that, according to the usage established at Charleston, the tickets of the delegates were prepared in packages to be delivered to the chairmen of the respective delegations.

Mr. HOWARD, of Tennessee. I desire to make a motion in regard to the seats which I think will settle the matter. It is this: that the President—

A DELEGATE. The Convention is not in order.

The PRESIDENT. The Convention has not been called to order. The Secretary will again call the roll of the States reported as not fully represented.

The SECRETARY called the States aforesaid, and they were reported now full.

The PRESIDENT then called the Convention to order, stating that the hour for opening had already passed, the reason for such postponement being that there was a misunderstanding as to the hour. Some having thought that noon was the appointed time, whereas ten o'clock was the time. He announced that the Convention would be opened with prayer.

The opening prayer, by Rev. JOHN McCRON, was delivered as follows:

O Thou, who sittest upon the circle of the earth and observest the children of men—in whom our fathers trusted and were not confounded—by whose gracious assistance they wrenched the liberties of these confederated commonwealths from the iron grasp of unsympathizing power—to Thee we offer the grateful homage of our hearts and lips for the glorious inheritance which they have bequeathed to us. "Our lines are fallen to us in pleasant places—yea, we have a goodly heritage." We recognize Thy hand in the national blessings we enjoy, and we pray Thee to accept the praises that we bring, for a little one has now become a thousand and commands the admiration of the world.

And we pray Thee, O God, that the compact Thou hast blessed may be perpetuated in all its integrity and beauty by the cement of Thy favor, and in the shadow of the impenetrable shield of the guardianship of Omnipotence. To this end we beseech Thee to give us the wisdom that cometh from above, so that we may always place the administration of national affairs in hands that are pure and competent to discharge the obligations involved in the trust.

And as the waters of the political deep are agitated by the rising tempest of sectional discord, give the spirit of a large and liberal forbearance to every one, that "peace may be within our walls and prosperity within our palaces." May the hatchet of strife be buried and the damps of its sepulchre destroy its temper and corrode its edge, and the calumet of fraternal peace pass continually from hand to hand throughout the States and Territories of our beloved Confederacy.

And as this Convention has met to consider the interests vital to our country, and to select from their fellow-citizens candidates for Executive authority, give the healthful spirit of thy grace, that the result may redound to Thy honor and to the welfare of the land of our love. Say, in Thy mercy, "Land of the Pilgrim, may thy glory brighten! Land of Washington, may thy freedom be eternal! Land of Charity, may Thy hand never lack the means to gratify thy benevolent desires! May thy soil never be trodden by the foot of an invader, nor the walls of thy hamlets echo the war-whoop of conquest."

Our Father, who art in Heaven, hallowed be thy Name. Thy kingdom come; Thy will be done on earth as it is in Heaven; give us this day our daily bread; forgive us our trespasses as we forgive them who trespass against us; lead us not into temptation, but deliver us from evil; for thine is the kingdom, the power and glory, forever. Amen.

At the conclusion of the prayer, Mr. CUSHING proceeded to address the Convention as follows:

GENTLEMEN OF THE CONVENTION:—Permit me, in the first place, to congratulate you upon your being re-assembled here for the discharge of your important duties in the interests of the Democratic party of the United States, and I beg leave, in the second place, to communicate to the Convention the state of the various branches of its business, as they now come up for consideration before you.

Prior to the adjournment of the Convention, two principal subjects of action were before it. One, the adoption of the doctrinal resolutions constituting the platform of the Convention; the other, voting upon the question of the nomination of a candidate for the Presidency.

In the course of the discussion of the question of a platform, the Convention adopted a vote, the effect of which was to amend the report of the majority of the Committee on the Platform by substituting the report of the minority of that Committee; and after the adoption of that motion, and the substitution of the minority for the majority report, a division was called for upon the several resolutions constituting that platform, being five in number. The 1st, 3d, 4th, and 5th of those resolutions were adopted by the Convention, and the 2d was rejected. After the vote on the adoption of the 1st, 3d, 4th and 5th of those resolutions, a motion was made in each case to reconsider the vote, and to lay that motion of reconsideration upon the table. But neither of those motions to reconsider or to lay on the table was put, the putting of these motions having been prevented by the intervention of questions of privilege, and the ultimate vote competent in such case, to wit: of the adoption of the report of the majority as amended by the report of the minority, had not been acted upon by the Convention. So that at the time when the Convention adjourned there remained pending before it these motions, to wit: To reconsider—the resolutions constituting the platform, and the ulterior question of adopting the majority as amended by the substitution of the minority report. Those questions, and those only, as the Chair understood the motions before the Convention, were not acted upon prior to the adjournment.

After the disposition of the intervening questions of privilege, a motion was made by Mr. MCCOOK, of Ohio, to proceed to vote for candidates for President and Vice President. Upon that motion the Convention instructed the Chair (not, as has been erroneously supposed, in the recess of the Convention, the Chair determining for the Convention, but the Convention instructing the Chair,) to make no declaration of a nomination except upon a vote equivalent to two-thirds in the Electoral College of the United States, and upon that balloting, no such vote being given, that order was, upon the motion of the gentleman from Virginia, (Mr. Russell,) laid on the table, for the purpose of enabling him to propose a motion, which he subsequently did, that the Convention adjourn from the city of Charleston to the city of Baltimore, and with a provision concerning the filling of vacancies embraced in the same resolution, which resolution the Secretary will please to read.

The SECRETARY read the resolution, as follows:

"*Resolved*, That when this Convention adjourns to-day, it adjourns to re-assemble at Baltimore, Md., on Monday, the 18th day of June, and that it be respectfully recommended to the Democratic party of the several States to make provision for supplying all vacancies in their respective delegations to this Convention when it shall re-assemble."

The PRESIDENT. The Convention will thus perceive that the order adopted by it provided, among other things, that it is respectfully recommended to the Democratic party of the several States to make provision for supplying all vacancies in their respective delegations to this Convention when it shall re-assemble. What is the construction of that resolution?—what is the scope of its application?—is a question not for the Chair to determine or to suggest to the Convention, but for the Convention itself to determine.

However that may be, in the preparatory arrangement for the present assembling of this Convention there were addressed to the Chair the credentials of members elected, or purporting to be elected, affirmed and confirmed by the original Conventions and accredited to this Convention. In three of those cases, or perhaps four, the credentials were authentic and complete, presenting no question of controverting delegates. In four others, to wit—the States of Georgia, Alabama, Louisiana, and Delaware, there were contesting applications. Upon those applications the Chair was called to determine whether it possessed any power to determine *prima facie* membership of this Convention. That question was presented in its most absolute and complete form in the case of Mississippi, where there was no contest either through irregularity of form or of competing delegations, and so also in the cases of Florida, Texas, and Arkansas. In those four States, there being an apparent authenticity of commission, the Chair was called upon to determine the naked abstract question whether he had power, peremptorily and preliminarily, to determine the *prima facie* membership of all alleged members of this Convention. The Chair would gladly have satisfied himself that he had this power, but upon examining the source of his power, to wit—the rules of the House of Representatives, he was unable to discern that he had any authority, even *prima facie*, to scrutinize and canvass credentials, although they were such as, upon their face, were free from contest or controversy, either of form or of substance, and therefore he deemed it his duty to reserve the determination of that question to be submittd to the Convention. And in due time the Chair will present that question as one of privilege to this body.

And now, gentlemen, having thus presented to you the exact state of the questions pending or involved in the action of the Convention when it adjourned, the Chair begs leave only to add a single observation of a more general nature. We assemble here now at a time when the enemies of the Democratic party—when, let me say, the enemies of the Constitution of the United States, are in the field (applause) with their selected leaders, with their banners displayed, advancing to the combat with the constitutional interests and party of the United States; and upon you, gentlemen, upon your action, upon your spirit of harmony, upon your devotion to the Constitution, upon your solicitude to maintain the interests, the honor and the integrity of the Democratic party as the guardians of the Constitution—upon you, gentlemen, it depends whether the issue of that combat is to be victory or defeat for the Constitution of the United States. (Renewed applause.)

It does not become the Chair to discuss any of the personal or political demands of that question. It may be permitted, however, to exhort you in the spirit of our community, of party interests, in the faith of our common respect for the Constitution, in the sense of our common devotion to the interests and honor of our country; I say to exhort you to feel that we come here this day not to determine any mere technical questions of form, not merely to gain personal or party triumphs, but we come here in the exercise of a solemn duty, in a crisis of the condition of the affairs of our country, such as has never yet befallen the United States. Shall we not all enter upon this duty in the solemn and profound conviction of the responsibilities thus devolved upon us, of our high duty to our country, to ourselves, and to the States of this Union? (Applause.) Gentlemen, the Convention is now in order for the transaction of business.

Mr. HOWARD, of Tennessee, had taken the floor for the purpose of making a motion.

Mr. HOWARD, of Tennessee, offered the following resolution:

Resolved, That the President of this Convention direct the Sergeant-at-Arms to issue tickets of admission to the delegates of the Convention as originally constituted and organized at Charleston.

Mr. KAVANAGH, of Minnesota. I move to lay the resolution upon the table, and upon that I call for a vote by States.

Mr. RUSSELL, of Virginia. I rise to ask a few questions of the Chair for information. I suppose they relate to a privileged question, so that I am entitled to ask them, notwithstanding the motion which has been made. I would ask the Chair if he has not undertaken to decide that the gentlemen who have seats here as delegates from the State of Virginia have a right to sit here? If he has undertaken to decide that question, I ask him to state to this Convention upon what ground he has decided that we are entitled to be here? I ask him to state if it was upon the ground that we had appeared and been recognized as proper delegates to this Convention when it was formerly in session? If he acted upon that ground with regard to the delegates from Virginia, and other delegates here, I ask him to state, for our information, why he has not, upon the same ground, issued tickets to all those formerly seated in this Convention with uncontested seats, or with seats which, if they were contested, were decided to be properly occupied by those gentlemen? I ask the Chair to state whether he has undertaken, in consequence of any action which those delegates themselves have taken, or in consequence of any rumored or reported action elsewhere in the country, to decide that they have deprived themselves of the right to return, as we have returned, with the permission of the Chair? I desire the Chair to state whether the same grounds do not apply, in his opinion, to all those delegations with uncontested seats here, as to Virginia?

The PRESIDENT. With the permission of the Convention, the Chair will respond to the questions of the gentleman from Virginia (Mr. Russell,) if it be understood by the Convention that it is competent for the Chair to do so, pending the motion of the gentleman from Minnesota (Mr. Kavanagh) to lay on the table the resolution of the gentleman from Tennessee (Mr. Howard.)

Mr. STUART, of Michigan. I hope there will be unanimous consent given to the Cnair, but with the understanding that neither the Chair nor the gentleman from Virginia (Mr. Russell) had the right to make any statement in the present condition of the business. (Cries of "leave," "leave.")

The PRESIDENT. The Chair will then state, in response to the inquiry of the gentleman from Virginia (Mr. Russell,) that the Chair did not undertake to judge anything, neither to decide that there were or were not vacancies. All the Chair undertook to say was that the gentlemen borne upon its roll as members of this Convention at the time of its adjournment at Charleston, were entitled to recognition of membership precisely to-day as they would had the Convention adjourned yesterday. [Applause.] To have gone beyond this point would have been to enter into the canvass of conflicting credentials upon new elections of members. The Chair was thoroughly convinced that he had no power to enter into that inquiry of conflicting credentials of persons alleging to have been elected to this Convention by State Conventions held since the adjournment of this Convention at Charleston. The Chair will suggest to the gentleman from Virginia that the question did not present itself in the form of simplicity and unity in which his inquiry would suppose, inasmuch as several States to which he refers, did not assume that the resolution in the adjournment created vacancies to be filled by new action of the respective States; and if the Chair had entered into any inquiry of the new credentials, as for instance to discriminate upon the question whether these credentials came from a new State Convention called anew, and that Convention vacating anterior commissions; or whether they emanate from a Convention called anew and simply confirming anterior commissions;—in either case if the Chair had gone into the question it would have been necessary for him to hold hearings and investigations of credentials and of facts in regard to eight States of the Union, as to which he had no more power under the rules of the House of Representatives than any other member of the Convention.

Whilst the Chair is disposed to exert the whole power, in any contingency, of the Speaker of the House of Representatives—having entered upon the discharge of this most unwelcome and responsible duty with a determination to act without favor and also without fear—yet the Chair knows that it is impossible that he shall maintain order in this Convention, that the deliberations of this Convention shall go on in any system of regularity, unless the Chair takes care to walk carefully and rigorously in the simple line of routine and of technical authority. [Applause.] Within the line of technical authority, and upon the rules of the House of Representatives, as constituting the guide of the Chair, the Chair will take leave to decide all questions as they may arise, in or out of the Convention. But the Chair does not propose to assume any judicial or quasi-judicial authority in regard to the canvass of credentials and the authenticity of membership; an authority manifestly not conferred upon the presiding officer, according to precedent and the uniform usage, of the two houses of the Congress of the United States never preliminarily determined by the presiding officer of either house of Congress. In issuing tickets to the gentlemen borne on the roll of the Convention, already sufficiently authenticated by the proceedings of the Convention itself, at the time of adjournment the Chair did that at least which was in the sphere of the duties of the Chair; and in doing that he in no degree involved or prejudiced the question of what was the right of any gentleman; that depending upon the action of this Convention. The Chair, as he before intimated, will now make this the first question, a question of privilege, that the Convention may instruct the Chair regarding his duty concerning the delegations of the other States.

Mr. CHURCH, of New York. I will ask the gentleman from Minnesota, (Mr. Kavanagh) to withdraw his motion to lay the resolution of the gentleman from Tennessee (Mr. Howard) upon the table, in order to enable me to offer an amendment which I think will dispose of this whole matter of contested seats.

Mr. KAVANAGH. The gentleman can read his amendment even if my motion is not withdrawn.

The PRESIDENT. If the gentleman insists upon his motion to lay upon the table, it will not be in order for any proposition to be read.

Mr. JOHN COCHRAN, of New York, asked consent of the Convention that the resolution be read for information.

No objection being made, the proposed amendment of Mr. Church was read as follows:

Resolved, That the credentials of all persons claiming seats in this Convention made vacant by the secession of delegates at Charleston be referred to the Committee on Credentials, and said Committee is hereby instructed, as soon as practicable, to examine the same and report the names of persons entitled to such seats, with the district—understanding, however, that every person accepting a seat in this Convention is bound in honor and faith to abide by the action of this Convention and support its nominations.

Mr. KAVANAGH, of Minnesota. I will withdraw my motion to lay upon the table, and accept the amendment of the gentleman from New York (Mr. Church,) and upon that I call the previous question

Mr. Saulsbury. I rise to a privileged question. It must be apparent to the whole Convention that its fate, and the fate of the whole party, depends upon that resolution. I think I have indicated as far as—

Mr. Kavanagh. I rise to a question of order. The gentleman from Delaware rose to a privileged question. I believe he is attempting to make a general speech on politics, and I hold that that is not a privileged question, even in a Democratic Convention.

Mr. Saulsbury. The question is debatable.

The President. The gentleman from Delaware will please to pause. The Chair does not understand that any debatable question is pending. The gentleman from New York (Mr. Church,) by unanimous consent had leave to read an amendment. That having been read, conversation occurred upon the applause in the galleries. That conversation having ceased, the question recurs upon the motion of the gentleman from Minnesota (Mr. Kavanagh) upon laying the resolution of the gentleman from Tennessee (Mr. Howard) on the table.

Mr. Saulsbury. My privileged question is this, that the Convention has no right to prescribe terms to its members, which terms are not made in the authority of the States from which they come. The resolution proposes to annex a condition to the admission of delegates to this floor. I wish to say—

Mr. Kavanagh. Is that a privileged question?

Mr. Saulsbury. I am perfectly in order. I say I come here intending, if this Convention makes any nomination [calls to order] to support it.

The President. The gentleman from Minnesota again calls the gentleman from Delaware to order. The Chair begs leave to state that the suggestions the gentleman from Delaware is making are substantially arguments in opposition to the amendment of the gentleman from New York, (Mr. Church,) and would be in order if the motion to lay on the table were not pending.

Mr. Montgomery, of Pennsylvania. I understand that the resolution of the gentleman from New York was accepted by the gentleman from Minnesota, who withdrew his motion to lay the resolution of the gentleman from Tennessee (Mr. Howard) on the table, and called the previous question upon that amendment.

The President. The Chair was unaware that any such action had been taken by the gentleman from Minnesota. The gentleman from Minnesota will be good enough to state whether he did accept the amendment of the gentleman from New York, and move the previous question upon it.

Mr. Kavanagh. Upon the request of the gentleman from New York I withdrew the call for the previous question—accepted the gentleman's amendment, and moved the previous question on that amendment.

Mr. Phillips, of Pennsylvania. It is not in the power of the gentleman to accept the amendment. In the first place, his motion was to lay upon the table, not to amend. In the next place, the resolution of the gentleman from Tennessee was read for information, and was not presented to the body. It was read by leave, while the motion to lay on the table was pending, which was not debatable. The gentleman did say he accepted it, but he had no power to do so. If he had been the mover of the original motion, he might have done so, not otherwise. He only, therefore, withdrew his motion to lay on the table, and that being done, and the floor being yielded, it was in order for the gentleman from New York to offer his amendment.

The President decided both points of order raised by Mr. Phillips well taken.

Mr. Church, of New York. I would inquire of the Chair if it is now in order for me to offer an amendment to the resolution of the gentleman from Tennessee? (Mr. Howard.)

The President. If the gentleman from Minnesota (Mr. Kavanagh) states to the Chair that he withdraws his motion to lay upon the table, and his motion for the previous question, then the Chair will rule that the gentleman from New York (Mr. Church) is in order. He can move his proposition as an amendment.

Mr. KAVANAGH. I do withdraw those motions.

The CHAIR. The gentleman from New York (Mr. Church) is now in order.

Mr. CHURCH. Then I move the resolution which has been read as an amendment to the resolution of the gentleman from Tennessee (Mr. Howard), and upon that I call the previous question.

Mr. GILMORE, of Pennsylvania. I wish to offer an amendment to the amendment.

The PRESIDENT. That will not be in order pending a call for the previous question.

Mr. RANDALL, of Pennsylvania. I understand that there is now before the Convention a proposition of the gentleman from New York (Mr. Church). As it is a distinct proposition, I desire to say a few words upon it.

The PRESIDENT decided Mr. Randall not to be in order in his remarks.

Mr. RANDALL, of Pennsylvania. As the proposition before the Convention contains two distinct propositions, I call for a division of the question.

The PRESIDENT. The Chair cannot entertain any proposition at this time.

Mr. AVERY, of North Carolina, called for a division of the question.

Mr. MONTGOMERY, of Pennsylvania. I rise to a point of order that there can be no division now, as the previous question has been demanded.

The PRESIDENT. The Chair begs leave to state to the gentleman from Pennsylvania (Mr. Montgomery) that he is perfectly correct. The Chair has already determined that it is the duty of the Chair first to call for a second to the demand for the previous question.

Mr. ———, of Tennessee. I rise to a point of order that there is no Committee on Credentials to which to refer this matter.

The PRESIDENT. The Chair will inform the gentleman from Tennessee that that is not a question of order but of substance, and that the Convention may at any time revive the Committee on Credentials by an order of reference. The duty of the Chair now is to put the question upon seconding the demand for the previous question.

The question was stated to be upon seconding the demand for the previous question. Being taken *viva voce*,

The PRESIDENT stated that the noes appeared to have it.

Mr. RICHARDSON, of Illinois, doubted the announcement, and asked that the vote be taken by States, which was ordered.

Mr. BRODHEAD, of Pennsylvania, stated that the gentleman from New York (Mr. Church) was willing to withdraw his call for the previous question.

Mr. MONTGOMERY, of Pennsylvania. The vote having been ordered to be taken by States, it is not now in order to withdraw the call for the previous question.

The PRESIDENT. The Chair will suggest to the gentleman from New York (Mr. Church) that the previous question having been demanded, the Chair put the question to the Convention whether they seconded that demand, and in the judgment of the Chair it was negatived. Thereupon the gentleman from Illinois (Mr. Richardson) called for the verification of that vote by States. After the vote thus made and taken, the Chair does not understand that it is competent to withdraw the call for the previous question.

Mr. SAULSBURY, of Delaware, moved that the Convention take a recess until four o'clock this afternoon.

Mr. SAMUELS, of Iowa, appealed to the gentleman from Delaware (Mr. Saulsbury) to withdraw his motion for one moment. If, after the suggestion he desired to make, the gentleman desired the motion for a recess, he would renew it.

Mr. SAULSBURY said he would withdraw upon that condition.

Mr. MONTGOMERY, of Pennsylvania, objected to any suggestions or discussions.

Mr. RYNDERS, of New York, rose to a point of order that the motion to take a recess having been withdrawn, the demand for the previous question was then operative, and no debate was in order.

The PRESIDENT sustained the point of order.

Mr. SAMUELS, of Iowa. Then I will renew the motion for a recess, though I shall vote against it.

Mr. LUDLOW, of New York, called for a vote by States upon this motion, which was ordered.

The SECRETARY proceeded to call the roll of States on the motion to take a reeess till four o'clock, which resulted as follows :

	Yeas.	Nays		Yeas.	Nays.		Yeas.	Nays.
Maine	1½	6½	North Carolina	10		Ohio		23
New Hampshire	½	4½	South Carolina			Indiana		13
Vermont		5	Georgia			Illinois		11
Massachusetts		13	Florida			Michigan		6
Rhode Island		4	Alabama			Wisconsin		5
Connecticut	1	5	Louisiana			Iowa		4
New York		35	Mississippi			Minnesota	1½	2½
New Jersey	5	2	Texas			California	4	
Pennsylvania	6	21	Arkansas		1	Oregon	3	
Delaware	3		Missouri	6½	2½			
Maryland	6	2	Tennessee	8½	3¼		73¼	178¼
Virginia	15		Kentucky	3	9			

So the motion to take a recess was lost, and the question being then taken by States upon recording the demand for the previous question, it was not agreed to. Yeas 107½, nays 140½, as follows :

	Yeas	Nays.		Yeas.	Nays.		Yeas	Nays
Maine	6	2	North Carolina	10		Ohio	23	
New Hampshire	5		South Carolina			Indiana	13	
Vermont	4½	½	Georgia			Illinois	11	
Massachusetts	4½	4¼	Florida			Michigan	6	
Rhode Island		4	Alabama			Wisconsin	5	
Connecticut	3½	2	Louisiana			Iowa	4	
New York		35	Mississippi			Minnesota	2½	1½
New Jersey	2¼	4½	Texas			California		4
Pennsylvania	9¼	16½	Arkansas		1	Oregon		3
Delaware		2	Missouri	2¼	6½			
Maryland	2	6	Tennessee	3	8		108¼	14[illegible]¼
Virginia		15	Kentucky	1¼	10½			

The question was then stated to be upon the amendment to the amendment.

Mr. GILMORE, of Pennsylvania, offered the following amendment to Mr. Church's resolution :

Resolved, That the President of the Convention be directed to issue tickets of admission to seats in the Convention to the delegates from the States of Texas, Florida, Mississippi and Arkansas, in which States there are no contesting delegations.

Mr. RANDALL, of Pennsylvania. I believe it will be better for the harmony of this body that we should now take a recess, but I do not desire to contravene the wishes of the Convention. If it is understood that I shall be entitled to the floor, I will move that this Convention now take a recess till four o'clock this afternoon.

Mr. SPINOLA, of New York, moved that the Convention adjourn till ten o'clock A. M. to-morrow.

Mr. RANDALL, of Pennsylvania. At the request of several friends, I accept the modification of the gentleman from New York (Mr. Spinola.)

The motion to adjourn was put, and the President decided it to be lost, and a division was called for, and

Mr. SPINOLA, of New York, called for a vote by States, which was ordered, and the following is the result of the vote. Yeas 35, nays 216.

So the motion to adjourn was not agreed to.

Mr. PHILLIPS, of Pennsylvania, then moved that the Convention take a recess until five o'clock P. M., which motion was agreed to, and the Convention took a recess.

EVENING SESSION.

The Convention was called to order at five o'clock.

The PRESIDENT said: Mr. Randall, of Pennsylvania, has the floor, upon an amendment moved by Mr. Gilmore, of Pennsylvania. Before proceeding in the debate, the Chair begs leave to state to the Convention that he has had placed in his hands credentials of gentlemen claiming seats in the Convention from the States of Delaware, Georgia, Alabama, Florida, Mississippi, Louisiana, Texas and Arkansas, including in that enumeration the letter presented to the Convention in his place, by Mr Howard, of Tennessee, in behalf of the gentlemen claiming seats from the State of Mississippi, and in addition to that, there has been addressed to the Chair a communication from Mr. Chaffee, claiming a seat from the State of Massachusetts. The Chair deems it his duty to communicate the fact to the Convention that those several documents have been placed in his hands, to be presented at the proper time to the consideration of the Convention.

Mr. GILMORE, of Pennsylvania. I have made a small addition to the amendment I offered this morning to the amendment of the gentleman from New York (Mr. Church), for the purpose of covering the cases mentioned by the Chair just now.

The amendment, as modified, was read as follows:

Resolved, That the President of the Convention be authorized to issue tickets of admission to seats in this Convention to the delegates from the States of Arkansas, Texas, Florida and Mississippi, in which States there are no contesting delegations, and that in those States, to wit: Delaware, Georgia, Alabama, and Louisiana, where there are contesting delegations, a Committee on Credentials shall be appointed, by the several delegations, to report upon said States.

Mr. CLARK, of Missouri, called for the reading of the original resolution, and the amendment of the gentleman from New York (Mr. Church). They were accordingly read.

Mr. CLARK. I will now ask that my friend from Pennsylvania (Mr. Gilmore) accept as a substitute for his amendment what I will send to the Chair to be read for information. If it be accepted it will then stand in the condition of an amendment to an amendment.

Objections were made to the modification of Mr. Gilmore's resolution, and also to Mr. Clark's proposition being read.

Mr. GILMORE. Then, for the purpose of arranging all difficulties, I ask to withdraw the amendment I offered this morning, and substitute the one I have just offered, and which has been read.

The question was stated to be upon the amendment to the amendment as modified.

Mr. CLARK of Missouri. I ask that my amendment be read, that the gentleman from Pennsylvania (Mr. Gilmore) may accept it in lieu of his own, if he prefers it.

Mr. SAMUELS, of Iowa, said he would withdraw the objection he had made in order that the Convention may ascertain what the proposition is.

The proposition was then read, as follows: Strike out the proviso in the amendment of Mr. Church, of New York, and add the following:

Resolved, That the citizens of the several States of the Union have an equal right to settle and remain in the Territories of the United States, and to hold therein, unmolested by any legislation whatever, their slave and other property; and that this Convention recognizes the opinion of the Supreme Court of the United States in the Dred Scott case as a true exposition of the Constitution in regard to the rights of the citizens of the several States and Territories of the United States upon all subjects concerning which it treats; and that the members of this Convention pledge themselves, and require all others who may be authorized as delegates, to make the same pledge, to support the Democratic candidates, fairly and in good faith, nominated by this Convention according to the usages of the National Democratic Party.

Mr. COCHRAN, of New York. What is the position of this proposition just read?

The PRESIDENT. It was read merely for information.

The question was stated to be upon the amendment to the amendment, when Mr. Randall, of Pennsylvania, addressed the Convention.

Mr. RICHARDSON, of Illinois, addressed the Convention on the proposition submitted.

MR. GILMORE opposed its adoption.

Mr. COCHRAN, of New York, addressed the Convention upon the several propositions under consideration, and opposed the amendment of Mr. Gilmore.

Mr. RUSSELL, of Virginia, addressed the Convention, and was in favor of the adoption of the amendment offered by Mr. Gilmore.

Mr. MONTGOMERY addressed the Convention in opposition to the last amendment offered, and in favor of the resolution offered by Mr. Church, of New York.

Mr. EWING, of Tennessee, addressed the Convention.

Mr. CLAIBORNE, of Missouri. With the permission of my friend from Tennessee (Mr. Ewing), I will say that it has been hinted by the gentleman from Virginia (Mr. Russell), and repeated by the gentleman from Tennessee (Mr. Ewing) that there is no contest before this Convention as to the seats claimed by the delegates from Arkansas, who held seats in the National Democratic Convention at Charleston. I will ask the President of this Convention if he has has not this day received evidence of the fact that there is a contest here about the seats of the delegation from Arkansas?

A communication to the President of the Convention was then read, and

Mr. CLAIBORNE asked if there was not another paper from the delegation of Arkansas? One was sent by a messenger to the President, by Gen. Rust, of Arkansas, this morning.

The PRESIDENT, after examining the file of papers before him, stated that no such communication had been received.

Mr. EWING, of Tennessee, resumed his remarks.

Mr. LORING, of Massachusetts, addressed the Convention in favor of the second amendment.

Mr. MERRICK, of Illinois, addressed the Convention in favor of the amendment offered by Mr. Church, and in opposition to the amendment offered by Mr. Gilmore.

Mr. SAMUELS asked the President whether there were any credentials presented to him from the Florida delegation? He had understood they did not ask for an admission.

The PRESIDENT. The delegation have placed in my hands a published report in one of the journals of Florida, of the proceedings of the Convention in that State.

Mr. SAMUELS. Are they accredited to this Convention?

The PRESIDENT. I do not know. The gentleman can have them read.

Mr. KING, of Missouri, claimed the floor, and the Florida proceedings were not read. Mr. King then addressed the Convention in opposition to the second amendment.

Mr. WEST, of Connecticut, addressed the Convention in opposition to the amendment of Mr. Gilmore.

Mr. HUNTER, of Missouri, addressed the Convention in favor of the Gilmore amendment.

Mr. AVERY, of North Carolina, addressed the Convention in favor of the Gilmore amendment.

Mr. ATKINS, of Tennessee, addressed the Convention at some length, and then moved the previous question.

Mr. MOFFATT, of Virginia, moved that the Convention do now adjourn, which motion was not agreed to.

The vote seconding the demand for the previous question was then put, and a vote by States was demanded, and the demand for the previous question was recorded by the following vote, viz : yeas 233, nays 18½.

The question was then announced to be on ordering the previous question to be put, when,

On motion of Mr. RICHARDSON, of Illinois, the Convention adjourned.

SECOND DAY.

TUESDAY, JUNE 19, 1860.

The Convention was called to order at 10½ o'clock A. M., by the President, Hon. CALEB CUSHING.

Prayer was offered by the Rev. Dr. FULLER, of Baltimore.

On motion of Mr. LUDLOW, of New York, the reading of the Journal of Monday was dispensed with.

The PRESIDENT stated the question to be upon ordering the main question to be put, the demand for the previous question having been seconded yesterday upon the amendment of Mr. Gilmore, of Pennsylvania, to the amendment of Mr. Church, of New York, to the resolution of Mr. Howard, of Tennessee.

Mr. CHURCH, of New York. I desire to ask the unanimous consent for the purpose of submitting a proposition calculated to harmonize all the questions now pending before the Convention. (Cries of "hear," "hear.")

Upon a consultation with the gentleman who moves an amendment to my amendment (Mr. Gilmore, of Pennsylvania), he has agreed, if it meets with the approbation of this Convention, for the purpose of harmonizing the action of this Convention, to an arrangement alike honorable to both sides, and which, if carried out, will terminate the controversy as to all pending questions. The proposition which has been made and accepted is simply this : The gentleman from Pennsylvania (Mr. Gilmore), is to withdraw his amendment to my amendment, and then I am to withdraw the latter part of my resolution, leaving only a simple resolution of reference to the Committee on Credentials. I will now ask the unanimous consent of the Convention for the purpose of carrying out that understanding.

The PRESIDENT. The Chair will suggest to the gentleman from New York (Mr. Church), and to the Convention, that, as there has been a second to the demand for the previous question, the object which he proposes can only be reached either by putting the vote upon the main question and rejecting it, or by the unanimous consent of the Convention.

No objection being heard, unanimous consent was granted.

Mr. Gilmore, of Pennsylvania. For the purpose of carrying out the arrangement that has just been announced, I beg leave to withdraw my amendment to the amendment of the gentleman from New York (Mr. Church).

The amendment of Mr. Gilmore was as follows:

Resolved, That the President of the Convention be directed to issue tickets of admission to seats in the Convention to the delegates from the States of Texas, Florida, Mississippi and Arkansas, in which States there are no contesting delegations.

The amendment to the amendment was accordingly withdrawn.

Mr. Church, of New York. For the purpose of perfecting the arrangement, I will now modify my resolution by striking out the latter part of it, leaving it simply a resolution of reference to the Committee on Credentials.

The reading of the original resolution of Mr. Howard, of Tennessee, together with the amendment of Mr. Church, of New York, as proposed yesterday, was called for, and they were read as follows:

Mr. Howard's original resolution:

Resolved, That the President of this Convention direct the Sergeant-at-Arms to issue tickets of admission to the delegates of the Convention as originally constituted and organized at Charleston.

Mr. Church's amendment:

Resolved, That the credentials of all persons claiming seats in this Convention made vacant by the secession of delegates at Charleston, be referred to the Committee on Credentials; and said Committee is hereby instructed, as soon as practicable, to examine the same, and report the names of persons entitled to such seats, with the distinct understanding, however, that every person accepting a seat in this Convention is bound in honor and good faith to abide by the action of this Convention and support its nominees.

The amendment, as modified by Mr. Church, was then read as follows:

Resolved, That the credentials of all persons claiming seats in this Convention made vacant by the secession of delegates at Charleston, be referred to the Committee on Credentials, and said Committee is hereby instructed, as soon as practicable, to examine the same and report the names of persons entitled to such seats.

The President. The next question is, Shall the main question now be put upon the modified amendment which occupies the place of the original before the modification was made.

The question being taken, the main question was unanimously ordered.

The question recurred upon the amendment of Mr. Church, of New York, as modified.

Mr. Ward, of Ohio. I desire, before the question is put, to inquire what the exact question is? I desire now to know whether that is a substitute for the original proposition, or merely an addition by way of amendment to it.

The President. The Chair will state that he understands the question to be upon the substitution of the proposition of the gentleman from New York, for the original proposition of the gentleman from Tennessee.

The question being then taken on the amendment of Mr. Church, of New York, was agreed to, and the resolution of Mr. Howard, of Tennessee, as amended, was adopted.

Mr. Cochran, of New York, made a motion to reconsider the last vote and to lay the motion to reconsider on the table, which was agreed to.

Mr McCook, of Ohio, moved that the Convention do now adjourn.

Mr. Hallett, of Massachusetts, rose to a question of privilege.

Mr. Stuart, of Michigan. There can be no higher question of privilege than that of adjournment.

The President. The gentleman is right, but the Chair suggests that he understands the explanation of the gentleman from Massachusetts to relate to a contested seat in that delegation.

Mr. BRODHEAD moved to amend the motion to adjourn by inserting "to 5 o'clock this afternoon."

The PRESIDENT. The motion to adjourn is not amendable.

Mr. PHILLIPS, of Pennsylvania. I move that when this Convention adjourn to-day it be to meet at 5 o'clock this afternoon.

The PRESIDENT. The Chair is of opinion that that motion is in order.

Mr. STUART. I beg leave to suggest that that motion cannot be in order.

Mr. MONTGOMERY, of Pennsylvania. I would state to the Convention that the delegation from Massachusetts desire, before the House adjourns, to submit a proposition. There is a contested seat in that delegation, and it may as well be disposed of at once. I would suggest to my colleague (Mr. Phillips) that he withdraw his motion.

Mr. PHILLIPS. The motion I made does not interfere with anything the gentleman from Massachusetts (Mr Hallett) may desire to present. I would also state that it is, I believe, the universal practice to allow the House, by its vote, to fix the time to which it will adjourn before it does adjourn. That certainly must be so, for unless that vote is taken before adjournment it never can be taken.

Mr. McCOOK, of Ohio, withdrew his motion to adjourn.

Mr. PHILLIPS, of Pennsylvania, then moved that when this Convention adjourn it be to meet at 5 o'clock this afternoon.

Mr. STURMAN, of Arkansas, asked the gentleman to withdraw his motion to allow him to present to the Convention a statement from his colleague. This morning he had the protest of the contesting delegates from Arkansas handed to him, with a polite request to present it to the Convention. He would send it to the Chair and request that it be read.

Mr. HALLETT, of Massachusetts, obtained the floor.

Mr. STUART, of Michigan, desired to submit some remarks upon the motion of the gentleman from Pennsylvania.

The PRESIDENT stated that the Chair would receive the document from the gentleman from Arkansas, but at present he could not entertain any new proposition pending the motion to adjourn.

A DELEGATE from New York inquired if it would be in order to refer the paper to the Committee on Credentials?

The CHAIR. Not pending the present motion to fix the hour to which the Convention will adjourn.

Mr. STUART. On that motion I claim the floor.

The PRESIDENT. The House having given its unanimous assent to the gentleman from Arkansas to present this paper, it will now be read.

Mr. STUART. The consent of the Convention was not given.

Mr. COCHRAN moved that the paper, without reading, be referred to the Committee on Credentials.

The PRESIDENT. That is not in order. It can be read by unanimous consent, not otherwise.

Many Delegates objected.

The PRESIDENT. The question then is on the motion to adjourn till 5 o'clock.

Mr. PHILLIPS, of Pennsylvania, read from the rules of the House of Representatives, to show that the motion to adjourn was always in order, and that the motion to fix a day to which the House will adjourn takes precedence of any other, and that both these motions, together with the motion to lay on the table, must be decided without debate.

The PRESIDENT suggested that that might not apply to fixing an hour to which to adjourn.

Mr. PHILLIPS believed that it did.

Mr. STUART said the rule applied to fixing a day, and had no application to this case. It was always in order to proceed to show that the hour designated was an impracticable one.

Mr. COCHRAN, of New York, suggested that the rules of the House of Representatives were applicable to this body as far as they were practicable. The House sat for months, this Convention for days. Hours of a day were to this Convention as days were to the sessions of the House.

Mr. STUART moved to lay the motion on the table.

The PRESIDENT said that that motion was not in order.

Mr. COCHRAN. The motion to fix a time is a privileged motion, the same as the motion to lay on the table.

Mr. STUART. It would be strange if we could not get rid of a subject.

Mr. HALLETT, of Massachusetts, desired to submit a matter to the Convention in reference to a contested seat in Massachusetts. His alternate at Charleston claimed to retain his seat in this Convention. He desired to have a hearing before the Committee on Credentials upon that question, and would submit the question whenever it was in order, or now, by general consent.

Mr. CLARK and Mr. CLAIBORNE, of Missouri, stated that a similar case had occurred in the Missouri delegation.

Mr. BRIGGS, of New York, inquired whether, under the resolution adopted this morning, all these cases did not go necessarily to the Committee ?

The SECRETARY read the resolution of the gentleman from New York, from which it appears that only credentials from seceding States went to the Committee.

Mr. STUART suggested that unanimous consent be given to have all such cases referred to the Committee.

No objection being made, the order was made.

The PRESIDENT here announced that Mr. Stout, of Oregon, Mr. Whitely, of Delaware, Mr. Wood, of Kentucky, and Mr. Gregory, of California, desired to be excused from serving on the Committee on Credentials.

By unanimous consent of the Convention, the following delegates were substituted in their place : Mr. Stevens, of Oregon; Mr. Buley, of Delaware ; Mr. Morrow, of Kentucky ; and Mr Dudley, of California.

The COMMITTEE ON CREDENTIALS now stands as follows :

Arkansas, Van. H. Manning ; Connecticut, James Gallagher ; California, John S. Dudley, Delaware, John H. Buley ; Indiana, S. A. Hall ; Illinois, William J. Allen ; Iowa, D. G Finch ; Kentucky. G H. Morrow; Maine, Charles D. Mason ; Massachusetts, Oliver Stevens ; Michigan, Benj. Follett ; Minnesota, Henry H. Sibley ; Maryland, William S. Gittings ; Missouri, John M. Krum ; New Hampshire, Aaron P. Hughes ; New York, D. DeWolf: New Jersey, Alfred R. Spear ; North Carolina, R R. Bridges ; Ohio, James B. Steedman ; Oregon, Isaac J. Stevens ; Pennsylvania, H. M. North ; Rhode Island, George H. Browne ; Tennessee. Wm. H. Carroll ; Vermont, Stephen Thomas ; Virginia, E W. Hubbard ; Wisconsin, P. H. Smith.

The question was then taken on the motion to adjourn till 5 o'clock. Before the vote was announced,

Mr. McCOOK called for a vote by States.

The question being taken by a call of the States, resulted as follows :

	Yeas.	Nays.		Yeas.	Nays		Yeas.	Nays.
Maine,	8		North Carolina	10		Ohio		28
New Hampshire	5		South Carolina			Indiana		13
Vermont	5		Georgia			Illinois		11
Massachusetts	13		Florida			Michigan	6	
Rhode Island	4		Alabama			Wisconsin		
Connecticut	2½	3½	Louisiana			Iowa		
New York	35		Mississippi			Minnesota	4	
New Jersey	7		Texas			California	4	
Pennsylvania	26	1	Arkansas	1		Oregon	3	
elaware	2		Missouri	3	6			
Maryland	8		Tennessee	12			185½	66½
Virginia	15		Kentucky	12				

On motion of Mr. BUTTERWORTH, of New York, the Convention then adjourned.

EVENING SESSION.

The Convention re-assembled at 5 o'clock.

Messrs. Fisher, of Virginia, Stetson, of New York, and King, of Missouri, desired information from the Chair, in relation to tickets of admission to the Convention.

MR. STUART. Mr. President, I rise merely to state that, according to my understanding, there can be no business that ought to occupy the attention of this Convention this evening. The Committee on Credentials will not report till to-morrow. I therefore move that the Convention adjourn.

The PRESIDENT. The Chair requests the gentleman to withdraw his motion for a moment, that the Chair may present a communication he has received to the Convention.

Mr. STUART. Certainly.

The motion to adjourn was accordingly withdrawn.

The PRESIDENT. Before proceeding to make that communication, the Chair desires to make a suggestion to the gentleman from Virginia (Mr. Fisher), and at the same time to make a suggestion to the Convention itself. At the assembling of this Convention at Charleston, a system of organization was adopted which involved the delivery of tickets for admission of members to the floor, the hall, and to their seats in the hall. That system was resumed at the assembling of the Convention in the city of Baltimore; and the duty devolved, as a matter of necessity, upon the Chair to direct the distribution of those tickets of admission. Was the Chair to give directions that all persons assuming to be members of this Convention should be admitted without tickets? Gentlemen, have we not been occupied in a debate of an entire day, the whole of which assumes that no gentleman shall come into this hall as a member, and take the seat of a member, without such a ticket of admission? What would have been the condition of things in this hall if there had been no system at the door of checking the admission of persons, and discriminating between those who were recognized as of right members of this Convention, and those who were not so recognized? Would it have been possible to have continued the deliberations of this body, with the free admission of persons at the doors of this hall, without any check or guard to their admission? The Chair submits it to the good sense of every member of this body that it would have been materially and morally impossible to go on without some provision for the delivery of tickets of members of this body at the door of this Convention. In this state of facts, in this evident necessity for some such provision, it appears that the gentleman from Virginia (Mr. Fisher), had not obtained the ticket which, as the Chair is informed by the Sergeant-at-Arms, was, in the ordinary course of business, delivered to the Chairman of the Virginia delegation. If that was so, surely the Sergeant-at-Arms and the officers of the Convention can only regret that the accident occurred.

But beyond that fact, the Chair will submit to the gentleman from Virginia (Mr. Fisher), that the solemn appeal he has made to the country against this ordinary expedient of tickets for the admission of members to the Convention, is an appeal to the country against a primary and obvious necessity of order in the Convention. If the Convention shall desire to change that system, no person will accept that change more gratefully than the Chair. (Cries of "no change," "no change") The duties devolved upon me as the presiding officer of this Convention; the necessity of preserving order in the Convention; putting motions; hearing and deciding questions of order, and the other necessary duties of the Chair, are quite enough occupation for him, and he deeply regrets, that in addition to that occupation—in itself quite enough for him to discharge—there is devolved upon him, in regard to the admission of members and spectators, an amount of duty incomparably greater than all the other duties of the Chair. He deplores this, and would be deeply grateful to the Convention if they would adopt some other order, if any other order be possible, by which there can be regularity of admission to the Convention.

With these remarks, the Chair submits the whole subject to the Convention; and if the Convention will be good enough to pass an order designating some other person to attend to this duty, the Chair will be deeply gratified to be relieved from this, the most onerous duty devolved upon the Chair.

Mr. STUART, of Michigan. I think that the whole subject is disposed of satisfactorily, and I hope that the motion will be put that the Convention adjourn.

The PRESIDENT. The Chair begs leave before putting the question to lay before the Convention a communication from Mr. Krum, the Chairman of the Committee on Credentials.

COMMUNICATION FROM THE COMMITTEE ON CREDENTIALS.

The SECRETARY read the following letter:

Hon. Caleb Cushing, President, &c.:

MY DEAR SIR: I am instructed by the Committee on Credentials to say they will be unable to report at the afternoon session of this day, and beg permission of the Convention to continue our session during the sitting of the Convention. Very respectfully, &c.,

19th June, 1860. JOHN M. KRUM, Chairman.

The PRESIDENT. As no objection is made, the Chair will take it for granted that the permission is given.

Mr. STUART, of Michigan, moved that the Convention do now adjourn.

The motion to adjourn was agreed to, and the Convention accordingly adjourned.

THIRD DAY.

WEDNESDAY, JUNE 20, 1860.

The Convention was called to order at twenty minutes past 10 o'clock A. M.

The PRESIDENT introduced the Rev. Mr. BOWEN, who offered up a prayer.

Mr. LUDLOW, of New York. Mr. President, I would ask whether there is any information in the possession of the Chair, or any member of this Convention, as to the probable time when the Committee on Credentials will be prepared to report.

The PRESIDENT. The Chair has not yet received any information upon the subject, but is informed that presently it will be communicated to the Chair.

Mr. LUDLOW. I will, therefore, in order to facilitate the business of the Convention, move that the reading of the journal be dispensed with.

The motion prevailed.

Mr. KING, of Missouri, rose to a privileged question and stated it.

Mr. CLARK, of Missouri, made a statement upon the privileged question stated by Mr. King.

Mr. LUDLOW, of New York. I rise to a point of order. It is this: The Chair recognized Gov. King. Gov. King has yielded the floor. Having made his explanation, he has exhausted his question of privilege. I now want to know what the question is before the Convention.

The PRESIDENT. The Convention will understand that no question is pending, and that the remarks of the gentleman from Missouri (Mr. King), as also those of the other gentleman from Missouri (Mr. Clark), are only proceeding under the assumed indulgence of the Convention. If objection be made, it is the duty of the Chair to arrest the course of remark.

Mr. LUDLOW. Who is entitled to the floor?

The PRESIDENT. Mr. Clark, of Missouri, was recognized.

Mr. LUDLOW. Is he in order?

The PRESIDENT. He is not in order unless by unanimous consent.

Mr. LUDLOW. I object.

The PRESIDENT. The gentleman from Missouri will observe that objection is made from various quarters, and he will not, therefore, be in order to proceed.

Mr. CLARK. I only want to place the record of my State right.

Mr. LUDLOW. I now move, sir, that this Convention take a recess until five o'clock P. M.

The PRESIDENT. The Chair requests the gentleman to withdraw the motion a moment in order that he may have read a letter from the delegation from Florida, for the purpose of correcting a misapprehension arising in the public mind, and possibly in the Convention, in consequence of a misconstruction of a statement made by the Chair.

The Secretary then read the following letter:

ROOMS OF THE FLORIDA DELEGATION TO THE DEMOCRATIC CONVENTION AT RICHMOND, BALTIMORE, June 19th, 1860.

Gen. Caleb Cushing, President Baltimore Convention:

SIR: In yesterday's proceedings of the Convention over which you preside, you are reported as stating that crédentials of gentlemen claiming seats in the Convention from Florida had been placed in your hands. In this you have—unintentionally, doubtless—done the State of Florida great injustice.

By reference to the proceedings of the recent Democratic Convention of that State, a newspaper copy of which was placed in your hands by one of our delegation, as we learn from him, for your private information only, and not as "credentials," you will perceive that Florida accredited her delegates to Richmond only. It is true her delegates to Richmond are entrusted with a large discretion for the purpose of harmonizing the Democracy, if possible, upon the principles rejected at Charleston.

In the exercise of that discretion the Florida delegates, during the recess of the Richmond Convention, are in attendance at Baltimore, observant spectators of your proceedings, and prepared to avail themselves of the first honorable opening for a re-union with their Democratic brethren; but as yet they have seen nothing to induce them to suppose that such opening will occur, and until it does they have unanimously determined not to participate in your proceedings in any manner whatever.

They have therefore to request that Florida may be omitted from the list of those States represented, or seeking to be represented, in the Convention over which you preside, until they shall themselves notify you of their desire to participate in your proceedings.

N. BAKER, Chairman.
GEO. W. CALL,
JAS. B. OWENS,
W. D. BARNES,
JOS. JOHN WILLIAMS,
B. F. WARDLAW,
Florida Delegation, Richmond.

The PRESIDENT. The Chair will only add in further explanation that his remark to which the letter refers was undoubtedly misapprehended. His statement was that the official proceedings of the Convention contained in a newspaper had been placed in his hands. He did not mean to be understood as saying that the delegation had presented credentials to the Convention, for he well understood at the time that it was otherwise; and in view of the respectful and dignified tone of this letter, further explaining the matter, the Chair had asked this indulgence of the Convention.

Mr. LUDLOW, of New York. I am informed from an authentic source that the Committee on Credentials will not be prepared to report until five o'clock this afternoon, and in view of that fact, and also in view of the additional fact that there is no other business and can be no other business before the Convention, I move that we take a recess until five o'clock.

The motion was put and carried, and accordingly, at 10 minutes before 11 o'clock, the Convention took a recess.

EVENING SESSION.

The Convention was called to order at precisely five o'clock.

Mr. STUART, of Michigan. I have, within the last five minutes, had an interview with the Chairman of the Committee on Credentials, as I passed along by the building, in order to ascertain, if possible, when they would be able to report; and I understand from him that it will not be possible for them to report until to-morrow morning. Therefore, sir, without taking further time, I will move that the Convention adjourn, which will be an adjournment until to-morrow morning at 10 o'clock.

The motion was put and carried, and accordingly the Convention adjourned.

FOURTH DAY.

THURSDAY, JUNE 21, 1860.

The Convention was called to order by the President, at 10 o'clock A. M.

Prayer was offered by the Rev. HENRY SLICER.

Mr. DAWSON, of Pennsylvania, moved to dispense with the reading of the journal, which was agreed to.

The PRESIDENT announced that reports of Committees were in order.

At this point of the opening proceedings, just at the moment when the most intense anxiety prevailed as to the presentation of the report of the Committee on Credentials, and when the Chairman, Mr. Krum, was expected to rise, a loud crash proceeded from the center of the floor. For a moment a scene of the wildest excitement ensued, which was communicated to all parts of the house, though fortunately the ladies who filled the dress circle, and the crowded upper tiers of male spectators, were able in a moment to comprehend the nature of the accident.

The floor being cleared, it was ascertained that the front of the stage and the portion covering the orchestra had given away, and suddenly sunk about three feet in the center, throwing the settees and those who were on them, within a circle of about fifty feet, into one wedged mass, from which they extricated themselves as rapidly as possible, and fled in all directions to distant parts of the house. Fortunately no one was injured, as would doubtless have been the case if the floor had sunk down all the way to the basement underneath.

The extent of the damage done was proved upon investigation to be very slight. The simple slipping of an upright support to the transverse beams upon which the joist and floor rested, caused the floor to be lowered to the ground. The floor itself being laid in battoned sections, was easily taken up, other supports placed in the proper places and the floor speedily relaid.

Mr. LUDLOW, of New York. In view of the fact that there are now three times the number of delegates present on the floor, I move that we take a recess for one hour. (Cries of "No," "no," "no!")

The PRESIDENT. How can the seats be otherwise repaired?

The motion to take a recess was put and declared carried.

Mr. STUART. We cannot do any business as a Convention. I, therefore, make the suggestion to the Chair that all tickets, whether held by delegates or reporters, after this floor shall have been cleared, be given up as gentlemen come in, as being the only remedy for this abuse.

[The object being to prevent delegates, after they have obtained admittance, from sending out their tickets to other parties, who again use them.]

Several MEMBERS. "That's right."

The PRESIDENT. During the sitting at Charleston the Chair ventured to take that step, and he would have renewed it now except for suggestions made in regard to his exercise of authority that tended to render him reserved upon that point. He will now, in view of the accident that has occured, assume to direct that every ticket, upon being presented by any gentleman having a right to admission, shall be delivered up to the officer, upon entering, and that a check be given to each gentleman admitted, with which he may resume his seat.

The Chair begs leave to make a further suggestion—that with the understanding that a proper arrangement shall be made by which it shall be rendered impossible that other gentlemen shall be introduced upon delegates' tickets, the Chair will adopt some process for that purpose. Meanwhile, in order that the injury may be repaired, he respectfully requests of gentlemen to vacate the hall, in order that the workmen may proceed to their work.

Mr. RYNDERS, of New York. I doubt if an hour will be time enough to do it.

The floor was then slowly cleared, and the workmen at once proceeded to make the necessary repairs. The damage was found to be easily remedied, and within the hour the floor was entirely replaced, with such additional precautions as to avoid a recurrence of the mishap.

At twelve o'clock M. the Convention was called to order by

The PRESIDENT, who said: Gentlemen:—The members of the Convention appear to have re-assembled; the period of the recess has expired; the Convention will please come to order.

Mr. CRAIG, of Missouri. I desire to offer some resolutions, which I will send to the Secretary to have read.

Mr. McCOOK, of Ohio. I object to the introduction of resolutions at this time as out of order.

The PRESIDENT. The only question is the point of order raised by the gentleman from Ohio (Mr. McCook).

Mr. CRAIG. I would beg the gentleman from Ohio to withdraw his point of order.

The PRESIDENT. Until the gentleman from Ohio (Mr. McCook) has withdrawn it, the Chair must enforce the rules of order. The gentleman from Ohio objects to the proposed resolutions as not in order. The Chair requests the Convention to revert to the fact that at the moment when the cause arose this morning that led to our separation an hour ago, the Chair had announced that the business in order was the reports from Committees, and the Chair was waiting for a report to be presented from the Committee on Credentials. And without deciding the general question whether if no report is to be made, resolutions would be in order, the Chair is of opinion that under the rules of the Convention and the call of the Chair, the first business is to receive reports of Committees.

Mr. CRAIG. Will the Chair allow me to appeal to the gentleman from Ohio

(Mr. McCook) to allow the resolutions to be read? I will not ask for any action of the Convention.

Objection was made by several delegates.

Mr. CRAIG. I would ask, if the Chairman of the Committee on Credentials demanding his privilege, am I not in order?

The PRESIDENT. The Chair will decide that question when it arises. The Chair perceives that the gentleman from Missouri (Mr. Krum) is upon the floor, as the Chair supposes, for the purpose of presenting his report.

REPORTS FROM THE COMMITTEE ON CREDENTIALS.

Mr. KRUM, of Missouri. The Committee on Credentials is now prepared to report.

Mr. CLARK, of Missouri. I ask the Chairman of the Committee (Mr. Krum) to proceed to the Secretary's desk to read his report from there.

Mr. KRUM. I think I can make myself heard from here. I trust my brother members of the Convention will give their attention while the Committee present their report. And allow me, before proceeding to the reading of that report, to advert to a fact or two, which I regard as not inappropriate. This is the first time in the history of the Democratic party when questions of the kind which have undergone investigation before your Committee have ever arisen. The remarkable question has arisen that after the beginning of the session of a National Convention questions of vacancies have——

Mr. DAVIS, of Virginia. I rise to a point of order. Is this speech in order, or is the report first in order? If the speech is in order, I want to hear it; if it is not, I do not want to hear it. I demand the decision of the Chair upon the point of order.

The PRESIDENT. The gentleman from Virginia (Mr. Davis) makes a point of order on the remarks the gentleman from Missouri (Mr. Krum) is making.

Mr. KRUM. Allow me before that question is decided——

Mr. DAVIS. Let the Chair decide the question.

Mr. KRUM. In the remark I was about to make I was not going to discuss the merits of the report. I was designing to make some prefatory remarks which I did not deem inappropriate, not affecting the subject matter of the report, or any question of privilege of this body. I had supposed that the courtesy of gentlemen would be extended to the Committee to say at least a word of explanation in regard to the labors which they have undergone. I had hoped to have had that courtesy from the Old Dominion.

Mr. DAVIS, of Virginia. I want to have it understood that some courtesy is due also to the Old Dominion to be heard if the gentleman says anything that the Old Dominion does not like. Is that also to be accorded to them?

Mr. KRUM. If I shall say anything that is disagreeable to the Old Dominion or her representatives here I trust that this Convention will unanimously allow me to retire to my distant home in the West. I hope my friend will be satisfied to listen to a dozen words.

Objection was made by delegates from several States.

The PRESIDENT. Objection is made to the gentleman from Missouri (Mr. Krum) going on. The Chair will suggest as a solution of the whole question, that the Chairman of the Committee should offer his report, and then he will be entitled to go on with his remarks after he has submitted his report. If the Chair is required to rule upon the point of order, he must rule that the Chairman of the Committee is to first submit his report, and then he will have the floor to make his remarks upon the report.

Mr. KRUM. I will then send up my report to be read.

THE MAJORITY REPORT.

The report was then read as follows:

To the Persident of the National Democratic Convention:

Mr. PRESIDENT: The Committee upon Credentials respectfully report that prior to the adjournment of this Convention at Charleston, on the 3d of May last, the following resolution was adopted:

"*Resolved*, That when this Convention adjourns to-day it be adjourned to re-assemble at Baltimore, Md., on Monday, the 18th of June next, and that it be respectfully recommended to the Democratic party of the several States to make provision for supplying all vacancies in their respective delegations to this Convantion when it shall re-assemble."

On the re-assembling of this Convention in Baltimore, the following resolution was adopted:

Resolved, That the credentials of all persons claiming seats in this Convention made vacant by the secession of delegates at Charleston, be referred to the Committee on Credentials; and said Committee is hereby instructed, as soon as practicable, to examine the same, and report the names of persons entitled to such seats.

By the further order of the Convention, the claims of all other persons claiming seats were also referred to your Committee. Your Committee thus instructed have proceeded to examine the claims of all persons which have been brought before them. Your Committee found that the delegations of the several States of Alabama, Mississippi, Louisiana, Texas and Florida had become wholly vacant by reason of the secession of the entire original delegations from this Convention; the delegations of the States of Georgia, Arkansas and Delaware had become vacant in part only from the same cause. In no other State had there been any secession, but individual seats were contested in the delegations from the States of Massachusetts and Missouri.

Aside from the above, no question touching the seats of delegates was brought to the notice of your Committee. After patient and full investigation, your Committee are of opinion that the persons hereinafter named in the resolutions, which are herewith submitted as a part of this report, are severally entitled to seats as delegates in this Convention, and they respectfully recommend that they be so received by this Convention.

From the State of Florida no credentials of any delegates were presented to your Committee. From the States of Mississippi and Texas no contesting claimants appear. From Alabama, Louisiana, Georgia and Arkansas there appeared contesting claimants for all the vacant seats. Of the four votes to which the State of Arkansas is entitled, the now sitting delegates represent one vote. The seats representing the remaining three votes had become vacant by the secession of the original delegates. These seats were all contested, one set of contestants consisting of six persons, and the other set consisting of three persons. Your Committee are of opinion that all of these contestants should be admitted to seats as delegates, with the power of voting as hereinafter declared in the resolution herewith reported in that behalf.

In the Fifth Congressional District of Massachusetts it appeared that B. F. Hallett and another person were appointed delegates to this Convention, and R. L. Chaffee and another person were appointed substitutes. That Mr. Hallett, not being able to attend at Charleston, notified Mr. Chaffee of that fact, who thereupon proceeded to Charleston, presented his credentials, and was duly admitted to his seat, which he continued to fill at the time of the adjournment of this Convention to Baltimore. At the re-assembling of the Convention at Baltimore, Mr. Hallett appeared, claimed the seat which had been awarded to Mr. Chaffee, and receiving the entrance ticket from the Chairman of the Massachusetts delegation, actually took possession of the seat. Your Committee are of opinion that when Mr. Hallett had notified

Mr. Chaffee that he could not fulfill his duty as delegate, and Mr. Chaffee repairing to Charleston had been duly admitted to this Convention, his rights to his seat became absolute, and not subject to be superseded at the pleasure of Mr. Hallett, and that Mr. Chaffee is now the rightful delegate to this Convention.

In the Eighth Electoral District of Missouri the facts are precisely parallel to the above Massachusetts case. The only difference is in terms, Johnson B. Clardy having been elected delegate, and John O'Fallon, Jr., having been elected alternate. Your Committee, for reasons above stated, are of opinion that Mr. O'Fallon is now the rightful delegate

In regard to the contesting claimants from Georgia, your Committee have to report that the evidence adduced before your Committee by the respective parties, presented a great variety of novel, as well as complexed facts and questions, touching the rights of either parties to seats. Your Committee, in attempting to solve these difficulties, encountered embarassments on every hand. After a most patient consideration of the whole matter, it seemed to your Committee that the only way of reaching a satisfactory adjustment is to admit to seats both delegations, with power to each of said delegations to cast one half of the vote of the State, in the manner expressed in the resolution herewith submitted. This solution seems equitable to your Committee, and therefore they recommend the adoption of said resolution. All of which is respectfully submitted. JOHN M. KRUM, Chairman.

1. *Resolved*, That George H. Gordon, E. Barksdale, W. F. Barry, H. C. Chambers, Joseph R. Davis, Beverly Matthews, Charles Clark, Wm. L. Featherston, P. F. Liddell, C. G. Armistead, Wm F. Avant, and T. J. Hudson, are entitled to seats in this Convention, as delegates from the State of Mississippi.

2. *Resolved*, That Pierre Soule, F. Cottman, R. C. Wickliffe, Michael Ryan, Manuel White, Charles Brenveneau, Gustavus Leroy, J. E. Morse, A. S. Herron, M. D. Colmer, J. N. T. Richardson, and J. L. Walker, are entitled to seats in this Convention, as delegates from the State of Louisiana.

3. *Resolved*, That R. W. Johnson, T. C. Hindman, J. P. Johnson, DeRoan Carroll, J. Gould, John A. Jordan, N. B. Burrows, and F. W. Hoadley be admitted to seats as delegates from the State of Arkansas, with power to cast two votes, and that Thos. H. Bradley, M. Hooper, and D. C. Cross, be also admitted to seats as delegates from the same State, with power to cast *one vote*, and in case either portion of said delegates shall refuse or neglect to take their said seats, or to cast their said votes, the other portion of said delegates taking seats in this Convention, shall be entitled to cast the entire three votes of said district.

4. *Resolved*, That Guy M. Bryan, F. R. Lubbock, F. S. Starkdale, E. Greer, H. R. Runnells, Thos. P. Ochiltree, M. W. Covie, and J. F. Crosby, are entitled to seats as delegates from Texas.

5. *Resolved*, That James A. Bayard and Wm. G. Whitely are entitled to seats from the county of New Castle, Delaware.

6. *Resolved*, That R. L. Chaffee, who was duly admitted at Charleston as a delegate from the Fifth Congressional District of Massachusetts, is still entitled to said seat in this Convention, and that Benjamin F. Hallett, who has assumed said seat, is not entitled thereto.

7. *Resolved*, That John O'Fallon, Jr., who was duly admitted at Charleston as a delegate from the Eighth Congressional District of Missouri, is still entitled to said seat in this Convention; and that John B. Clardy, who has assumed said seat, is not entitled thereto.

8. *Resolved*, That R. A. Barker, D. C. Humphrey, John Forsyth, William Garrett, J. J. Seivels, S. C. Posey, L. E. Parsons, Joseph C. Bradley, Thomas B. Cooper, James Williams, O. H. Bynum, Samuel W. Weaxley, L. V. B.

Martin, John W. Warrack, W. R. R. Wyatt, Benjamin Harrison, Thomas M. Mathews and Norment McLeod, are entitled to seats in this Convention as delegates from the State of Alabama.

9. *Resolved*, That the delegation from the State of Georgia, of which H. L. Benning is Chairman, be admitted to the Convention, with power to cast one-half of the vote of said State; and that the delegation from said State, of which Col. Gardner is Chairman, be also admitted to the Convention, with power to cast one-half the vote of said State, and if either of said delegations refuse or neglect to cast the vote as above indicated, that in such case the delegates present in the Convention be authorized to cast the full vote of said State.

Mr. KRUM. Mr. President, when the question of order was made by the gentleman from Virginia, I was about to submit a few prefatory remarks, which I deemed as due to the Committee itself, but being one of those that always submit with cheerfulness to the rules and actions of Democratic Conventions, I yielded to the question of order thus made.

The remarks I was about to submit have no relation to the merits of the report. I was about to refer to the remarkable fact that has been developed since the session of this body in a distant Southern city, and I refer to it for the purpose of saying a word in respect to the labors of the Committee on Credentials and the manner in which those labors have been performed by that Committee. The report just submitted to you, as doubtless you all know, involves new, complex and unusual questions, that have arisen since the session at Charleston. The Committee to whom those questions were referred have, in the discharge of their duties, desired to do justice and to discharge those duties with fidelity, and in their behalf I desire to say that they have labored with an industry that I have never seen surpassed and rarely equaled. A limited time was allowed to your Committee, for, Mr. President, we were aware that you were sitting here impatiently. We had the conviction thrust upon us that it was necessary to have our labors completed at an early day. We come before you, therefore, knowing that our work has been but imperfectly performed. If further time had been allowed to us, we doubtless could have perfected it and presented a more elaborate report. These remarks, I thought, were due to the Committee.

Now, Mr. President, I have only to say that it has been communicated to the Chairman of the Committee that a portion of that Committee desired to present a minority report, and in addition to that, that one of the Committee desires to present another minority report, and I trust an opportunity will be given to those gentlemen to do so.

MINORITY REPORT.

Mr. STEVENS, of Oregon, then rose and submitted the minority report as follows:

To the President of the Democratic National Convention:

SIR:—We, the undersigned, members of the Committee on Credentials, feel constrained to dissent from many of the views and a large portion of the action of the majority of the Committee in respect to the rights of delegates to seats referred to them by the Convention, and to respectfully recommend the adoption of the following resolutions:

1. *Resolved*, That B. F. Hallett is entitled to a seat in this Convention as a delegate from the 5th Congressional District of Massachusetts.

2. *Resolved*, That John B. Gardy is entitled to a seat in this Convention as a delegate from the 8th Congressional District of the State of Missouri.

3. *Resolved*, That James A. Bayard and W. C. Whitely are entitled to seats in this Convention as delegates from the State of Delaware.

4. *Resolved*, That the delegation headed by R. W. Johnson are entitled to seats as delegates in this Convention from the State of Arkansas.

5. *Resolved*, That the delegation of which Guy M. Bryan is Chairman are entitled to seats as delegates in this Convention from the State of Texas.

6. *Resolved*, That the delegation of which John Tarlton is Chairman are entitled to seats in this Convention as delegates from the State of Louisiana.

7. *Resolved*, That the delegation of which L. P. Walker is Chairman are entitled to seats in this Convention as delegates from the State of Alabama.

8. *Resovled*, That the delegation of which Henry L. Benning is Chairman are entitled to seats in this Convention from the State of Georgia.

9. *Resolved*, That the delegation from the State of Florida, accredited to the Charleston Convention, are invited to take seats in this Convention and cast the vote of Florida.

The principles involved in these resolutions and the facts on which they rest are of such gravity and moment that we deem it due to the Convention and to ourselves to set them forth with care and particularity. We differ radically from the majority of the Committee, both in much of the action we reccommend to the Convention and the principles which should control such action. It is a question not simply of the integrity, but the existence of the Democratic party in several States of this Union. It is a question whether the Democratic party in said State shall be ostracized and branded as unworthy of affiliation with the national organization.

It is a question whether persons irregularly called, or withdrawing from the regular Convention, shall have the sanction of the National Convention to raise the flag of rebellion against their respective State organizations. It is a question whether the Convention itself shall repudiate its own deliberate action at Charleston. We do not magnify the importance of these questions when we assert that upon their proper solution depends the fact as to whether there shall be a National Democratic party or not. The task will not be difficult to show that the action recommended by the majority of the Committee is grossly inconsistent, and should be reprobated and condemned by this Convention. But to the task, without further preamble.

Reserving to the closing portion of this report the cases of contested seats in the Massachusetts and Missouri delegation, we come at once to the cases of the delegates who withdrew from the Charleston Convention. This Convention, on the eve of its adjournment at Charleston, and in the great cause of the restoration of harmony to our distracted party, "respectfully recommended to the Democratic party of the several States to make provision for supplying all vacancies in their respective delegations to this Convention when it shall re-assemble." We call particular attention to the wording of the resolution. Certain delegates had withdrawn. They had placed on the Convention the reasons of their withdrawal.

They still, however, were the representatives of the Democratic party of their several States. Their withdrawal was not a resignation. It was not so considered by the Convention. The vacancies referred to had reference to the contingency of vacancies *at the time of re-assembling*, and the resolution proposed to provide for supplying them. The Convention did not presume to touch the question as to whether the withdrawal of the delegates constituted a resignation, nor had it any right to interfere in the matter. A resignation must be made to the appointing power, and to be complete and final must be accepted by the appointing power. It was well known on the adjournment of the Convention at Charleston that the withdrawing delegates desired the instruction of their several constituencies before deciding on their future course.

Such was the spirit and purpose of their deliberations at Charleston. They consulted their respective constituencies. In every case except the case of

South Carolina, their constituencies directed or authorized them—the vacancies being filled as contemplated in the resolution of the Convention—to repair to Baltimore, and there in earnest efforts with their brethren of the Convention, to endeavor once more to unite their party and promote harmony and peace in the great cause of their country. The resolution of the Convention did not prejudge the question since so strenuously raised that their withdrawal was a resignation, but left the whole question to the said delegates, and their respective constituencies, to the end that every State in this Union might be represented in Baltimore.

The Committee has passed resolutions, declaring by a vote of 16 to 9, that the delegation from Louisiana, headed by Pierre Soule—by a vote of 14 to 11, that the delegation from Alabama, headed by Parsons—and by a vote of 13 to 10, that half of each delegation claiming seats from Georgia, are entitled to seats in the Convention. The resolutions recommended by the undersigned to the Convention declare the right of the delegations elected to Charleston, with vacancies supplied, as contemplated in the resolution of the Convention to which reference has been made, and accredited to Baltimore, to said seats. The Committee which thus recommend the irregular delegates from these three States, have rejected the regular delegates from Delaware, and admitted the Charleston delegates.

It has admitted irregular delegates from Arkansas, and rejected a portion of the Charleston delegates, as modified, by the filling of vacancies. It has admitted the Charleston delegates from Mississippi by a vote of 23 to 2, and the Charleston delegates from Texas by a vote of 19 to 6. The fact that delegations are not contested does not establish the right to seats in the Convention. There may be irregular delegates without contest, and there may be a contest between two sets of irregular delegates. The right of persons to seats as delegates is to be determined by the fact as to whether they were appointed by the constituency which they claim to represent, and appointed according to the usages of said constituency. Wanting these essential pre-requisites, they are not entitled to seats, even if there be no contestants; and having these, their right to seats is not impaired or affected by contestants.

The Committee, in deciding by a vote of 23 to 2, that the Charleston delegates from Mississippi are entitled to seats in the Baltimore Convention, have decided rightly, just because they were duly accredited to Charleston, have never since resigned, and have received instructions from the State of Mississippi, through a Convention called by the Democratic Executive Committee of the State, to return to Baltimore.

The Charleston delegates, both from Alabama and Georgia, stand in precisely the same position. They were also duly accredited to Charleston. They withdrew and never resigned. They returned to their respective constituencies. The Executive Committees in these States, as in the case of Mississippi, called a Convention of the party. The Convention met. The delegates, as in the case of Mississippi, submitted their action to the Conventions, and these Conventions approved their course, continued their powers, and accredited them to Baltimore. Their rights stand on precisely the same basis, and are sustained by the same authority as in Mississippi. The contestants were appointed by nobody authorized to meet according to the usages of the party in these States, and are not entitled to any consideration whatever.

In the case of Alabama, the Convention assembled on the call of the Democratic Executive Committee (addressed to the Democracy of the State,) was very largely attended, nearly every county in the State having been represented. A small number of persons, however, issued a notice, which was published in only three newspapers in the State—in two papers the notice was without signers, and in the third paper (Mobile Register) it was signed by John Forsyth and thirty-five others. The notice in one paper called upon all Democrats *and all other persons*—in the second paper upon Democrats and *all conservatives*, and the third paper (Mobile Register) upon *the people of Alabama*, to hold county meetings and send delegates to a State Convention, to be held in Montg mery or Selma, the 4th day of June, to appoint delegates to Baltimore. Twenty-eight counties only out of fifty-two were represented.

It was the coming together of persons from all parties outside of the regular organization to strike down the Democracy of the State. It was a call without any official authority whatsoever. We thus find the Democracy of the State assembling in Convention according to the usages of the party, and we find at the same time persons assembling at the call of unauthorized individuals. In the former case the whole State was represented. In the latter about half the State. Yet the majority of the Committee have indorsed the action of the Democracy of Alabama, and have repudiated, contrary to all precedent, usage, right and justice, the action of the former; not only this, they have repudiated the principles of their own action in the case of the Mississippi delegation.

But the action of the majority of the Committee in the case of Georgia has gone one step further in its disregard of the acknowledged principles of the party. The Convention which the Committee put on an equality with the regularly authorized Convention, consisted in great part of persons who just participated in the regular Democratic Convention of the State. The regular called Convention consisted of nearly four hundred delegates, representing all the counties of the State. The resolutions of the Convention having been adopted by a vote of 299 to 41, these latter withdrew from the Convention and organized anew. Thus the majority of your Committee have exalted the pretensions of less than one-eighth of the delegates of the State Convention to an equality with the rights of seven-eighths of the Democracy of the State.

In the case of Louisiana, the old Convention, which originally appointed the delegates to Charleston, was re-assembled on the call of the Executive Committee of the State, and by a decisive majority accredited the Charleston delegates to Baltimore. The reasons for this action have their parallels in the cases of Texas and Delaware, which have received the sanction of the Committee. In Texas, the delegates come back accredited by the Democratic Executive Committee simply—it being a manifest impossibility, from want of time, to assemble the party in a State Convention; and in Delaware, under the usages and rules of the party, the old Convention was re-assembled. In Louisiana there was time to assemble the old Convention, but not to order an election of delegates in the several parishes to meet a new Convention. The Executive Committee did every thing it could to get the expression of the views of the State. It re-assembled the old Convention, nearly every parish in the State being represented, and accredited the Charleston delegates to Baltimore.

But the Convention whose delegates to Baltimore have been indorsed by the majority of your Committee, was called at the instance of two local organizations, and of Dr. Cottman, a former member of the National Executive Committee of the party. The calls were somewhat conflicting. The notice did not reach many parishes in the State. Only twenty parishes out of thirty-nine are pretended to be represented, and in several of these there is no reason to doubt the fact that the delegates did not leave behind them a single constituent agreeing with them in sentiments. In not a single parish was this call responded to by a majority of the Democratic voters. The Convention only represented a very small portion of the party—it was totally irregular, besides.

The majority of the Committee object to the action of the old Convention on its re-assembling at the call of the Executive Committee, on the ground that it was defunct and could not be brought to life. Yet it indorses the action of the other Convention on the call in part of the equally defunct member of the National Committee, Dr. Cottman. The following the usage of Delaware, by the Executive Committee of Louisiana, though manifestly a necessity for the reasons stated, has no weight as a precedent with this majority. Conceding their ground of its being irregular, seats as delegates should be given to the body called by the regular authority and not to the body assembled by no responsible authority whatever, and especally when the former represented the great body of the party and the latter did not. All these considerations, however, have been disregarded by the majority of the Committee, who have persisted by a vote of 16 to 9 to award the seats as delegates to the representatives of the disorganizing minority Convention.

In the case of Arkansas, the majority of the Committee propose to divide out the seats to all applicants. In this State the Democratic party were about assembling in their District Conventions, consisting of delegates from the several counties of the State, for the nomination of member of Congress, when their delegates returned from Charleston. As in Texas, there was not time for the assembling of a State Convention. In these District Conventions, delegates were selected to represent the party at Baltimore. A call was however issued in a Memphis paper, without any signature whatever, calling upon the people of the Northern District to assemble in mass meeting at Madison, to elect delegates to Baltimore.

Some four or five hundred men from ten to twelve counties thus assembled and appointed three delegates to Baltimore. The majority of the Committee propose to allow these men to vote in the Convention. There are twenty-seven counties and twenty-five thousand voters in the district. Col. Hindman, a delegate, elected by the District Convention, to Baltimore, was elected to Congress, in 1858, by eighteen thousand majority, and was unanimously renominated by the Convention which selected him as a delegate to Baltimore. These facts show the significance of the action of the District Convention in electing delegates to Baltimore as representing truly the sentiment of the Democratic party of the district, and they exhibit the utter insignificance of the anonymously called Convention, for it will be borne in mind that it was held at a central point, at the western terminus of the railroad from Memphis, and where several stage and wagon routes meet. They were elected as delegates generally from the State to the National Convention, with the hope that they might get in without any definite claim.

In Massachusetts and Missouri, the contests are between principals now holding their seats and substitutes who held their places at Charleston. In each case the principal was detained at home by sickness in his family. In eaeh case the principal gave notice to his substitute that he should take his seat at Baltimore. The majority of the Committee hold that the principals, elected as such by the proper Conventions, are not entitled to their seats and have reported accordingly. We hold that a substitute is appointed simply to act in the absence of the principal, and that his authority ceases whenever the principal makes his appearance and takes his seat. We emphatically declare that such has been the invariable usage in all Conventions of the party, whether National or State, and that it is based on reason and the representative principle

All which is respectfully submitted.

ISAAC J. STEVENS, Oregon,
H. M. NORTH, Pennsylvania,
E. W. HUBBARD, Virginia,
WM. H. CARROLL, Tennessee,
A. R SPEER, New Jersey,
JOHN H. BULEY, Delaware,
R. R. BRIDGES, North Carolina,
GEO. H. MORROW, Kentucky,
D. S. GREGORY, California.

In the points of difference between the majority and minority reports of the

Committee on Credentials, I concur in the conclusion of the minority report in the cases of Georgia, Alabama, Missouri and Massachusetts.

AARON V. HUGHES, New Hampshire.

Mr. STEVENS. It will be observed that the Committee are nearly unanimous, and the two reports agree in the case of Texas, Missouri and Delaware. I am requested to state that the delegate from Tennessee dissents from a portion of the conclusion of the Committee, but votes under instruction of his co-delegates; also that the gentleman from New Hampshire agrees with the report of the minority, in the case of Georgia, Alabama, Massachusetts and Missouri.

A SECOND MINORITY REPORT.

Mr. GITTINGS, of Maryland. Mr. President : Being unable to agree with either wing of the Committee on Credentials, I have drawn up a report, which I submit to the Convention.

The report was then read as follows :

Hon. Caleb Cushing, President:

SIR :—The undersigned, a delegate from the State of Maryland, and representing that State upon the Committee on Credentials, begs leave to say to the Democratic National Convention that, while he concurs in and indorses the report of the majority of the Committee upon Credentials—so far as relates to the contested seats of the State of Massachusetts; the contested seat in the State of Missouri; the contested seats in the State of Delaware; as also in regard to the contested delegations in the States of Arkansas, Georgia and Louisiana, and agreeing with them also in their recommendation to admit the delegations now present and claiming seats from the States of Texas and Mississippi—he differs from and protests against their action with regard to the State of Alabama.

Upon a careful examination of all the facts concerning this State, the undersigned believes and so reports, that the delegation of which L. P. Walker is chairman is the regularly elected representative of the State of Alabama, and as such is clearly entitled to seats in the Democratic National Convention.

Coming here as they do, not alone by virtue of the commission under which they held their seats at Charleston, but having been re-elected and accredited by a State Convention called together in accordance with the usages of the Democratic party of the State of Alabama, the undersigned holds it to be the imperative duty of this National Convention to recognize their claims as the only authorized delegates from the State of Alabama.

The undersigned therefore offers the following:

Resolved, That so much of the majority report of the Committee on Credentials as relates to Massachusetts, Missouri, Delaware, Arkansas, Georgia, Louisiana, Mississippi and Texas be adopted.

Resolved, That the delegation of which L. P. Walker is Chairman, be and they are hereby declared the only regular authorized representatives of the State of Alabama, and as such, are entitled to seats in this National Democratic Convention.

All of which is respectfully submitted.

Baltimore, June 21, 1860. W. S. GITTINGS.

Mr. GITTINGS. I move that the report be printed, and that we take a recess till 3 o'clock. [Many voices, "no," "no."]

Mr. GITTINGS. I withdraw it.

Mr. KRUM resumed the floor.

Mr. PHILLIPS desired to make a suggestion to the gentleman from Maryland.

Mr. KRUM declined to yield the floor. He then said : Mr. President and gentlemen of the Convention, by the majority and minority reports you are now possessed of the questions which arise in respect to those reports, and it is not my purpose now to enter upon a debate in respect to any of those questions, but merely to make a suggestion in order that we may understand each other in our future action in regard to those reports. And, in the first place, I am thoroughly convinced that an extended debate in regard to any one of the questions will result in little if any good to the harmony of this Convention; and, as the propositions are plainly stated and addressed to the judgment of the Convention in the several reports, I desire to state that, within a resonable time, I shall move the previous question, in order that we may come to direct action. [Applause, and cries from all quarters, "move it now," "now," "now."] I am appealed to on every hand to move it now. I desire to state that I am under such obligations to brethren of the Committee, with whom I have acted with entire harmony and good faith, that I could not do so. [Renewed cries of "question," and "move it now."]

Mr. PHILLIPS, of Pennsylvania. I suggest that as the reports of the majority and minority agree as to recommending the admission of the delegates from Mississippi, Texas and Delaware, I ask the unanimous consent of the Convention to let the vote be taken upon them now. [Many voices—"no," "no."] Mr. President, tell me with what fairness it can be refused?

Mr. CESSNA, of Pennsylvania. I call my colleague to order.

The PRESIDENT. The Chair begs leave to inquire whether the gentleman from Missouri (Mr. Krum) made a motion or yielded the floor? He did not know which, it was done so abruptly.

A DELEGATE. He yielded the floor to the gentleman from Oregon (Mr. Stevens).

The PRESIDENT. The Chair did not so understand, and therefore wishes to inquire of the gentleman from Missouri?

Mr. KRUM No, sir—I only yielded temporarily.

The PRESIDENT. Then the gentleman from Missouri has the floor.

Mr. PHILLIPS. I submit that the gentleman cannot yield the floor temporarily, but must yield it absolutelv—and I understood the gentleman to say that he did yield it to the gentleman from Oregon.

Points of order were made by Mr. Schell, of New York, Mr. Atkins, of Tennessee, and Mr. Waterbury, of New York, upon Mr. Krum, each claiming that Mr. Krum had yielded the floor.

The PRESIDENT stated that he must determine the question of order by ascertaining the question of fact. If the gentleman from Missouri says to the Convention that he had finished what he had to say, and had ceased to speak in order to enable the gentleman from Oregon (Mr. Stevens) to speak —if that was his intention when he left his position, the Chair will be bound to say that the gentleman from Missouri (Mr. Krum) had lost the floor and could not resume it, and upon that question of fact and intention the Chair will be bound to accept the declaration upon honor of the gentleman from Missouri.

Mr. KRUM, of Missouri. I trust that whenever I speak it will be regarded that I speak upon honor. I speak to you now upon honor. I state now, as I did before, that the fact is I supposed I had the right to yield the floor temporarily to the gentleman from Oregon (Mr. Stevens) that he might make some explanation or comment to this Convention. I did so, and it was my design to resume the floor. And I did not suppose I had lost my right to the floor simply because I stepped from this elevation.

The PRESIDENT. The gentleman from Missouri now explains that what he said was, "I yield the floor temporarily to the gentleman from Oregon" Now the Chair does not understand that any gentleman in this body can yield the floor to any other gentleman to speak, until the gentleman so proposing to speak shall be recognized by the Chair. If it were otherwise, there would be an end of all order of debate, as well as interchange of fair rights of inequality upon the floor of the Convention. And now as the gentleman from Missouri (Mr. Krum) says that in sitting down he said, "I yield the floor, &c.," the Chair rules that that is a yielding of the floor; and if the gentleman from Oregon (Mr. Stevens) had got the floor so that he could be recognized, he would have been recognized. But in this case the Chair recognized the gentleman from Pennsylvania (Mr. Phillips), and the Chair is of opinion that he is entitled to the floor.

Mr. PHILLIPS submitted some remarks upon the subject of the several reports of the Committees, and was called to order by Mr. Stuart, of Michigan, and by Mr. Pugh, of Ohio.

Mr. PHILLIPS. I did not mean to submit any motion of amendment at this time. My object is merely to call the attention of the Convention to some points presented by the different reports of the Committee on Credentials, and upon that it occurred to me that the duty of the Convention would be plain. I repeat, I invite the attention of the Convention to the fact that the Committee on Credentials report unanimously in favor of the admission of the delegations of Mississippi, Texas and Delaware. Upon all those delegations there is unanimity.

Mr. STEVENS, of Oregon. I do not rise to inflict a speech upon this Convention. I am content, for the most part, to rest the views of the minority of the Committee on Credentials on the report which they have presented to the Convention. That report has been read, and shows entire unanimity in the Committee as regards Delaware, Texas and Mississippi. Those three cases involve the principles which the minority of the Committee have adopted in reference to the action they ask of this Convention upon the resolutions they have submitted. My friend from Pennsylvania (Mr. Phillips) has well put the case of those three States, and I need add nothing further. I now call the previous question.

Mr. GOULDEN, of Georgia. I appeal to this Convention to hear me for a few moments.

The PRESIDENT. I must state the question, as it is called for. It is the duty of the Chair now to put the preliminary question, which is upon the second of the demand for the previous question. Is the Convention ready for that question?

Mr. GOULDEN, of Georgia. Before the question is put, allow me to say a word.

The PRESIDENT. The gentleman from Georgia (Mr. Goulden) is out of order.

Mr. AVERY, of North Carolina. I rise to a privileged question. Before the question is put upon seconding the demand for the previous question, I call for a division of the question upon the resolutions.

The PRESIDENT. That can be done as well after the previous question is ordered.

The question was then put to the Convention—

"Shall the demand for the previous question be seconded?"

And the Convention agreed to the seconding of the demand for the previous question.

The PRESIDENT. The question now is—

"Shall the main question be now put?"

A vote was taken, and the main question was ordered.

Mr. COCHRAN, of New York. We of the New York delegation, wish to consult before voting upon this question. And for the purpose of affording us that opportunity, I move that when this Convention adjourn, it be to meet at 5 o'clock this afternoon.

Cries of "no adjournment," "let us vote."

The question was then taken upon the vote of Mr. Cochran, and the Chair announced that it was not agreed to.

Mr. RANDALL, of Pennsylvania, moved that the Convention take a recess until half-past four o'clock, and upon that he called for the vote by States.

Mr. STUART, of Michigan. I would suggest to the Chair that after the house has ordered the main question to be put, nothing can take precedence of it but a motion to adjourn generally.

Mr. SEYMOUR, of New York. I move that the Convention now adjourn till five o'clock this afternoon. We wish an opportunity to look through the reports.

Mr. STUART, of Michigan. There is no motion in order but a general motion to adjourn.

Mr. SEYMOUR. Then I move to adjourn.

Mr. AVERY, of North Carolina. I will withdraw my motion for a division of the question.

Mr. PHILLIPS, of Pennsylvania, and others renewed the call for the division of the question.

The PRESIDENT. The division of the question has now been called for. The first question is now upon the motion of Mr. Seymour, of New York, to adjourn.

The question being taken, the motion to adjourn was not agreed to.

Mr. RANDALL, of Pennsylvania. I move the Convention adjourn to half-past four o'clock.

Mr. STUART, of Michigan. I must insist upon my point of order, that after the house has ordered the main question to be now put, it cuts off every question except the motion to adjourn generally.

Mr. LUDLOW, of New York. I have a suggestion to make in favor of a recess. It is that the large delegation of New York has had no opportunity of consultation upon the questions now before the Convention. I now move that the Convention take a recess until 5 o'clock this afternoon.

The PRESIDENT. There is no question before the Convention except the motion of the gentleman from New York (Mr. Ludlow,) to take a recess until 5 o'clock, and the Chair does not understand that in this stage of the previous question a motion for a recess is in order. A motion to adjourn is in order, but not a motion for a recess.

Mr. BRADFORD, of Pennsylvania. I move that when the Convention adjourn to-day, it be to half-past four o'clock this afternoon.

Mr. SAMUELS, of Iowa. I ask the Chair, in connection with that motion, to pass upon the question of order made by the gentleman from Michigan, (Mr. Stuart,) and that is that such a motion is not in order after the previous question has been ordered.

Mr. STUART, of Michigan. I would suggest that the Convention go on with the business of the Convention, so that we may be able to proceed to a vote immediately upon assembling again.

The PRESIDENT. The Chair understands that the main question having been ordered, the first question is upon the amendments to the majority report, the amendments consisting of the two minority reports.

Mr. STUART, of Michigan. With that understanding, I will withdraw my objection.

Mr. CESSNA, of Pennsylvania. The delegation from Pennsylvania upon consultation are willing to withdraw their opposition, and to vote in favor of the motion, if the call of the States is withdrawn.

MR. RANDALL, of Pennsylvania. If the call of the vote by States is withdrawn, the motion will probably now be carried.

Mr. SAULSBURY withdrew the call.

The question was then taken upon the motion to take a recess and was agreed to.

Thereupon the Convention took a recess until half-past four o'clock.

EVENING SESSION.

The Convention was called to order by the President at 5 o'clock.

Mr. Ludlow, of New York. Mr. President :—On behalf of the delegation from New York, I tender their apology for having kept this Convention waiting beyond the time of the recess. And I am authorized by them in view of the fact that they are now in consultation, and will be unable for some length of time to record their votes upon the question now before the Convention. I am deputized by them to appear before you and ask a further recess and time to—

Many voices. "No, no," "yes, yes."

Mr. Johnson, of Maryland. I would suggest, in order to save the time of this Convention, that the vote be now taken, and the vote of New York be recorded when she is ready to give it.

Responses of "good, good," and "no, no."

Mr. Bradford, of Pennsylvania. I move a recess till 8 o'clock this evening.

Voices, "no, no."

Several Delegates moved to adjourn.

Mr. Bradford. I move we do now adjourn.

Mr. Saulsbury, of Delaware. I call for the vote by States.

A Delegate from Massachusetts inquired if the Convention adjourned, to what hour it would be?

The President. Till 10 o'clock to-morrow morning.

The call of the States having been completed, and all having responded with the exception of the New York delegation, who were absent in consultation,

The President inquired, as a matter of form, of the Chairman of the New York delegation, if present, whether the vote of that State was ready to be recorded? It was not material, but receiving no answer, he would assume that there was no one here authorized to cast the vote of that State.

The Chair begged leave to state, before declaring the vote just taken, that he had received this afternoon a communication from gentlemen of the State of Arkansas, which he had had no opportunity to present this afternoon, but would offer to the Convention to-morrow morning. He desired to state this lest he might be supposed to have overlooked it.

The vote was then announced on the motion to adjourn—ayes 161½, nays 48, as follows:

	Yeas.	Nays.		Yeas.	Nays.		Yeas.	Nays.
Maine	8		North Carolina	7½	2½	Ohio	23	
New Hampshire	½	4½	South Carolina			Indiana	13	
Vermont			Georgia			Illinois	11	
Massachusetts	4½	8	Florida			Michigan	6	
Rhode Island	4		Alabama			Wisconsin	5	
Connecticut	2	4	Louisiana			Iowa	4	
New York			Mississippi			Minnesota	4	
New Jersey	4	8	Texas			California	4	
Pennsylvania	15	11	Arkansas			Oregon	3	
Delaware	2		Missouri	6	3			
Maryland	4	4	Tennessee	5	7		161½	48
Virginia	14	1	Kentucky	12				

Whereupon the Convention adjourned.

FIFTH DAY.

Friday, June 22, 1860.

At 10 o'clock the President called the Convention to order, and it was opened by the Rev. Mr. Schwartz with prayer.

Mr. Wright, of Massachusetts, called for the reading of the journal.

Mr. McCook, of Ohio, moved to dispense with the reading of the journal.

Mr. Wright. I desire to have it read because there is a difference of opinion as to the state of the motions before the Convention. It is proper that we should know how the journal stands, and I submit to the gentleman the propriety of having it read.

Many VOICES. "No," "no."

Mr. McCOOK. We can have the state of the questions from the Chair.

The question was taken, and the reading of the journal was dispensed with.

The PRESIDENT. At the adjournment of the Convention yesterday, it had ordered that the main question be now put. If it be the pleasure of the Convention, the Chairman will have reported in due form, the order of questions as they arise to which the main question applies.

The Secretary here read the resolutions of the majority of the Committee.

Mr. KRUM rose to a question of privilege. His attention had been directed to the fact that errors had occurred in the names of the delegates in both the report of the majority and the minority, and he asked permission to correct the same.

The PRESIDENT stated that he had been informed of the errors by the gentlemen who made the several reports, and if the Convention pleased the Chairman would understand that by unanimous consent the gentlemen from Missouri have permission to correct the misnomers.

Mr. STEVENS, of Oregon, desired to state that an omission had occurred, in the minority report, of a resolution in regard to the delegates from Mississippi, and he would ask the unanimous consent of the Convention to have it incorporated.

Resolved, That George H. Gordon, E. Barksdale, W. F. Barry, H. C. Chambers, Joseph R. Davis, Beverly Matthews, Charles Clark, Wm. L. Featherston, P. F. Slidell, C. G. Armistead, Wm. F. Cevant and F. G. Hudson are entitled to seats in this Convention as delegates from the State of Mississippi.

The PRESIDENT. The Chair will undersstand that unless objection is made, the unanimous consent of the Convention will be given that the clerical errors be corrected.

The resolutions of the minority report (Mr Stevens') were then read as corrected; also the resolution reported by Mr. Gittings, of Maryland.

Mr. SIBLEY, of Minnesota. Mr. President, I desire to propound a single respectful interrogatory. It will be recollected that yesterday the Chairman of the Commitee on Credentials, while proceeding to address the Convention upon the presentation of the majority report, under a misapprehension of his right, yielded the floor to the gentleman from Oregon (Mr. Stevens), for explanation, and was thus unable to proceed. I now submit to the Chair the question whether, according to the rules and practice of the House of Representatives, which govern this body, the Chairman of the Committee has not a right to close the debate before the previous question is put?

The PRESIDENT. If the gentleman from Missouri (Mr. Krum) desires to close debate, it is, as the Chair understands, his privilege to do so, even after the main question has been ordered. Before doing so, the Chair desires to inquire of the gentleman from Maryland (Mr. Gittings) whether he wishes to make an amendment to his resolution?

Mr. GITTINGS. It has been suggested that as there has been no new matter in my first resolution it is out of order. I readily see that it is so, and to save the Chair the pain of calling me to order, I shall ask permission of the Convention to withdraw it, leaving but one resolution.

The PRESIDENT. The Chair will understand the Convention as giving its unanimous consent to the amendment desired by the gentleman from Maryland (Mr. Gittings).

Mr. WRIGHT, of Massachusetts. Before that question is decided I wish to raise a question of order whether the gentleman from Maryland did submit a motion to the Convention to amend the report before the Convention by the substitution of his resolution yesterday for the majority resolution? I did not hear it. I heard him submit a motion to print.

Mr. GITTINGS. I undoubtedly made the motion. If my friend did not hear it, either his hearing is bad, or my voice is very feeble.

Mr. WRIGHT. I receive the gentleman's explanation, but respectfully submit that the gentleman omitted to do it, though he intended to make the motion.

The PRESIDENT. The Chair understood the gentleman from Maryland to make the motion.

Mr. WRIGHT. Do I now understand the first resolution moved to be out of order as a proposition to amend the majority report?

The PRESIDENT. The first resolution has been withdrawn by unanimous consent. [Voices, "oh, no."] Does not the gentleman from Maryland withdraw the proposition?

Mr. WRIGHT. I do not consent, it is out of order.

The PRESIDENT suggested to the gentleman from Maryland, in order not to require the Chair to rule his amendment out of order, to ask the consent of the Convention to withdraw his resolution.

Mr. WRIGHT now rose to another question—whether the second resolution, being identical with a proposition in the majority report, is not also surplusage and out of order?

The PRESIDENT stated that he would rule upon that question when it came up for action upon it.

Mr. GITTINGS. Inasmuch as there is some disposition to debate, I will withdraw both the resolutions.

The PRESIDENT. By unanimous consent the gentleman from Maryland wishes to withdraw his proposition.

Unanimous consent was given, and Mr. Gittings withdrew his Minority Report and Resolutions.

Mr. KRUM. I rise to a further question of privilege, to correct the list of names, Mr. Burrows and Mr. Manning belonging to the Arkansas delegation instead of Florida.

He then asked leave, in behalf of the majority of the Committee on Credentials, to file a brief statement of their reasons.

Mr. SIBLEY, of Minnesota, inquired whether a single objection was sufficient to prevent the speech of the Chairman of the Committee being made?

Mr. KRUM. If the Convention will allow me to present this brief statement I will consent to make no speech whatever.

Mr. WRIGHT rose to a point of order. There had been no debate upon the resolutions and therefore the claim of the Chairman of the Committee could not be allowed.

The PRESIDENT. The gentleman from Missouri has the floor. The Chair desires to understand whether he wishes to exercise his presumed right to be heard.

Mr. KRUM. Yes, sir.

Mr. WATERBURY, of New York, insisted that the point of order taken by the gentleman from Massachusetts was correct—that there had been no debate, and therefore the gentleman from Missouri had no right to speak as Chairman of the Committee.

Mr. ATKINS, of Tennessee. I trust the gentleman from New York (Mr. Waterbury) will withdraw the point of order he has made upon the gentleman from Missouri, (Mr. Krum.) There certainly was some little debate yesterday upon this proposition.

Mr. WATERBURY, of New York. I am not aware of any debate upon this proposition, unless it be the few remarks made by the gentleman from Missouri himself (Mr. Krum) and the suggestion made by the gentleman from

Pennsylvania (Mr. Phillips.) But the gentleman from Pennsylvania did not debate the merits of the propositions before the Convention. And there has not been, in the proper sense of the term, any debate whatever upon these propositions.

Mr. CLARK, of Missouri. Before the Chair announces its opinion, I wish to call the attention of the President to the remarks of the gentleman from Pennsylvania, (Mr. Phillips.) and some remarks of the gentleman from Oregon, (Mr. Stevens,) in reference to the various reports. I make these suggestions merely to enable the Chair to determine whether there has been any debate at all or not.

The PRESIDENT. The Chair is aware of that, and the Chair was about to say that yesterday, upon the report of the Committee on Credentials being rendered, the gentleman from Missouri, (Mr. Krum,) the Chairman of the Committee, made a speech within the rules of the Convention. The Chair would be bound to consider that as debate, although it was only on one side of the question. After that followed—although it may have been but a single sentence—yet there followed a remark or two from the gentleman from Oregon, (Mr. Stevens,) and after that there followed more suggestions from the gentleman from Pennsylvania (Mr. Phillips,) upon which suggestions the gentleman from Michigan (Mr. Stuart,) made a point of order whether or not debate was in order at that time, and whether what the gentleman from Pennsylvania, (Mr. Phillips) was saying, constituted debate in order? The Chair expressly ruled at that time that the several propositions before the Convention were debatable propositions, and that the Chair understood the gentleman from Pennsylvania to be debating those propositions in order; therefore, the Chair is of opinion that there was debate, and that upon that state of facts, in concurrence with the usage of the House of Representatives—which the Chair assumes to bind him in all matters not expressly set down in the rules, the Chair rules that the gentleman from Missouri (Mr. Krum) has the right to address the Convention.

Mr. KRUM, of Missouri. I will submit to this Convention a few remarks, and in order that they may be concisely stated, I have taken the trouble to condense them in as brief a space as the circumstances in which I am placed will allow. The gentleman then proceeded to read as follows:

It will be observed that the majority report contains only the *conclusions* and *recommendations* of the Committee. This is the usual course. Committees are the chosen organs for investigation of deliberative bodies. Their reports are confided in, and unless assailed, stand unquestioned. In the matter now before the Convention, the report of the Committee is assailed by a minority report, (signed by I. J. Stevens and eight others,) and a statement of certain premises and labored argument have been presented by the minority of the Commitee, to support the conclusions of this minority.

The statements contained in this minority report, on which the main argument of these gentlemen is founded, are for the most part naked assumptions, not established by any evidence before the Committee, and depend entirely for their verity upon the mere *ipse dixit* of the gentlemen who make them.

The task of exposing the misstatements contained in this minority report is an easy one, and it will be done in terse but unmistakable language. In the brief space of fifteen minutes the most salient points can only be noticed. If the facts *assumed* by these gentlemen have no foundation, as a matter of course their argument based upon them falls to the ground. Now to the work:

First. It is asserted that the withdrawal from this Convention of certain delegates, was *not a resignation;* that *the vacancies referred to* (in the resolution of this Convention,) *had reference to the contingency of vacancies at the time of re-assembling, &c., i. e.* prospective vacancies! A balder absurdity was never uttered. Now what was the subject matter of which the Committee had jurisdiction? Was it not the "*Credentials of all persons claiming seats, &c., made vacant by the secession of delegates at Charleston?*" This Convention decided for itself whether *vacancies* had occurred. The Democracy of the States, affected by such withdrawal, in every instance, by appointing delegates anew, virtually admitted that vacancies had occurred. The claimants who appeared before your Committee, by accepting a new appointment admitted the fact, and the gentlemen of the minority stultify their own statement by acting on these very cases.

If there were no *vacancies* by secession, there was nothing for the Committee to do in respect to such cases. Out upon such nonsense!

Secondly, In attempting to show the inconsistency of the majority report, these gentlemen state that delegates were recommended to seats who had not been *re*-appointed or re-accredited to Baltimore after their secession at Charleston. To this a flat denial is given. This denial is based upon the evidence that was before the Committee. In every case, to wit, in Alabama, Georgia, Mississippi, Louisiana, Arkansas, and Texas, the parties admitted to seats by the majority report had been severally elected, appointed or re-accredited in some form, *since* the adjournment at Charleston. Of this fact, (if the evidence is reliable,) successful contradiction is challenged.

The minority gentlemen again stultify themselves, for they show that re-elections took place in three States, but they strangely forgot to state the fact, (established before the Committee,) that Messrs. Bayard and Whitely were *re-appointed* according to the *rules* of the Democracy of New Castle county, Delaware, and the Texas delegation were *directed* by the Executive Committee of that State to repair to Baltimore. It was in evidence before the Committee that this was a customary mode in those States of making nominations and appointing delegates, &c. The Committee considered it tantamount to a re-appointment. But what of Mississippi? Is it not the boast of some of the Mississippi delegation, that they have been re-appointed since their secession without opposition? If there has not been a new election, how comes it that delegates are here from Mississippi who were not at Charleston? The credentials of this delegation show upon their face that they were appointed by the Convention that sat on the 30th and 31st of May, 1860! The temerity of the gentlemen is without a parallel. No *new* election in Mississippi?

The following are some of the reasons which influenced the decision of the majority of the Committee in respect to the claimants from Alabama, of which L. P. Walker is Chairman. He and his associates claim to have been appointed by a Convention that sat on the 4th of June inst. Several of these were not *seceders* at Charleston. Mark this fact. But where were these delegates appointed on the 4th of June to go?—to what Convention? They were instructed by the Convention that appointed them to *repair to Richmond and to co-operate with the delegates of that Convention, &c.*

This is written upon the face of the credentials which were before your Committee. It is true, a little lower down in the same paper, they are "accredited" to this Convention!

These gentlemen were considered by your Committee, for this and other reasons, as delegates to the *Richmond* Convention and not to this. A roving commission! Suppose their instructions had included Conventions of the Black Republicans of Chicago, and of the Mormons of Utah—would this Convention allow them seats after they had boxed the compass under such a roving commission? Your Committee said no, and every true Democrat throughout the land will respond no! (Applause and some hisses.)

In the Arkansas case, the applicants for seats show no regularity of record. The seceders from Charleston having vacated their seats by the act of secession, the Committee felt it their duty either to recommend to the Convention the exclusion of both sets of applicants on the score of irregularity, or to admit both. The two District Conventions that are alleged to have sustained the action of the seceders and to have accredited them to Baltimore, had, by their own admission, no power to act in the premises, and therefore their action does not entitle the applicants to seats in the Convention. The opposing claimants were appointed by a Convention called, upon notice, in the usual way, by individuals not possessing an official character, and they are therefore, technically speaking, no more entitled than the others to seats; but the Committee, disregarding technicalities and not desiring to leave the Democracy of Arkansas unrepresented on this floor, decided to recommend that all the claimants be admitted to seats in the Convention, on the terms and conditions specified in their report.

In the Louisiana case it is clearly demonstrated likewise, that according to strict usage neither of the delegations were entitled to be received by this Convention. The seceders from Charleston did not present themselves before a new Convention, fresh from the people, but the *old* Convention which had adjourned *sine die*, (and therefore had by its own act and the usages of the party terminated its legal existence,) was called together to indorse the action of the seceders. That so called Convention had therefore no more right than any other like number of individual Democrats to *assume* to act as the representatives of the Democracy of Louisiana. Their proceedings in any case were of no force or validity, and their action in re-accrediting the seceding delegates to Baltimore was a gross usurpation of power on their part.

On the other hand, the delegation whose admission has been recommended by the Committee was appointed by a Convention assembled at Donaldsonville, composed of delegates from twenty-one parishes, (including the city of New Orleans,) out of thirty-nine parishes in the State. It is true that the call for the Democracy of the State to send delegates to the Convention was made by individual Democrats and by two distinct Democratic clubs, but inasmuch as the State Executive Committee refused to call a new Convention, and thus appeal to the Democracy to indorse or condemn the action of their delegates at Charleston who withdrew from the Convention, there was no other course to be pursued than for known and distinguished members of the party to issue the call, and for the Democracy to sustain it by the appointment of delegates in accordance with such call. An emergency had arisen, and inasmuch as the Executive Committee had refused to act, it seemed to the Committee that there was no other course left to the Democracy of Louisiana, but to assemble in Convention upon the spontaneous call of individual Democrats.

The admission of both of the delegations presenting themselves from Georgia, was recommended because the Committee believed that each of those delegations represent the opinions and sentiments of a part of the Democracy of the State. The withdrawal from the Convention of a part of its members was occasioned, as the evidence before the Committee demonstrated, by a difference of construction between them and their associates upon oertain points in the Democratic platform. Two Conventions, each claiming to be the correct and only exponents of the Democratic sentiment of the State, were held, and each appointed a delegation to this Convention. The regularity of both of these Conventions was involved in doubt. At all events one does not seem more regular than the other. After a full investigation of the facts in this case, the Committee, deeming it of the highest importance that the harmony of the party in Georgia required that both delegations should be admitted upon the floor of the Convention, with equal privileges, so recommended to the Convention in their report. It is undeniable that the appointing power in both cases was composed of delegates fresh from the ranks of the Democracy, and in the opinion of the Committee, the irregularities alleged in either case were not sufficient to justify the exclusion of either of the delegations.

The Committee consisted of twenty-five members, and the majority report received the sanction of sixteen, as to the greater portion of it, and the whole is approved by fifteen. The minority report is approved altogether by nine and but partially by one member.

Practically, then, the question is presented by the minority report, shall the statements and opinions of nine gentlemen outweigh and overbalance the statements and opinions of fifteen of equal respectability, touching the same matter?

Mr. BROWN, of North Carolina. It is with very great reluctance that I venture to interpose a few words upon this occasion. Sir, it would give me infinitely more pleasure to pour oil on the agitated waves which now disturb us, than to say anything which would have a contrary effect.

Mr. SIBLEY, of Minnesota. I rise to a point of order.

Mr. BROWN, of North Carolina. I ask leave of the Convention to make an explanation as to a matter of fact within my personal kowledge?

Mr. SIBLEY. The gentleman has anticipated my point of order by asking consent to speak.

Mr. GORMAN, of Minnesota. The necessity of the case requires that I shall insist upon the point of order.

The PRESIDENT. The Chair must decide that no debate is now in order.

Mr. STEVENS, of Oregon. I rise to a personal explanation.

Mr. STUART, of Michigan. I must object.

Mr. STEVENS. I have only two sentences to say.

Mr. STUART. I must object.

The PRESIDENT. The Chair must administer the rules of the Convention, which preclude debate in this stage of the business.

Mr. STEVENS. I appeal to the gentleman to allow me to make a personal explanation.

Mr. STUART. No gentleman will go farther than myself in relation to personal matters, but it is obvious to all that we must proceed with business.

The PRESIDENT. The Chairman will state that the first question in the order of motion and of vote is the proposition of the gentleman from Oregon (Mr. Stevens); that gentleman moves certain matter as a substitute for the report of the Committee. The Chair understands that motion to be equivalent to a motion to strike out and insert, and although the Chair feels that there may be some doubt as to what should be the construction of a case like this, and, indeed, of what is the true construction of the universal rule that a motion to strike out and insert is indivisible, without going to the extent that that universal declaration applies to this motion, or what is behind the motion. The Chair has, on reflection, come to the conclusion to rule that this motion to strike out and insert is indivisible; and, therefore, unless overruled by the Convention, the Chair will be prepared to put the question upon the series of resolutions in block. Having come to that conclusion, of course, upon a *prima facie* reflection upon the subject, the Chair will be subject to be instructed and directed by the Convention. The Chair had conceived that if the resolutions of the gentleman from Oregon (Mr. Stevens), should be adopted, then they would be divisible, and the separate propositions contained in the report of the minority would be susceptible of being voted upon separately; or if the motion for substitution should be rejected, then, upon the Convention being brought to a vote upon the resolutions of the gentleman from Missouri (Mr. Krum) those propositions would be separable. Upon this view of the whole case, the Chair has arrived at this *prima facie* conclusion, subject to be instructed or directed by the Convention.

Mr. COCHRAN, of New York. I shall appeal from the decision of the Chair, merely to make an explanation to the Convention upon the ruling of the Chair; and having made that explanation, I shall leave it to the contemplation and judgment of the Chair and withdraw the appeal. It is undoubtedly true that the motion to strike out and insert is indivisible ; the motion to strike out and inserting one independent proposition of the majority report is indivisible. But the rule is applicable to that and nothing more; that is, if upon the first branch of the majority report the motion should be made to strike out that branch and insert the first branch of the minority report, that motion would be indivisible. That is the extent of the application of the rule of the House. But that does not reach an amendment in the nature of a substitute. That motion, I think, is as divisible being a substitute as it would be if it was a simple motion to amend ; for the substitute is nothing more than an amendment of the nature of a substitute. I now withdraw my appeal.

Cries of "question," "question !"

The PRESIDENT. The Chair will repeat that he suggested the doubt in his mind, behind this question, whether the motion of the gentleman from Oregon (Mr. Stevens), might or might not involve divisible matter ; but he concluded still that it would be more convenient for him to rule upon that which is the *prima facie* construction of the rule of the Convention. If that *prima facie* construction be not correct, then the Chair would be most gladly instructed or overruled by the Convention.

Cries of "question," "question !"

The PRESIDENT. Before putting the question the Chair desires to remind the Convention that he informed the Convention yesterday that he had been requested to lay before the Convention a communication from gentlemen from Arkansas. He had no opportunity of having it read then ; he again informs the Convention that he has been requested to present that communication in order to have it read.

Mr. GORMAN, of Minnesota, and others, objected to the reading of the communication.

Objections being made, the President stated the communication could not be read.

The question recurred upon the motion to substitute the resolutions of Mr. Stevens, of Oregon, on part of the minority of the Committee on Credentials, for the resolutions of Mr. Krum, of Missouri, on part of the majority of the same Committee.

Upon that question, Mr. McCOOK called for a vote by States, which was ordered.

The PRESIDENT. The vote by States has been called for by the State of Ohio. The Secretary will, in the first place, report the resolutions now to be voted upon, as they have been corrected by Mr. Stevens, of Oregon, and then the Secretary will proceed to call the vote by States.

The resolutions were then read as follows :

1. *Resolved*, That B. F. Hallett is entitled to a seat in this Convention as a delegate from the 5th Congressional District of Massachusetts.

2. *Resolved*, That Johnson B. Clardy is entitled to a seat in this Convention as a delegate from the 8th Congressional District of the State of Missouri.

3. *Resolved*, That James A. Bayard and W. G. Whitely are entitled to seats in this Convention as delegates from the State of Delaware.

4. *Resolved*, That the delegation headed by R. W. Johnson are entitled to seats as delegates in this Convention from the State of Arkansas.

5. *Resolved*, That the delegation of which Guy N. Bryan is Chairman, are entitled to seats as delegates in this Convention from the State of Texas.

6. *Resolved*, That the delegation of which John Tarleton is Chairman are entitled to seats in this Convention as delegates from the State of Louisiana.

7. *Resolved*, That the delegation of which L. P. Walker is Chairman are entitled to seats in this Convention from the State of Alabama.

8. *Resolved*, That the delegation of which Henry L. Benning is Chairman are entitled to seats in this Convention from the State of Georgia.

9. *Resolved*, That the delegation from the State of Florida, accredited to the Charleston Convention, are entitled to take seats in this Convention and cast the vote of Florida.

10. *Resovled*, That George H. Gordon, E. Barksdale, W. S. Barry, H. C. Chambers, Joseph R. Davis, Beverly Matthews, Charles Clark, William S. Featherstone, P. F. Siddell, Wirt Adams, C. G Armistead, A. M. Clayton, and F. G. Hudson, are entitled to seats in this Convention as delegates from the State of Mississippi.

The Secretary proceeded to call the roll of States.

The Chair then announced the vote upon the question of substituting the resolutions of the minority in place of the majority resolutions—yeas 100½, nays 150—as follows:

	Yeas.	Nays.
Maine	2½	5½
New Hampshire	½	4½
Vermont	1½	3½
Massachusetts	8	5
Rhode Island		4
Connecticut	2½	3½
New York	35	
New Jersey	4	8
Pennsylvania	17	10
Delaware	2	
Maryland	5½	2
Virginia	14	1
North Carolina	9	1
Arkansas	½	½
Missouri	5	4
Tennessee	10	1
Kentucky	10	2
Ohio		23
Indiana		13
Illinois		11
Michigan		6
Wisconsin		5
Iowa		4
Minnesota	1½	2½
California	4	
Oregon	3	
	100½	150

Maryland ½ vote not voted; Tennessee 1 vote not voted.

So the motion to substitute the minority for the majority resolutions was rejected.

The PRESIDENT. The Secretary will now repeat the original resolutions in block if no division is called.

The SECRETARY read the resolutions.

Mr. FLOURNOY, of Arkansas, by unanimous consent, read the list of delegates from Arkansas. Mr. Hoadley's name should be transferred from Texas to Arkansas, and the name of Mr. Leroy Carroll should be De Rosa Carroll.

Mr. JONES, of Tennessee, and Mr. CHURCH, of New York, called for a division of the question on the resolutions—the vote to be taken on each resolution separately.

The PRESIDENT inquired of the gentleman from Ohio (Mr. McCook), whether he limited his call of the States to the whole matter, or intended it to apply to a single proposition?

Mr. McCOOK, of Ohio, said he limited his call to the vote just taken. There were propositions which did not require the vote to be taken by States, and it would consume time to do so.

The CHAIR. Then the call already made has exhausted the motion.

Mr. SAULSBURY, of Delaware, and Mr. GILMORE, of Pennsylvania, renewed the call of States.

The PRESIDENT. On each one of the propositions or one only?

Mr. SAULSBURY and Mr. GILMORE. Each one.

MISSISSIPPI.

The SECRETARY then read the first of the series of resolutions:

1. *Resolved*, That George H. Gordon, E. Barksdale, W. S. Barry, H. C. Chambers, Joseph R. Davis, Beverly Matthews, Charles Clark, William S. Featherstone, P. F. Siddell, Wirt Adams, C. G. Armistead, A. M. Clayton, and F. G. Hudson are entitled to seats in this Convention as delegates from the State of Mississippi.

The question being taken by States, resulted—ayes 250, nays 2½; the nays being a half vote from Iowa and two from Pennsylvania.

The resolution was accordingly adopted.

Mr. RYNDERS called for the admission of the delegates from Mississippi instanter, in accordance with the vote just taken.

Several delegates signified their dissent.

Mr. RYNDERS. I make that motion. I don't care whether you say aye or no.

Mr. COCHRAN said that the propositions were being voted upon *seriatim*, and until the last one was adopted, the whole question had not been put as determined, so that the delegates from Mississippi could not take their seats.

The PRESIDENT ruled in accordance with the suggestion of Mr. Cochran.

Mr. MASON, of Kentucky, respectfully differed with the Chair, but did not take an appeal.

Mr. STUART, of Michigan. The Chair is undoubtedly correct.

LOUISIANA.

The SECRETARY then read the second resolution, to wit:

2. *Resolved*, That Pierre Soule, F. Cottman, R. C. Wickliffe, Michael Ryan, Manuel White, Charles Brenveneau, Gustavus Leroy, J. E. Morse, A. S. Herron, M. D. Colmar, J. N. T. Richardson, and J. L. Walker, are entitled to seats in this Convention as delegates from the State of Louisiana.

The question being taken on the second resolution by States, resulted—ayes 153, nays 98—as follows:

	Yeas.	Nays						
Maine	5½	2½	Delaware	2		Illinois	11	
New Hampshire	4	½	Maryland	2½	5½	Michigan	6	
Vermont	4½	½	Virginia	1	13	Wisconsin	5	
Massachusetts	5	8	North Carolina	2	8	Iowa	4	
Rhode Island	4		Arkansas	½	½	Minnesota	2½	1½
Connecticut	3½	2½	Missouri	4	5	California		4
New York	36		Tennessee	2	10	Oregon		3
New Jersey	2¼	4½	Kentucky	2	10			
Pennsylvania	10	17	Ohio	23			153	98
			Indiana	13				

The resolution was accordingly adopted.

ARKANSAS.

The third resolution was then read:

3. *Resolved*, That R. W. Johnson, T. C. Hindman, J. P. Johnson, De Rosa Carroll, J. Gould, John A. Jordan, B. B. Burrow and F. W. Hoadley be admitted to seats as delegates from the State of Arkansas, with power to cast two votes, and that Thos. H. Bradley, M. Hooper and D. C. Cross be also admitted to seats as delegates from the same State, with power to cast *one vote*, and in case either portion of said delegates shall refuse or neglect to take their said seats, or to cast their said votes, the other portion of said delegates taking seats in this Convention shall be entitled to cast the entire three votes of said State.

Mr. SAULSBURY moved to divide the resolution and take the question on three distinct branches of it, to wit: first, in regard to the admission of Mr. Johnson and his coadjutors, with power to cast two votes; second, as to the admission of Mr. Hooper and coadjutors, with power to cast one vote; and third, as to how the vote of the State is to be cast in case either one of those delegates does not choose to take his seat.

The PRESIDENT ruled the resolution divisible, as each part makes sense with the other parts rejected.

The question was then stated on the first part of the resolution, and the State of Maine called.

Mr. WRIGHT, of Massachusetts, appealed from the decision of the Chair as to the divisibility of the question.

Mr. STURMAN made a point of order that the State of Maine, having been called, the appeal came too late.

The PRESIDENT. The State of Maine has not answered.

Mr. Gorman, of Minnesota, inquired how it would be possible, if the Convention rejected the latter part of the resolution, for the State of Arkansas to be represented by any other than two votes? It would disfranchise the State of one vote.

The President stated that it was not in the power of the Convention to adopt a proposition which was unjust or which would disfranchise a State.

Mr. Stuart moved to lay the appeal from the decision of the Chair on the table, which was agreed to.

The vote was then taken by States on the first part of the resolution, and resulted—ayes 182, nays 69—as follows:

	Yeas.	Nays.		Yeas.	Nays.		Yeas	Nays.
Maine	5½	2½	North Carolina	1	9	Ohio	23	
New Hampshire	5		South Carolina			Indiana	13	
Vermont	5		Georgia			Illinois	11	
Massachusetts	13		Florida			Michigan	6	
Rhode Island	4		Alabama			Wisconsin	5	
Connecticut	6		Louisiana			Iowa	3½	1½
New York	35		Mississippi			Minnesota	4	
New Jersey	7		Texas			California		4
Pennsylvania	10	17	Arkansas			Oregon		3
Delaware	2		Missouri	9				
Maryland	2½	5½	Tennessee	11½	1½		182	69
Virginia		15	Kentucky		12			

The vote was then taken on the second branch of the resolution, and resulted—ayes 150, nays 100½—as follows:

	Yeas.	Nays.		Yeas.	Nays.		Yeas.	Nays.
Maine	5½	2½	North Carolina	1	9	Ohio	23	
New Hampshire	5		South Carolina	0	0	Indiana	13	
Vermont	4½	½	Georgia	0	0	Illinois	11	
Massachusetts	5	8	Florida	0	0	Michigan	6	
Rhode Island	4		Alabama	0	0	Wisconsin	5	
Connecticut	3½	2½	Louisiana	0	0	Iowa	4	
New York	35		Mississippi	0	0	Minnesota	2½	½
New Jersey	2½	4½	Texas	0	0	California		4
Pennsylvania	10	17	Arkansas	0	0	Oregon		3
Delaware		2	Missouri	4	5			
Maryland	2	6	Tennessee	½	11		150	100½
Virginia	1	14	Kentucky	2	10			

Arkansas declining to vote.

Mr. Brodhead, of Pennsylvania, for the purpose of saving time, appealed to the gentleman who called for the vote by States to withdraw it on the remainder of the resolution.

The call was accordingly withdrawn, and the question taken *viva voce*, resulting in the adoption of the last branch of the resolution.

So the entire resolution was adopted.

TEXAS.

The fourth resolution, in regard to Texas, was then read as follows:

4. *Resolved*, That Guy M. Bryan, F. R. Lubbock, F. S. Stockdale, E. Greer, H. R. Runnells, Thos. P. Ochiltree, M. W. Covie and J. S. Crosby, are entitled to seats as delegates from Texas.

Mr. Brodhead, of Pennsylvania, suggested that the vote upon this resolution be taken *viva voce*, but objection being made,

The Secretary proceeded to call the roll of States, which having been concluded the vote was announced: Yeas 250, nays 2½, the nays being Pennsylvania 2, Iowa ½.

The resolution was accordingly adopted.

DELAWARE.

The fifth resolution was then read, as follows:

5. *Resolved*, That James A. Bayard and Wm. G. Whitely are entitled to seats from the county of New Castle, Delaware.

Mr. Brodhead, of Pennsylvania, suggested that it would save time to take the vote *viva voce*, which was agreed to.

The question being taken, the resolution was adopted.

MASSACHUSETTS.

The sixth resolution was then read, as follows:

6. *Resolved*, That K. S. Chaffee, who was duly admited at Charleston as a delegate from the Fifth Congressional District of Massachusetts, is still entitled to said seat in this Convention, and that Benjamin F. Hallett, who has assumed said seat, is not entitled thereto.

The question being taken upon this resolution by States, resulted—yeas 138, nays 112½—as follows:

	Yeas.	Nays.		Yeas.	Nays.		Yeas.	Nays.
Maine	5½	2½	North Carolina		10	Ohio	23	
New Hampshire	2½	2½	South Carolina			Indiana	13	
Vermont	3	2	Georgia			Illinois	11	
Massachusetts	3	8½	Florida			Michigan	6	
Rhode Island	4		Alabama			Wisconsin	5	
Connecticut	3½	2½	Louisiana			Iowa	3½	1½
New York	35		Mississippi			Minnesota	2½	1½
New Jersey	1½	4½	Texas			California		4
Pennsylvania	9½	17½	Arkansas		1	Oregon		3
Delaware		2	Missouri	4	5		—	—
Maryland	2½	5½	Tennessee		12		138	112½
Virginia		15	Kentucky		12			

The resolution was accordingly adopted.

Mr. Stuart, of Michigan. I rise to a privileged question. I move to reconsider the vote just taken, and move to lay that motion on the table. I understand that that motion cannot now be taken up, but it can be received. I also make the same motion in regard to each of the other votes taken this morning upon the propositions from the Committee on Credentials, including the vote on the minority reports.

The President said the several motions of Mr. Stuart would be receeived and entered upon the journal.

So the motions of Mr. Stuart were considered and entered, as having been so many distinct motions made and entered in their order, upon the rejection of the Minority Report, and the adoption of each resolution reported by the majority of the Committee on Credentials, to be acted upon when properly called up, in their order.

MISSOURI.

The seventh resolution was then read as follows:

7. *Resolved*, That John O'Fallon, Jr., who was duly admitted at Charleston, as a delegate from the Eighth Congressional District of Missouri, is still entitled to said seat in this Convention; and that John B. Clardy, who has assumed said seat, is not entitled thereto.

The question being taken by States upon the resolution—it resulted—yeas 138½, nays 112—as follows:

	Yeas.	Nays.		Yeas.	Nays.		Yeas.	Nays.
Maine	5½	2½	North Carolina		10	Ohio	23	
New Hampshire	2½	2½	South Carolina			Indiana	13	
Vermont	3	2	Georgia			Illinois	11	
Massachusetts	5	8	Florida			Michigan	6	
Rhode Island	4		Alabama			Wisconsin	5	
Connecticut	3½	2½	Louisiana			Iowa	3½	1½
New York	35		Mississippi			Minnesota	2½	1½
New Jersey	1½	5½	Texas			California		4
Pennsylvania	10	17	Arkansas	½	1½	Oregon		3
Delaware		2	Missouri	1½	6		—	—
Maryland	2½	5½	Tennessee		12		138½	112
Virginia		15	Kentucky		12			

The resolution was accordingly adopted.

Mr. CESSNA, of Pennsylvania, moved that the vote just taken be reconsidered, and that the motion to reconsider be laid upon the table.

The motion was received and ordered to be entered upon the journal.

ALABAMA.

The eighth resolution was then read, as follows :

8. *Resolved*, That R. A. Baker, D. C. Humphreys, John Forsyth, Wm. Garrett, J. J. Seibles, S. C. Posey, L. E. Parsons, Joseph C. Bradley, Thomas B. Cooper, James Williams, O. H. Bynum, Samuel D. Weakley, L. V. B. Martin, John W. Wornack, W. R. R. Wyatt, Benjamin Harrison, Thomas M. Mathews and Norment McLeod, are entitled to seats in this Convention as delegates from the State of Alabama.

The question then being taken by States upon this resolution, it resulted—yeas 148½, nays 101½,—as follows :

	Yeas.	Nays.		Yeas.	Nays.		Yeas.	Nays.
Maine	5½	2½	North Carolina	1½	8	Ohio	28	
New Hampshire	2½	2	South Carolina			Indiana	13	
Vermont	4½	½	Georgia			Illinois	11	
Massachusetts	5	8	Florida			Michigan	6	
Rhode Island	4		Alabama			Wisconsin	5	
Connecticut	3½	2½	Louisiana			Iowa	4	
New York	35		Mississippi			Minnesota	2½	1½
New Jersey	3	4	Texas			California		4
Pennsylvania	10	17	Arkansas	½	½	Oregon		3
Delaware		2	Missouri	4	5			
Maryland	2	6	Tennessee	2	10		148½	101½
Virginia	½	14½	Kentucky	1½	10½			

New Hampshire ½, declined voting.

The resolution was accordingly adopted.

Mr. CESSNA, of Pennsylvania, moved to reconsider the vote just taken, and that that motion be laid upon the table.

The motion was received and ordered to be entered upon the journal.

Mr. SEWARD, of Georgia, sent the following communication to the Secretary's desk to be filed, a copy of which had also upon the assembling of the Convention in the morning, been placed in the hands of the President of the Convention :

BALTIMORE, JUNE 22, 1860.

Hon. Caleb Cushing, President of the National Democratic Convention :

SIR :—In obedience to instructions herewith enclosed, I withdraw the application of the National Democratic Delegates from Georgia, for seats in the Convention over which you preside, and I request that the instructions be read to the Convention.

Yours respectfully, JAMES GARDNER,
Chairman Georgia National Democratic Delegation.

CONSULTATION ROOM OF THE GEORGIA NATIONAL DELEGATION,
BALTIMORE, JUNE 22, 1860.

Resolved, That our Chairman, Mr. Gardner, be and is hereby instructed to withdraw the application of the National Democratic Delegates of Georgia, for seats in the Convention now sitting in this city.

Resolved, That we are prompted to this course by a sincere desire to relieve the Convention of embarrassment, and to promote as far as possible the harmony of the Convention.

Resolved, That we do not hereby admit that the delegation headed by the Hon. Henry L. Benning, as Chairman, represents the National Democracy of Georgia, nevertheless, we shall rejoice sincerely to see them adhere to the Convention, and in good faith support its nominees.

JAMES GARDNER, *Chairman.*

B. Y. MARTIN, *Secretary.*

GEORGIA.

The ninth and last resolution of the series was then read, as follows :

9. *Resolved*, That the delegation from the State of Georgia, of which H. L. Benning is Chairman, be admitted to the Convention, with power to cast one half of the vote of said State ; and that the delegation from said State of which Col. Gardner is Chairman, be also admitted to the Convention, with power to cast one-half the vote of said State, and if either of said delegations refuse or neglect to cast the vote as above indicated, that in such case the delegates present in the Convention be authorized to cast the full vote of said State.

The SECRETARY proceeded to call the roll, and as he called the State of Maine—

Mr. WILLIAMSON, of Kentucky, called for a division of the question upon the resolution.

Mr. STUART, of Michigan. I submit that that motion cannot be made. The rule is that if the remaining portion will by itself stand so as to make sense, and the portion included in the first division, will also by itself stand so as to make sense, then it may be divided, but not otherwise. I have examined this resolution, with a view to call for the division myself, but I am satisfied that it is incapable of division.

Mr. SIBLEY, of Minnesota. I call the gentleman to order; the Secretary had commenced the call of the roll, and the State of Maine had responded.

The PRESIDENT. The Chair thinks that the gentleman from Kentucky, (Mr. Williamson) addressed the Chair before any response was given from Maine.

Mr. STUART, of Michigan. The rule is that the portion to be voted upon must make sense by itself, and the portion left must make sense by itself, or else the proposition is not divisible.

The PRESIDENT. The Chair is informed by the Secretary that the State of Maine had been called, and the response entered upon the record, before the Chair was addressed. If that be so, the Chair is bound to decide that the call for the division is too late.

Mr. WILLIAMSON, of Kentucky. I think there must be an error on the part of the Secretary. I addressed the Chair before the State of Maine responded to the call of the Secretary ; but I did not get my proposition fully submitted before that State responded.

Mr. RYNDERS, of New York. I can say that we here understood the vote of Maine to be announced before the Chair was addressed.

Mr. JONES, of Tennessee. I wish to know if I did not demand a division of the question upon every distinct proposition susceptible of division ?

The PRESIDENT. That was the understanding of the Chair of the effect of the demand of the gentleman from Tennessee (Mr. Jones) and the gentleman from Delaware (Mr. Saulsbury.)

Mr. JONES. Then I submit to the Chair whether we cannot vote upon each portion of the resolution now reported to the Convention ?

The PRESIDENT. If the gentleman from Tennessee (Mr. Jones) claims that right now, the Chair will be bound to rule as he did in the case of Arkansas. The Chair will be bound to look into the question of divisibility. It will not be a division upon the demand of the gentleman from Kentucky, (Mr. Williamson,) but the demand of the gentleman from Tennessee, (Mr. Jones.)

Subsequently the President said : The Chair, on inspecting the 9th resolution, pertaining to the State of Georgia, perceives that it is constructed on precisely the same principles with the resolution pertaining to the State of Arkansas. And the Chair having ruled that that was divisible, is bound to make the same ruling in this case. If the Chair is in error upon this subject he has no pride of opinion about it, and of course submits it to the Convention.

But the Chair must make the decision that it is divisible. The Secretary will report the first branch of the resolution.

The SECRETARY reported it as follows:

"*Resolved*, That the delegation from the State of Georgia, of which H. L. Benning is Chairman, be admitted to the Convention, with power to cast one-half of the vote of said State."

Mr. WATERBURY, of New York. Is it in order to divide the first part of the resolution?

Mr. STUART, of Michigan. That is the very point that I raised. If you divide the first part of the resolution, and reject the first part and retain the last part, it will have no sense.

The PRESIDENT. The Chair has ruled that the part just read by the Secretary constitutes the first branch of the resolution.

Mr. BRODHEAD, of Pennsylvania. I would suggest that the first division should end with the word "Convention," so that it will read—

"*Resolved*, That the delegation from the State of Georgia, of which H. L. Benning is Coairman, be admitted to the Convention."

Mr. STUART, of Michigan. The idea is this: The Chair cannot anticipate what the vote will be; the proposition may be carried or rejected. But it is not susceptible of division unless, in either event, the remaining words have a substantive meaning by themselves. Suppose the first part is voted down and the latter part adopted—"with power to cast one-half of the vote of said State." Those words would have no meaning at all by themselves.

Mr. COCHRAN, of New York. The gentleman from Michigan (Mr. Stuart) states the proposition correctly. If the first branch of the resolution be abstracted the last is naught.

The PRESIDENT. The Chair has two or three times endeavored to state what he means to rule; but gentlemen have interposed with suggestions from time to time so that he has not as yet been able to do it. The Chair takes the same view of this resolution as he did of the resolution in regard to Georgia. The resolution begins—

"*Resolved*, That the delegation from the State of Georgia, of which H. L. Benning is Chairman, be admitted to the Convention with power to cast one-half of the vote of that State."

The Chair finds there a proposition having sense. It may or may not, if adopted alone, operate unjustly. That is not a qnestion of order; the question of justice or injustice is independent of the question of sense.

As to the decision suggested by the gentleman from Pennsylvania (Mr. Brodhead), if the first part he proposes be rejected, then there remain words of no possible application to any part of the resolution, to wit: "with power to cast one-half of the vote of said State." The view, therefore, of the Chair is that the division must be at the end of the words, "of said State."

Mr. SEWARD, of Georgia. I rise to a question of privilege on behalf of the contestants from the State of Georgia. I send a communication to the Chair, which I desire to have read. It is intended as a peace measure, and to relieve this Convention of this perplexing and troublesome question. [Cries of "object," "object," and "question."]

Mr. WILLIAMSON, of Kentucky. I withdraw the call for a division of this resolution, if it is upon my motion.

The PRESIDENT. The Chair understands that the call is upon the motion of the gentleman from Tennessee (Mr. Jones.)

Mr. WILLIAMSON. Then I hope that gentleman will withdraw the call.

Mr. JONES. I cannot withdraw it.

Mr. SEWARD, of Georgia. I insist upon my question of privilege, and that no gentleman has a right to object to it, because it affects the rights of members upon this floor.

The PRESIDENT. The Chair will state to the Convention that the gentleman from Georgia (Mr. Seward) presents this letter and desires that it be read.

Mr. BUTTERWORTH, of New York. I object to the reading of it at this time.

The PRESIDENT. The Chair understands, in the first place, that in the present stage of the question—that is, under the operation of the previous question—it is not competent to introduce any document to be read, except by unanimous consent of the Convention, or under a suspension of the rules. And the Chair is not aware how, in this stage of the question, there can be a motion to suspend the rules. Therefore, the Chair understands that in this stage of the question there must be unanimous consent for the reading of a document.

[It was understood that the letter was from Col. Gardner, the Chairman of the contesting delegation from the State of Georgia, notifying the Convention that they withdrew from all further contest, and which letter had been placed on the Secretary's files.]

Mr. JONES, of Tennessee. At the request of several gentlemen I withdraw my call for a division of the question.

The PRESIDENT stated the question to be upon agreeing to the entire resolution, as originally reported by the Secretary to the Convention.

The question being then taken by States upon the resolution, it was rejected—yeas 106½, nays 145—as follows:

	Yeas.	Nays.		Yeas.	Nays.		Yeas.	Nays.
Maine	4	4	Maryland	2	6	Michigan	6	
New Hampshire	2	3	Virginia	1	14	Wisconsin	5	
Vermont	3½	1½	North Carolina	1	9	Iowa	4	
Massachusetts	5	8	Arkansas	½	½	Minnesota	2½	1½
Rhode Island	4		Missouri	4	5	California		4
Connecticut	3½	8½	Tennessee		12	Oregon		3
New York		35	Kentucky		11½			
New Jersey	2	5	Ohio	28			106½	145
Pennsylvania	9½	17½	Indiana	13				
Delaware		2	Illinois	11				

Mr. CHURCH, of New York. The delegation from New York have had no opportunity

The PRESIDENT. Will the gentleman excuse the Chair a moment? The Chair will state that as he now understands it all the resolutions reported from the Committee on Credentials have been acted upon, and therefore the previous question, so far as it is applicable to this subject matter has been exhausted.

Mr. CHURCH, of New York. The New York delegation have had no opportunity to vote upon the question of the admission of delegates from the State of Georgia in accordance with their wishes, or as they believe would be right and just to the Democracy of that State. Coming here, as the New York delegation did, with the determination, so far as it lay in their power, to reconcile the Democracy of this great nation, and to harmonize the party, so that the results of this Convention would be indorsed by the Democracy of this nation, we propose now to submit a motion in relation to that State—Georgia—which I have no doubt will meet with the approbation of this Convention. That motion is that the delegation from the State of Georgia, claiming seats in this Convention, of which H. L. Benning is Chairman, be admitted to this Convention, and upon that I call the previous question.

Mr. BRODHEAD, of Pennsylvania. I have a similar proposition, reduced to writing, in the form of a resolution, which I hope the gentleman will accept.

Mr. CHURCH. I will accept it.

The PRESIDENT. The Chair wishes to understand whether the proposition sent to the Chair by the gentleman from Pennsylvania (Mr. Brodhead), is the same proposition as that submitted by the gentleman from New York (Mr. Church ?)

Mr. BRODHEAD. It is the same.

Mr SEWARD, of Georgia. I rise to a point of order.

The PRESIDENT. The Chair asks the gentleman to let the resolution be reported.

The resolution was then read as follows :

Resolved, That the delegation of which Henry L. Benning is Chairman are entitled to seats in this Convention from the State of Georgia.

Mr. SEWARD. My point of order is this : That the majority report, as amended, has not been acted upon. And although the previous question may have been exhausted, that is the pending proposition before the Convention, and the Convention must be brought to a direct vote upon the report as amended before it is finally disposed of.

The PRESIDENT. In regard to the question of order raised by the gentleman from Georgia (Mr. Seward), the Chair considers that, according to his understanding of the state of proceedings, all matters reported from the Committee, upon which it is competent to vote, have been voted upon, and, therefore, the previous question is exhausted, and no additional motion need be put or is in order to be put.

Mr. HALLETT, of Massachusetts, here obtained the floor, but was called to order by several delegates.

Mr. CHURCH, of New York. I rise to a point of order. I submit that having myself offered a resolution and called the previous question upon it, no debate is in order.

The PRESIDENT. The gentleman from New York undoubtedly has reason in his suggestion. The gentleman from Massachusetts has risen to something, the Chair cannot tell what. It may or may not be some competent motion, notwithstanding the gentleman has moved the previous question.

Mr. CHURCH. The gentleman has announced that he rose for the purpose of discussing my resolution.

The PRESIDENT. The Chair did not so understand him. The gentleman from Massachusetts will state to what question he has arisen.

Mr. HALLETT. I understand that a motion was made by the gentleman from New York to admit the Georgia delegation accredited to the Charleston Convention ?

The PRESIDENT. Yes, sir.

Mr. HALLETT. And that the motion is before the Convention ?

The PRESIDENT. The gentleman from New York demanded the previous question, and it is the duty of the Chair to put it unless some privileged motion intervenes. The Secretary will please read the resolution of the gentleman from New York.

The resolution was read accordingly.

The PRESIDENT. The question is on seconding the previous question.

The question being then taken on seconding the previous question, it was agreed to.

The question recurring on ordering the main question, it was also agreed to.

The question being then taken on the resolution of the gentleman from New York (Mr. Church), it was adopted, and the Georgia seceding delegates declared entitled to their seats.

Mr. HALLETT and numerous others addressed the Chair at the same instant.

The PRESIDENT recognized the gentleman from Massachusetts, and

Mr. HALLETT addressed the Convention and moved that the Convention take a recess till 5 o'clock.

Mr. Stuart. I now move to lay on the table the motion to reconsider, made by the gentleman from Massachusetts.

Mr. Cochran. I now move that when the Convention adjourn it be to meet at 5 o'clock.

The President inquired if the gentleman from Michigan asked for a vote on each one of the resolutions to lay it on the table, or if his motion referred to the 9th only?

Mr. Russell, Chairman of the Virginia delegation. Mr. President, I wish, before the Convention adjourns, to make an announcement in behalf of the Virginia delegation. I wish to do it at the proper time.

The President. The Chair would like to be informed by the gentleman from Michigan whether his motion is intended to be applied to each of the resolutions *seriatim?*

Mr. Stuart. I have no choice. I suppose the proper mode of proceeding would be to call up one at a time. If the Chair deems it his duty to take them up in this order, I am entirely satisfied.

The President. The Chair does not deem it his duty to volunteer, but if any gentleman wishes to call for the vote in that order he can do so.

Mr. Stuart. I will call for them in their order.

The President. The question is now upon the motion of the gentleman from New York (Mr. Cochran,) that when the Convention adjourn it be to meet at 5 o'clock this afternoon.

Upon that question Mr. Saulsbury called for a vore by States, which was ordered. The question being then taken by States, the motion was not agreed to—Yeas 82½, nays 168.

Mr. Cessna, of Pennsylvania, called up the several motions to reconsider, with the accompanying motions to lay on the table.

The President stated the first question to be upon laying upon the table the motion to reconsider the vote by which the Convention refused to substitute the resolutions reported by the minority of the Committee on Credentials for those reported by the majority of said Committee.

Upon this question the State of Tennessee demanded a vote by States which was ordered. The question being then taken by States, the motion to lay on the table was not agreed to—yeas 113½, nays 138½, as follows :

	Yeas.	Nays.		Yeas.	Nays.		Yeas.	Nays.
Maine	5½	2½	Maryland	2	6	Michigan	6	
New Hampshire	3	2	Virginia		15	Wisconsin	5	
Vermont	4½	½	North Carolina	1	9	Iowa	4	
Massachusetts	5	8	Arkansas	½	½	Minnesota	2½	1½
Rhode Island	4		Missouri	4½	4½	California		4
Connecticut	3½	2½	Tennesee		12	Oregon		3
New York		35	Kentucky	2	10			
New Jersey	3½	3½	Ohio	23			113½	138½
Pennsylvania	10	17	Indiana	13				
Delaware		2	Illinois	11				

The question recurred upon the motion to reconsider the vote rejecting the minority resolutions.

Mr. Cochran, of New York, moved that when this Convention adjourn, it be to meet this evening at 7 o'clock, which was agreed to.

Mr. Cochran moved that the Convention do now adjourn, which was agreed to.

And the Convention accordingly took a recess until 7 o'clock P. M.

EVENING SESSION.

The Convention was called to order at a few minutes past 7 o'clock.

The President stated that the pending question to be upon reconsidering the vote by which the Convention refused to substitute the resolutions submitted upon the part of the minority of the Committee on Credentials in place of the resolutions submitted by the majority of said Committee.

Mr. CESSNA, of Pennsylvania, called for the previous question upon this motion, which was seconded, and the main question ordered to be put.

The question recurred upon the motion to reconsider.

Mr. SAULSBURY, of Delaware, called for a vote by States, which was ordered.

The question being then taken by States, the motion to reconsider was not agreed to—yeas 113, nays 139—as follows:

	Yeas.	Nays.		Yeas.	Nays.		Yeas.	Nays.
Maine	2½	5½	Maryland	6	2	Michigan		6
New Hampshire	2	3	Virginia	15		Wisconsin		5
Vermont	1	4	North Carolina	9	1	Iowa		4
Massachusetts	8	5	Arkansas	½	½	Minnesota	1½	2½
Rhode Island		4	Missouri	4½	4½	California	4	
Connecticut	2½	3½	Tennessee	10	2	Oregon	3	
New York		35	Kentucky	10	2			
New Jersey	4½	2½	Ohio		23		113	139
Pennsylvania	17	10	Indiana		13			
Delaware	2		Illinois		11			

The next question was upon the motion to lay upon the table the motion to reconsider the vote by which the Convention adopted the first resolution of the majority report in relation to delegates from Mississippi.

The question being taken, the motion to lay on the table was agreed to.

The next question was upon the motion to lay upon the table the motion to reconsider the vote by which the Convention adopted the majority resolution in relation to delegates from Louisiana.

Mr. SAULSBURY, of Delaware. At the request of others, not that I care so much about it myself, I call for a vote by States.

The question being taken by States, the motion to lay on the table was agreed to—yeas 150½, nays 99,—as follows:—

	Yeas.	Nays.		Yeas.	Nays.		Yeas.	Nays.
Maine	5½	2½	Maryland	2	6	Michigan	6	
New Hampshire	4½	1½	Virginia		15	Wisconsin	5	
Vermont	4½	½	North Carolina	1	8½	Iowa	4	
Massachusetts	5	8	Arkansas	½	1½	Minnesota	2½	1½
Rhode Island	4		Missouri	4½	4½	California		4
Connecticut	3½	2½	Tennessee	2	10	Oregon		3
New York	35		Kentucky	2	10			
New Jersey	2½	4½	Ohio	23			150½	99
Pennsylvania	10	17	Indiana	13				
Delaware		2	Illinois	11				

The next question was upon laying upon the table the motion to reconsider the vote by which the Convention adopted the majority resolution in relation to delegates from Arkansas.

The question being taken, the motion was agreed to.

The next question was upon the same motion in relation to Texas.

The question being taken, the motion to reconsider was laid upon the table.

The next question was upon the same motion in relation to Delaware, and the motion to lay upon the table was agreed to.

The next question was upon laying upon the table the motion to reconsider the vote by which the Convention adopted the 6th resolution in relation to the claim of Mr. K. S. Chaffee, as against Mr. B. F. Hallett.

The motion to reconsider was laid upon the table.

The next question was upon laying upon the table the motion to reconsider the vote by which the Convention adopted the 7th resolution of the majority report, giving John O'Fallon, Jr., the seat in the Missouri contest.

The motion to reconsider was laid upon the table.

The next question was upon the motion to lay upon the table the motion to reconsider the vote upon the resolution in relation to Alabama—the motion was agreed to.

The same with regard to the vote of the Convention, rejecting the resolution of the majority in relation to Georgia.

The next question was upon the motion to lay upon the table the motion to reconsider the vote adopting the resolution offered by Mr. Church, of New York, admitting the original delegates from the State of Georgia to vote in the Convention.

The motion was laid upon the table.

Mr. CESSNA, of Pennsylvania. I now offer the following resolution :

Resolved, That this Convention do now proceed to nominate candidates for President and Vice President of the United States.

And on that resolution I call the previous question.

Mr. STANSBURY. I move that the Convention do now adjourn *sine die.*

The PRESIDENT. The gentleman from Pennsylvania (Mr. Cessna) moved a resolution to proceed to ballot for nominations for President and Vice President, and upon that motion he demanded the previous question. It is the duty of the Chair to call for a second to that question in the ordinary course of business. The Chair understands the gentleman from Maryland (Mr. Stansbury) interposed with a motion the Convention do adjourn *sine die.*

Mr. McKIBBEN, of Pennsylvania. I second that motion.

The PRESIDENT. The Chair supposes that motion to be in order.

Mr. CESSNA, of Pennsylvania. Certainly ; there is no doubt about it; and on that motion I demand a vote by States.

Mr. McKIBBEN. The gentleman has no right to speak for the Pennsylvania delegation and demand a vote by States.

A VOICE. New York demands it.

Mr. MOFFATT, of Virginia. I rise to a question of privilege.

Mr. STANSBURY, of Maryland. As gentlemen object to my motion I withdraw it.

Mr. MOFFATT, of Virginia. Have I the right to the floor ?

The PRESIDENT. The gentleman is entitled to the floor.

Mr. MOFFATT, of Virginia. I understand that the proceedings in which we have been engaged this evening have been fully consummated ; and that the question of contested seats here is at an end. I therefore raise this point, whether or not it is the duty of the Chair at once to issue tickets to the admitted delegates, in order that they participate in the proceedings of this Convention.

The PRESIDENT. The Chair will state that he so understands his duty, and has already given that direction.

The demand for the previous question was then seconded.

Mr. RUSSELL, of Virginia. If it be the pleasure of yourself, Mr. President, and the Convention, I will now make the brief announcement of which I made mention this morning.

Mr. GORMAN, of Minnesota. I object to the gentleman's proceeding, and I raise the point of order that he has no right to make any debate, or any other announcement pending the call for the previous question.

Mr. RUSSELL. I rise to a question of privilege.

The PRESIDENT. The gentleman from Virginia (Mr. Russell) rises to address the Chair, and the Chair desires to know what proposition he desires to make.

VOICES. Let the gentleman proceed.

Mr. RUSSELL. I consider it a question of privilege, and the Chair will decide whether it is so or not when I submit it. I will detain the Convention but a very brief time. I understand that the action of this Convention upon the various questions arising out of the reports from the Committee on Credentials has become final, complete and irrevocable. And it has become my duty now, by direction of a large majority of the delegation from Virginia, respectfully to inform this body that it is inconsistent with their convictions of duty to participate longer in its deliberations.

The delegates from Virginia, who participate in this movement, have come to the conclusion which I have announced, after long, mature and anxious deliberation, and after, in their judgment, having exhausted all honorable efforts to obviate this necessity. In addition to the facts which appear upon your record, I desire the attention of this body long enough only to state that it is ascertained that the delegations to which you, sir, under the order of this Convention have just directed tickets to be issued—some of them at least, and all of them whom we regard as the representatives of the Democracy of their States—will decline to join here in the deliberations of this body. For the rest, the reasons which impel us to take this important step will be rendered to those to whom only we are responsible, the Democracy of the Old Dominion. To you, sir, and to the body over which you preside, I have only to say in addition, that we bid you a respectful adieu.

Mr. MOFFATT, of Virginia, obtained the floor.

The portion of the delegation from Virginia which retired then left their seats.

Mr. MOFFATT resumed If it be your pleasure, Mr. President, and the pleasure of this Convention, I desire to do what I have not done since the time of my first connection with this body, and that is to occupy some portion of your time in defining the position which I occupy as one of the representatives from the Commonwealth of Virginia, and to say a few words on behalf of my colleagues who remain as members of this Convention. I will commence by saying that I was appointed, as was my colleague who represents jointly with me the Eleventh Electoral District of Virginia, by a District Convention, composed of delegates elected by the sovereign people of that district. I owe allegiance to that district Convention and to none else. I was elected by that district Convention a delegate to this National Convention, and was given a charter to represent that constituency in the Convention.

But I never was elected to any other Convention. I was authorized to represent that constituency in this Convention, but I never was authorized to withdraw from it. I was appointed to carry out the wishes of the people, who are national and not sectional—men who are willing to stand by the banner now, as they have in times past, of the National Democracy. Therefore, acting here in the absence of instructions from that constituency, I can never feel justified in separating from this body. I desire to say a few words in regard to the action that has precipitated upon the country the fearful issue which we now behold. What is the spectacle that presents itself?

Mr. AUGUSTUS SCHELL, of New York, called the gentleman to order, and objected to his proceeding further in his remarks.

Mr. LANDER, of North Carolina. Mr. President, painful as the duty is, it is, nevertheless, my duty to announce here, as a representative of the delegates from North Carolina, that a very large majority of them are compelled to retire permanently from this Convention on account of the unjust action, as we conceive, that has this day been perpetrated upon some of our sovereign States and fellow-citizens of the South. We of the South have heretofore maintained and supported the Northern Democracy, for the reason that they are willing to attribute to us in the South equality in the Union. The vote to-day has satisfied the majority of the North Carolina delegates that that being refused by our brethren of the Northern Democracy, North Carolina—Rip Van Winkle as you may call her—can no longer remain in this Convention. The rights of sovereign States and of gentlemen of the South have been denied by a majority of this body. We cannot act, as we conceive, in view of this wrong. I use the word "wrong" with no intention to reflect upon those gentlemen of the North Carolina delegation who differ with me or with the majority of the delegation. For these reasons, without assigning any more, as I have no idea of inflicting a speech upon this Convention, who are

10

in no state of preparation to receive it, I announce that eight out of ten of the votes of North Carolina ask to retire.

Mr. EWING, of Tennessee. Mr. President, in behalf of the delegation from Tennessee, I beg leave to address this Convention upon this occasion, so important, and, to us, so solemn in its consequences. The delegation from Tennessee have exhibited, so far as they knew how, every disposition to harmonize this Convention, and to bring its labors to a happy result. They were the first, when the majority platform was not adopted, to seek for some proposition for compromise—something that would enable us to harmonize. They have a candidate who was dear to them. They cast away his prospect for the sake of harmony. They have yielded all that they can. They have endeavored with all their power to accomplish the result they came here for, but they fear that the result is not to be accomplished in a manner that can render a just and proper account to their constituents. We have consulted together, and after anxious and long deliberation, without knowing exactly what phase this matter might finally present, we have not adopted any decisive rule for our action; but a large majority of our delegates—some 20 to 4—have decided that upon the result which is now obtained, we shall ask leave of this Convention to retire, that we may consult and announce our final action? We shall take no further part in the deliberations of this Convention, unless our minds should change, and of that I can offer you no reasonable hope.

Mr. CALDWELL, of Kentucky. Mr. President, I am instructed by a majority of the Kentucky delegation to state that circumstances have arisen that make it exceedingly doubtful in their minds whether they should continue in this body. We have arrived now at a point when a grave question arises in the minds of a large majority of our delegation, whether it is not our duty to retire and report to our constituents that we have failed in our mission. We have not yet determined to withdraw, but we ask permission to retire for consultation.

The PRESIDENT. The Chair will understand that leave is granted.

Mr. STUART. That cannot be the understanding of the Convention. I object to it.

The PRESIDENT. The Chair desires that there may be some understanding for his own guidance. It has repeatedly occurred heretofore that delegations have retired on leave for consultation. Kentucky now makes that request. Is the Chair to understand that the Convention does or does not consent to the application?

Many VOICES. Yes, yes.

Mr. STUART and others. No, no.

Mr. MCCOOK, of Ohio. According to the rule adopted at Charleston, the effect of a delegation retiring is to suspend business. Every member is willing that the Kentucky delegation should have time for deliberation, but our proceedings have been protracted and the time of those who remain is to be considered, as well as of the few who wish to retire. I am therefore opposed to granting leave, if it is to suspend our proceedings.

Mr. STUART. Mr. President, I understand that the delegation wish to retire but a very few minutes. I therefore withdraw my objection.

Mr. JOHNSON, of Maryland. Mr. President, I am authorized by my colleagues to report the state of facts in regard to a portion of the Maryland delegation. Mr. Johnson stated that a portion of the delegates thought it no longer consistent with their rights and honor to participate in the proceedings of the Convention, but did not state what portion of the delegates s ould withdraw from the Convention.

Mr. GLASS, of Virginia. It is due to me, Mr. President, to state that I, as one of the representatives of Virginia, have not concurred with the majority of my delegation in the important steps which they have just announced to this Convention. I have done everything in my power to preserve the nationality of the Democratic party, and the harmony and successful termination of this Convention, believing that upon that harmony depends the most momentous consequences to our country. I have, however, in deference to the overwhelming expression of the purpose of the majority of my delegation, declined any further participation in the deliberations of this Convention. But in doing so, I wish it distinctly placed on record, that I do not intend to indorse their action. That I reserve to myself and constituency in the future, as circumstances may determine. My sole purpose in going out and declining any further action on this occasion, is to preserve, if possible, the union and harmony of the Democracy of Virginia. With that view I decline any further participation with this body.

Mr. WATERSON, of Tennessee. I was a member of the Baltimore Convention twenty years ago, and since that time I have voted for every Democratic candidate for President, and for every Democratic nominee in my bailwick, and I shall be among the last to leave the ship; I shall cling to the last spar; and having voted for the last twenty years, as I have said, I announce to this Convention that, if I live until the next Presidential election, I shall vote for the nominee of this Convention. (Loud applause.)

Mr. JONES, of Tennessee, here got and claimed the floor.

Mr. WATERSON. I am not through yet. But I am proud that my friend by my side is actuated by the same sentiments and the same considerations that animate me. (Renewed applause.) There are some gallant spirits here from the land of Jackson who will remain. (Applause) I had the honor of being a member of the State Convention that accredited the delegates to this Convention. I had the honor of being a member of the Committee who drew up the resolutions adopted by that Committee. We labored for hours, intending if we could to erect a platform upon which every national man in every portion of our beloved country could stand. We did so, as I verily believe. That Convention recommended for the Presidency a distinguished citizen of my own State, Gov. Johnson. I am only sorry that I have not the resolutions in my pocket. But I well remember what was declared in the resolution; it recommended Gov. Johnson for the Presidency, and after declaring that he was our first choice, we pledged ourselves to give our hearty support to the nominee of the party whether he lives in the North or the South, (applause,) provided he cordially indorses the Cincinnati platform.

I have no fears that this Convention will nominate a candidate that does not cordially indorse the Cincinnati platform. Upon the principle of that platform we have gone into every contest for the past twelve years, and we have achieved triumph after triumph. I trust that never while the feeling of gratitude warms my bosom towards the gallant men of the North, who have fought our battles, will I ever be found acting otherwise than with the Democratic party. I do not remember any time when the gallant Democrats of the North were called upon to come to our rescue that they did not march forth by our side. There has been no unconditional resolve on the part of the Tennessee delegation, and I trust that better counsels will prevail. They are my friends of days past; we have labored shoulder to shoulder against the common enemy, and I trust that in the approaching canvass it will not be necessary for us to turn our shields against them. But if the battle must come, let it come; I am prepared to do my duty. (Applause.) This is not of my seeking; I have witnessed these indications for some time past; I see that there is obliged to be a battle among the Democracy; that somebody must be beaten. I shall discharge my duty as a Democrat, and a National Democrat, let the result be what it may. (Loud applause.) I shall follow my convictions of right. I have given no vote that I did not believe was right in itself, that I should not believe to be Democratic; and I am proud to see sitting around me the representatives from the 4th Congressional district—the Memphis district—who are my friends. They will not abandon their post. I am the only representative who is here, or who has been here from the Congressional district which I have the honor to represent. That makes two votes. My friend sitting by my side is the sole representative from the Knoxville district in the State of Tennessee, the only representative from that district who is here or who has been here during the sittings of this Convention. That makes three votes, and here is my friend Mr. Cooper (laughter and loud applause), who is the editor of a Democratic newspaper in another Congressional district, and I know that he does not believe in bolting. (Applause.) And I see by my side another friend, his colleague, and if I were to see him leave it would cause me sorrow. I do not believe that he will do it, I shall believe it when I see it, and not before. I have felt it my duty to say this much, and now I take my seat.

Mr. JONES, of Tennessee. I shall not detain the Convention long. I desire to state that I have been connected with this Convention from its very beginning. I was in the city of Charleston before this Convention assembled; I staid there until it adjourned to this place; I voted for that adjournment; I counseled it, because I believed it would tend to harmonize the great Democratic party, the national party of this country. And although I have been a Democrat ever since I first drew milk from my mother's breast, (laughter and applause,) I do not believe that I am aged and experienced enough to undertake the work of breaking up the Democratic party. (Applause.) I went back from Charleston and reported my action to my constituents. I supported Gov. Johnson, the choice of Tennessee, to the very last, even after every other Tennesseean had pulled down his flag. I believe that the people of Tennessee, and especially the Democracy of the Gibraltar of the Knoxville district, supported me in the course I have pursued. What grounds had Alabama and all those other States for leaving this Convention? They said they left because they could not get Congressional protection, and the words had hardly came from their lips in the Convention before you could hear them upon the streets saying that if a certain man was not nominated they would support the nominee. Then there is a contest here about men, it would seem. I have never cast my vote for that individual.

But I do think that gentlemen have attempted to break up the Democratic party upon hostility to a man and not upon principles that affect the interests of the South. (Applause.) I do hope that the Tennesseean delegation who have retired to consult, will, with the wisdom and the philosophy of old, and with the patriotism of a Washington who fought and bled for his country, with the devotion of that great man who said "the Union must and shall be preserved" will reconsider their action and come back into this Convention.

Mr. SMITH, of California, rose and addressed the Convention, but his remarks being of an uncivil and personal character, he was called to order by several delegates.

The PRESIDENT. The gentleman is not in order—the Chair is constrained to say.

Mr. SMITH. Very well, then, I will withdraw from the Convention.

Mr. STEVENS, of Oregon. I can say in behalf of the delegation from Oregon, that I have a most melancholy duty to perform. It is somewhat significant, Mr. President and gentleman of this Convention, that that district of country which is entirely aloof from the theater of this turmoil feels compelled to take a certain decisive step. I participated in the proceedings of the Convention at Charleston, and I have done my part as well as I could at Baltimore. At no period at either place have I allowed my feelings to get the better of my judgment, and I approach this question and this exigency with as much coolness and am prepared for it with as much deliberation as I ever approached any event in my life. Mr. President, there is remarkable significance in the fact that the Democratic party on the Pacific coast feel compelled to take this course. We have a growing empire on that coast that has been wrought out by the sacrifice of the blood and the peril of the last twelve years. On every route that leads from the Mississippi valley to that Western shore the bones of your emigrants are scattered. At every step almost, the tombstones of the suffering, way-worn travelers are found. We are still on that Western coast, planting our footsteps in blood in endeavoring to develop the country. We have come to this Convention and we have labored earnestly to bring about harmony. We have sought to stand upon principles alone. We did hope when this Convention re-assembled at Baltimore, that it would bring together the Democratic party in every sovereign State.

We find ourselves grievously mistaken. By your action to-day, gentlemen as much entitled to seats as ourselves, in our opinion, are excluded from the floor. We do not mean to impugn the motives of others, but are conscious that a most grievous wrong and insult has been given to sovereign States. Those States are the weak parties in this contest, and we have resolved to stand by them and assert their rights. I now announce that the delegation from Oregon have come to the conclusion to withdraw from the deliberations and take no further part in them.

Mr. Moffatt, of Virginia. concluded the remarks he was about to make, when called to order by Mr. Schell, of New York.

Mr. Davis, of Virginia, announced his determination to remain in the Convention, and give his reasons therefor.

Mr. Riley, of Pennsylvania, moved to adjourn.

Mr. McCook called for the vote by States on the motion to adjourn.

Appeals were made to the gentleman to withdraw the call, but without avail.

Mr. Moffatt begged leave to announce the introduction into the Convention, of Col. Dillard, as an alternate from one of the Eastern Districts of the State of Virginia.

The vote was taken by States on the motion to adjourn, and resulted as follows: —Ayes 18½, nays 210½.

So the motion to adjourn was rejected.

Mr. Cessna, of Pennsylvania. I now ask the Chair to ascertain from the Convention, whether or not there is a second to my demand for the previous question upon the resolution to proceed to ballot for candidates for the Presidency and Vice Presidency.

Mr. Clark, of Missouri. I desire to be heard on the part of Missouri before that question is taken. The object of my rising now is to ask permission for a portion of the delegation from Missouri to consult as to their further action. I am the Chairman of that delegation, but I do not ask this for myself; my purpose is fixed. But it is due to my colleagues who desire an opportunity for consultation that they should be allowed a little time for that purpose. I therefore request that instead of the Convention proceeding with their business to-night, they will adjourn until to-morrow morning. This is an important crisis in our history. We must have some consultation before any other vote is taken. I propose this to the gentleman from Pennsylvania (Mr. Cessna,) that as there are several delegations who desire to consult before further action, that the previous question be sustained, and then the Convention adjourn, and they proceed at once in the morning to business, with the understanding that we will then announce our determination.

Mr. Cessna, of Pennsylvania. I will state to the gentleman from Missouri (Mr. Clark,) that so far as my own views are concerned, whatever may be the wishes of the majority of the Convention, which I cannot undertake to explain, the purpose for which I made my motion was, that we might get through as much of the preliminary business as possible to-night. I would not myself be willing to withdraw the demand for the previous question, or delay in any way the action of this Convention before we reach that point, if we ever do reach it, at which the previous question shall have been seconded and the main question ordered, in order that if this Convention shall then be disposed to adjourn, the first business to-morrow morning shall be balloting for nominations. But I have no right to say what the majority of this Convention will do.

Mr. CLARK. I have no right to press this matter. If it is not agreed that this Convention will adjourn after ordering the previous question, I will proceed now, but I would prefer to wait.

Mr. STUART, of Michigan, said that it was his understanding that the previous question had been seconded.

After some consultation, it seemed to be understood that the previous question had been seconded, and the question was upon ordering the main question to be now put.

Mr. CRAIG, of Missouri. I hope the suggestion of my colleague, (Mr. Clark,) may be adopted, and fearing that at least the course of one delegate from Missouri may be misapprehended, I will say, that although I am proud to follow almost anywhere my distinguished colleague may lead, I never will follow him out of a Democratic Convention, or out of the Democratic party.

Mr. CLARK. As the remarks of my colleague (Mr. Craig) might place me in a false position, I will announce now what I would not have done but for his remarks. I remarked when I got up before that my own purpose was fixed, and the delay I asked was in behalf of a portion of the Missouri delegation, who wanted time to consult. My own purpose is fixed. For weal or woe, as the representative of a large constituency in this Convention, and as the representative in the Congress of the United States of 100,000 people, and having to vote in the House of Representatives for President, if the question ever goes to that House. I am in this Convention, and intend to stay in it. [Great applause.] I place myself upon the organization of the great party of which I am an honorable member, and will have to throw myself upon the good sense and patriotism of my constituency, in whatever theater of action they may place me, to justify me in adhering to the old time honored usages of the party which have brought us renown and glory in this great Union. [Renewed applause.]

I will not extend my remarks, but will ask this Convention to adjourn, as the demand for the previous question has been recorded.

Mr. CLARK withdrew the motion to adjourn, at the request of Mr. Gaulden, of Georgia.

A Delegate from Virginia asked if the alternates of the Virginia delegation would be allowed to hold the seats of those delegates who had withdrawn from this Convention.

Cries of "yes, yes."

The PRESIDENT. The Chair does not understand that that is a question competent for him to determine.

The Delegate from Virginia. I wish to say, in addition, that as the Vice President for Virginia has also seceded, we have elected Hon. William G. Brown in his place. [Applause.]

Mr. GAULDEN, of Georgia, here announced his determination to continue to act in this Convention, and addressed the Convention in an eloquent manner, advocating the maintenance of the integrity of the National Democratic party.

Mr. WHITNEY, of Massachusetts. I am instructed by a majority of the

Massachusetts delegation, to ask leave of this Convention to retire for consultation.

Mr. SAULSBURY, of Delaware, announced that on a future ballot the Delaware delegation should decline to vote, resuming the right to change their course at any time.

Mr. STEELE, of North Carolina, gave his reasons for continuing to act in the Convention.

Mr. EWING, of Tennessee. Mr. President, the majority of the delegation from Tennessee, who asked the indulgence of this Convention to retire for consultation, have done so, and as the result of their deliberations I have to announce that nineteen out of the twenty-four representatives have decided to retire, and five to remain.

Mr. CLAIBORNE, of Missouri. For nearly three weeks, I have listened patiently to everything that has been said in this Convention, both at Charleston and Baltimore. I desire now to state the reasons for pursuing the course that I now take, so far as my connection with this Convention is concerned; and let me say, I hope there will be no adjournment to-night, until we shall make a national nomination. [Applause.]

I have ever been taught to believe that the cardinal principle of Democracy is, that the majority shall govern. To day, I have seen the majority of the Committee on Credentials report to admit certain delegates, and exclude others, and the majority of the Committee adopt that report. To-day, for the first time in the history of Democracy, I have seen the mother of States starting madly from a National Convention. I am a Southern man, born and raised beneath the sunny sky of the South.

Not a drop of blood in my veins ever flowed in veins north of Mason and Dixon's line. My ancestors for 300 years sleep beneath the turf that shelters the bones of Washington, and I thank God that they rest in the graves of honest slave-holders. [Applause.] Sir, it has been the fortune of a distinguished candidate at Charleston to be reproached with having, like Esau, sold his birth-right for a mess of pottage. They tell me I am a traitor to the institutions of the South because I voted there and shall vote here for Stephen A. Douglas. I hurl back the ephithet.

When the delegation from Alabama withdrew from the Charleston Convention under the instructions of their State, I felt that the heavens should have been hung in crape, for I feared that the example of the distinguished son of that State would work the ruin of the national Democratic party of the country. But since then, Southern State after State has closed up the ranks, and the Domocracy is still, I believe, omnipotent and triumphant.

Sir, I trust this Convention will soon proceed to the nomination, and that to-morrow will witness the Democratic party united and harmonious, and that the shout will go up from every hill and valley in the land announcing the triumphs of the party that still carries before it, as its shield, the Constitution, and that strikes and crosses swords with the enemies of that Constitution and the Union. [Applause.] The Democratic party has passed through ordeals before, and it will pass this one, as sure as there is a God in heaven. The success that attended with our fathers in the revolutionary struggle will be ours in this great struggle, and we shall be victorious over every foe.

The gentleman concluded his remarks by saying, that with Douglas, Missouri would give twenty-five thousand majority.

Cries of "question, question."

The PRESIDENT. Shall the main question be now put?

The motion "shall the main question be now put," to go into a nomination of candidates for President and Vice President was carried.

The PRESIDENT. The motion has been carried. Will the Convention now vote upon the main question?

Mr. CESSNA, of Pennsylvania. I move an adjournment. (Cries of "No, no.")

Mr. Clark. I will claim the right to make the statement I proposed in the morning.

The President. A motion to adjourn has been made. All who are in favor of it will vote aye, &c.

The vote being taken *viva voce*, the President decided that the question had been determined in the affirmative, whereupon the Convention, at 10:30, adjourned.

List of Delegates for the State of Alabama, in the National Convention, with their Post Office addresses.

William Garrett, Socopotay.
John Forsyth, Mobile.
Robt A Baker, Summerfield.
John J. Seibler, Montgomery.
D. C. Humphreys, Huntsville.
Sidney C. Posey, Florence.
Hugh Monroe, Mobile.
T. M. Mathews, Cahaba.
A. J. McGinney, Lowndesboro.
W. R. R. Wyatt, Autaugaville.
Bush Jones, Uniontown.
John W. Wornack, Eutaw.
L. V. B. Martin, Tuscaloosa.
O. H. Bynum, Courtland.
Samuel D. Weakley, Florence.
W. S. Throckmorton, Tuscumbia.
J. C. Bradley, Huntsville.
James Williams, Bridgeport.
Thomas B. Cooper, Center.
Lewis E Parsons, Talladega.
William Jenkins, Mardeiville.
Benj Harrison, Montgomery.

SIXTH DAY.

Saturday, June 23, 1860.

At 10½ o'clock, the President, Hon. Caleb Cushing, took his seat and called the Convention to order, when the Rev. Dr. Cummings opened with prayer.

On motion of Mr. Dodge, of Iowa, the reading of the journal of yesterday was dispensed with.

At the request of Mr. Garrett, of Alabama, the Secretary read a corrected list of the Alabama delegation as admitted to this Convention.

Mr. Garrett also announced that the delegation from Alabama had chosen Hugh Monroe Vice President, and Bush Jones Secretary for the State of Alabama

Mr. Caldwell, of Kentucky. After the withdrawal of the Kentucky delegation last evening, we held a hurried consultation, and, under the circumstances, hastened back to the hall for the purpose of announcing our determination. After making one or two ineffectual efforts to be heard by the President, an adjournment intervened before I succeeded. It is proper that I should state that after the meeting that we had last evening, the night intervened, and upon a consultation this morning there were some slight changes in the opinions of some of our delegation, and it is my duty now to report to the Convention the determination at present arrived at. The circumstances in which we are placed are exceedingly embarrassing, and we have not therefore been enabled to come to an entirely harmonious conclusion. The result is, however, that the delegates of Kentucky remain in the Convention. (Applause.) There are ten delegates who withdraw from the Convention.

The exact character of their withdrawal is set forth in a single paragraph, with their names appended, which I shall desire the Secretary to read before I sit down. There are five others—completing that delegation—who desire for the present to suspend their connection with the action of this Convention. I need not go into any reasons for it, because from the remarks that I made last evening our views will have been understood. I will add here, that there may be no misunderstanding, that I myself am one of those five, and we have also signed a short paper, which I shall also ask the Secretary to read to the Convention.

Not desiring to detain the Convention longer, it only remains for me to say that having placed in nomination before this Convention a distinguished and favored son of Kentucky, being actuated in our withdrawal by circumstances that impel us to think that it is our duty to retire for the present. I also deem it my duty in justice to that distinguished, patriotic, and national Democrat, to withdraw his name from before the Convention, which I now do. I will ask the Secretary to read the papers I have indicated, and also one which a gentleman of our delegation has handed me, which he desires to be read. I ask that the three papers be read.

The first paper, signed by James G. Leach, was then read.

Mr. Payne, of Ohio, said he considered the paper just read an abuse of the privilege of this body, and an insult to its members; and he moved that it be returned to the gentleman who signed it, and be not received by the Convention; and he gave notice that he should object to any communication, from any source, reflecting upon the action of this body.

Mr. Leach disclaimed any intention of disrespect.

The question being taken on the motion of the gentleman from Ohio, declining to receive the paper, it was agreed to.

So the Convention declined to receive the paper.

The Secretary then read the communication signed by the retiring and remaining delegates from Kentucky, as follows:

To the Hon. Caleb Cushing, President of the Democratic National Convention, assembled in the city of Baltimore:

The Democratic Convention for the State of Kentucky, held in the city of Frankfort, on the 9th day of January, 1860, among others, adopted the following resolution:

Resolved, That we pledge the Democracy of Kentucky to an honest and industrious support of the nominee of the Charleston Convention.

Since the adoption of this resolution, and the assembly of this Convention, events have transpired not then contemplated, notwithstanding which we have labored diligently to preserve the harmony and unity of said Convention, but discord and disintegration have prevailed to such an extent that we feel that our efforts cannot accomplish this end.

Therefore, without intending to vacate our seats, or to join or participate in any other Convention or organization in this city, and with the intention of again co-operating with this Convention, should its unity and harmony be restored by any future event, we now declare that we will not participate in the meantime in the deliberations of this Convention, nor hold ourselves or constituents bound by its action, but leave both at full liberty to act as future circumstances may dictate.

N. W. WILLIAMSON,
G. A. CALDWELL,
Delegates for State at large.
W. BRADLEY,
SAMUEL B. FIELD,
THOMAS J. YOUNG.

Resolved, That the Chairman of our delegation be instructed to inform the Convention in our behalf that in the present condition of that body we deem it inconsistent with our duty to ourselves and our constituents to participate further in its deliberations. Our reasons for so doing will be given to the Democracy of Kentucky.

JNO. DISHMAN,	J. S. KENDALL,
JOS. B. BECK,	D. W. QUARLES,
COLBERT CECIL,	L. GREEN,
R. M JOHNSON,	CAL. BUTLER,
R. NICKEE,	JAS. G. LEACH.

Mr. West, of Connecticut, inquired what motion was now pending?

The PRESIDENT. The motion to proceed to the vote for candidates for President and Vice President of the United States.

Mr. WEST. I hope the motion will now be put.

Mr. REED, of Kentucky. I do not rise to make a speech—God knows I am tired of speaking—but simply to announce the fact that I, as one of the Kentucky delegation, together with others, have seen no cause as yet for abandoning this Convention. (Applause.) I read in the history of the ancient city of the plain that an angel of the Lord was sent to inquire whether there were any righteous men to be found that that city might be saved, the promise being that if five could be found it should not be destroyed. (Applause.) I am happy to say that from Kentucky there are not only five but nine men who will stand by this Convention. (Applause) It is a Democratic Convention. It belongs to the Democratic party. We, of Kentucky, stand here opposing secession and sectionalism North and South. We will stand with you as a wall of fire in opposing both extremes. (Applause.) We will rally upon the principles of equal rights and exclusive privileges to none. We will form a nucleus here around which all conservative men of both sections can rally and save the nation. I am not going to abandon the Convention because it is apparent that one of our glorious chieftains is not likely to receive the nomination. (Applause.) No. I have gratitude in my heart to the man whose pathway from the city of Washington to his house in the far West is lighted by his own effigies. (Applause.) We in Kentucky owe to him, and to the North and West, our homes and firesides. Gentlemen who own a hundred slaves each say I am right. I will go home to my constituents and to the campaign, and camp-fires will he lighted in the mountains and valleys, and in less than seventy days you will hear a shout that will turn the course of affairs and set things right. (Applause.) We will take this matter out of the hands of politicians and the Administration and return it to the people. (Applause.) I stand pledged to stand by the nominee of the Convention by solemn resolution binding upon me and every Kentuckian. I will stand by it though the heavens fall. (Applause.) I have been a Democrat from my infancy. I regard this as a strife between Democracy and Federalism. Non-intervention I regard as Democracy, and Congressional intervention as Federalism. (Applause.)

My colleague (Mr. Caldwell) has withdrawn the name of Mr. Guthrie, the choice of Kentucky. I put his name again in nomination—Kentucky's favorite son.

Mr. CLARK, of Missouri. Before the Convention proceeds to a ballot, in accordance with my promise of last night, I desire to state what is the conclusion the Missouri delegation have reached after consultation.

Mr. KING, of Missouri. I would like the gentleman, in making that announcement, to state that it is the action of but a part of the Missouri delegation. A number of us here had no desire to consult. I wanted to consult with no one.

Mr. CLARK. My colleague would have had no need for an explanation if he had had a little patience. I announced to the Convention yesterday that there was a portion of the Missouri delegation who asked me to request of the Convention time for consultation. I did not include myself, nor did I include my colleague. That portion of my delegation have consulted, and it is my duty now to announce to the Convention the conclusion of that consultation. I have to announce that two of the Missouri delegation desire to withdraw from this Convention. In doing this, I claim that it is right that they should take the responsibility, and that the honor attaching to such a movement should be theirs entirely.

Mr. HILL, of North Carolina. Mr. President, the Convention has knowledge that on yesterday a portion of the delegation from North Carolina retired for reasons satisfactory to themselves. At the time I thought my colleagues were wrong, having perceived no sufficient reason in the action of this Convention to justify a retirement from the Convention. Since that time I feel it due to my constituents and the State to which I owe allegiance to join my destiny to theirs.

I part with my brethren here to-day, as the gentleman from Kentucky said, more in sorrow than in anger; but a sense of duty requires that I declare that I no longer can take part in the proceedings of this Convention.

Mr. JONES, of Tennessee, rose to correct some newspaper report of his remarks, and also to announce that instead of nineteen delegates retiring from the Tennessee delegation, but thirteen had withdrawn from the Convention.

Mr. JONES, of Pennsylvania, raised the point of order that no speeches were in order, as the previous question had been called on the resolution of Mr. Cessna, of Pennsylvania, to proceed to the ballot for nomination of President and Vice President.

The PRESIDENT ruled that no gentleman could proceed with any remarks without the unanimous consent of the Convention.

Several Delegates asked Mr. Jones, of Pennsylvania, to withdraw his objection, but he refused to do so.

The PRESIDENT said he had received two papers which he deemed it as his duty to communicate to the Convention. One was a paper signed by Mr. Sturman, of Arkansas, and the other a paper from the State of Georgia.

Objection was made to the reading of the papers.

Mr. STURMAN, of Arkausas, desired leave to state why he retired from the Convention.

Mr. JONES, of Pennsylvania, insisted upon his point, that pending the question before the Convention no gentleman was in order to address the Convention.

The PRESIDENT ruled that the gentleman from Arkansas (Mr. Sturman) could not proceed, as objection had been made.

Mr. CESSNA, of Pennsylvania, called for the vote upon his resolution to proceed to nominate candidates for President and Vice President.

The PRESIDENT. Gentlemen of the Convention, a motion has been made by the gentleman from Pennsylvania (Mr. Cessna,) to the consideration of which the Chair will now proceed.

But before doing so, I beg the indulgence of the Convention to say that whilst deeply sensible of the honor done me by the Convention in placing me in this chair, I was not less deeply sensible of the difficulties, general and personal, looming up in the future to environ my path Nevertheless, in the solicitude to maintain the harmony and union of the Democratic party, and n the face of the retirement of the delegations of several States, I continued at my post, laboring to that end, and in that sense had the honor to meet you, gentlemen, here in Baltimore. But circumstances have since transpired which compel me to pause. The delegations of a majority of the States of this Union have, either in whole or in part, in one form or another, ceased to participate in the deliberations of this body. At no time would any consideration of candidates have affected my judgment as to my duty. And I came here prepared, regardless of all personal preferences, cordially to support the nominations of this Convention, whosoever they might be. But under the present circumstances I deem it a duty of self-respect, and I deem it still more a duty to this Convention as at present organized—I say I deem it my duty in both relations, whilst tendering my most grateful acknowledgments to gentlemen of all sides, and especially to those gentlemen who may have differed with me in opinion in any respect—whilst tendering my most grateful acknowledgments to all gentlemen for the candid and honorable support which they have given the Chair, even when they differed in opinion upon rulings, and whilst tendering also the gentlemen present my most cordial respects and regards. not knowing a single gentleman upon this floor as to whom I have other than sentiments of cordiality and friendship—I deem it my duty to resign my seat as presiding officer of this Convention. [Applause.] I deem it my duty to resign my place as presiding officer of this Convention in order to take my seat on the floor as a member of the delegation of Massachusetts, and to abide whatever may be its determination in regard to its further action in this Convention. And I deem this above all a duty I owe to the members of the Convention as to whom my action would no longer represent the will of the majority of the Convention.

Mr. CUSHING here left the chair, and took his place with the Massachusetts delegation.

Hon. DAVID TOD, of Ohio, immediately assumed the chair and was greeted with enthusiastic and hearty cheers. After order was restored, he said:

As the present presiding officer of this Convention by common consent of my brother Vice Presidents, with great diffidence I assume the chair. When I announce to you that for 34 years I have stood up in that district so long misrepresented by Joshua R. Giddings, with the Demmocratic banner in my hand, [applause,] I know that I shall receive the good wishes of this Convention, at least, for the discharge of the duties of the chair. If there are no privileged questions intervening, the Secretary will proceed with the call of the States.

Mr. BUTLER, of Massachusetts, addressed the chair.

Objection was made to his speaking.

The PRESIDENT. The gentleman from Massachusetts will take his seat.

The SECRETARY proceeded to call the States amid great confusion and struggles for the floor.

Mr. STOUGHTON, of Vermont, challenged the vote of that State.

The PRESIDENT. That cannot be entertained before the result is announced. The Chair appealed to the honor of members of the Convention to preserve order until the vote was taken.

Mr. BUTLER. I assure the Convention that I will not detain them but a moment.

The PRESIDENT. Objection being made, the gentleman from Massachusetts must take his seat.

Mr. BUTLER. I desire to present, as a question of privilege, a protest respectful in its character and terms to this Convention. I ask for Massachusetts the same respectful hearing that has been given to everybody else.

The PRESIDENT. Is the objection withdrawn?

Several VOICES. "No, no."

Many DELEGATES appealed in behalf of allowing Mr. Butler to proceed.

The PRESIDENT directed the call to proceed.

The resolution ordering the Convention to proceed to vote for candidates for the office of President and Vice President of the United States was adopted.

The President then directed the Secretary to call the States for the purpose of recording their votes for a candidate for the office of President of the United States.

Mr. CLAIBORNE, of Missouri, appealed to the Convention to allow Mr. Butler to address them.

Mr. SAYLES, of Rhode Island, seconded the appeal. The privilege had been accorded to every State.

Objection being still made, the Secretary proceeded to call the States. Massachusetts being called—

Mr. BUTLER said: Mr. President, I have the instruction of a majority of the delegation from Massachusetts to present a written protest. I will send it to the Chair to have it read. And further, with your leave, I desire to say what I think will be pleasant to the Convention. First, that while a majority of the delegates from Massachusetts do not purpose further to participate in the doings of this Convention, we desire to part, if we may, to meet you as friends and Democrats again. We desire to part in the same spirit of manly courtesy with which we came together.

The following is the protest of the Massachusetts delegation :—

MASSACHUSETTS DELEGATION, BARNUM'S HOTEL,
BALTIMORE, June 22, 1860.

To the President of the Convention .

The undersigned, a majority of the delegates from Massachusetts to the National Democratic Convantion, in view of the action this day taken by the Convention in excluding the Hon. Benj. F. Hallett from the seat occupied by him as a delegate from the Fifth Congressional District of our State, and the assignment of his seat to Mr. K. S. Chaffee, who was selected only as a substitute by the District Democratic Convention which elected Mr. Hallett as one of the delegates, do hereby protest against the action of this body in thus excluding an old, faithful and most efficient servant of the National Democratic cause—a regularly elected and commissioned delegate, for circumstances arising from a mournful domestic affliction which prevented him from attending the earlier sittings of this body, and caused the substitution of Mr. Chaffee in his place.

We therefore desire to lay before the Convention our respectful protest against the aforesaid action, and also our request that it may be entered upon the records.

JAS S. WHITNEY, Del. at large.
W. C. N. SWIFT, 1st Dist.
ALEXANDER LINCOLN, 2d Dist.
JAMES RILEY, 4th Dist.
CORNELIUS DOHERTY, 5th Dist.
E. S. WILLIAMS, 6th Dist.
BENJ. F. BUTLER, 8th Dist.
D. N. CARPENTER, 11th Dist.
C. S. CUSHING, Del. at large.
P. W. LELAND, 2d Dist.
BRADFORD L. WALES, 3d Dist.
ISAAC H. WRIGHT, 4th Dist.
GEO. R. LORING, 6th Dist.
GEO. JOHNSON, 7th Dist.
A. W. CHAPIN, 10th Dist.

A portion of the Massachusetts delegation here retired.

Mr. DAWSON, of Pennsylvania, asked leave for the Pennsylvania delegation to retire for consultation merely in reference to their choice for the Presidency?

The request was granted by unanimous consent.

The SECRETARY then proceeded with the call, calling again the State of MASSACHUSETTS.

Mr. STEVENS, of Massachusetts, said—I am not ready at this moment to cast the vote of Massachusetts, the delegation being in consultation as to their rights. But I cannot permit the call of Massachusetts to be made twice without some response, and in doing so I propose to reflect in no way upon the action of those delegates who have withdrawn. It is my conviction that should I withdraw from this Convention it would meet with the deepest reprobation of my constituents. (Applause.) I profess, as one of the delegates at large, to know the sentiments of the people of Massachusetts, and I say that they are for the principle of non-intervention and for Stephen A. Douglas. (Applause.) Our party has been laboring hard to stem the side of abolitionism and fanaticism. The Democracy of Massachusetts never split upon any platform, and are ever ready to maintain the integrity of our organization.

At the call of the State of MARYLAND,

Mr. BRENT said—Before my vote is cast I desire to submit an explanation. Not one word would have passed my lips but for the remarks of my colleague yesterday (Mr. Johnson). The Democracy of Maryland, assembled in this city, by a platform of resolutions passed in March, 1860, unanimously declared that they would plant themselves on the doctrine of non-intervention by Congress with slavery in the Territories, reaffirming the Cincinnati platform, and declaring at the same time that a difference of opinion upon questions of Territorial and Congressional power was a matter of toleration. After that declaration I have no hesitation in standing upon the Charleston platform, and standing on that platform I cast my vote for Douglas.

At the call of the State of NORTH CAROLINA,

Mr. DICK, of North Carolina, said—I stand alone for North Carolina. I stand by the national Democracy and by the gallant champion of the North-West.

Mr. JONES, of Pennsylvania, insisted that gentleman should not be allowed, in explaining their votes, to make stump speeches.

Mr. DICK. I had hoped that I could claim the courtesy of the Convention after patient, anxious, silent waiting for sixteen days. I have a birth-right amidst the national Democracy which I never intend to forfeit. (Applause.)

Although my friends have gone—friends with whom I have heretofore rallied in many a fiercely-fought contest, I bid them good bye with sorrow, saying naught against their motives. They have gone from us, and, as I think, with strange gods, but I intend to worship where I have done heretofore. My constituents sent me here knowing that I would vote for Stephen A. Douglas. (Applause.) I have seen no cause of secescion. I stand by the Northern Democracy that have stood by me in the hour of trial. Soon a great battle is to be fought, which, in all probability, will decide the destinies of my country. I see arrayed three hostile armies—one disorganized, the other two organized with their chosen leaders. True, one is but a small army, with no ammunition, and with old rusty guns long since condemned. (Laughter.) But the other is a foe to be dreaded. They are falling into line and advancing. They have an experienced chieftain, and above their heads waves the dark banner of treason and disunion, stained with the blood of Virginia's sons. (Applause.)

Mr. JONES, of Pennsylvania, raised a question of order.

The PRESIDENT ruled that the gentleman had a right to proceed, but it rested with himself whether he exceeded the bounds of the courtesy extended to him by the house.

North Carolina was again called.

Mr. DICK resumed. I expect to stand upon the deck of the old Democratic ship. launched eighty-four years ago, freighted with the hopes and interests and destinies of the country, as I have stood upon her when "she walked the waters like a thing of life," and seemed to dare the elements to strife. Now, in the midst of storms and tempests, I expect to stand by her, and I hope and believe she will outride the storm, and lead us to the haven of a glorious destiny. [Applause.] But if she must go down amid the dark waters of division and sectionalism, I expect to cling to the last spar that floats upon the troubled waters, and go down with the hopes and interests of the country. Believing, as I do, that old North Carolina will do all she can, she now casts her one vote in this Convention for Stephen A. Douglas. [Applause.]

When the State of GEORGIA was called,

Mr. GAULDEN, of, Georgia, took the floor and said: I hold in my hand some resolutions of the Benning delegation, from Georgia, which has been admitted by a vote of this Assembly, to seats upon the floor.

Mr. GAULDEN read the resolutions and continued his remarks:—

Now these learned gentleman of the majority seem to have been very much disgusted at the course I have pursued here. I have as much pity and contempt for them as they possibly can have for me. Majorities have no terrors for me. I was notified by the Secretary of the Georgia delegation, to meet them at their room yesterday evening, with an intimation that they were disposed to put me on trial, and see whether I was worthy to go with them. I told him that if that was the idea I plead to the jurisdiction, and was responsible to the State of Georgia, and not to them. However he gave me to understand that that was not really the idea, but that they merely wanted to see me down there; I went, but it soon become obvious that they desired to put me in a position where I would be obliged to go with them. I told them I considered myself a delegate to this Convention under my original appointment to Charleston; I had gone there and refused to secede. Two Conventions in Georgia, their Convention and another, had indorsed me and sent me here, and that I claimed the right to participate in the proceedings of this Convention, and under the decision at Charleston to cast a *pro rata* vote. I distinctly warned them that I would not be bound to go with them finally in any course they might pursue; that I belonged to the great National Democratic party of the United States, and was here representing the State of Georgia, under their indorsement, and had the right to act with them up to a certain time, but reserved to myself the right, when the final rupture came, to go where I pleased, and act upon my individual reponsibility. We had a great deal of discussion, they trying to bring me down to pledges, which I scorned then as I do now, and have as much disgust for them as they can have for me.

I told them that under the peculiar circumstances of the case, though I claimed the right to participate in the proceedings of this Convention, and should do so, I would not attempt to cast the vote of the State of Georgia. That is the only pledge I made them. That seemed to be their holy horror; they seemed to have a terrible dread that I would come here, under my Charleston appointment, and cast the whole ten votes of Georgia. I told them I would not do that; that under the peculiar circumstances of the case I doubted my right to vote at all; and that until I gave them formal notice of the final dissolution of all connection between them and me, I would not attempt to cast a vote at all. But I did reserve to myself the right to come here and participate with what I believed to be the National Democracy of these United States, the men with whom I cast my fortunes, and upon whom in my humble judgment, depends not only the perpetuity of this Union, but the perpetuity of civil liberty itself. I told them I considered it a duty I owed to myself and this Convention, and to the country not to come here and cast the vote of the State of Georgia at any rate until the connection between them and me had been dissolved. And I now publicly do dissolve all connection between that delegation and myself. [Applause.] I trust I shall be excused for the present from voting.

When the State of ALABAMA was called,

Mr. PARSONS, of Alabama, said: I have been instructed by my delegation to announce briefly the principles which have governed us in the result to which we have come. Coming from the extreme South, representing a Conservative constituency, devoted to the Constitution and rights of the several States in this Union, we look to the preservation of those rights now with more than ordinary solicitude by clinging to the Democratic organization. We prefer non-intervention and union to intervention and disunion. [Applause.] And in urging this I am confident I speak the sentiments of a large majority of the people of Alabama. [Applause.] We come here prepared to see the most desperate efforts to break up the Democratic party. Shall that be done? [Cries of "no, no."] Shall it be said that in 1860, here in Baltimore, the grave of this Union was dug? The Star Spangled Banner still waves over us—shall it still continue to wave? [Applause, and cries of "yes, yes."] You will find a response come up from the Gulf States—the Cotton States—such as never before has been heard since this Republic was established. [Applause.] You have been told by distinguished gentlemen of our State that we do not speak the sentiments of our people. We appeal to the verdict of the ballot box. We made the issue with them in 1850 and 1854, and we tell them to take warning from the result of that issue. The struggle for disunion is putting forth its last efforts. But the people will rally around us.

Such being the principles and convictions we entertain in the depths of our hearts, we cast our votes as a unit—nine votes for STEPHEN A. DOUGLAS. [Loud applause.]

When the State of LOUISIANA was called,

Hon. PIERRE SOULE, of Louisiana, rose and was received with enthusiastic cheers and applause. After silence had been restored, the gentleman proceeded as follows:

Though mindful of what she owes to her sister States of the South, and ever ready to act in concert with them, when actual aggression shall call for actual resistance, Louisiana is unwilling to risk her future and the future of this Union upon impracticable issues and purely theoretical abstractions. She cannot be so far oblivious of past services as to disown that fearless and indomitable champion of popular rights and of State equality, who, in that great and memorable struggle which initiated, in his State, the war now so unrelentingly waged against him, bore so gallantly the brunt of the battle, victoriously vindicating the rights of the South against infuriated opponents, and, by the lurid glare of his burning effigies, rode triumphant the storm which unprincipled and discredited politicians, in league with the high priests of Black Republicanism, had raised around him:—Louisiana casts her vote for STEPHEN A. DOUGLAS.

When the State of ARKANSAS was called,

Mr. STURMAN, of Arkansas, said—I am positively instructed to vote for a certain platform, and one of a certain set of men on that platform, and, therefore, failing in that, I must retire from this Convention.

Mr. FLOURNOY, of Arkansas. It was not my purpose, knowing the impatience of this body, to have made anything like a speech on this occasion; but the hearty welcome you give me inclines me to believe that you will hear me patiently for a few minutes.

First, let me explain my position as connected with this Convention, for it is rather a delicate one. I was nominated as a delegate for the Charleston Convention when it was known that I was called the head and front of the Douglas party in my State. It was a personal compliment, for I believed that I was in a minority in that Convention. But, sir, it was not a hopeless minority—it was a strong one, for they were afraid to make an issue before the Convention, which was strong enough to have voted down any anti-Douglas resolutions. I will explain how those resolutions were passed upon us. We had kept a boat some thirty-six hours waiting, as the only means by which we could get home, waiting for the Convention to close. When we got through with the appointment of delegates and other business we took our leave. Before we got to the boat those instructions were passed.

Though I did not feel bound to follow those instructions, still I did respect them at Charleston and carried them out to the letter—though it frequently brought Flournoy, the individual, in conflict with Flournoy, the delegate. (Laughter.) I am at this moment peculiarly circumstanced in regard to that matter. When I came here this morning I expected to follow out my convictions and to vote for Douglas on the first ballot. I was instructed before I went to Charleston to vote for Mr. Breckinridge, amongst others; but I have exhausted the instructions, except that I have not had an opportunity to vote for Mr. Breckinridge, and as I wish to have a record wthout impeachment, I propose to cast my own vote for him.

If I can be indulged a moment longer, I desire to say that I am a Southern man, born and reared amid the institution of slavery. I first learned to whirl the top and bounce the ball with the young African. Everything I own on earth is the result of slave labor. The bread that feeds my wife and little ones is produced by the labor of slaves. They live on my plantation with every feeling of kindness as between master and slave. Sir, if I could see that there is anything intended in our platform unfriendly to the institution of slavery—if I could see that we did not get every constitutional right we are entitled to, I would be the last on earth to submit in this Union; I would myself apply the torch to the magazine and blow it into atoms before I would submit to wrong. (Applause.) But I feel that in the doctrine of non-intervention and popular sovereignty are enough to protect the interests of the South. I would scorn to entertain the belief that this heart could not embrace the whole of this mighty Union—that it was so narrow and contracted as to recognize only the flag of a section in the stars and the stripes. Sir, it is the flag of the whole country. (Applause.)

Under the circumstances, I cast one-half a vote for Breckinridge and one vote for Douglas.

At the call of the State of MICHIGAN,

Mr. STUART responded—Michigan will not detain this Convention long in giving arguments in favor of her devotion to the party and the Union. She will manifest it by conforming to the usages of the Democratic party, and abiding by the result of all Conventions in which she takes part. She casts six votes for DOUGLAS.

At the call of the State of IOWA,

Mr. DODGE said—Mr. President, knowing, as I do, the impatience of this Convention, I will not at this stage of the proceedings detain you long. My colleagues have expressed a wish that I, as a North-Western man, should make some reply to the remarks of the gentlemen from Alabama (Mr. Parsons), and Louisiana (Mr. Soule). Their language is that of true Democrats and patriots, and has imparted joy and gladness to the hearts of every member of this Convention, and to none more than to the delegation from Iowa.

It was my fortune to have served in the Senate with my eloquent friend from Louisiana at the time of the passage of the measures to which he has referred. My votes, I can aver, were given to sustain what I deemed to be sound, constitutional principles, and are perhaps a true reflex of the sentiments of the Democracy of my section of the Union and of our distinguished candidate for the Presidency. How strange and unnatural, that Stephen A. Douglas, covered with wounds inflicted by fanatical abolitionists, should not be esteemed a true friend of the South, or that the gallant old warrior and veteran of Democracy (Col. Richardson), the indefatigable and self-sacrificing friend of Judge Douglas on this floor, should now be regarded with feelings of opposition, if not hostility, by Southern men.

In war he has periled his life in defense of a Southern State. In the House of Representatives he fought the most memorable legislative battle on record, to relieve the South from the odious and unconstitutional Missouri restriction. To Dougias in the Senate and Richardson in the House, do the South owe, more than to any other two living men, that great measure of deliverance and justice—the repeal of the so called Missouri Compromise. Sir, the Democracy of the North-West have been alike true and loyal to the whole country. We have risked everything to do justice to our brethren of the South, and we think that the time has now arrived when they should be willing to hazard something for our sake. We know that the candidate whom we present is a man in whom all sections can safely confide. (Applause.) Judge Douglas has earned for himself, by his unconquerable energy, untiring industry, and extraordinary talents, united to an undying attachment to the Union, a reputation and a name which will adorn the brightest pages of our country's history. (Applause.)

Never, since the days of General Jackson, were the people, the Democratic voters, so overwhelmingly in favor of any man for the Presidency. (Applause.) His supporters in the North-West are the men whose pride and glory it was and is to have voted against the "Wilmot Proviso" in all its shapes and phases—to have voted for all the Compromise measures of 1850, the Fugitive Slave Law includ d—and for the Kansas and Nebraska Bill of 1854. The mal-administration of affairs in Kansas, and the audacious interference of the people of Massachusetts and Missouri in the affairs of that Territory, caused the overthrow of the Democratic party in the North-West, while it only gained Kentucky and Tennessee in the South. Surely States which owe their redemption from the opposition to our self-immolation for them, should be slow to ask us to join in forming new issues, such as must prove disastrous both to our party and country.

Allow me to say *en passant* that Delaware was for the "Wilmot Proviso" when Iowa was helping to fight the battle of the South against it. Our fathers were defeated for voting with your fathers for the Missouri restriction of 1820; their sons have been overwhelmed with defeat for voting with you for its repeal. Let us, now that all obstacles are removed, strictly adhere to the wise and just principle of non-intervention, leaving to the people interested the right to determine their domestic institutions in their own way, subject, of course, to the Constitution of the United States. (Applause.)

The Democracy of the North-West believe Mr. Douglas to be eminently qualified for the Presidency, and worthy to fill that exalted station; but we would not be his friends or supporters if we did not know him to be in favor of the equality of the States and of even and exact justice to the people of every one of them. If he had the slightest taint of abolition about him, or if all his past life were not a guaranty that he would use the army, navy, and every power with which he may be clothed for the protection of the South, and do it justice in the formation of his Cabinet and the distribution of his patronage, we would, instead of supporting, scorn and spurn him. Iowa casts four votes for STEPHEN A. DOUGLAS. (Applause.)

Before the vote was anounced,

Mr. STOUGHTON, of Vermont, challenged the vote of that State.

Mr. SMITH. It becomes necessary for me to say that Vermont votes as a unit for Douglas, until directed otherwise by a majority of delegates. And the instructions by which we are governed apply to the delegate who declines to vote with us. [Mr. S. here read the resolution of instruction to cast the vote for such candidate as a majority of the delegates shall, after consultation, select.] I submit that with such instructions, the gentleman is not at liberty to decline to vote so long as he remains in it.

The PRESIDENT. The Chair is of opinion that the Chairman of the delegation is authorized, in view of the action at Charleston, to cast the entire vote of the State, so long as all the delegation are present.

Mr. STEVENS, of Massachusetts, here rose and stated that, although some of the delegation from Massachusetts had withdrawn, he was instructed by the remainder of the delegation to cast the entire vote of the State.

Mr. BISSELL, of New York, rose to a question of privilege. He desired the Secretary should announce the vote of the State of Pennsylvania.

The Secretary announced it. Douglas 10, Breckinridge 3, Guthrie 3, and Seymour 1.

Mr. BISSELL. I did not hear the name of Seymour announced from the Chairman of the delegation. Sir, I have been from the first instructed to withdraw his name as a candidate, whenever presented. [Applause.] I will now beg leave to read his letter addressed to me:

"UTICA, JUNE 14, 1860.

GENTLEMEN:—Allusion having been made to my name in connection with the nominations to be made at Baltimore, I wish to state in writing what I have heretofore said to you in conversation, that I am averse to being placed in nomination by the National Democratic Convention. I do not suppose my name will be presented on that occasion, but if it is, I request that you will, as delegates from this district, withdraw it from consideration. I cannot, under any circumstances, be a candidate for the office of President or Vice President. Yours, truly, HORATIO SEYMOUR."

To Messrs. John Stryker, D. P. Bissell, Delegates, &c.

The reading of the letter was followed by applause. Mr. B. then proceeded to say:

It is due to Mr. Seymour to say that he has ever expressed to me, his neighbor and friend, the same feeling. I withdraw his name, as his friend and neighbor.

One of the delegates from Maryland desired to withdraw his vote for Breckinridge, and to decline to cast any vote. The Chairman of the delegation had made a mistake in annnouncing half a vote for Breckinridge.

The delegation from the State of Pennsylvania, desired to have placed upon the records of the Convention, the manner in which the several delegates from that State cast their votes, and the Chairman of the delegation filed the following statement:

Messrs. Cassidy, Cessna, Coffroth, Cunningham, Gibson, R. M., Grant, Grey, Griffith, Halderman, Montgomery, Nill, Painter, Rufsnyder, Ross, Shattuck, Smith, Ward, Weir, Wilson, Wright, voted for Stephen A. Douglas.

Messrs. Baker, Bigler. Bradford, Dent, Ent, Evans, Guernsey, McHenry, McKibben, Megargee, Packer, Plummer, Randall, Roberts, Phillips, Swarr, Hottenstein, declined to vote.

Messrs. Blood and Glossbrenner voted for Horatio Seymour.

Messrs. Brodhead, Clymer, Hughes, Jones, Van Zant, Lauer, voted for James Guthrie.

Messrs. Campbell. Dawson, Gibson, J. A., Gloninger, McKee, Magee, Reilley, voted for Breckinridge.

RESULT OF THE FIRST BALLOT.

The Secretary here announced the result of the first ballot as follows:
Whole vote cast, 190½.

STATES.	For Stephen A. Douglas	For John C Breckinridge	For Henry A. Wise	For Thomas S. Bocock	For Daniel S. Dickinson	For James Guthrie	For Horatio Seymour.	STATES.	For Stephen A. Douglas	For John C. Breckinridge	For Henry A. Wise	For Thomas S. Bocock	For Daniel S Dickinson	For James Guthrie	For Horatio Seymour
Maine	5½	0	0	0	0	0	0	Arkansas	1	0½	0	0	0	0	0
New Hampshire	5	0	0	0	0	0	0	Missouri	4½	0	0	0	0	0½	0
Vermont	5	0	0	0	0	0	0	Tennessee	3	0	0	0	0	0	0
Massachusetts	19	0	0	0	0	0	0	Kentucky	0	0	0	0	0	4½	0
Rhode Island	4	0	0	0	0	0	0	Ohio	23	0	0	0	0	0	0
Connecticut	3½	1	0	0	0	0	0	Indiana	13	0	0	0	0		0
New York	35	0	0	0	0	0	0	Illinois	11	0	0	0	0	0	0
New Jersey	2½	0	0	0	0	0	0	Michigan	6	0	0	0	0	0	0
Pennsylvania	10	3	0	0	0	3	1	Wisconsin	5	0	0	0	0	0	0
Maryland	2½	0	0½	0	0	0	0	Iowa	4	0	0	0	0	0	0
Virginia	1½	0	0	1	0½	0	0	Minnesota	2½	0½	0	0	0	1	0
North Carolina	1	0	0	0	0	0	0								
Alabama	9	0	0	0	0	0	0	Total	173½	5	½	1	½	9	1
Louisiana	6	0	0	0	0	0	0								

Mr. CHURCH, of New York. Mr. President, I offer for the consideration of the Convention the following resolution—

Mr. FLOURNOY. I want to insist that we take at least another ballot before we pass any resolution, for we can make it stronger, a great deal.

Many DELEGATES. "Agreed," "agreed," "another ballot."

Mr. CHURCH. Let me say to my friend that he can make it just as strong as he pleases upon this resolution.

Cries of "read it," "read it."

The resolution was then read, as follows:

"*Resolved*, That STEPHEN A. DOUGLAS, of the State of Illinois, having now received two-thirds of all the votes given in this Convention, he is hereby declared, in accordance with the rules governing this body and in accordance with the uniform custom and rules of former Democratic National Conventions, the regular nominee of the Democratic party of the United States for the office of President." [Loud applause]

Mr. CHURCH then stated that this resolution came under the order of the previous question.

Mr. JONES, of Pennsylvania, rose and was proceeding to speak, when

Mr. GORMAN, of Minnesota, called the gentleman to order.

Mr. JONES then insisted that the resolution was out of order.

The PRESIDENT ruled that it was in order.

Mr. JONES. I insist that it cannot be submitted without giving one day's notice, under the rules adopted at Charleston.

Mr. CHURCH. The original rule of this Convention required that when two-thirds of all the votes were cast for any candidate, that candidate shall be declared the nominee. During the sitting of the Charleston Convention, after the secession, a resolution was offered instructing the President to declare no person nominated until he had received two-thirds of all the votes of a full Convention. A question of order was raised that it required one day's notice. The Chair ruled that the resolution was only one of instruction to the Chairman of that Convention, in regard to the original rule, and that it did not alter or change that rule. Now my resolution is one changing the instructions to the presiding officer, and, as such, it is strictly in order, according to the decision heretofore made.

Now I desire to say a single word with reference to the action of the delegates from New York upon the question of the number of votes required to nominate a candidate. New York came to this Convention for peace and harmony. We represent a larger constituency than any other delegation—numbering 200,000 honest, loyal, faithful Democrats—and from the first assembling of the Convention at Charleston down to the present moment, for sixteen long days and nights, have we honestly and faithfully endeavored to carry out the instructions of our constituents. We have yielded everything but personal honor in order to heal up the divisions of the Convention. One question after another has been presented to us, and we have been asked to yield this point, and that point, and the other point, and we have never failed to respond whenever we have been asked until we were required to yield everythidg which distinguishes our manhood—nay more, everything which distinguishes the manhood of the 200,000 Democrats behind us. [Applause.] When we came to that point—though we say it with pain, and sorrow, and anguish—when we were asked to admit, without question or examination, the whole body of seceders who came here to our doors—not repentant, not determined to abide by our action, but demanding the surrender of our principles into their hands—when we were asked to do that, and, besides, to give up our candidate and the candidate of the choice of the Democracy of New York—a candidate who will sweep New York as with a whirlwind—

[applause]—when we were asked to do all that, we said firmly we cannot in honor comply with your demands.

Now, in relation to this resolution. After the secession at Charleston we were asked by those Southern States who did not secede to unite with them in preventing a dissolution of this body, and in making some adjustment of the various difficulties with which we were surrounded. We were told by those gentlemen that, if we would pass a resolution of instructions to our presiding officer, that it should require two-thirds of a full Convention to nominate, and also, when we got through, make some slight amendment to our platform, they would remain in the Convention, stand by its action, and fight the seceders and disunionists to the very bitter end. They told us that the question was brought before our delegation of altering the rule of the Convention in relation to the number required to nominate. We were opposed to it, we thought it an outrage to require two-thirds even of the body deliberating to nominate. New York has often given its vote in National Conventions to repeal that rule. I remember well, when in 1844, New York had a favorite candidate of her own, and when this rule was thrust upon us and enforced for the purpose of defeating that candidate. We have always been opposed to the two-third rule. But by the construction we were asked to give that rule we were asked to increase the number necessary to nominate from two-thirds to five-sixths of the Convention. We thought that was outrageous, undemocratic, despotic, wrong. But we said—I said to our delegation, in God's name let us sacrifice all we can for peace and harmony. Kentucky, that gallant State, has held communion with us; Tennessee, the land of the hero Jackson, who had more worshipers in New York than—I was going to say—in all the rest of the Union besides; all these States have communed with us, and they have asked this of us as a peace offering. I advised it to be done; we agreed to do it; we did it, and we did it as a peace offering, for harmony and for no other purpose, and not because it was in accordance with our wishes. It seems now that this peace offering has been spurned. Notwithstanding the sacrifice we have made for peace and harmony, we have had no peace and had no harmony.

And now, gentlemen, I am willing, the New York delegation is ready to take all the responsibility of this resolution which I have offered. [Great applause.] No State will go further now or hereafter to unite or cement the Democratic party, to heal up the unfortunate division which has been made. Yet I say, in behalf of the glorious Democracy of the Empire State, that we will stand by the right and fight it through. [Renewed applause.] The difficulties which have attended this Convention have been most unfortunate; but the worst result that can happen is that those gentlemen, by their action, will have elected a Black Republican President of the United States. And if that result shall happen, then I say that they, and they alone, will be responsible for that result. [Loud applause.]

Mr. Jones, of Pennsylvania. When the gentleman from New York (Mr. Church) speaks of "those gentlemen," does he refer to those here who refuse to break down the previous action of this Convention, or to those who have seceded?

Mr. Church. I speak of those who have retired from this Convention, who have violated the obligations which every man is under who enters into a Convention to abide in firmness, in honesty, in good faith by its action, and to support its nominees [applause:] and I say if this division, caused by themselves merely because we have decided the cases of contesting delegations, shall cause the defeat of the party, they alone will be responsible. They say we decided wrongly. Suppose, merely for the sake of the argument, that we have, we had a right to decide, and when that decision was made by a majority of the Convention, every good Democrat was bound to acquiesce in it. [Applause.] Why, sirs, it is a new theory, a new doctrine, that a minority of the Convention, or any portion of that minority, have the right to set up their judgment against that of the majority of the Convention. And even if it should be admitted that we were wrong in our decision, that is no reason for seceding from this Convention, yet that is the only reason I haveheard for the secession here.

The seceders at Charleston said they went out of the Convention because we had not adopted principles that they could stand upon ; that they differed with us upon vital principles, and yet they came back to our doors and asked admission, although we had refused to change the principles we had adopted.

I have but one or two remarks more to make. All that I have said is in grief rather than in anger. Sir, no portion of the Democracy of this country have fought Black Republicanism with more courage and more fidelity than the Democracy of New York.

The CHAIR informed the gentleman that his time had expired.

Mr DAVIS, of Virginia. On the ballot taken to-day, as I understand the announcement from the Chair, some 190 votes were cast in this Convention. Now how in the name of common sense do you expect to get two-thirds of the votes of the Electorial College ? If the Democratic voters of the United States were asked to-day their choice for the President of the United States, nineteen-twentieths would say Stephen A. Douglas, of Illinois. [Applause.] I have no doubt that every village post office in the United States has been eagerly watched since the sitting of this Convention, and the inquiry made by many men, " what is the Convention doing ?" If the delegates to the great National Democratic Convention were as true and generous as the people who have appointed them, they would have nominated Stephen A. Douglas long since. [Applause.] We are called upon now to do what we ought to have done at Charleston, otherwise we must stay here and ballot and ballot, and ballot without ever nominating. If we had adopted this resolution at Charleston, as we ought to have done, we would have concluded long since.

Mr. HOGE. of Virginia, asked leave, on the part of the Virginia delegation, for five minutes to consult, at the end of which time he thought they could present a proposition that wolud settle this whole matter ? Leave was granted.

Mr. DUNNING, of Indiana. The State of Indiana having voted 58 times for Stephen A. Douglas, as many other States have done, I desire to say that I hope the resolution will be so amended as to declare him the unanimous nominee of the Democratic party, as he is the unanimous choice of the honest voters of the Democratic party of this great country.

Mr. GITTINGS, of Maryland. I rise to enter a protest on the part of the constituency I represent ; and a large portion, almost the entire majority of the Democratic voters of the State of Maryland, against this resolution. The rule was laid down at Charleston that two-thirds of the electoral college—202 votes should be required to nominate. I am not prepared to say whether or not before that Convention had proceeded to buisness I would have voted to rescind that rule and have a candidate nominated by a bare majority,

Mr. GALLAGHER, of Connecticut. As I understand this motion, the President of this Convention at Charleston decided that it required two-thirds of all the votes of the electoral college to nominate, notwithstanding several States had seceded from the Convention. From that decision an appeal was taken, and by the vote of New York, I am sorry to say the Chair was sustained, and all that is now necessary is to rescind the vote sustaining the decision of the Chair.

The CHAIRMAN (Mr. Tod, of Ohio.) The Chair will explain. The resolution passed at Charleston, as understood by the then President of this Convention, as understood by the present occupant of the Chair, was not a change in the rule requiring two-thirds of the vote given to nominate, but merely a direction to the Chair from the Convention not to dec'are any one nominated until he had received two-thirds of the votes of the electoral college. And the present occupant of the Chair will not feel at liberty, under that direction, to declare any one nominated until he gets 202 votes, unless the Convention shall otherwise instruct him. But the Chair does not understand the original rule, requiring two-thirds of the votes cast necessary for a nomination, to have been altered in the slightest degree at Charleston.

Mr. GITTINGS. I hope we will adhere to the rule. I have voted fifty times for Mr. Douglas, and will vote fifty times more for him, if that will secure his nomination. I hope he will be nominated. There are delegates enough here to make two thirds of the electoral college, if they will only vote. I do not believe any man who remains here is inclined to be factious. Thank God the factious men, as I believe, have all gone hence. [Applause.] I hope that this resolution will be withdrawn for the present. at least, so that we can have a few more ballots, and see what we can do. I think it is premature, and I appeal to my friends of the Douglas party, not to press it now, for you have always been fair and consistent. I served for two days on the Committee on Credentials, and I say to you and to the world that the only spirit of compromise, the only desire for harmony, came from the Douglas men on that Committee. Upon one particular point, where their feelings were, perhaps, more enlisted than upon any other question, upon my appeal, knowing I was conservative in my views, the gentlemen from Illinois and Ohio on that Committee were kind enough to change their votes for the sake of harmony.

Mr. HOGE, of Virginia. The voice that has heretofore been uttered from Virginia in this Convention, is the voice of politicians—not the voice of the people. [Applause.] While we are deserted by the politicians, you will find that the voice of the people of Virginia will be pronounced in favor of the nominees of this Convention. [Applause.]

Now, in reference to the resolution before us, I honestly believe when the rule was changed at Charleston it was iniquitously done, though I submitted that the vote of Virginia should be cast as a unit for that change. I did it hoping that good might come out of evil. Now if it be true that any gentleman has remained in this Convention and refused to vote, and thereby deprived the members here — who desire to act conscientiously — of the opportunity to make a fair and regular nomination according to the rule adopted, if, after another opportunity is afforded them, they do not vote, I will submit a motion on behalf of the Old Dominion to declare the nomination unanimous. I, therefore, on behalf of the Virginia delegation, and my friend from Maryland (Mr. Gittings,) and the rest of us who stand here deserted by our late colleagues, entreat that an opportunity may be given to every gentleman present to vote. And then if they decline to vote, I will treat them as out of the Convention; and if there is not enough votes then given to make up a two-third vote of the elctoral college, I will myself move to declare the nomination unanimous. [Applause.]

Mr. CHURCH, of New York. There seems to be a disposition on the part of several gentlemen to have another ballot. [Cries of "yes!" "yes!"] And New York, standing as she has stood from the beginning in this Convention, will not stand in the way of any fair and honest proposition. [Applause] I therefore will withdraw the resolution I have offered, and suggest that we at once proceed to another ballot for President.

The SECRETARY then proceeded to call the roll of States for the second ballot for a candidate for the office of President of the United States.

When the State of ARKANSAS was called,

Mr. FLOURNOY, of Arkansas, said that he now considered himself absolved from the instructions of his State Convention, and had great pleasure in casting the vote of Arkansas for Stephen A. Douglas.

When the State of MINNESOTA was called,

Mr. GORMAN, of Minnesota, said that a portion of his delegation being absent or declining to vote, in behalf of the majority of that delegation, he cast the four votes of Minnesota for Stephen A. Douglas.

Mr. BECKER, of Minnesota, announced that he and two of his colleagues had vacated their seats in the Convention.

The call of the States having been concluded, the following was announced as the result of the

SECOND BALLOT.

Whole number of votes actually cast, 194½, as follows:

STATES	For Stephen A. Douglas	For John C. Breckinridge...	For James Guthrie	STATES.	For Stephen A. Douglas	For John C. Breckinridge..	For James Guthrie.......
Maine.	7	0	0	Arkansas	1½	0	0
New Hampshire ..	5	0	0	Missouri	4½	0	1½
Vermont	5	0	0	Tennessee	3	0	0
Massachusetts	1'	0	0	Kentucky	3	0	1½
Rhode Island	4	0	0	Ohio	23	0	0
Connecticut	3½	0½	0	Indiana	13	0	0
New York	35	0	0	Illinois	11	0	0
New Jersey	2½	0	0	Michigan	6	0	0
Pennsylvania	19	7	2½	Wisconsin	5	0	0
Maryland	2½	0	0	Iowa	4	0	0
Virginia.............	3	0	0	Minnesota	4	0	0
North Carolina ..	1	0	0				
Alabama............	9	0	0		181½	7½	5½
Louisiana	6	0	0				

Mr. HOGE, of Virginia, obtained the floor.

Mr. CLARK, of Missouri. Will the gentleman allow me to say a word before he proceeds?

Mr. HOGE. Certainly, with pleasure.

Mr. CLARK. It is known to this Convention that at Charleston as well as here, I have never cast a vote for Stephen A. Douglas. I have taken my course at Charleston and here, in obedience to what I thought were the wishes of my constituents, although in that I may have been mistaken. I endeavored to place in nomination a gentleman agreeing in all particulars more fully, as I thought, with the wishes of Missouri than Mr. Douglas. I have never had any hostility towards Mr. Douglas, but have always regarded him—and have so announced in Congress and elsewhere—as a great and patriotic statesman. [Applause.] I should feel the interests and destinies of my country entirely safe in his hands and under his administration. [Renewed applause.] I have my personal preference, in obedience to what I consider the will and sentiment of the State I in part represent. I was commissioned to the National Democratic Convention, and I know of none but this one. [Applause.] I have linked my destiny to this, and as I said yesterday, for weal or woe, I shall live and die in the Democratic party. With that view, in order that we may end our labors here, and give the country repose, until they begin to shout for victory, I intend to second the motion of the gentleman from Virginia, (Mr. Hoge,) to declare Stephen A. Douglas the nominee unanimously of this Convention.

Mr. HOGE, of Virginia. Before I submit the resolution I promised, I desire to submit one single remark. The Virginia delegates who remain in this, the National and the only National Convention of the Democratic party, have cast only the individual vote of their respective districts. We have not attempted to cast the vote of any gentleman who has left here, and I feel the utmost confidence that those gentlemen will not undertake elsewhere to cast any votes but their own.

I now beg leave to submit the following resolution, being the same as that offered by the gentleman from New York (Mr. Church,) with a slight modification that he and I have made:

"*Resolved unanimously*, That Stephen A. Douglas, of the State of Illinois, having now received two-thirds of all the votes given in this Convention, he is hereby declared, in accordance with rules governing this body, and in accordance with the uniform customs and rules of former Democratic National Conventions, the regular nominee of the Democratic party of the United States, for the office of President of the United States."

Mr. SEYMOUR, of New York. I and some of my friends have occupied a somewhat peculiar position both at Charleston and here. We have among us a distinguished Democrat whose name has been frequently mentioned as the standard-bearer of the Democracy in this campaign. I have known him long, stood by his side through many contests, and was prepared to stand by him if he was the choice of the Democratic party at this time. And I have felt bound from time to time, during the deliberations of the New York delegation, to cast my vote for him. But now I feel, and I say it with great gratification, that I should be speaking the sentiment of my constituency, and the sentiment of the entire Democracy of the State of New York more correctly, if I should coincide with my political friends, which I most cheerfully do, in the vote now about to be pronounced. [Applause.] And I rejoice that it is to be pronounced in a tone that will reach every heart in this confederacy. Stephen A. Douglas, of Illinois, for ten years in the Senate of the United States, has been the champion and the leader of the Democracy, and he is now, as I believe, to be the honored instrument of one now more glorious triumph of the old Democracy. [Applause.] Whatever disturbances and disruptions may have exhisted, by the vote now to be given it will appear that the good and true men who have remained here will with one voice, hail the name of their standard-bearer, Stephen A. Douglas, of Illinois [Loud applause.]

The reading of the resolution being called for, the SECRETARY again read it.

Mr. MASON, of Kentucky. Mr. President—The resolutian offered by the gentleman from New York would bear criticism. Now, if you will not say in the resolution that this is the rule which has heretofore governed the Democratic party—because you voted at Charleston, that it was not, and for our accommodation; if you will not make this new construction, but simply declare that, under all the circumstances, Mr. Douglas ought to be the unanimous nominee of this party, I should not be surprised if the State of Kentucky would agree with you, and that quite likely you may get the vote of that State, though I cannot say it with certainty.

Mr. RICHARDSON, of Illinois. There has never been a nomination for President under any other construction than that made by my friend from New York in his resolution. It is true you agreed at Charleston that you would not do it this time, but always heretofore you have nominated the candidate by a two-third vote. Mr. Stevenson, of Virginia, in 1848, when the New York delegation was excluded, and Gen. Cass was nominated, declared that 170 votes were two-thirds. The action of the Conventions has been uniform upon this subject.

The question being taken on the resolution of Mr. Church, of New York, as offered by Mr. Hoge, of Virginia, an overwhelming and unanimous "aye" was given.

The negative vote was called for and there being no response,

The PRESIDENT said—Gentlemen of the Convention, as your presiding officer I declare Stephen A. Douglas, of Illinois, by the unanimous vote of this Convention, the nominee of the Democratic party of the United States, for President. And may God, in his infinite mercy protect him, and with him this Union.

This announcement was received by the Convention with profound attention and responded to with the most enthusiastic acclamations and cheers. The cheering continued for several minutes, in the midst of which the banner of the Keystone Club was displayed from the upper gallery, and the band struck up "Hail to the Chief."

A second banner inscribed with the name of "Douglas, the next President of the United States," "Pennsylvania good for 40,000 for Douglas," was received with a fresh outburst of enthusiasm.

Cheer followed cheer, hats were waving in all parts of the house, the bands playing, and a general scene of congratulation going on among the delegates.

Calls followed for various speakers, interrupted by renewed propositions for three more cheers for Douglas, which were given with a will as often as called for.

RESPONSES OF THE STATES

Loud calls were then made for Mr. Dawson.

Mr. DAWSON, of Pennsylvania, thereupon addressed the Convention as follows :—

Mr. President, and Gentlemen of the Convention :—It is scarcely necessary for me to say that at no time during the sittings of this body did Judge Douglas receive the united voice of the delegation from Pennsylvania. And, I may further add, that in the consideration of a platform a majority of us united with our Southern friends, ready to give them all that we believed them entitled to under the Federal Constitution. In our judgment they asked for nothing more, and we were not willing to give them less. [Applause.] In our actions then we have been overruled by a decided majority of this body, and for Pennsylvania, I am free to say that, attached as we are to the Democratic party, its principles, its discipline, its organization, standing true forever in the eloquent language of the President in his opening speech at Charleston, "Standing as perpetual sentinels upon the outposts of the Constitution," we will, I trust, abide by its decisions and support its nominees. [Cheers.]

Judge Douglas is a man of acknowledged talent, and everywhere regarded as the accomplished statesman, skilled in the art of ruling. Born under a New England sun, yet by adoption a citizen of the West, honored and cherised in the valley of the Mississippi, and on the slopes of the Atlantic, he now should belong to the whole country. [Cheers.] Unrestrained, to some extent, in early life, in the learning of the schools, the deficiency, if any exists, has been largely compensated by the generous measure in which nature has dealt upon him her choicest gifts of intellect and charactor. [Applause.] Like Henry of the Revolution, like Peel of England, these noble qualities have made him the architect of his own fortune. (Cheers.]

That the Union is a confederacy endowed with special powers, the States composing it retaining all the undelegated attributes of sovereignty, is the fundamental truth of our political system. In defense of this truth we are about to engage in a new contest, and in the comprehension of its true character we have thoroughly to educate the public mind. The popular heart is to be won back to loyalty by holding up to its contemplation the image of the Constitution in this severe beauty of lineament and proportion. The erring conclusions of our fellow citizens of all sections are to be corrected by a thorough and persevering exposition of their fallacy, and in place of these are to be inculcated the paramount claims of the Federal compact to the hearty allegiance, in letter and spirit, of every American who can comprehend and appeciate the institutions of his country, and who really cherishes a desire for their perpetuity. [Applause.]

If here in this beautiful city which looks out upon the Chesapeak, we could have needed any incitement to a broad patriotism in our deliberations, it should have been found in the associations in the midst of which we are assembled, for it was at Annapolis at the close of the Revolution that Washington resigned his commission. It is also within sight of the spot at which we are convened that imposing monuments rise to the greatness of his memory and to the patriotism of the sons of Maryland. [Cheers.]

Pennsylvania, the State in which independence was first proclaimed and the work of the Revolution secured by the construction of the federal compact, the State which holds within her bosom the ashes of Franklin and boasts the first battle-field of Washington, will be true to her noble memories. [Applause.] And in the fullness of that enlightened conservative sentiment for which she has been distinguished, will rally, I hope, in giant strength, cast the dust from her eyes, and aid the friends of the Democratic party once more to elect their nominee. [Loud and long continued cheering.]

Mr. SHEPLEY, of Maine, being loudly called for, he arose and said:

Mr. President, and Gentlemen of the Convention:—It is known to you that our own State, on the Northern frontier, which has occupied but little time of your Convention, has, until the last two bollots, been divided in its votes and in its preference for candidates. But, sir, that division in the expression of our opinions was not a division as to who was the preference of the Democracy of Maine. The Democracy of Maine have been in the habit of sacrificing their own preferences for the harmony of the Democratic party, and so long as any of us believe that by the sacrifice of individual preferences, either of our own or of our constituents, we can do anything for the harmony and the unity of the party, we are disposed to make that sacrifice for ourselves and for them.

But, Mr. President, there arose a delicate and responsible duty for those of us who were in the minority to perform. There was a time when some of those from New England, with whom we acted, withdrew from the Convention, and it then became the duty of the minority of our delegates to determine their course of action. We accordingly decided, in the first place, that if we went out of this Convention because some question, in regard to the admissibility of delegates, was decided contrary to our convictions, there would be an end to Conventions. But we decided that we might separate upon a question of principle, and that if, upon any question of principle, we were defeated, we would go out, even if we went out alone. But that was not the case, and so we determined to remain. I say this, merely as introductory to the point I am about to make—that when any delegate decided to remain in this Convention, he virtually agreed to the resolution which has just been passed. [Applause.] That he acknowleged the principle that there was a quorum present, with power to make a nomination, though there were not two-thirds of this Convention left.

I have only one word to say, in conclusion. We represent 55,000 Democrats in the State of Maine, and although it has been urged here that there is no Northern Democracy, in the coming election we will show those men of the lowlands, who have said it, that

> There are hills beyond Pentland,
> There are friths beyond Forth;
> If there are lords in the Southland,
> There are chiefs in the North."

Mr. COCHRAN, of New York, was then loudly called for. He rose and said:

Gentlemen—It is with no reluctance, though with much diffidence, that I rise to respond to the calls with which I have been honored. I congratulate the whole country upon the successful termination of your labors. (Applause.) My own individual efforts, it is due to you to say, have not been bent to this issue. I frankly say that, with all the efforts of which I am capable, but still with manly openness, I have opposed the course which has at last brought this Convention to the haven of its desires. But, sir, my course was adopted under the pressure of convictions and of affections otherwise given than to the favorite of Illinois. There was a gentleman from the far South-West, whose position we of New York had long contemplated with satisfaction, and it might not seem strange to our fellow-Democrats, in glancing along our own borders, our eyes had been directed to some of our own favorite sons. But the time has arrived when these differences of opinion are to be merged in the authoritative decrees of the great Democratic party, and as that decree is here announced to the people of the United States, I for one lend the feeble volume of my voice to those winds and currents that are now bearing to every portion of the Union the honored, illustrious, impregnable name of Stephen A. Douglas. (Loud cheers.)

Sir, it is the part of patriotism, when sacrifices are required upon the common altar of our country, to make them, and when those sacrifices are in accordance with the best feelings of loyalty and devotion to the whole country, it is better that they should be made with a volition that shows no reluctance, and with alacrity and with energy. I should do a great wrong, both to myself and my constituents, were I to suppress the declaration that he who stands forth now as the standard-bearer of the Democratic party is one who will command a roar of acclamation from the hills and fields, from the streets and groves of the State of New York, loud as from voices without number. (Cheers) I proclaim to this Convention here to-day assembled, that he who has commanded the suffrages of my fellow-delegates is the man who was demanded by the great Democratic party of the United States. (Applause.) Now that the toil is over and the controversy is at an end which has been so fairly and manfully conducted by all, I here come forward for myself, and those who feel with me, and declare that the reluctance of the past will be compensated by the cordiality of the future, (applause,) and notwithstanding secession after secession has taken place in the National Democratic Convention, with such a standard-bearer as you have this day given us, we shall be victorious against all opposition. (Cheers.) I have arisen only in response to the call of my fellow Democrats, not to make a speech, not to present an argument, but to declare that patriotism and honesty require that those who have been sent here as delegates are in strict honor bound by the action of this Convention. (Applause.) But above and beyond the obligations of honor, there is a volition that will expand from these walls to the whole country, which will resound in huzza upon huzza for Stephen A. Douglas. (Loud cheers.)

On motion of Mr. STUART, of Michigan, the Convention took a recess till 7 o'clock.

EVENING SESSION.

The PRESIDENT called the Convention to order at 7 o'clock.

The PRESIDENT requested each of the several delegations to name one of their own number to constitute a member of the Executive National Committee.

Mr. SAYLES, of Rhode Island, said that there was a resolution referring to that matter, and a Committee had been appointed.

The PRESIDENT then called the attention of that Committee to the discharge of their duty.

Mr. JONES, of Tennessee. Mr. President, the Southern delegates in their Convention have conferred together and have agreed unanimously to nominate for Vice President of the United States the Hon. Benjamin Fitzpatrick, of the State of Alabama. (Applause.)

Mr. CLARK, of Missouri. This nomination being made by consultation of the Southern States, including Missouri, (we claim to be a Western State, however—laughter,) I beg leave to second the nomination, and to say to the Convention that after long and somewhat intimate acquaintance with Gov. Fitzpatrick, a better nomination could not be made. He is a self-made man —a man in the prime of life—a man of vigorous intellect—a man of great administrative talent—a popular Governor of his own State—a national man —a life-long Democrat. He lives in the State that first seceded from this Convention. We have selected him for his peculiar fitness, his high qualfications, and because he lives in a State where his name will give such a majority as will astonish every portion of the country. (Applause.) His name is a tower of strength. (Applause,)

Mr. Gittings, of Maryland. I call for the vote by States. I consider it an eminently fit nomination, and I have an object in calling for the vote by States. I want it to go out that every State voted for Mr. Fitzpatrick, and their votes were so recorded.

THE FIRST GUN.

Mr. Sayles, of Rhode Island. I have a telegraphic despatch The first gun.

Providence, R. I.—4 o'clock. Your note is received. We are now firing a hundred guns, amidst great enthusiasm over the name of Stephen A. Douglas. (Enthusiastic cheers.)

Mr. Cagger, of New York. I have the

SECOND GUN.

Troy, N. Y. The nomination of Douglas received with immense enthusiasm. A salute now being fired. (Renewed applause.)

The President, (after calling the Convention to order repeatedly)—Gentlemen, you all know that the Chair feels so much disposition to join in these yells that *he* can't keep order. (Laughter.) The Secretary will now proceed with the call of States.

CALL OF THE STATES ON THE NOMINATION OF VICE PRESIDENT.

At the call of the States the response was promptly given in favor of Mr. Fitzpatrick, with no exception until the State of Pennsylvania was reached, when one vote was announced for William F. Alexander, of New Jersey.

Mr. Whiteburn, of New Jersey. I was authorized before the meeting of this Convention, by Mr. Alexander, not to allow his name to be presented as as a candidate.

The call having been completed, the vote was announced as follows:

Whole number of votes cast, 199½, as follows, viz:

BALLOT FOR VICE PRESIDENT.

	For Benjamin Fitzpatrick.		For Benjamin Fitzpatrick.		For Benjamin Fitzpatrick.
Maine	7	North Carolina	1	Ohio	23
New Hampshire	5	South Carolina	0	Indiana	13
Vermont	5	Georgia	0	Illinois	11
Massachusetts	10	Florida	0	Michigan	6
Rhode Island	4	Alabama	9	Wisconsin	5
Connecticut	6	Louisiana	6	Iowa	4
New York	35	Mississippi	0	Minnesota	4
New Jersey	7	Texas	0	California	0
Pennsylvania	14	Arkansas	4	Oregon	0
Delaware	0	Missouri	6		
Maryland	3	Tennessee	3	Total	198½
Virginia	8	Kentucky	4½		

Pennsylvania cast one blank vote.

The President.—The Chair, therefore, announces that the Democratic

Convention have made choice of Benjamin Fitzpatrick as their candidate for Vice President of the United States.

Mr. STEVENS, of Massachusetts, asked leave to file a statement of the delegate from Massachusetts, (Mr. Chaffee,) whose right to a seat had been sustained by this Convention, as against the contestant, in answer to the protest of a portion of the Massachusetts delegation, who withdrew.

Agreed to, and the following is the statement.

IN CONVENTION, JUNE 23d, 1860.

The undersigned respectfully represents, in reply to the protest presented by B. F. Butler, and others of his colleagues, from the State of Massachusetts, respecting his rights as a member of this Convention, the following brief considerations of fact and argument, namely: That on the 19th day of October, 1859, Benjamin F. Hallett and Cornelius Doherty, of Boston, were duly elected delegates from the Fifth Congressional District of Massachusetts, and K. S. Chaffee, of Cambridge, and Silas Pierce, of Boston, as substitute Delegates, to attend the National Democratic Convention at Charleston.

That on the 17th day of April, 1860, Mr. Hallett formally notified the undersigned of his determination not to attend the said Convention, for reasons of a private nature, which are immaterial here. That thereupon, the undersigned repaired to the city of Charleston, for the purpose of discharging his duty as a substitute delegate to the Convention, and that, upon the report of the Committee on Credentials in his favor, (his seat having been contested,) he was confirmed as a member of the Convention, and acted as such up to the time of the adjournment of the Convention to Charletson..

That upon the re-assembling of the Convention, at its present session, Mr. Hallett presented himself before the Convention, claiming, and in fact, assuming the seat of the undersigned, and that the question of contested right in the premises was referred to the Committee on Credentials for decision, and their report, in his favor, was adopted, with a large majority, by the Convention itself. To all which facts, in the opinion of the undersigned, the following considerations of argument properly applied:

1. That by the same authority by which Mr. Hallett was authorized to act as a delegate to the National Convention, the undersigned was invested with the right to act as such, in a certain contingency, to wit: the non-attendance of the former, for any cause whatever.

2. That the undersigned, therefore, was not the *personal* agent of Mr. Hallett, in any proper sense, or his mere *personal* substitute, but was the agent of the District Convention itself, expressly designated as its substitute *delegate*, and having authority to act as such, in case the former should, for any reason, decline to act.

3. That Mr. Hallett's notification to the undersigned, of his intention not to attend the Convention at Charleston, was, in effect, an act of resignation on his part, and that the undersigned was substituted in his stead, in this contingency, not by Mr. Hallett's own act, but by the act of the District Convention itself.

4. That in this view, the undersigned, having availed himself of his rights in this respect, and having attended upon the discharge of his delegated duties, is amenable to no other body than that by which he was appointed, and holds a seat in the Convention of absolute right.

All of which is respectfully submitted and subscribed.

K. S. CHAFFEE.

Mr. STEVENS, of Massachusetts, submitted the following resolution, which was adopted:

Resolved, That John G. Parkhurst, Recording Secretary of this Convention, be requested to prepare the proceedings of this Convention, to be printed in proper form, and that the National Committee cause 10,000 copies of the same when so prepared, to be printed and distributed among the delegates of this Convention.

REPORT ON RULES AND REGULATIONS.

Mr. KRUM, of Missouri, from the Committee on Rules and Regulations, submitted the following Report: —

Mr. PRESIDENT: The Committee on Rules and Regulations, to which was referred the several matters contemplated by the resolution of Mr. Pugh, of Ohio, beg leave to report:

That they have had the same under consideration, and as the result of their deliberations, submit to the Convention the following resolutions, and recommend their adoption:

1. *Resolved*, That in the next National Democratic Convention the number of delegates from each State shall not exceed double the number of the electoral votes of the State from which such delegates may be elected or appointed.

2. *Resolved*, That a Committee consisting of one from each State, be appointed, which shall be called *the Natioaal Democratic Committee;* and that said Committee shall have authority to call and designate the time and place of holding the next National Democratic Convention, and provide accommodation therefor; and said Committee, in conformity with usage, shall also have power and authority to take all such measures as in the opinion of said Committee may best promote the interests, insure the suscess, and preserve the unity and harmony of the Democratic party. And said Committee shall have power to fill any vacancy that may occur in their number by resignation, death, or refusal to act; but in filling vacancies, it shall be the duty of said Committee to appoint the person who may be designated for the place by the Executive or Central Committee or Convention of the State in which such vacancy may occur; but if no person be designated after reasonable notice, as herein provided, then said Committee may fill the vacancy at pleasure. And the said *National Democratic Committee* shall also have power to appoint from their own members an *Executive Committee;* and said National Committee shall continue in office until their successors shall be duly appointed.

3. *Resolved*, That in the *Call* of said National Democratic Committee for holding the next National Convention, they shall designate the number of delegates to which each State may be entitled.

4. *Resolved*, That the National Committee cause an Official Report of the Proceedings of this Convention to be prepared, published and distributed among and to each of the members thereof; which report shall contain a list of the names of the several members of this Convention, with the Post-office address of each delegate, and the number of electoral votes of each State.

All of which is respectfully submitted.

JOHN M. KRUM, *Chairman.*

On motion of Mr. PRATT, of Connecticut, the report was adopted.

NATIONAL DEMOCRATIC COMMITTEE.

The Convention then duly appointed the following named gentlemen to serve as the *National Democratic Committee,* as provided in the Report submitted by the Chairman of the Committee on Rules and Regulations, viz:

SYLVANUS R. LYMAN, of Portland, Maine.
ALPHEUS F. SNOW, of Claremont, New Hampshire.
CHARLES G. EASTMAN, of Montpelier, Vermont.

FREDERICK O. PRINCE, of Boston, Massachusetts.
JACOB BABBITT, of Bristol, Rhode Island.
WM. L. CONVERSE, of Norwich, Connecticut.
AUGUSTE BELMONT, of New York City, New York.
JACOB VAN ARSDALE, of Newark, New Jersey.
RICHARD J. HALDERMAN, of Harrisburgh, Pennsylvania.
THOS. M. LANAHAN, of Baltimore, Maryland.
JOHN. A. HARMAN, of Stanton, Virginia.
ROBERT P. DICK, of Greensborough, North Carolina.
WM. B. CAULDEN, of Huntsville, Georgia.
W. W. MOORE, of Jacksonville, Florida.
OATLEY H. BYNUM, of Portland, Alabama.
THOS. COTTMAN, of Donaldsonville, Louisiana.
THOMPSON B. FLOURNOY, of Arkansas.
JAMES CRAIG, of St. Joseph's, Missouri.
J. KNOX WALKER, of Memphis, Tennessee.
HENRY C. HARRISON, of Covington, Kentucky.
HUGH J. JEWETT, of Zanesville, Ohio.
H. W. HARRINGTON, of Madison, Indiana.
MURRAY McCONNELL, of Jacksonville, Illinois.
BENJ. FOLLETT, of Ypsilanti, Michigan.
JOHN R. SHARPSTEIN, of Milwaukee, Wisconsin.
WM. H. MERRITT, of Cedar Rapids, Iowa.
HENRY H. SIBLEY, of Minnesota.
JAMES A. McDOUGAL, of San Francisco, California.
WM. B. EARNEST, of Oregon.
SAMUEL TOWNSEND, of Delaware.
——— ———, of South Carolina.
——— ———, of Mississippi.
A. J. HAMILTON, of Texas.

COMMITTEE TO WAIT ON CANDIDATES.

Mr. LUDLOW, of New York, offered the following resolution, which was adopted :

Resolved, That a Committee of nine be appointed by the President to inform the candidates nominated for President and Vice President of the United States of their nomination by this Convention and request their acceptance.

The CHAIRMAN announced the following, as said Committee :

WILLIAM H. LUDLOW, of New York.
J. L. SEWARD, of Georgia.
J. L. DAWSON, of Pennsylvania.
ROBERT C. WICKLIFFE, of Louisiana.
W. A. GORMAN, of Minnesota.
T. B. FLOURNOY, of Arkansas.
A. A. KING, of Missouri.
BION BRADBURY, of Maine.
R. P. DICK, of North Carolina.

Mr. PAYNE, of Ohio. It is generally understood that the platform was adopted at Charleston. I understand that a distinguished member from Louisiana, (Mr. Wickliffe,) desires to present a resolution relating to the platform, and I hope he will be allowed to do so.

Gov. WICKLIFFE, of Louisiana. In behalf of the Committee on Resolutions, I beg leave to present the following. The adoption of it will give to Stephen A. Douglas forty thousand votes in two of the Southern States of this Union.

Resolved, That it is in accordance with the interpretation of the Cincinnati platform, that during the existence of the Territorial Governments the measure of restriction, whatever it may be, imposed by the Federal Constitution on the power of the Territorial Legislature over the subject of the domestic relations, as the same has been or shall hereafter be finally determined by the Supreme Court of the United States, should be respected by all good citizens, and enforced with promptness and fidelity by every branch of the General Government.

Mr. PAYNE. Mr. President, I undertake to say that no fair-minded man, North or South, can find fault with one word of that resolution. (Several voices, "not a word.") Now, with the permission of the Chair, I will read it again in the hearing of this part of the house.

The gentleman read the resolution from his seat, and moved the previous question.

Mr. DAVIS, of Virginia. I say that's unfair. I protest against it, and I want to be heard.

Mr. PAYNE withdrew the call.

Mr. DAVIS then gave his reasons for opposing the resolution.

Mr. PAYNE. I now demand the previous question.

The previous question was then seconded and the Convention ordered that it now be taken.

The resolution was adopted with one or two dissenting voices.

Mr. PRICE, of Louisiana, moved to reconsider the vote on its adoption, and to lay that motion on the table, which was agreed to.

SPEECH OF COL. RICHARDSON.—LETTER FROM MR. DOUGLAS.

Mr. RICHARDSON, of Illinois. Mr. Chairman, the labors of this Convention, arduous as they have been, are now drawing to a close. Arduous duties lie before us in the canvass that is to come, consequent upon the nomination that we have made here to-day. To the Convention, to those who have been our friends, for their support on behalf of our nominee for the Presidency, and on behalf of his State, as also to this entire Convention, I return my profound thanks. We have been involved in seeming difficulties, great and perilous during the time that we have been deliberating here. But the Democratic party have passed through greater difficulties than these, and come from the contest with their banner untorn and with triumph perched upon it. (Applause.)

I have no complaint to make against those who have seceded from this Convention. But I desire to say, before I leave, that I wish them to go to their constituents with all the responsibility of that act resting upon them if the Democratic party is broken down and destroyed. As for us, we have nothing to do but with our nominations to go forth to fight this battle for the success of the Democratic party and the perpetuity of this Government. And if those gentlemen who have seceded from us bring this Government into peril, the responsibility of the act will rest upon them, and not upon us. (Applause.)

Sir, what a spectacle do we present. Day after day during this discussion I have heard it said that this whole discussion was to secure the nomination of a particular man. My lips were sealed. When gentlemen have charged that all this effort on our part has been to nominate a single man, Mr. President, the time has arrived when I can put the denial straight, flat upon that statement, and produce the proof that will put them to blush whenever they repeat it again. (Applause.) I will not repeat the transactions that occurred at Charleston or here, I will refer to them only for the purpose of calling attention to another thing. At Charleston we were told by the seceders that they went off on account of the platform. How do they stand before the country to-day? They come back here upon that platform precisely as they left it at Charleston. (Applause.) They sought admission into your Convention, and the Convention acted upon their application. Then another set of gentlemen, who were in here and had pledged themselves to stand by the nominees, if they could get 202 votes in the nomination—these other gentlemen told you that unless you admitted those seceders, they would go out too. They made an issue not upon the candidate, not upon the platform, but upon the contest over the seats which the seceders claimed here. (Applause.)

I attribute none but patriotic motives to every gentleman. But I must say, I do not know how elevated that patriotism that leads men to go out of a National Democratic Convention, and seeks to break up the party, because you will not let this man or that man, or the other man, sit here in this Convention. (Applause.) So help me God! if I was influenced by such considerations, I would go home and seek the most insignificant town in my State and remain there the balance of my life, for I should not want to be seen by many people. (Great applause.)

Now, Mr. President, I am going to make an announcement that will account for the currency of a rumor prevalent here the other day. Judge Douglas will accept the nomination. (Loud cheers and applause.) But Judge Douglas was prepared, for the harmony of the party, for the success of the party, for the preservation of the government, always and at all times, to withdraw his name from the Convention. (Applause.) I mean those gentlemen shall meet that issue when they go home. I have had in my possession, since the session of this Convention here, his authority placed in my hands to withdraw his name, to be used by his friends whenever they deemed it necessary to do so. (Great applause.) And I now send to the Secretary's desk a letter which though marked "private," I ask may be read to this Convention.

The SECRETARY read the following letter:

[*Private.*]

WASHINGTON, 11 P. M., June 20, 1860.

MY DEAR SIR: I learn there is imminent danger that the Democratic party will be demoralized, if not destroyed by the breaking up of the Convention. Such a result would inevitably expose the country to the perils of sectional strife between the Northern and Southern partisans of Congressional intervention upon the subject of slavery in the Territories. I firmly and conscientiously believe that there is no safety for the country—no hope for the preservation of the Union, except by a faithful and rigid adherence to the doctrine of non-intervention by Congress with slavery in the Territories. (Applause.) Intervention means disunion. There is no difference in principle between Northern and Southern Interventionists. The one intervenes for slavery, and the other against slavery; but each appeals to the passions and prejudices of his own section against the peace of the whole country and the right of self-government by the people of the Territories. Hence the doctrine of non-intervention must be maintained at all hazards. But while I can never sacrifice the principle, even to attain the Presidency, I will cheerfully and joyfully sacrifice myself to maintain the principle. (Applause.) If, therefore, you and my other friends, who have stood by me with such heroic firmness at Charleston and Baltimore, shall be of the opinion that the principle can be preserved and the unity and ascendancy of the Democratic party maintained, and the country saved from the perils of Northern abolitionism and Southern disunion by withdrawing my name and uniting upon some other non-intervention and Union-loving Democrat, I beseech you to pursue that course. (Applause.) Do not understand me as wishing to dictate to my friends. I have implicit confidence in your's and their patriotism, judgment and discretion. Whatever you may do in the premises will meet my hearty approval, but I conjure you to act with an eye single to the safety and wel fare of the country, and without the slightest regard to my individual interest or aggrandizement. (Applause.) My interests will be but promoted, and ambition gratified, and motives vindicated by that course on the part of my friends which will be most effectual in saving the country from being ruled or ruined by a sectional party.

The action of the Charleston Convention in sustaining me by so large a majority on the Platform, and designating me as the first choice of the party for the Presidency, is all the personal triumph I desire. This letter is prompted by the same motives which induced my despatch four years ago, withdrawing my name from the Cincinnati Convention.

With this knowledge of my opinions and wishes, you and other friends must act upon your own convictions of duty.

Very truly, your friend, S. A. DOUGLAS.

Hon. WM. A. RICHARDSON, Baltimore, Md.

The reading of the letter was received with the most enthusiastic applause the whole Convention rising in their seats, waving their hats and cheering.

Mr. RICHARDSON resumed. Mr. President, we have discharged our whole duty. Whatever may befall us in that future so uncertain, we have the proud consolation that we have discharged our duty to just political associations; we have discharged our duty to this bright heritage that our fathers have given to us; we have discharged our duty to the country so connected with the hopes of all the future; we have discharged our duty to that God who placed us here that we might advance the great interests of our fellow-man. (Applause.)

So anxious was my friend, the nominee of this Convention, that this should be impressed upon the minds of all his friends here that he telegraphed the gentleman from New York (Mr. Richmond) on yesterday, I believe, to the same effect. I trust that no person who knows me believes that I would be guilty of manufacturing evidence for an occasion of this sort. (Cries of "no," "no.") I have borne this letter with me for three days, but those gentlemen who have seceded from this Convention placed it out of my power to use it. And the responsibility, therefore, is on them. I do not care if we have but ten friends in the South. In all time to come, I shall be found, so long as my heart continues to beat, striving to maintain all their constitutional rights. I have stood amid the storm of Northern fanaticism, and I understand what it is. I understand what you have to pass through in your section of the country, and appreciate your position. But in a just cause you cannot fail. We will be enabled with you to pass that crisis, and place the government where it will be so administered as to secure all the rights of all sections of the country. It is in hours of danger that true men are found, and in such hours alone. Meet this issue boldly, fearlessly, and for the right. In thirty days from this time we shall have established our ascendancy throughout the North-West, and we shall have such an organization and power then as will give us the control of that Northern empire now fast growing into such vast importance and power.

Sir, we shall have a terrible conflict. I expect to traverse the State in which I live from the lakes to the Ohio river. I expect to meet everywhere my fellow-citizens; I know their temper, and I know that they will put their mark upon that man who, when our army was winning for itself the proudest laurels, declared in Congress that it was an unnecessary and an unconstitutional war. (Applause.) We in the North have one sectional party to fight, and intend to whip them. You have an equally sectional party to fight in the South, and we expect you to whip them. When the election comes on in November next, we shall carry a majority of the electoral vote of the North, and we expect you to carry a majority of the electoral vote of the South. (Applause.) I am exceedingly obliged to the Convention for the kindness and patience with which they have listened to my remsrks.

Mr. CESSNA, of Pennsylvania. We were informed, upon the opening of this Convention in this city, by our late highly respected and most lamented presiding officer, that when we adjourned at Charleston there were pending three motions to reconsider, and three motions so lay those motions to reconsider on the table. I move that the question be now taken upon those motions.

The motion to lay on the table the motion to reconsider the vote by which the first resolution in the minority Report of the Committee on Platform was adopted was then put and carried.

The several motions to lay on the table, the several motions to reconsider the vote adopting the 3d, 4th and 5th Resolutions in the minority Report substituted for the majority Report of the Committee on Platform and Resolutions, were then put and carried, and the motions to reconsider pending before the Convention at the time of its adjournment from Charleston to Baltimore, were severally laid upon the table.

RESOLUTIONS OF THANKS.

Mr. SEYMOUR, of New York, offered the following resolution, which was adopted, the question being put by Vice President Elston, of Indiana:

Resolved, That the thanks of this Convention be presented to the Hon. David Tod, for the dignified, impartial and courteous manner in which he has presided over this Convention.

The following resolutions were also adopted:

Resolved, That our thanks are due and hereby tendered to the several railroad companies which have furnished us with half-fare tickets to this Convention; and especially to the Baltimore and Ohio Railroad Company, for their kind exertions with other companies to procure for us such tickets, and for the extra trains run for our accommodation; and also to the Adams Express Company, for their kindness in transmitting messages, &c., for the accommodation of delegates.

Resolved, That the thanks of this Convention be and are hereby tendered to R. Eaton Goodell, of Illinois, and E. O. Perrine, of New York, principal Reading Secretaries, and to John G. Parkhurst, of Michigan, and Franklin Vansant, of Pennsylvania, principal Recording Secretaries, for the energy, fidelity and attention with which they have discharged their respective duties.

Resolved, That the thanks of this Convention be tendered to the Marshal of the Police of Baltimore and those acting under him for the able manner in which they discharged their duties; also, to the Sergeant-at-Arms of this Convention, and those acting under him, and all the officers of the Convention, for the efficient and able manner in which they have discharged their duties.

Mr. MERRICK, of Illinois, offered the following resolution:

Resolved, That the thanks of this Convention be tendered to the Committee of Arrangements on the part of the State of Maryland and the city of Baltimore, and for the liberal and generous arrangements provided for the accommodation of this Convention, and the uniform courtesy displayed to its members.

Mr. WARWACK, of Alabama. I desire to return the thanks of Alabama to this Convention for the nomination you have made for Vice President of the United States. Alabama has her choice now for President and Vice President, and we pledge Alabama to give her electoral vote for the ticket you have this day nominated—such a vote as she has not given since she voted for Jackson in 1828. I wished, when I heard the speech of the gentleman from Illinois (Mr. Richardson), that I had such a friend as Judge Douglas has in him. (Applause.) In 1856 Alabama voted for Mr. Douglas eight times, and the intriguers saw that he stood next for the nomination at the end of the next four years, that he must certainly be our next President, and they resorted to every measure to break him down. But Alabama will be true to the Union and the Democratic party. We know not who may be the nominee of the seceding Convention, but let him be from the South or from the North, if he be nominated by them, the State of Alabama will cast her electoral vote for the nominees of this Convention.

Mr. Stuart, of Michigan. Mr. President, we shall never be able to adjourn in a better mood than we are now. I therefore propose that we adjourn, and let us go into the field where the enemy are and conquer them in a hand-to-hand fight. (Applause.)

THE PRESIDENT'S ADIEU.

The President. Before putting the motion, the Chair must not forget to say how profoundly grateful he feels for the vote of thanks so generously tendered to him for his conduct in presiding over your deliberations. Called, for the first time, to preside over some six hundred gentlemen, the Chair announced to you in the beginning that he never could succeed in preserving order, unless he had the help and support of every member. He is proud to say now that he was not disappointed in that expectation.

One word more. The victory in this contest, fellow Democrats, is in our hands. We have only to continue firmly, nationally, sternly, fairly, honorably in the discharge of our duties, as we have done since we met at Charleston, to crown our efforts with entire success.

Wishing you all a safe return to your homes, to your wives and children, and God grant that you may all have them at home waiting for you.

After putting the motion to adjourn,

The President said, I now declare this Convention adjourned, and bid you adieu.

The following is a statement of the number of Presidential electors to which each State is entitled, viz :

	States.		States.		States.
Maine	8	Virginia	15	Tennessee	12
New Hampshire	5	North Carolina	10	Kentucky	12
Vermont	5	South Carolina	8	Ohio	23
Massachusetts	13	Georgia	10	Indiana	13
Rhode Island	4	Florida	3	Illinois	11
Connecticut	6	Alabama	9	Michigan	6
New York	35	Louisiana	6	Wisconsin	5
New Jersey	7	Mississippi	7	Iowa	4
Pennsylvania	27	Texas	4	Minnesota	4
Delaware	3	Arkansas	4	California	4
Maryland	8	Missouri	9	Oregon	3

DAVID TOD, President.

John G. Parkhurst, for the Secretaries.

Recapitulation of the Fifty-seven Ballots at Charleston.

Ballots	Douglas	Hunter	Guthrie	Johnson	Lane	Dickinson	Davis	Ballots	Douglas	Hunter	Guthrie	Johnson	Lane	Dickinson	Davis
1..	145½	42	35	12	6	7	1½	30..	151½	25	45	11	5½	3	1
2..	147	41½	36½	12	6	6½	1	31..	151½	32½	47½	11	5½	3	1
3...	148½	36	42	12	6	6½	1	32..	152½	22½	47½	11	5½	3	1
4..	149	41½	37½	12	6	5	1	33	152½	22	47½	11	14½	3	1
5..	149½	41	37½	12	6	5	1	34...	152½	22	47½	11	14½	5	1
6..	149½	41	39½	12	6	3	0	35	152	22	47½	12	12½	4½	1
7..	150½	41	38½	11	7	4	1	36	151½	22	48	12	13½	4¼	1
8..	150½	40½	38½	11	6	4½	1	37	151½	16	64½	..	13½	5½	1
9..	150½	39½	41	12	6	1	1	38	151½	16	66	..	13	5½	0
10..	150½	39	39½	12	6	4	1½	39	151½	16	66½	..	12½	5½	0
11...	150½	38	39½	12	5½	4	1½	40...	151½	16	66½	..	12½	5½	0
12..	150½	38	39½	12	6½	4	1½	41	151½	16	66½	..	13½	5½	0
13..	149½	28½	39½	12	6	1	1	42	151½	16	66½	..	13	5	0
14..	150	27	41	12	20	½	1	43	151½	16	65½	...	13	5	1
15..	150	26½	41½	12	20½	½	1	44...	151½	16	65½	..	13	5	1
16..	150	26	42	12	20½	½	1	45	151½	16	65½	..	13	5	1
17..	150	26	42	12	20½	½	1	46	151½	16	65½	..	13	5	1
18..	150	26	41½	12	20½	1	1	47	151½	16	65½	..	13	5	1
19..	150	26	41½	12	20½	1	1	48	151½	16	65½	...	13	5	1
20..	150	26	42	12	20½	½	1	49..	151½	16	65½	..	14	4	1
21...	150½	26	41½	12	20½	½	1	50	151½	16	65½	..	14	4	1
22..	150½	26	41½	12	20½	½	1	51	151½	16	65½	...	14	4	1
23..	152½	25	41½	12	20½	½	1	52	151	16	65½	...	14	4	1
24..	151½	25	41½	12	20½	1½	1	53	151½	16	65½	..	14	4	1
25..	151½	35	41½	12	19½	11½	1	54	151½	20½	61	..	16	2	1
26..	151½	25	41½	12	19½	12	1	55..	151½	16	65½	..	14	4	1
27...	151½	25	42½	12	9	12½	1	56..	151½	16	65½	..	14	4	1
28..	151½	25	42	12	8	12½	1	57	151½	16	65½	..	14	4	1
29..	151½	25	42	12	8	13	1								

On the first ballot Mr. Toucey received 2½ votes and Mr. Pierce 1; and on the second ballot Toucey received 2½ votes.

MR. DOUGLAS' LETTER OF ACCEPTANCE.

WASHINGTON, JUNE 29, 1860.

GENTLEMEN :—In accordance with the verbal assurance which I gave you when you placed in my hands the authentic evidence of my nomination for the Presidency by the National Convention of the Democratic party, I now send you my formal acceptance. Upon a careful examination of the platform of principle adopted at Charleston, and re-affirmed at Baltimore, with an additional resolution, which is in perfect harmony with the others, I find it to be a faithful embodiment of the time-honored principles of the Democratic party, as the same are now proclaimed and understood by all parties in the Presidential contests of 1848, 1852, and 1856. Upon looking into the proceedings of the Convention, also, I find that the nomination was made with great unanimity in the presence, and with the concurrence, of more than two-thirds of the whole number of delegates, and in exact accordance with the long established usages of the party.

My inflexible purpose not to be a candidate, nor accept the nomination in any contingency, except as the regular nominee of the National Democratic party, and in that case only upon conditions that the usages, as well as the principles of the party, should be strictly adhered to, had been proclaimed for a long time and become well known to the country. These conditions having all been complied with by the free and voluntary action of the Democratic masses and their faithful representatives, without any agency, interference, or procurement on my part, I feel bound in honor and duty to accept the nomination.

In taking this step, I am not unmindful of the responsibility it imposes; but in a firm reliance on Divine Providence, I have faith that the people will comprehend the true nature of the issue involved and eventually maintain the right. The peace of the country and perpetuity of the Union have been put in jeopardy by attempts to interfere with and control the domestic affairs of the people in the Territories, through the agency of the Federal Government. If the power and duty of Federal interference be conceded, two hostile parties must be the inevitable result. The one inflaming the passions and ambition of the North, and the other of the South; and each struggling to use the Federal power and authority for the aggrandizement of its own section at the expense of the equal rights of the other, and in derogation of those fundamental principles of self government which were firmly established in this country by the American revolution as the basis of our entire Republican system.

During the memorable period in our political history, when the advocates of federal intervention upon the subject of slavery in the Territories had well nigh precipitated the country into revolution, the Northern interventionists, demanding the Wilmot proviso for the prohibition of slavery, and the Southern interventionists, then few in number, and without a single Representative in either House of Congress, insisting upon Congressional legislation for the protection of slavery, in opposition to the wishes of the people in either case, it will be remembered that it required all the wisdom, power, and influence of a Clay and a Webster, and a Cass, supported by conservative and patriotic men, Whig and Democrat, of that day, to devise and carry out a line of policy which would restore peace to the country and stability to the Union.

The essential living principle of that policy, as applied in the legislation of 1850, was, and now is, non-intervention by Congress with slavery in the Territories. The fair application of this just and equitable principle restored harmony and fraternity to a distracted country.

If we now depart from that wise and just policy which produced these happy results, and permit the country to be again distracted, if not precipitated into revolution by a sectional contest between pro-slavery and anti-slavery interventionists, where shall we look for another Clay, another Webster, or another Cass, to pilot the ship of State over the breakers into the haven of peace and safety?

The Federal Union must be preserved. The Constitution must be maintained inviolate in all its parts. Every right guaranteed by the Constitution must be protected by law in all cases where legislation is necessary to its enjoyment. The judicial authority, as provided in the Constitution, must be sustained, and its decisions implicitly obeyed and faithfully executed. The laws must be administered and the constitutional authorities upheld, and all unlawful resistance suppressed.

These things must all be done with firmness, impartiality, and fidelity, if we expect to enjoy and transmit, unimpaired, to our posterity, that blessed inheritance which we have received in trust from the patriots and sages of the Revolution.

With sincere thanks for the kind and agreeable manner in which you have made known to me the action of the Convention, I have the honor to be, very respectfully,

Your friend and fellow-citizen,

S. A. DOUGLAS.

Hon. W. H. LUDLOW, of New York, and others of the Committee.

DECLINATION OF SENATOR FITZPATRICK.

The following is the correspondence between the Committee and Mr. Fitzpatrick :—

WASHINGTON, JUNE 25, 1860.

SIR : You have been unanimously nominated by the National Convention of the Democratic party, which met in Charleston on the 22d day of April last, and adjourned to meet at Baltimore on the 18th day of June, as their candidate for the office of Vice President.

To us has been delegated the agreeable duty to inform you of such nomination, and to ask your acceptance of it.

In selecting you for this honorable post, the Convention have but appreciated the ability and high-toned nationality and patriotism which have long distinguished your public career.

We tender to you our congratulations, and have the honor to be your fellow-citizens,

WILLIAM H. LUDLOW, of New York,
R. P. DICK, of North Carolina,
J. L. SEWARD, of Georgia,
J. L. DAWSON, of Pennsylvania,
R. C. WICKLIFFE, of Louisiana,
W. A. GORMAN, of Minnesota,
T. B. FLOURNOY, of Arkansas,
A. A. KING, of Missouri,
BION BRADBURY, of Maine.

To Hon. BENJAMIN FITZPATRICK.

WASHINGTON, JUNE 25, 1860.

GENTLEMEN : Your letter of to-day, informing me that I "have been unanimously nominated by the Notional Convention of the Democratic party, which met at Charleston on the 23d of April last, and adjourned to meet at Baltimore on the 18th day of June, as their candidate for the office of Vice President," was duly received.

Acknowledging with lively sensibility this distinguished mark of your confidence and regard, it is with no ordinary feelings of regret, that considerations, the recital of which I will not impose upon you, constrain me to decline the nomination so flatteringly tendered. My designation as a candidate for this high position would have been more gratifying to me if it had proceeded from a united Democracy—united both as to principles and to men.

The distracting differences at present existing in the ranks of the Democratic party were strikingly exemplified both at Charleston and at Baltimore, and, in my humble opinion, distinctly admonish me that I should in no way contribute to these unfortunate divisions.

The Black Republicans have harmoniously (at least in Convention,) presented their candidates for the Presidency and Vice Presidency. So has the Constitutional Union party (as it is termed.) Each party is already engaged in the contest. In the presence of such organizations we still unfortunately exhibit a divided camp. What a melancholy spectacle! It is calculated to cause every Democratic citizen who cherishes the Constitution of his country to despond, if not to despair of the durability of the Union.

Desirous, as far as I am capable of exercising any influence, to remove every obstacle which may prevent a restoration of the peace, harmony, and perfect concord of that glorious old party to which I have been inflexibly devoted from early manhood—a party which, in my deliberate opinion, is the only real and reliable ligament which binds the South, the North, the East and the West together upon Constitutional principles—no alternative was left to me but that which I herein most respectfully communicate to you.

For the agreeable manner in which you have conveyed to me the action of the Convention, accept my sincere thanks.

Very truly, your friend and obedient servant,

B. FITZPATRICK.

To WM. H. LUDLOW, of New York, and others.

The foregoing correspondence was immediately placed in the hands of the National Democratic Committee, and therenpon a meeting of said Committee was held at the National Hotel, in the city of Washington, on the 25th day of June, at which meeting all the States were represented except Delaware, South Carolina, Mississippi, and Oregon.

The Hon. H. H. SIBLEY, of Minnesota, was made Chairman of the meeting, and F. O. PRINCE, of Massachusetts, was appointed Secretary.

After the Secretary had finished reading the correspondence between the Committee of the Convention and Mr. Fitzpatrick,

On motion of Mr. DICK, of North Carolina, the Hon. HERSCHEL V. JOHNSON, of Georgia, was by acclamation unanimously nominated as the candidate of the National Democratic party for the office of Vice President of the United States.

On motion of Mr. GAULDEN, of Georgia, it was voted that a Committee of five be appointed by the Chair, to notify Mr. Johnson of his nomination, and request his acceptance of the same; and Messrs. Gaulden, of Georgia, McConnell, of Illinois, Dick, of North Carolina, Eastman, of Vermont, and Cottman, of Louisiana, were appointed such Committee.

The Committee immediately waited upon Mr. Johnson and notified him of his nomination, and requested his acceptance; and the following is the speech of Mr. Johnson on accepting the nomination for the Vice Presidency:

Mr. Chairman, Gentlemen of the Executive Committee of the National Democratic Party, and Fellow-Citizens:—I was taken by surprise when I received a telegraphic despatch in Baltimore, at three o'clock this day, that the Hon. Benjamin Fitzpatrick had declined the nomination tendered him by the Democratic National Convention, and that it was demanded of me to accept it. It is known to many of you that my name was freely mentioned in Baltimore, in connexion with this nomination, and that I persistently refused to countenance it, but invariably urged that if Georgia were to be thus honored, it was due to another of her sons, distinguished for his talents and great public service. This was my earnest desire, and the desire of the delegation of which I was a member. But the Convention, in its wisdom, deemed it best to nominate a statesman of Alabama. It was entirely satisfactory. Alabama is the child of Georgia, and the mother cordially responds to any compliment bestowed upon her daughter. These are the circumstances under which I have been assigned this distinguished position, and which demand that disinclination should yield to the voice of duty.

The National Democratic party is in a peculiar condition. It is assailed in the house of its professed friends, and threatened with overthrow. The country is in a peculiar condition. It is on the eve of a sectional conflict which may sweep down all political parties, and terminate in a dissolution of the Union. It is the duty of patriots and statesmen to unite in averting these threatened calamities.

It may not be inappropriate to refer to the circumstances which imperil the National Democracy. The Alabama delegation went to the Convention at Charleston instructed to demand the incorporation into the platform of the party the proposition that Congress should intervene for the protection of slaves in the Territories, and to withdraw if the demand should be refused. That delegation did retire, and with them a large portion of the delegations from the Cotton States. Why should they have retired? The record shows that if they had remained at their posts they had the power to have prevented the nomination of any candidate who might be obnoxious to the South. Thus reduced by secessions, the Convention adjourned to Baltimore, and requested the States to fill the vacancies in their respective delegations. The Convention re-assembled on the 18th instant. The seceding delegations were returned, some accredited to Richmond, and others to Baltimore by way of Richmond, and instructed to make the same demand, and to withdraw if it should be refused. Delegates were appointed in Louisiana, Alabama, and Georgia, by the National Democrats of those States, to fill the vacant seats of the seceders. Those of Alabama and Louisiana were admitted, and the seceding delegates from Georgia were admitted to seats. They all took umbrage at the decisions of the Convention, touching the various contests for seats.

They retired, organized, and nominated candidates for the Presidency and Vice Presidency, and they claim to be the National Democracy of the United States. Now, if they were actuated by "principle;" if it was their purpose in good faith to obtain the recognition of the principle of Congressional protection for slavery in the Territories, why not wait until a proper time arrive to bring that subject before the Convention, and then according to their instructions, withdraw from the body? The reason is palpable; they were waging war against the distinguished man, not for the maintenance of the "principle;" they were willing to jeopard the integrity of the Democratic party and the triumph of its cherished principles, rather than see its will proclaimed in the nomination of its favorites

Admitting, for the sake of argument, Mr. Douglas to be as obnoxious as they allege he is, yet there never was a time when the South, united, could not have defeated his nomination. Why, then, should they have seceded? Why not remain at their post? Why seek to dismember and destroy the party? I question not the patriotism of any, but the people will hold them responsible sooner or later, for all the ills that may flow from their errors.

I said the demand for Congressional intervention was properly rejected at Charleston, and why do I say so? Becauie it was the agreement between the North and South that the slavery agitation should be removed from the halls of Congress, and the people of the Territories be left perfectly free to regulate their domestic institutions in their own way, subject to the Constitution of the United States.

This was the principle of the compromise measures of 1850, and practically applied in the Nebraska-Kansas act, in 1854. It was adopted by both the great parties of the United States in 1852. It triumphed in the election of Franklin Pierce in that year, and of James Buchanan in 1856. It is, perhaps, the best ground of compromise between the North and the South which human ingenuity can devise, and by it the Democratic party, at least, of all sections, should be willing to abide. It gives advantages to neither section over the other, because it refers all questions of dispute between them, either as to Congressional or Territorial power over the subject of slavery, to the final arbitrament of the Supreme Court of the United States. It is, therefore, safe for the South. Its practical working is not without satisfactory results. Where the people of a Territory desire slave labor, and the soil and climate are suited to it, slavery will go; where these conditions do not exist, it will not go. This finds an illustration in New Mexico, where slavery is established, and that in those Territories where it is excluded. only a few days ago propositions to repeal the slavery laws of New Mexico were made and rejected, on the one hand, and the anti-slavery law of Kansas, on the other, was made and rejected in the Senate.

Suppose these propositions, or either of them prevailed, is it not certain that the country would have been thrown into the highest excitement? but by their rejection non-intervention was practically adhered to, and the public mind is satisfied and quiet. Let us maintain it firmly and faithfully. We are bound to it by every consideration of interest and obligation of compact. Its abandonment will prove fatal to the National Democratic party, and ultimately to the Union itself. It will drive the South into intense sectionalism, and the North into the ranks of Black Republicanism. I do not say every man of the North, for I know that the great body of the Northern Democracy will remain true to the Constitution, despite the overwhelming flood of its relentless cohorts. But I mean that the free labor States would be controled by Black Republicans, and would not be able to return a single member to either House of Congress friendly to the constitutional rights of the South. I trust that such a condition of things may never exist; but if it should, I know of no way by which the Union can be saved.

Hence the doctrine of Congressional intervention, and advocated by this new-born sectional party, is fraught with peril to the country. The question is now distinctly presented to the people, whether they will adhere to the doctrine of non-intervention, or whether they will abandon it; whether they will re-open the slavery agitation by requiring Congress to take jurisdiction over it, or whether they will give repose to the public mind and security to the Union, leaving it where the compromise leaves it, to the free action of the people of the Territories and the Constitution of the United States. The issue is fairly made up. It is intervention or non-intervention. Its decision involves the destiny of this great Republic and the highest interest of the civilized world.

Compared with it, the aspirations of men and the fate of political parties sink into utter insignificance. Where shall we look for deliverance from these threatened evils? It has been the mission of the Democratic party of the Union, in a thousand perils, to rescue our country from impending calamities. Its past career abounds with heroic passages, and is illustrated with the most glorious achievements in the cause of Constitutional liberty. It is the party of Jefferson, and Madison, and Jackson, and Polk, whose administrations constitute grand epochs in our national liberty. It is the party of the Constitution. I look to it with confidence. Where else shall the patriot look in these times of political defection and sectional agitation? Let our integrity be permanently destroyed, and the doctrine of non-intervention overthrown, and then the best hopes of the statesman may well be clouded with gloom and darkness.

It is to maintain these that I consent to take the position now assigned me, and welcome the consequences of personal good or personal ill, which that position may bring. Nothing else could induce me to brave the detraction which it invites, and incur the heavy responsibility which it imposes. I have nothing to add but the expression of my profound thanks for the honor so unexpectedly conferred upon me, and my cordial acknowledgments for the flattering terms in which I have been notified of my nomination. Whatever may be honorably done, I shall cheerfully do to maintain the integrity of the party and the triumph of its principles.

www.ingramcontent.com/pod-product-compliance
Lightning Source LLC
LaVergne TN
LVHW011226110826
845150LV00006B/1556

* 9 7 8 1 4 2 5 5 1 5 1 0 2 *